W9-AAI-306

THE HARPER HANDBOOK

OF

COMMUNICATION SKILLS

THE HARPER HANDBOOK

OF

COMMUNICATION SKILLS

C. MERTON BABCOCK
MICHIGAN STATE UNIVERSITY

HARPER & BROTHERS, PUBLISHERS, NEW YORK

THE HARPER HANDBOOK OF COMMUNICATION SKILLS

Copyright © 1957, by Harper & Brothers

Printed in the United States of America

All rights in this book are reserved.
No part of the book may be used or reproduced
in any manner whatsoever without written per-
mission except in the case of brief quotations
embodied in critical articles and reviews. For
information address Harper & Brothers
49 East 33rd Street, New York 16, N.Y.

K-I

Library of Congress catalog card number: 57–6265

CONTENTS

FOREWORD

MASTERY OF ONE'S OWN LANGUAGE IS PROPerly regarded as the primary aim of education in all cultures of the world. The task of learning a language begins in the home immediately after birth and extends throughout the years of formal education. More time and effort are spent by parents and teachers in our society upon this goal of learning than on any other in the entire curriculum. Adequacy in language at the social level at which people live, work, and play is regarded as a *sine qua non*.

Realization among educators of the major importance of adequate language preparation for college students has given rise to new integrated courses that focus on reading, writing, speaking, listening, and thinking as related parts of a single unity. The central importance of communication courses is clearly evident from studies of higher education conducted since 1944. Such courses are designed to teach the use of language more realistically, more economically, and more adequately than has been possible with traditional courses in rhetoric and composition. The aim of the communication course is to help students achieve "complete" mastery of their language.

Communication courses have brought back into sharp focus the principal purpose of writing and speaking: to convey ideas clearly and effectively from one person to another. This important principle has been seriously neglected during recent years. The need for a suitable textbook and guide for students based on current facts about American English has become increasingly more apparent. The old dogmas have become obsolete in our time, and scholars have been reluctant to bring language studies up to date. Many of the communication courses have had to get along without a suitable textbook, or they have had to make whatever use they could of the existing ones.

For these reasons, *The Harper Handbook of Communication Skills* is a timely volume addressed to twentieth-century college students. The subject matter for this work has come out of years of honest effort on the part of educators to satisfy the demands of language instruction in a dynamic world of incessant change and alteration.

Any student who approaches his language problems with an open mind and with a sincere desire to achieve maximum skill in all facets of communication study should find this volume of inestimable value in enhancing his intellectual, social, and linguistic capacities.

PAUL D. BAGWELL
Chairman, Department of Communication Skills
Michigan State University

PREFACE

ONCE IN A GREAT WHILE THE TEMPO OF man's ingenuity quickens noticeably. Society explodes in a flood of new ideas, new standards, new tastes, new styles. A fresh and exciting era is born, marked by changed attitudes, changed customs, changed goals. Those who are first to recognize the new signposts, and have the courage and energy to take notice, discover a new world of expanded opportunities. Today's college youth are living in an extraordinary period in human history. The culture and economy of the United States have found an entirely new dimension. Progress in almost every phase of human activity has broken all bounds, upset man's wildest predictions.

Language, which keeps pace with man's intellectual, social, and spiritual progress, has also undergone revolutionary changes. The semantic and pragmatic dimensions of words, discussed by Charles W. Morris and others, have become in our day as much the concern of language arts as the syntactic dimension which has been of central importance in freshman courses for many years.

Communication skills is a new look in language study, designed to satisfy the needs of college students who are faced with linguistic problems peculiar to the present. The erstwhile notion that language is a social heritage to be protected at all costs and guarded against all innovators, that it is regulated, and must be regulated, by a set of fixed and unchangeable rules and conventions, has been replaced by the practical notion that language is the currency of communicative exchange, and that it should be regarded as an instrument for the transmission and reception of thoughts rather than mere expression.

The Harper Handbook of Communication Skills is designed to assist students in acquiring skill in reading, writing, speaking, and listening. This book is based on the theory that clear thinking is prerequisite to mastery of these skills. Consequently more attention is given to thought structure, and to conception and perception of ideas, than is usual in handbooks of this kind.

The Harper Handbook of Communication Skills is organized on the principle that communication of meaning is at once a personal, social, and linguistic affair; that success or failure to understand or be understood depends upon psychological factors, intellectual capacities, and social awarenesses, as well as on knowledge of how language shapes thoughts, how it reflects cultural history, and how it may be manipulated to achieve the purposes of those who employ it. Recognition of the fact that words are rooted deeply in human experiences has had much to do with the selection of materials and their organization in this book. Students who are sincerely interested in improving their ability to employ language effectively, under whatever circumstances, should find this text a practical guide to such improvement.

I am deeply indebted to a host of scholars, linguists, linguistic scientists, general semanticists, and philosophers who have by their insights and findings set the stage for this kind of language arts course. Special mention should be made of the contributions of S. I. Hayakawa, C. C. Fries, Hans Kurath, Charles W. Morris, Robert C. Pooley, Stuart Chase, Harry A. Overstreet, Edward Sapir, and Joseph Wood Krutch. I also owe a debt of gratitude to my colleagues at Michigan State University who have during the past decade expended much time and effort perfecting a communication skills program that will prepare students most adequately for a college career and for civic and vocational life. Finally, I am indebted to authors and publishers of quotations used in this text to support and clarify the ideas presented.

C. MERTON BABCOCK

East Lansing, Michigan
November, 1956

I

GET YOUR BEARINGS

1

UNDERSTAND THE PROCESS

COMMUNICATION IS THE SCIENCE AND ART of making sense with words. As a science it consists of a set of principles for discovering truth. As an art it offers abundant opportunities for self-expression and self-realization. The ability to manipulate words undoubtedly heads the list of requirements for success in any field of coöperative endeavor. Its basic importance in vocational success is well recognized:

"As soon as you move one step up from the bottom, your effectiveness depends on your ability to reach others through the spoken and written word. And the farther away your job is from manual work, the larger the organization of which you are an employee, the more important it will be that you know how to convey your thoughts in writing or speaking. In the very large organizations, whether it is the government, the larger business corporation, or the Army, this ability to express oneself is perhaps the most important of all the skills a man can possess."[1]

In addition to its vocational value, communication skill is probably the most important prerequisite to learning in any field of academic study, and to growth and development in the community. If you are to acquire intellectual, social, moral, aesthetic, and spiritual capacities; if you are to make any notable contribution to society, or if you are to benefit from participation in community activity, you must learn to clarify your thoughts, to express them efficiently and effectively, and to examine the expression of others in order to comprehend its meaning and significance.

[1] Peter F. Drucker, "How to Be an Employee," *Fortune*, May, 1952, p. 126.

Communication skill is skill in the clarification, transmission, and reception of meaning. It involves ideas, people, and words. This means that communication skill includes: (a) the ability to think constructively: to reflect, to imagine, to create ideas; (b) the ability to adapt ideas to particular people: to coöperate, to promote mutual agreement and understanding; (c) the ability to clarify thought by the use of accurate, precise, and meaningful diction.

1.1 Analysis of the Process

An analysis of the process of communication points up four distinct operations: (a) abstraction of meaning from experience, (b) creation of ideas by reflection, (c) expression of ideas in symbolic language, and (d) transmission and reception of ideas between and among people.

Abstraction of Meaning from Experience

Communication is most successful when the physical senses have been actively engaged in direct observation of facts. Understanding is knowing, and knowing comes from doing. First-hand knowledge of a subject is always preferable to second-hand knowledge or hearsay.

Abstraction means selecting or choosing particular features of experience that satisfy the needs and designs of the observer. For example, when you consider a bottle of ink, you select color and fluidity from a total organization of qualities. Unless you are a very unusual person, you ignore such qualities as odor, chemical composition, density, and weight, until you have some particular reason for noting them. Abstraction is always regulated by purpose. When Martin Luther threw a bottle of ink at the devil, he was seeing something entirely different from what he saw when he was writing a sermon.

The importance of experience in communication is too often overlooked. Many people attempt to communicate from ignorance rather than from knowledge. Experience gives zest, flavor, and life to otherwise impotent words—words which unless acquired actively may turn out to be "as colorful as a concrete walk" or "as tasteless as a mailorder cake." Students who focus their undivided attention on grammatical arrangements, vocabulary choices, and stylistic matters often produce sad specimens of verbal discourse: what one writer has called "unflunkably respectable, studiously second-hand, soullessly perfunctory recitatives in Middle C which are droned out frankly for credit."

"Life is our dictionary," said Emerson in *The American Scholar;* "the preamble to thought, the transition through which it passes from the unconscious to the conscious, is action. Only so much do I know, as I have lived. Instantly we know whose words are loaded with life, and whose not." Speakers and writers who attract and influence readers and listeners have discovered this simple secret: to talk about something to which they were eyewitnesses.

The trouble with many beginning college students is that they don't trust their own thought. They think other people's words are more expressive than their own. They attempt to force ideas into a mold of words rather than fashion words to fit an idea. Don't get the cart before the horse. Capture an idea first, and find words suitable for its transmission afterwards.

Creation of Ideas by Reflection

"Good writing," said Emerson, "results from a proper blending of experience with the present action of the mind." This union or marriage of mind and sensual impression produces ideas —or problem solutions. When you are faced with a real need or confronted with a real problem, creative imagination goes to work. If there is no need, no urgency, no demand for a solution, nothing happens. But, given the desire and a reservoir of experience and proper intellectual capacity, ideas come in focus. The whole process of creative thinking takes place before words enter the picture.

Communication does not begin with the machinery for saying things but with things to say and the need to say them. The stuff of experience is cut up, rearranged, and then pasted back together again according to a pattern or design determined by purpose. Unless words are intimately related to thoughts, they are meaningless. The notion that you can string them together in sentences and group them in units of discourse, according to established rules and conventions, and thus produce clear-cut ideas is sheer nonsense. When words become substitutes for thoughts, communication breaks down.

Expression of Ideas in Verbal Symbols

Contrary to some opinion, ideas are not made up of words. They are rather images of reality projected on the screen of your mind. Before they can be shared with others they must be converted into a medium of exchange. Language is one such medium, perhaps the most important one. It is quite obviously of major concern for our present purposes.

Effective communication requires a selection of words which will most adequately represent your thought. But since words are always approximations of reality, ideas will usually be sold short. Something will be lost in translation: initially, in abstracting facts from experience; and secondly, in finding words to match mental images of experience. The moment a word passes your lips, the thought it contains is twice removed from reality. By the time the thought is reconstructed in the minds of others, numerous opportunities for distortion have been afforded. For this reason clarity is of utmost importance in communication.

Transmission and Reception of Ideas by Signals

Communication of ideas is often explained by analogy with a telephone system. Messages (ideas), originating with a sender (speaker or writer), are coded (expressed) in signals (words) and transmitted (spoken or written) through a channel (medium of communication) to a receiver (listener or reader), who decodes the message and determines the meaning. Disturbances and difficulties in the communication system are called *noise*. A noisy system is one in which errors are likely to occur in the form of misinterpretation, distortion, or ambiguity, caused by absence of clear-cut ideas, inappropriate language, or lack of empathy, *i.e.* mutual understanding, between sender and receiver. If you ask someone for bread, and he gives you a stone; or if you ask for a fish and receive a serpent—to borrow a Biblical phrase—you can be sure the communication system is badly in need of repair. Effective communication takes place when all the parts of the system work smoothly and efficiently and noise is reduced to a minimum.

1.2 Dynamics of Communication

A dynamic system is one in which all elements are so inter-related and synchronized that whatever affects one part of the system affects all other parts. The human organism is such a system: physical incapacity causes emotional disturbances, and vice versa. Shakespeare's Richard III is a dramatic example of psychosomatic behavior:

> Cheated of feature by dissembling nature,
> Deform'd, unfininish'd, sent before my time
> into this breathing world, scarce half made up . . .
> I am determined to prove a villain.

A communication system is dynamic in the sense that the meanings of particular words depend upon the circumstances in which they are employed. One way to isolate the factors that alter meanings from situation to situation is to think of a communication event as a dramatic episode. The elements of drama —act, scene, agent, agency, and purpose—may be used to explain verbal transactions. They are the what, who, when, where, how, and why of communication. Ideas conceived (act) by an individual or individuals (agent) under specific circumstances of place and time (scene) are expressed and transmitted in language (agency) for desired ends (purpose). This is a way of saying that effective communication is intellectually sound, or rational; emotionally controlled, or poised; socially and culturally oriented, or appropriate; verbally accurate, or clear; and purposefully directed, or intentional.

The context in which a word appears frequently defines the intended meaning. When Patrick Henry said, "Give me liberty, or give me death," there was little misunderstanding of his meaning of *liberty*. But the circumstances, not the dictionary, supplied this meaning. When Calvin Coolidge, prior to the presidential primaries in 1927, issued the statement, "I do not choose to run," hundreds of people scurried to the dictionary for a clue to his meaning, but in vain. The precise meaning of *choose* was strictly a matter of the President's personal intention. Notice how the contexts supply the very special meanings of the italicized words in these sentences:

> There are no *atheists* in the foxholes.
> One with God is a *majority*.
> The man who does only what is expected of him is a *slave*.
> This world is *tumbling* round our heads.
> I shall *return!*

Whenever you take words at face value, ignoring the contexts in which they are placed or the special circumstances which invest them with meaning, you are almost sure to miss the author's intention. S. I. Hayakawa supplies an example of such misunderstanding:

> There is the incident of an Armistice Day speaker, a university teacher, who declared before a high-school assembly that the Gettysburg Address was "a powerful piece of propaganda." The context clearly revealed that "propaganda" was being used according to its dictionary meanings rather than according to its popular meanings; it also revealed that the speaker was a very great admirer of Lincoln's.

However, the local newspaper, completely ignoring the context, presented the account in such a way as to convey the impression that the speaker had called Lincoln a liar. On this basis, the newspaper began a campaign against the instructor. The speaker remonstrated with the editor of the newspaper, who replied, in effect, "I don't care what else you said. You said the Gettysburg Address was propaganda, didn't you?" This appeared to the editor complete proof that Lincoln had been maligned and that the speaker deserved to be discharged from his position at the university.[2]

1.3 Acquiring Communication Skill

Communication skill is a matter of making appropriate verbal adjustments to ideas, purposes, people, and occasions. It is characterized by: honesty and sincerity of expression, clarity and specificity of thought, importance and significance of ideas, appropriateness of diction, centralization of purpose, logical organization of materials, and consistency of development.

Here are specific points to help you acquire such skill.

Focusing Attention on an Idea Which You Want to Communicate

If you are to engage in writing or speaking, you must have something to say. If you are to engage in reading or listening, you must be able to comprehend the essential meaning intended by the author or speaker. The commodity of a communicative transaction is not words, but ideas. Words are merely the vehicle by which thoughts or ideas can be transmitted from one person to another.

There is a vast difference between a theme or speech topic and an idea. A theme topic can be handed to you on a platter, but an idea is self-conceived. It may flash across your consciousness as a spontaneous psychological insight, or it may develop slowly from a happy and fruitful marriage of reason and intuition. In any event, it is the result of your own creative imagination's

[2] S. I. Hayakawa, *Language in Thought and Action*, New York, 1941, 1949, pp. 61–62.

making novel arrangements of your personal experiences. No one can do this for you.

Directing your Ideas to Specific People

Any realistic attempt to communicate meaning involves, in addition to having something to say, someone to say it to. Effective communication influences people. The artificial exercise of filling up pages with words directed to no one in particular is not communication. It is talking to oneself. Communication is purposeful: it urges others to act, to believe, to understand, to do. Themes must be written for someone to read; speeches must be directed to live audiences. Even though exercises in communication are assigned and required, they can and must be directed to other individuals than the instructor of the class. Much of the dull, insipid "nonsense" that characterizes ineffective communication would come alive if authors directed their efforts to real rather than imaginary people.

Employing Diction Which Is Clear, Specific, and Socially Acceptable

A given word may be perfectly clear to one individual and totally incomprehensible to another. In clarifying meaning, you must employ symbols which have significance in the social group to which you belong. The simplest way of saying a thing is not necessarily the best way. Neither is the most erudite. The diction employed under whatever circumstances must be directly related to the nature and complexity of the idea concerned and to the experiences of the persons to whom it is directed.

Whether a given expression is socially acceptable or not depends to a large extent on where you live and whom you are addressing. You probably have discovered that certain expressions which are common currency in your home town are frowned upon in college circles. The converse may be equally true. You must, therefore, acquaint yourself with the taboos and restrictions that are placed on language choices by people with whom you associate. For most practical purposes, you must learn to speak, write, read, and understand the living language of America as it is employed by those who carry on the affairs of society.

Having a Definite Reason for Communicating an Idea

Purpose is undoubtedly the most important of all the basic essentials of communication skill, because it operates as a master control over all other considerations. The unfolding of an idea is related to purpose. Selection of supporting details is decided by purpose. Arrangement and organization of material are determined by purpose. Diction and matters of usage are regulated by purpose. And, to some extent, even grammatical structure and syntax are governed by purpose. Unless a communication has definite purpose it is meaningless. You must know where you are going if you hope to arrive. You must know what you are trying to achieve if you hope to succeed in the communication of ideas.

Selecting Facts and Details Which Support Your Idea

Far too frequently a student chooses material for a theme or speech which is vaguely related to his subject and purpose. Such practice throws the communication out of focus and makes the thought ambiguous. Even if you wish to communicate psychological experiences, you must depend on facts. You must select words, examples, situations which will dramatize the emotion you want to incite.

Making Your Communication Sincere, Honest, and Truthful

Language, like atomic energy, has a twin potential. It may be both beneficial and harmful, depending on how it is employed. The communication of meaning should be the execution of a sacred bond or trust. Since it is a coöperative undertaking, its purpose should always be to improve rather than to destroy society. If this is to be accomplished, we must gear our efforts to such traditional virtues as honesty, integrity, and sincerity. As George Gobel says, "Even if it's aggravatin', we like honesty!"

We must learn to shun hypocrisy, part-truths, and gross exaggerations. We must lower the boom on emotional feelings that promote irrational prejudices. We must make diligent efforts to understand the other man's point of view, and freight our own words with respectable thoughts. The man who does not tell the truth sets a snare in which he himself is almost sure to be caught.

1.4 Analysis of Skills

Communication skill includes proficiency in four specific verbal activities—speaking, reading, writing, and listening. Two of these activities—speaking and writing—are skills of transmission; the other two—listening and reading—are skills of reception. All four activities require the ability to think straight, clearly, and critically.

Thinking

Before you can engage in any of the verbal activities just mentioned, you must perform what has been called "the hardest task in the world!" You must think. There is no way out of it. Before you can manage words, you must engage the mind. Just how you go about it is determined by your own personality, including your experiences at home, in school, on the job, in church, and in the whole web of social relationships which make up your past and present.

Thinking is of two kinds: logical and nonlogical. While logic and orderly thinking may be taught in a college course, there is no systematic way to develop and control the powers of nonlogical thought. "You can send a boy (or girl) to college, but you can't make him think." Thinking is an extremely personal matter. It concerns appetites and emotions as well as mental capacities. No one can do it for you. No one can tell another how to construct ideas. Each mind has its own method and each method is a mystery. The mind is somehow conditioned and nature does the rest. The conditioning consists of stocking the mind with facts from experience and study which may be used as necessity arises. Intelligence or native capacity is quite obviously a boon. Study supplements the process by introducing facts, ideas, patterns, and designs that would fail of perception through undirected observation. As Chester Barnard has said: "There seems to be no substitute for using the mind, applying it, working it, to develop its power." And even though we can scarcely fathom the mystery of thought creation, we can learn to discipline our mental powers and thereby control our efforts to communicate meaning.

Creating a thought or idea is best described as solving a problem. It is nothing that we have not done over and over many times while growing into maturity. Here are the essential steps in the process:

a. Setting: contact with environment in which changes occur.
b. Observation: recognition of these changes through sense impression.
c. Definition of problem: realization of a need to alter the environment in harmony with established goals, wants, needs, desires.
d. Evaluation of problem: emergency preparation for self-defense in the form of emotional tension, or conflict, which engages the entire organism.
e. Consideration of trial solutions: determination of possible modes of action based on previous experiences.
f. Finding a solution: selection of one of these modes of action as most suitable in the existing situation.
g. Experimentation: engagement of the organism in the selected mode of action.
h. Verification: testing the soundness, suitability, and efficacy of the selected mode of action.
i. Resolution and reconstruction: acceptance of the idea as satisfactory; relaxation of tension and of emergency status.

Listening

Most of us are on the receiving end of oral communication about 40 percent of our waking hours. We are not actually listening all of this time, but we are exposed to the spoken word. Anyone with open ears can hear what is going on about him, but it requires an open mind to comprehend and judge the significance of what is said. Listening is a verbal skill which requires thoughtful, constructive, purposeful, and critical powers of mind.

The kinds of reception that pay small dividends in communication are passive reception, spasmodic reception, and submissive reception. Passive reception is best described as "in one ear and out the other." Spasmodic reception is "off and on, hit and miss, touch and go." Submissive reception is "hook, line, and sinker" reception. Some people sit quietly and offer no overt resistance to spoken discourse but at the same time do not actually "tune in" on what is being said. Their own preoccupations jam the communication channel and nothing comes through. Others "tune in" from time to time as interest directs, but take frequent mental side trips and wind up with a very hazy and foggy notion of what was transmitted. Still others prepare religiously a transcript of every word that is uttered but do not bother to assemble the verbal elements into ideas or to question the validity and practicality of the speaker's convictions.

Effective listening is similar to working a jigsaw puzzle. Words, sentences, phrases must be properly notched together by conscious, disciplined, and directed effort to produce a complete picture or idea. The pieces or verbal elements do not automatically fall in place. They must be carefully and constructively managed. Such management requires thinking.

Reading

The ability to read entails much more than mere recitation of words or recognition of their standard meanings. Effective reading, like listening, requires disciplined, creative, and critical thinking. A skillful reader digs beneath the surface meanings of words to their subtle associations and hidden implications. He comprehends not only what appears on a page, but also how it is put together and for what precise reasons. The real problem of reading, as one writer puts it, "lies back of the eyeball" where comprehension takes place in mysterious ways. Before a college student can say his training in reading is adequate, he must be able to read with comparative ease the various types of written discourse which confront him in school, in his vocation, and in civic and domestic life.

Reading skill has three facets or dimensions: speed, comprehension, and critical appraisal. A reader who ponders too long over simple arrangements of words in ordinary prose contexts wastes valuable time. A reader who also misconstrues the author's intended meaning wastes both time and effort. A reader who is unable to distinguish between true, partly true, and false statements in written discourse is at the mercy of a writer. A reader who accepts whatever appears in print as gospel is an easy mark for unscrupulous propagandists. Effective reading is an active, aggressive acquisition of ideas.

Because written communication so often lacks the intimacy, informality, and freedom of spoken discourse, a slightly greater burden is placed upon a student to comprehend the full significance of printed texts. The necessity for a large working vocabulary is immediately apparent, as well as the necessity for familiarity with difficult patterns of organization and style. One of the most taxing problems of getting an education is comprehending the heavy, abstruse, and complex styles of textbooks. This problem makes emphasis on reading skill a positive "must" for college freshmen.

Speaking

The spoken language is much more frequently employed in communication than is the written language. The ratio, even among professional writers, is better than 99 to 1. People invariably learn to speak before they learn to write. In fact, written symbols are merely graphic representations or pictures of spoken symbols. A pictographic language was designed for recording the spoken word and for permitting communication among people widely separated by space and time. The spoken word has ever been the great carrier of culture and tradition.

No wonder some people argue that the way we talk is more personal, more authentic, more communicative, and therefore more important than the way we write. Spoken words are experimental, revolutionary, and daring; they are unpretentious, elemental, and disarming. Speech idioms blaze a trail for written idioms to follow. "Colleges and books only copy the language which the field and work-yard made." Telephone messages are eminently more communicative than are telegrams. Personal interviews are preferable to written messages of any kind when the aim is to transmit meaning from one person to another. Oral communication is characterized by an intimacy and genuineness that can only be simulated in writing. People understand each other better when they meet face to face. Extra-verbal factors—personal appearance, gestures, facial expressions, mannerisms, vocal qualities, and physical bearing—play an important part in communication, especially when they are employed to clarify meaning rather than to call attention to the speaker himself.

Writing

Writing is the least frequently employed of the agencies of communication. It differs from speaking in its rigid conformity to standards, in its permanence of forms, and in its characteristic formalty. Speaking is self-corrective. Writing is immutable. If a listener fails to grasp the meaning of a statement, a speaker can repeat his thought in different words and clear up any amibiguity, which in writing must stand as stated. A writer must, therefore, be critically aware of unity, of organization, of diction, as well as of mechanical matters such as spelling, punctuation, paragraph structure, and grammar.

Many people think of writing as almost solely a matter of grammar, sentence structure, and syntax. Such people have great difficulty developing or acquiring verbal skill. "You can't," as Wendell Johnson has said, "write writing." The focus in communication must be on ideas: their clarification and transmission. Grammar and syntax are important, but not more important than other considerations.

Because of its disciplinary value, writing not only functions as a specific means of communicating ideas but also trains one to think clearly and to express thoughts in a rational, orderly manner. Writing is excellent training for effective speaking. Words on paper show up their inadequacies more clearly than they do when spoken. Improper word choices, tangled sentences, and misplaced phrases glare at you and demand correction. Since writing is less frequently employed than other forms of communication, a great deal of practice and critical judgment is necessary for acquiring skill and proficiency.

EXERCISES

1. Determine the similarities and differences in spoken and written discourse by comparing a printed speech and an editorial or magazine article on the same subject. Pay special attention to the author's awareness of audience, method of approach, style, vocabulary, tone, devices used to create interest, and patterns of development.

2. Listen to a talk or lecture in any of your college courses, and jot down any words employed by the speaker which you do not understand. Look these words up in the dictionary and determine what words might have been substituted that are familiar to you. Would the substitution of these words in any way affect the idea concerned?

3. Read orally to the class a passage assigned by your instructor. Try to make the reading sound natural and unaffected. Make direct eye-contact with your audience as often as you can. Make careful note of any criticism offered you and begin immediately to im-

prove your difficulties in pronunciation, enunciation, rate, volume, and fluency.

4. Write a paper in which you explain to your instructor the nature of any difficulties you have experienced heretofore in listening, reading, speaking, and writing. Be clear and precise. Describe the difficulties in detail. Mention such things as stage fright, incapacity to pay attention, inadequate vocabulary, paucity of ideas, etc.

5. Cite a number of examples, with which you are familiar, of the breakdown or failure of attempts to communicate an idea. Analyze one of these instances and be prepared to explain to the class where the difficulty lay.

6. In the following sentence the words *thousands* and *few* are unprecise: Fish give birth to thousands of young every few weeks. The word *birth*, in this sentence, is also used in an unusual sense. Find examples in your assigned readings or in magazine advertisements of words for which you must supply your own meanings or definitions. How could the meaning of these words be clarified?

FOR FURTHER READING

Beall, Paul R., "Pass the Word Along," *Vital Speeches of the Day,* May 15, 1953, pp. 465–470.

Bunche, Ralph J., "The International Significance of Human Relations," address, Springfield, Illinois, February 12, 1951.

Chase, Stuart, *Roads to Agreement: Successful Methods in the Science of Human Relations,* New York, 1951.

Dewey, John, *How We Think,* New York, 1933.

Hayakawa, S. I., *Language, Meaning, and Maturity* (Selections from ETC: A Review of General Semantics, 1943–1953), New York, 1954.

Hayakawa, S. I., *Language in Thought and Action,* New York, 1949.

Hazlitt, William, "On the Differences Between Writing and Speaking."

Lee, Irving J., *Customs and Crises in Communication* (Cases for the Study of Some Barriers and Breakdowns), New York, 1954.

Lee, Irving J., *Language Habits in Human Affairs,* New York, 1941.

Lloyd, Donald J., "Our National Mania for Correctness," *The American Scholar*, Summer, 1952.

Meerloo, Joost A. M., *Conversation and Communication* (A Psychological Inquiry into Language and Human Relations), New York, 1952.

Murray, Elwood, "Communication in Human Relations," *Journal of Communication*, May, 1951.

Overstreet, Harry A., *Influencing Human Behavior*, New York, 1925.

Rapoport, Anatol, "Semantics: The Problem of Meaning," in *American Philosophy*, edited by Ralph B. Winn, New York, 1955.

Thouless, Robert A., *How to Think Straight*, New York, 1939.

UNDERSTAND YOURSELF

LANGUAGE IS STRICTLY A PERSONAL AFFAIR. Each of us speaks his own tongue and employs words in his own unique way. You can learn very little about your own difficulties in communication if you keep your attention focused on other people's words. Spoken or written signals invariably release private meanings. Something personal goes out with every utterance, and words once spoken never have quite the same meanings again. This chapter is devoted to a number of specific factors that affect your own ability to use words effectively.

2.1   Perception

What you perceive in a given phenomenon, that is, what meaning you give to a particular experience, or what interpretation you make of observed facts, depends on who you are and what you are up to. "We do not determine what we will think. We only open our senses, clear away as we can all obstructions from the fact, and suffer the intellect to see." But what the intellect sees or perceives is conditioned by past experience and by present needs, feelings, and emotions. Each mind has its own method. We all wear our own brand of "colored glasses," and whatever we perceive through them we regard as "truth."

This so-called "truth" is subject to at least two kinds of errors: errors in sensation and errors in interpretation. Errors in sensation are caused by defects in the sense organs. Color blindness is an example. Errors in interpretation, much more frequent, are due to a variety of subtle causes which are treated in this chapter. The accompanying chart demonstrates how erroneous our interpretations of phenomena may be. In order that you may acquire accurate information about the world of experience, it is

Source: John Wiley & Sons, Inc.

Is This a Spiral? Close examination will reveal a series of concentric circles.

necessary that your sensation-perception equipment be working properly. There is little excuse for going through life making the same mistakes day after day. If your communicative eyeglasses distort your vision, you need to have them corrected.

Thoughts as Mental Counterparts of Reality

What we see in a given set of circumstances depends to some extent on what we want to see, or need to see. We select from any experience those features which are useful for our own purposes. A lumberman considering a tree sees something quite different from what an artist, a landscape architect, or a botanist sees. The particular features we select in observing reality make up mental images, our private versions of how things are. We react to these images as though they were true carbon copies of reality. We hold up a mirror to nature and then swear that it reflects the truth, the whole truth, and nothing but the truth. We assume that objects, people, events make identical impressions on everyone. Our vision is adjusted to personal motives which regulate behavior and we see what we see because we leave out what we leave out.

Words as Connecting Links between Mind and Matter

Idealists believe that nothing is real except images created in the mind. Realists, on the other hand, believe that nothing is real except what exists apart from mind. Without accepting either point of view unreservedly, we can agree that words constitute a necessary link between mind and matter. They are instruments by which we probe reality. They are both sign and symbol. They reflect qualities of both observer and thing observed. (These matters are discussed in detail in Chapter 3.)

As signs, words represent or replace objects. As symbols they reflect our personal evaluations or attitudes toward objects. Every experience is judged as good, bad, indifferent, satisfactory, unsatisfactory, important, unimportant in various degrees by the language we use in describing it. Notice the subjective evaluation of a sunset in the following passage:

"They are soft, sensuous, lovely—they are exquisite, refined, effeminate, but we have seen no sunsets here like the gorgeous conflagrations that flame in the track of the sinking sun in our high northern latitudes."[1]

Perception Governed by Needs

How long can you remember your home address, your telephone number, your age? Only as long as you have need of the

[1] Mark Twain, *Innocents Abroad*, Vol. I.

information. When you move from one place to another, you quickly forget your former address, and people who have had no reason to remember their ages have no accurate idea how long they have lived. The details you can set down about the college or university campus all have some bearing, directly or indirectly, on your need to remember them. Out of the total environment in which you live, you abstract, select, and remember those features which are related to what you are at present interested in. Suppose you have just been jilted by your girl friend. The chances are ten to one that you will suddenly "see" for the first time another girl who has been in your immediate circle of acquaintances all along.

Stages in Perception

The process of perception consists of three distinct stages: (a) contact with a chaos or blur of experience in which nothing is clearly distinguished; (b) analysis of the blur into differentiated units or parts, based on a need to distinguish them; (c) synthesis of the parts into an organized, integrated, and meaningful whole.

This final integrated whole you record in your consciousness. It is your image of reality. A visit to a factory, an assembly plant, Grand Central Station, the stock exchange is likely to appear first as a conglomerated blur. But as you differentiate the several parts of the milieu and then relate the parts so as to form a complete picture, you make sense of what was initially non-sense.

Notice what happens when you try to read the following sentence:

THEWORLDOFHUMANRELATIONSISMUCHLESSUNIFORM
THANTHEWORLDOFNATURE

You must muster past experience and verbal habits to act as guides, first in breaking the "blur" into understandable units, and then in putting these units together again in an integrated and meaningful fashion. This same process is evident in your day-to-day struggles with new or novel situations or problems: a modern painting, a foreign language, an interpretive dance, a musical composition, a pantomime, the stars in the sky. Your success or failure will depend to a great extent on the need, pressure, tension, curiosity with which you approach the particular problem.

2.2   Emotional Maturity

The human organism is equipped with a special security system called the emotions. This is fortunate, because whenever one is threatened by outside forces the emotions sound a general alarm. All the functional elements of the body are mustered to defend against the attack. "Impossible" feats of strength and endurance can be performed under emotional stress. In the case of fear, the action of the heart is speeded up by adrenalin; the blood is redistributed to critical parts of the body; the liver puts glycogen into the blood to produce energy; the lungs take in additional oxygen; and the spleen produces more red corpuscles. All of these adjustments and many more are made automatically and involuntarily.

Control of conscious thoughts is extremely difficult in the face of violent emotional experience. Marjorie Kinnan Rawlings, when face to face with a deadly coral snake, testified: "I found that I had still the blind, unthinking, 'instinctive' horror of coming on a poisonous serpent. Nothing could warm the frozen column that replaced my spine."

Emotional experiences of this kind have powerful effects on linguistic behavior. Considering Mrs. Rawlings' testimony, it is almost certain that the words *coral, snake,* or *rattler* became so tinged or colored by the frightful experience as to recall or stir up the dormant fears every time the words were subsequently pronounced. "Poor words!" says one writer. "Like innocent victims of prejudice, they may be compromised forever."

What happens is that words produce conditioned responses in the same way the sight of food causes the saliva to flow.

When words are emotionally charged in the manner just described they may easily trap readers and listeners in fixed associations. This, of course, plays havoc with successful communication of ideas by short-circuiting normal, rational processes of thought. Effective communication is emotionally controlled —at least ideally so. We often respond quite unconsciously, of course, to the emotional tones of words, having long since forgotten the initial experiences that colored them.

Emotional maturity is characteristic of persons with an open or communicative personality. The qualities of such a personality are initiative, self-confidence, respect for others, emotional detachment, insatiable curiosity, sense of direction, and adaptability.

INITIATIVE.   Communicative initiative is creative ability. An effective communicator has a fertile imagination. He is able to shape a welter of disconnected experiences into a single novel entity or idea. He is not tied to the apron strings of tradition but is willing to think for himself. His speech is fresh, original, spontaneous, and engaging. He holds his audience at attention because he speaks his own mind. He realizes, as Lincoln Steffens put it, that "everything in the world remains to be done or done over," and he elects himself to do it.

SELF-CONFIDENCE.   Communicative success is directly related to self-assurance, confidence, and physical and emotional poise. Convictions are a necessary part of great personalities. A successful communicator believes in himself, in his own ideas, and in his ability to transmit them to others. He makes up his mind to pursue his course despite the opprobrium and scorn others may heap upon him. He understands the difference between integrity to honest conviction and braggadocio—between exhibitionism and communication. He understands that to doubt his own qualifications as a speaker or writer is to fail before he gets started. He knows that if he doesn't believe in himself, it is almost certain that no one else will.

RESPECT FOR OTHERS. Social sensitivity means having respect for and confidence in other people—especially people with whom you want to communicate. Communication thrives in a free atmosphere, unsophisticated, uninhibited, and unrestrained. A too reserved, too scientific, too mundane attitude toward readers and listeners may militate against you. Lack of faith in others is a danger signal in any coöperative enterprise. Hypocrisy is the archenemy of social communication. Intimacy, agreement, affability, and good will turn the trick. When you are able to identify yourself with another's point of view, see things as he sees them, surrender momentarily to his verbal associations, assume his interests, tolerate his ideas, and respect his opinions, successful communication can be established.

EMOTIONAL DETACHMENT. An effective communicator is able to consider objects, persons, events with an impersonal, unbiased, and unprejudiced eye. He is able to delay judgment of a speaker and his subject until he has heard an entire discourse. He is able to face and adjust to new and strange situations without becoming blocked by psychological hangovers from his past. He keeps the sand out of his eyes, the cobwebs out of his brain, and the skeletons out of his emotional closets.

INSATIABLE CURIOSITY. We have a way of looking at the world without seeing anything but a vague outline. We take in whole vistas of sights and ranges of sounds without discriminating any details. Our world is for the most part one big blur. A child learns to make sense out of this blur, this whirling chaos, by being curious, naïve, direct, and penetrating. He finds "books in running brooks" and "sermons in stones" where adults see only the absence of bridges and impediments to progress.

Curiosity may have killed the proverbial cat, but it will pay rich dividends for you in the communication of ideas. An effective communicator has a lust for learning. He exercises the courage to doubt, and challenges his own beliefs and assumptions by direct observation of facts. His interests are wide, his experiences broad.

SENSE OF DIRECTION. An effective communicator is governed by purpose. He is oriented to attainable goals and he keeps these goals in sight at all times. He knows where he is going and what he hopes to accomplish. He does not let temporary failures or setbacks cause communicative rigor mortis.

ADAPTABILITY. Effective communication demands that a person adapt himself to new and strange circumstances without becoming frustrated and going to pieces. H. A. Overstreet has declared that "the person who is mature in his communicative powers is noted as an exception to the rule. The person who is immature—halting, clumsy, obscure, mumbling, dull, platitudinous, insensitive—is the rule."

Adaptability suggests growth, progress, improvement. Some people, of course, have a higher "communicative metabolism" than others. They are able to maintain a balanced perspective in spite of radical changes in circumstance and in the face of chaotic environmental pressures and influences. They are able to convert strangeness into familiarity by predicting the probable results of various projected actions and modes of behavior. They control a situation rather than succumb to it. People who can take an adventurous attitude toward new situations, who can talk to children as well as adults, who can play a dozen roles equally well, who assume an active, positive, dynamic attitude toward whatever tasks are required of them are the people who make successful communicators.

2.3 Motives and Communication

Motivation has been likened to a compass which guides and directs the onward course of behavior. Such a compass is an invaluable aid to successful communication adjustments. The acquisition of verbal skill may be thought of as a succession of motivational stages from infancy to maturity. How you talk, how you write, how you read and listen are indicative of what is important to you and what unimportant.

Levels of Motivation

Motives may be classified as biological, psychological, and sociocultural.

BIOLOGICAL MOTIVES. The drives which have to do with maintenance of physiological equilibrium are called biological motives. They include the need or desire for food, water, oxygen, temperature regularity, sexual satisfaction, activity, rest, protection from harm, and avoidance of pain. All of these needs are intimately related to survival, which is the basic motive of human existence.

PSYCHOLOGICAL MOTIVES. Defending, protecting, and enhancing your personal conception of "self" involve psychological motives. You may actually defend your "self" conception at the risk of your life. Such motives include:

Prestige: desire for affection, recognition, companionship, and approval.
Self-assertion: desire for independence and self-sufficiency.
Power: desire to control others or to be controlled by them.
Manipulation: desire to create, build, design, compose, achieve.
Expression: desire to communicate, to express, to emote, to sound off.
Ownership: desire to acquire possessions, wealth, property.
Exploration: desire to discover new things, to satisfy curiosity, to find out the nature of things.

SOCIOCULTURAL MOTIVES. The motives concerned with the interrelations of self and society may include such specific needs as: the need to think creatively, the need to exercise moral judgment and responsibility, the need to believe in a higher power than human beings, the need for social participation, the need for economic security, the need for civic and political participation, the need for psychosomatic balance or health, the need to live in family units, the need to discover and create beauty, and the need for recreation.

Purposes as Motives

The essential difference between motives and purposes is simply this: motives may be and usually are involuntary guides to behavior; purposes are thoughtful, willful, and voluntary. Purposes, aims, goals, ambitions give unity to one's life and career, keep one from scattering his forces.

Purpose, as is shown in Chapter 6, is of utmost importance in communication. Three positive suggestions are offered here:

a. Purposes should be self-conceived, not merely assumed or borrowed from others. This means that you must be sincerely concerned with what you say or what you read or listen to. Arbitrarily assigned or assumed purposes are artificial and produce artificial results.

b. Purposes should be possible of attainment. Many people become frustrated because they dream themselves into positions which they can never actually realize or experience.

c. Purposes should be clearly thought out. Vague, embryonic, and foggy purposes give no direction to discourse. You must know exactly what you hope to accomplish before you can achieve a goal.

Conflict in Motives

We have Sigmund Freud's word for it that "a neurosis . . . can never arise except from a conflict between two tendencies." While all conflicts are certainly not neurotic, indecision, frustration, and insecurity are stumbling blocks to successful communication.

Conflict is very often due to causes that are not immediately apparent. One of the most serious conflicts in its effects on speech behavior is that caused by differences between personal idioms of language and socially approved idioms. Robert A. Hall, Jr., in *Leave Your Language Alone*, argues that untold psychological harm is the result of overinsistence on grammatical correctness.

Conflict in motives may produce any of the following types of non-communicative behavior: (a) avoidance of social contacts for fear of having nothing to say; (b) avoidance of expressing an idea or conviction for fear of its probable effect on a listener; (c) avoidance of giving speeches in class for fear of being embarrassed or frightened; (d) avoidance of criticizing another's speech for fear of offending the speaker; (e) avoidance of answering questions in class for fear of giving wrong answers; (f) avoidance of writing assignments for fear of making mistakes; (g) irresolution in choices of speech and theme topics for fear topics of personal interest will sound silly to others; (h) avoidance of spending proper time in study for fear of ridicule.

Whenever you find yourself between the horns of a dilemma, you should clarify your purposes as best you can, be sure you are right, and then speak your mind with a will. No one is greatly admired who is always on the fence waiting to hear what others say before deciding what to think.

2.4 Habits and Skills

We are all largely creatures of habit. What we have done repeatedly before, we are almost certain to do again and again. Developing a personality is really nothing more than acquiring unique ways of doing things. Our peculiar tricks of thought, patterns of behavior, attitudes and prejudices, verbal mannerisms, and communicative idiosyncrasies are all matters of habit.

As we grow and develop into maturity, we cling tenaciously to types of verbal behavior which we acquired young and gradually fixed by continual usage. Psychologists say that resistance to linguistic change is one of the most stable aspects of personality. This fact makes the formation of appropriate language habits of utmost importance in the development of communication skill.

William James has shown that the period below twenty years of age is the most important period in a person's life for the "fixing" of adequate habits of vocalization, pronunciation, gesture, motion, and address. "Hardly ever," he says, "is a language learned after twenty spoken without a foreign accent; hardly ever can a youth transferred to the society of his betters unlearn the nasality and other vices of speech bred in him by the association of his growing years."

This same principle quite naturally holds for other skills of communication. Previous experiences very often set the stage for new and novel experiences. Habits and skills acquired during high school are part of your qualifications for college work. Verbal skills acquired during college years will help to determine your success or failure to adjust yourself to problems of education and vocational life.

The following maxims, supplied by William James, should furnish invaluable guides to the formation of appropriate habits and skills of communication:

Make automatic and habitual, as early as possible, as many useful actions as you can.

Guard against growing into ways that are likely to be disadvantageous.

In learning a new habit, never suffer an exception to occur till the new habit is securely rooted in your life.

Seize the very first possible opportunity to act on every resolution you make and on every emotional prompting you may experience in the direction of the habits you aspire to gain.

Keep the faculty of effort alive in you by a little gratuitous exercise every day.

2.5   Beliefs

Another factor in personality that powerfully influences behavior is belief. Belief is conviction, assurance, and faith in particular ideas. Since ideas are problem solutions, beliefs are explanations of life's mysteries that have been assimilated into your scheme of values or frame of reference. Your own peculiar constellation or cluster of beliefs determines how you will be classified by others: radical, conservative, reactionary, progressive, fatalistic, agnostic, idealistic, relativistic, rationalist, transcendentalist, realist, etc. Roughly speaking, people may be divided into three major classes with respect to belief: dogmatists, skeptics, and doubters. The dogmatists firmly assert; the skeptics vehemently protest; and the doubters confidently doubt.

The intellectual and emotional aspects of belief are so intricately related as to be inseparable. A doubter, for example, is often wholly unaware of the emotional roots of his persistent doubts. Many of the beliefs you yourself cherish lie dormant just beneath consciousness and cause types of behavior that you cannot easily explain. Personal meanings of words are, in the final analysis, the best indicators of subconscious beliefs.

An experiment conducted in England demonstrates how belief influences the meaning attached to verbal statements. A group of 56 subjects wrote down their interpretations of the following statement:

The judge says the prisoner is probably guilty.

Various degrees of certainty were apparent in the several interpretations of the expression "probably guilty." The table[2] indicates these variations:

(1) Certain	4
(2) Almost but not quite certain	29
(3) More likely guilty than not guilty	15
(4) Could be equally guilty or not guilty	8
	56

[2] John Cohen and Mark Hansel, *Risk and Gambling*, New York, 1956, p. 83.

An effective communicator will ask himself three pertinent questions concerning his own beliefs: Are my beliefs grounded in verifiable facts? Are my beliefs consistent with one another? Are my beliefs subject to alteration in the face of new evidence?

Irrationality, "thinking" based on false assumptions and unsubstantial evidence, has been called the "largest single vested interest in the world." When ideas are grounded in facts and are continually revised with the accumulation of new evidence, they may be called sound. But how infrequently do people bother to inspect the facts. They jump to the wildest conclusions, in harmony with their own preconceived notions and unchallenged beliefs. Bergen Evans hit the nail on the head when he said:

"The popular mind, irrational and prejudiced, makes some effort to examine evidence, but it has very little knowledge of the true nature of what it is looking for or of the forces at work to frustrate and confuse it in its reach. It generalizes from exceptions, and from a mass of experience, selects only those elements that confirm its preconceptions—without the faintest awareness of what it is doing. Most of what is called thinking . . . even up to and including much of what goes on in the brains of college faculties . . . is actually a seeking for confirmation of previous convictions. The true scientific spirit that leads men to be particularly suspicious of all beliefs they hold dear is utterly incomprehensible to most people."[3]

Inflexibility of belief is one of the worst stumbling blocks to successful communication. Ideas thrive in free soil. A man or woman with new ideas is our best safeguard against stagnation. People who have persistently lived by such rigid codes as "Spare the rod and spoil the child," "An eye for an eye and a tooth for a tooth," are unoriented to the dynamic nature of the world. Times change, people change, circumstances change, language changes. If you close your eyes to the normal changes in the

[3] Bergen Evans, "A Tale of a Tub," in *The Natural History of Nonsense,* New York, 1946.

world, your ideas will soon become as obsolete as a mustard plaster. Here is a statement of belief that exhibits a healthy, open orientation:

"I believe finally that we are only at the threshold of wisdom concerning how human beings learn, why they forget, what motivates their search for knowledge, what knowledge is of most worth, and all the other aspects of education which perplex the minds of thinking men; therefore, I believe we must constantly be experimenting and evaluating, never resting, never worshipping the status quo, never satisfied, realizing that the higher we ascend in our search the wider becomes the horizon of our vision."[4]

2.6   Attitudes

Attitudes are inclinations or predispositions to particular types of action or reaction. People's attitudes are, generally speaking, in favor of, indifferent to, or opposed to particular objects, persons, places, or processes. Attitudes are very like habits and beliefs, except that they are less fixed and stable. No attempt is made here to classify all human attitudes. The following categories are familiar ones:

Aggressive-Submissive

Whenever persons are engaged in communication, the attitude of one toward the other is roughly one of the following: A feels superior to B, A feels equal to B, A feels inferior to B. Whether one of these attitudes is more conducive to successful exchange of ideas depends entirely on the circumstances. Talking to the boss and talking to a schoolmate, for example, may call for entirely different attitudes. For most class exercises in communication, equality of speaker and listener or writer and reader is appropriate. Over-aggressiveness dispels confidence; over-submissiveness creates resentment.

[4] Elwin A. Lee, "This I Believe," *School and Society*, April 17, 1954, p. 119.

Positive-Negative

Most people dislike a Scrooge. And many people weary of
Pollyanna. Dorothy Thompson said in 1941, "In this democracy,
it has become a public duty to be as happy as one can be."
Happiness is usually thought of as a positive virtue. Of course,
if you are opposed to legal graft and political corruption, no
one can rightly expect you to take a positive attitude toward
such issues. Your attitude, in any case, must be gauged by your
purpose. But it must be said that a consistently negative attitude
toward anything and everything is detrimental to effective communication. An optimistic, forward, dynamic, or positive attitude usually pays good dividends in social communication.
Arthur H. Motley tells of a girl in a candy store who was a favorite with the customers. People would wait in line to have her
serve them, even though another clerk happened to be free.
This girl would take up a very modest amount of candy when
filling an order. Then she would add more and more until the
correct weight was reached. The other girls took one tremendous
scoop of candy and dumped it in the bag. Then they would take
out candy until they had reached the right amount. Customers,
not liking things taken away from them, naturally preferred the
girl they thought was giving them more. Notice the difference
between the positive and negative approach in this business
correspondence:

Negative: If you fail to pay your account within the next five days,
your neglect of this obligation will injure your credit rating.
Postive: Payment of your account within the next five days will protect your credit standing in the community.

Coöperative-Antagonistic

Coöperation, as we have shown, is the lifeblood of communication. Through social necessity we have learned to get along
with others. Hostility, opposition, and stubbornness gain few
favors. But even coöperation has its limitations. President Johnson's impeachment was thwarted by one man who refused to

coöperate. Falsely accused persons have been saved from execution by one jury member who refused to coöperate. The American Revolution was a rebellion against a type of coöperation that exploited the people. Let us never become so narrow as to assume that "rebellion is in itself a sign of the inferior mind."

Conformative-Nonconformative

The "band wagon" device of propagandists depends upon an attitude of conformity for its success. It takes little doing to show how inappropriate following the crowd may be. While language depends upon social conventions for its currency, successful writing and speaking are characterized by independence, originality, and spontaneity. Creativity thrives in an atmosphere of nonconformity. Thornton Wilder, in "The Silent Generation," speaks of the "liberty of belonging to oneself and not to a social fiction." An incident in a tearoom, reported in the news, shows how disconcerting nonconformity may be for people whose attitudes of conformity are frozen by convention:

"Val Peterson, former governor of Nebraska, shed his coat in the poshy dining room of the Grand Hotel on Mackinac Island. All the head waiters in the place couldn't make him put it back on again. It was a horrible dilemma, because he is a celebrity of sorts and the head waiters decided it wouldn't be good form, either, to pitch him out on the gubernatorial ear. But the real treat in the yarn concerns an unnamed, not celebrated man, who thereupon peeled off his own coat and loosened his tie, invoking all the privileges of democracy when threatened with expulsion."[5]

This story also demonstrates how regard for social status regulates attitudes of conformity or nonconformity.

Objective-Subjective

A person whose attitude is predominantly subjective is oriented to feelings rather than to facts. Communication is always

[5] *The State Journal* (Lansing, Michigan), August 5, 1955, p. 8.

a compromise between objective and subjective extremes. Neither attitude is better than the other except for selected purposes. A scientific report presupposes an impersonal, objective attitude on the part of the experimenter. A poem, novel, or drama may quite appropriately be subjective, although certainly it need not be. George R. Stewart's novels, for example, are quite objective: *Storm, Fire, Ordeal by Hunger,* and *U.S. 40.* For most exercises in communication skill, objectivity is preferable to subjectivity, because little opportunity is afforded thereby for opinions and feelings to cloud the truth.

2.7   Interests

Interests are also predispositions to particular lines of activity. They are especially important in communication because they regulate and facilitate attention. Interest in any task, whether educational, vocational, or communicative, supplies a natural drive toward achievement. Interest determines what one will read or listen to. It also determines what ideas selected for transmission will find an audience. If you bring to a lecture, talk, essay, or book a sincere interest in the subject, your chances of comprehending the author or speaker's ideas will be greatly enhanced. If you want to insure satisfactory reception of your ideas, you must appeal to the interests of readers and listeners. Interests are governed by familiarity, pleasant associations, personal experience, and intelligibility.

2.8   Values and Value Judgments

Values are feelings or expressions of the usefulness of perceived objects in satisfying motives. They are developed by interaction of self and environment. The interpretation we make of the facts of experience determines the value we assign to these facts and the responses we will make to them. The experience of Marjorie Kinnan Rawlings coming face to face with a deadly coral snake, mentioned earlier in this chapter (Section 2.2), shows how facts may be interpreted as threatening to the well-being and integrity of self.

All knowledge is saturated with values of one degree or another; otherwise facts would be meaningless. The splitting of the atom, for example, would be nothing more than a scientist's pastime, except as we interpret its significance as a means of dealing with our environment, both physical and social.

When a set of values is cherished by a community of people we usually refer to it as a value system. Thus, the "American way of life" is a value system, as is the nudists' way of life, the Communists' ideology, the Christians' doctrine or creed, the scientists' code of ethics, the medical doctors' Hippocratic oath, and the educators' belief in academic freedom. The expression "There is honor among thieves" points to a value system arrived at by mutual agreement of the people who hold to such a code.

When values are matters of individual or personal interpretation of facts, we usually refer to them as value judgments. Thus, the feeling that "All professors are bores," that "Women's place is in the home," that "Children should be seen and not heard," or that "Athletics has no proper place in higher education" may be your own evaluation of these matters.

Roughly speaking, we interpret facts, with reference to our motives and purposes, as advantageous, neutral, or detrimental. The very words we employ in relating experiences, explaining processes, or pleading causes reflect the values we place upon objective facts. Eric Berne, explaining why people act and feel the way they do, says:

"When we say that we love someone, we mean that the image of that person in our minds is highly charged with constructive, affectionate, and generous feelings. When we say that we hate someone, we mean that that person's image is charged with destructive, angry, and hostile feelings. What the person is actually like, or how he appears to other people and how they feel about him, does not come into the picture, except indirectly."[6]

Semanticists usually classify words according to the following scheme in an attempt to show how value judgments influence the expression and communication of meaning:

Honorific	Neutral	Degrading
generous	liberal	spendthrift
officer	policeman	cop
public servant	government official	bureaucrat
statesman	policy maker	politician
youthful	young	immature

2.9 Mechanisms of Self-Defense

In order to insure the integrity of self, protect it from devaluation, and maintain self-consistency, we establish all sorts of barriers against internal and external attacks. The less status we give to self the more barriers we set up for its defense. These barriers, or defense mechanisms, are very like habits, attitudes, and values in that they become part and parcel of the total self. Because such mechanisms shut out reality, they seriously interfere with effective communication both in transmission and in reception of ideas.

Identification

Identification is a defense mechanism by which one person assumes the role of another, and acts and behaves accordingly. We are quite accustomed to observing this type of behavior among children, who assume the observed roles of adulthood. They borrow adult clothing, ape adult mannerisms, and mock adult words, often to the embarrassment and chagrin of parents. But identification is not all child's play. Adults themselves play this same game—going so far as to accept the very thoughts and

[6] From *The Mind in Action*, New York, 1947.

ideas of others without reserve. "Most people are other people," says Oscar Wilde; "their thoughts are someone else's opinions, their lives a mimicry, their passions a quotation." People who do not trust their own thinking loudly expound the phrases, creeds, doctrines, ideologies, and prefabricated ideas of others. Such avoidance of brain work is retreat from reality. When the retreat becomes neurotic, identification becomes complete in fantasy, as witness "Teddy Roosevelt" in *Arsenic and Old Lace*.

Projection

Projection is a mechanism of defense by which one attributes his own motives, thoughts, experiences, and values to others. An individual defending himself in this fashion assumes that words have identical meanings and associations for everyone. By projection, listeners put words in a speaker's mouth—words which the speaker never uttered at all. Whatever the listener thinks the speaker means becomes what he actually said. The transmitter's words are bent to the receiver's thoughts.

Displacement, or scapegoating, is a form of projection by which personal inadequacies are transferred to others. Hitler's treatment of the Jews during World War II is an example.

Rationalization

Rationalization is a device by which one justifies, reconciles, and defends his own failures. It is a variety of wishful thinking designed to protect an idealized conception of self from ridicule or loss of status. A student, for example, may defend his incapacity to learn by calling attention to inadequate study conditions, insufficient time, or failure to understand an assignment. Making profuse excuses, belittling others, cirticizing existing circumstances, debasing the unattained goal, obscuring motives, transferring blame—all these are forms of rationalization.

Negativism is a particular variety of rationalization by which one aggressively resists outward forces—parental demands, social, political, or economic pressures—which interfere with personal plans. If you find yourself persistently criticizing others, antagonizing your instructors, or blocking group activity, you are probably defending your own feeling of inferiority.

Substitution and Distraction

Verbal substitutes are antidotes for unpleasant realities. They are employed as defense mechanisms against unpalatable truths or unsavory facts about self. Euphemisms offer excellent examples of such substitution. H. L. Mencken in *Supplement I* to *The American Language* supplies many examples of euphemistic evasions. His account of the substitution of *ecdysiast* for *strip-tease artist* is especially enlighting (pp. 584–587). A form of hypocrisy is apparent in such turgid substitutions as *underprivileged* for *poor*, *retarded* for *stupid*, and *vocational school* for *penal institution*.

When a boy is caught red-handed stealing someone's property, he is likely to say he is "borrowing" it, thus protecting his own position by substituting a much less offensive term. Such familiar expressions as *preventive war, strategic retreat, official sources, selective service, boys will be boys, business is business* are examples of verbal substitutes which camouflage truth.

Distraction is a device for calling attention away from a subject or idea which threatens to put self in a poor light. In propaganda analysis, it is called the "red herring" device. A candidate for public office who is asked to state his views on increasing taxes for support of education may draw a red herring across the trail and divert attention to the real issue by criticizing low standards of teacher qualification. Students sometimes use this device to get a professor wound up on an idea that has nothing to do with the current class assignment or the course of study. Depreciating the character, habits, or political views of an opponent in debate or discussion is a common variety of distraction. Humor—the telling of stories in order to avoid discussion of ideas—is another variety. Davy Crockett used this device to win a seat in Congress at a time when he knew little or nothing about politics and had no firm convictions on the public issues of his day.

Compensation

Compensation is a mechanism designed to make amends for personal deficiencies of one kind or another. In communication courses, a student may try to compensate for lack of ideas by taking great pains with penmanship, neatness of manuscript form, accuracy of spelling, and other mechanical matters. "Apple polishing" is a popular term for all types of scholastic compensation.

Achievement, of course, is the only reasonable test of communication skill. An instructor should be little concerned with how much midnight oil you have burned in completing an assignment. Your efforts in reading, writing, speaking, and listening should be judged by objective, impersonal, and impartial standards.

Retreat

Another method of self-protection is escape or retreat from reality. A student who has failed to prepare an assignment for class may simply not show up. A person stumped by a particularly knotty problem may say, with Scarlet O'Hara, "I'll think about that tomorrow." Some go so far as to deny the existence of "insoluble" problems by silencing all conversation about them. Going to the movies, burying oneself in a book, and taking a vacation are methods of retreat from boredom, worry, incompetence, insecurity, domination, gloom, or drudgery.

Regression—evident in temper-tantrums, jealous fits, talk strikes—is a type of retreat in which one avoids unpleasantness by reverting to infantile behavior.

EXERCISES

1. Make an inventory of your listening difficulties by comparing your personal reactions and responses to a lecture or talk with

the reactions and responses of your classmates. Your instructor will explain how to go about it.

2. Diagnose your personal reading difficulties by taking a standardized reading test which your instructor will administer.

3. Give a short speech or talk before the class in which you relate an unusual personal experience. Take particular note of any physical and emotional reactions you have to the audience, such as stage fright, forgetfulness, or rigidity.

4. Write a 500- to 750-word autobiography of your personality. Direct your thoughts to your instructor, who will hold what you say in strict confidence. Focus your attention on such things as are suggested in the following questions:

   a. What people have had the greatest influence on your life?
   b. What experiences in your early life do you remember most vividly?
   c. What do you think of your grade-school and high-school education? What teacher influenced you most? Why?
   d. What are your principal likes and dislikes?
   e. How do you get along with other people? Are you popular? Are you a wallflower?
   f. Have you won honors for some achievement you have accomplished?
   g. Do you have a definite goal in life, or are you searching for such a goal?
   h. Why did you come to college?
   i. What do you consider your strongest and weakest traits of character?
   j. How much have you traveled?
   k. What subject do you prefer to talk about among friends?
   l. What hobbies or special talents do you have?
   m. What do you do for amusement and entertainment?
   n. What type of books and magazines do you read?
   o. What is your favorite movie or television program?

5. What evidence can you find to support the idea that the average run of American people are superstitious, or cling to a number of groundless beliefs?

6. Write a short paper in which you explain how you went about breaking an irritating or repulsive habit.

7. Think of an instance in which you misjudged the motives of one

of your acquaintances. Tell the class about it, explaining the nature of your mistake.

FOR FURTHER READING

Allport, Gordon W., "Prejudice: A Sickness of Individuals and Society," *Scientific American*, June, 1950.

Bailey, Bernadine, "Pre-fabricated Thinking," *International Altrusan*, June, 1946.

Barzun, Jacques, "The Educated Man," *Life*, October 16, 1950.

Berne, Eric, "Why People Act and Feel the Way They Do," in *The Mind in Action*, New York, 1947.

Boatright, Mody C., "On the Nature of Belief," *Southern Review*, Spring, 1954.

Bruce, H. Addington, "The Importance of Being Interested," *Outlook*, July 18, 1914.

Cohen, Felix S., "The Reconstruction of Hidden Value Judgments," from *Symbols and Values*, edited by Lyman Bryson, and others, New York, 1954.

Easton, David, "Shifting Images of Social Science and Values," *The Antioch Review*, Spring, 1955.

Evans, Bergen, "Autointoxication," *Harper's Magazine*, May, 1947.

Frankel, Charles, "Are We Really Crazy?" *Harper's Magazine*, June, 1955.

Fromm, Erich, "The Illusion of Individuality," in *Escape from Freedom*, New York, 1941.

Fry, Christopher, "On Keeping the Sense of Wonder," *Vogue*, January, 1956.

Gosse, Edmund, "The First Consciousness of the Self," in *Father and Son*, New York, 1907.

Highet, Gilbert, "The Necessity for Reason," in *Man's Unconquerable Mind*, New York, 1954.

Horney, Karen, *Our Inner Conflicts*, New York, 1945.

James, William, "On a Certain Blindness in Human Beings," in *Essays on Faith and Morals*, New York, 1939.

Johnson, Wendell, *People in Quandaries*, New York, 1946.

Krutch, Joseph Wood, "The Genesis of a Mood," in *The Modern Temper*, New York, 1929.

Morrison, Theodore, "Dover Beach Revisited," *Harper's Magazine*, January, 1940.

Overstreet, Harry A., "The Gentle People of Prejudice," *Saturday Review of Literature*, January 21, 1950.

Overstreet, Harry A., *The Mature Mind*, New York, 1949.

Overstreet, Harry A., *The Mind Alive*, New York, 1954.

Rollo, May, *Man's Search for Himself*, New York, 1953.

Steffens, Lincoln, *The Autobiography of Lincoln Steffens*, New York, 1931.

Winn, Ralph B., "Axiology: The Problem of Human Values," in *American Philosophy*, New York, 1955.

3

UNDERSTAND THE USES
OF LANGUAGE

LANGUAGE HAS BEEN CALLED THE "HIGH-est and most amazing achievement of the human mind." It is, of course, the scepter by which man defends his position as "monarch of all he surveys." By this magic wand the world as we know it was created. Words have transformed human chaos into social order, savagery into civilization, and ignorance into knowledge. Language makes it possible for us to experience what is absent in space and remote in time, to recreate the past and to anticipate and fashion the future.

But despite its inestimable usefulness, language can be an instrument of destruction. In the hands of irresponsible and malicious persons, it can be used to destroy what it has created, to rob us of our birthright, to enslave our minds, and to thwart our purposes. This makes it mandatory that we understand the functions of language in the communication of thought.

Language has three primary functions: sign, signal, and symbol. As signs, words make it possible for us to discover natural truth, to record, classify, condense, and organize experience. As signals, words allow us to exchange thoughts, ideas, sensations, emotions, and feelings with others. As symbols, words allow us to create ideas, to focus attention on abstract truth, and to satisfy our personal needs and desires.

46

3.1   Words as Signs

A sign is the name of anything—person, place, object, event, process—arbitrarily assigned to specify or distinguish it. A sign announces the existence of whatever has been, can be, or is observed with the senses. It is an instrument of science by which phenomena are analyzed, classified, differentiated, and recorded. The following words may properly be called signs:

Euarctos americanus	(American black bear)
Cambarus diogenes	(crawfish)
Centaurea cyanus	(cornflower)

High-precision sign language, such as is employed by scientists in recording observations of the natural process world, is quite unintelligible to the average person:

What happens in photosynthesis may be presented as an interchange in which six molecules of carbon dioxide combine with six molecules of water in the presence of light and chlorophyll to produce one molecule of glucose sugar and six molecules of free oxygen:

$$\text{Six } CO_2 + \text{ six } H_2O \xrightarrow[\text{chlorophyll}]{\text{light}} C_6H_{12}O_6 \text{ and six } O_2.[1]$$

Inflexibility of Words

The phenomena we observe with our senses are ever changing, but verbal statements arrest the flux of reality. Ideas become crystallized and frozen the moment they are phrased in language. Words cannot possibly keep pace with the unreined imagination or the fluid nature of experience. "The result of today, which haunts the mind and cannot be escaped, will presently be abridged into a word." We think of words as the changing coins of communication, when actually things, not words, refuse to be arrested. We say, "The sun is coming up," even though we have

[1] George W. Gray, "Our Bridge from the Sun," *Harper's Magazine*, September, 1955.

long since decided that the sunrise is an optical illusion. We say, "A man boards a ship," even though the ship is made of steel; and we speak of "sailing" in ships that have no sails. We are unable to figure out how "exceptions prove the rule," until we discover that *prove* originally meant *test* or *try*.

Whenever you read a statement that purports to represent the state of present reality, you can be sure that it is at best an approximation of ever changing facts: The population of the United States is 161,000,000. The number of employed persons in the United States is 62,000,000. The American people purchase 8,000,000 new automobiles annually. American consumers eat 25,000,000 meals each year made from frozen foods.

Abstraction and Concreteness

An abstraction is the result of selecting particular facts of experience from a total aggregate of facts which make up an object or phenomenon. One way to explain this is to say: we see what we see because we leave out what we leave out. We cannot, with our limited senses, experience all that exists in the world of reality. We are necessarily selective.

In the first place, our sensual capacities—that is, our powers of observation—are circumscribed. No eye has been invented which can see all that exists. The most detailed report you can imagine, such as the specification of the constituency of a drop of blood as seen under a powerful microscope, is incomplete. Scientists are able to show that the spectrum is not actually a band of separate colors, as we visualize it, but a continuous scale of light waves which we, by sense perception, cut into fragments of red, orange, yellow, green, blue, indigo, and violet. What we call infrared and ultraviolet are parts of the continuous scale which lie beyond our capacity to observe directly.

Another reason for the selectivity of our observations is that we are limited by our motives and purposes while making an observation. When we look at a clock, for example, we usually see only what time is indicated. A thirsty man on a desert sees a mirage of a running stream of water (which doesn't exist) partly because his need is so strong.

When we translate experience into language, we employ words which are abstractions of the objects they stand for. Thus, the word *automobile,* which may be applied to the car I drive, leaves out any consideration of make, model, accessories, mileage, or condition. The more abstract a word is, the fewer characteristics which distinguish the object it represents are specified. The more concrete a word is, the more observable characteristics are included.

If we think of words as having degrees of abstractness, we might chart selected words applying to the same object as follows:

ABSTRACT

wealth	vessel	vegetation
possessions	ship	farm produce
assets	sailing craft	fruit crop
livestock	whaler	apples
cattle	*Pequod*	Winesap

CONCRETE

When we use "high-level abstractions" like *democracy, freedom, communism,* and *capitalism,* we should take care to make our meanings perfectly clear. One writer has said that a word is like a check drawn against the world of experience, and that it has no meaning unless we can "cash it in" by pointing to the thing in experience to which it refers.

Both abstract and concrete words are necessary in communication. Abstract words are necessary to give ideas form and compactness. Concrete words are necessary to make ideas clear. Notice how the idea in the first sentence of the following passage is clarified by the subsequent concrete details: "He had the emotional stability of a six-year old. When he felt out of sorts, he would rave and stamp, or sink into suicidal gloom and talk darkly of going to the East to end his days as a Buddhist monk. Ten minutes later, when something pleased him, he would rush out of doors and run around the garden, or jump up and down on the sofa, or stand on his head. He could be grief-stricken over the death of a pet dog, and he could be callous and heartless to a degree that would have made a Roman emperor shudder."[2]

General and Specific Words

Words may also be classified according to degree of precision they denote. A general word or expression refers to a class, group, or type of particular objects. A specific word refers to a particular instance or object included in a class, group, or type. Thus, *percale, gingham, silk, cotton* are specific examples of the more general *cloth* or *fabric*. The difference between general and specific words is illustrated in the following statements:

General: The Army furnishes the enlistee with food, clothing, and housing.
Specific: In the infantry, Pfc. Jones eats "C" rations, wears fatigues, and lives in a pup tent.

The word *army*, in the first statement, is more specific than *military services*, but less specific than *infantry*. *Pfc. Jones* is more specific than *enlistee; "C" rations* more specific than *food; fatigues* more specific than *clothing;* and *pup tent* more specific than *housing*.

As with abstract and concrete words, both general and specific words are essential to communication of meaning. As a rule, however, specific words clarify meaning better than general ones do. Notice the clarity of the following editorial about "Federal Gobbledegook," expressed in specific language:

"The idea of seven Pentagons stuffed to the attic with letters, documents, files and other assorted varieties of Government paper is an appalling one; but we have the Hoover Commission's word for it that there is enough federal records on hand to fill all

[2] Deems Taylor, "The Monster," *Of Men and Music*, New York, 1937, pp. 4–5.

those Pentagons if anyone wanted to take the trouble to do it.

"And that isn't all. There are enough federal employees handling the Government's paper work to occupy all the office space in thirty-six Empire State Buildings. A billion official letters a year are written at an annual cost to the taxpayer of a dollar per letter. . . ."[3]

3.2 Words as Signals

As signals words are bridges between people. Signals make it possible for us to exchange ideas, thoughts, points of view. In order for any two people to understand each other, there must be agreement on what words will mean in particular contexts, for particular purposes, and on particular occasions.

In the quotation from the *New York Times* just given, the following sentence occurs: "A billion official letters a year are written at an annual cost to the taxpayer of a dollar per letter." Does the word *letter*, which appears twice, have the same meaning in both instances? The second *letter* could mean (a) a missive, message, piece of correspondence, communication or (b) an alphabetic character, a unit of orthography. The import of the text would be radically altered if we should interpret it wrong. In this case, the second use of the word derives its meaning from the first use, so that there is little question as to the intent. But it is very easy to get one's signals crossed and misunderstand a simple statement or convey meaning in no wise intended. As Rudyard Kipling says, "There are nine and sixty ways of constructing tribal lays, and every single one of them is right." Just so with language: the important question is one not of correctness but of adequacy, or fitness, or appropriateness. This passage from Melville's *White Jacket* is a good example of language perfectly appropriate to a particular situation:

"Now take my advice, and steer clear of all trouble. D'ye see,

[3] *New York Times*, February 22, 1955, p. 20.

touch your tile whenever a swob speaks to you. And never mind how much they rope's end you, keep your red rag belayed; for you must know as how they don't fancy sea-lawyers; and when sarving out of slops comes round, stand up to it stiffly; it's only an Oh Lord or two, and a few Oh my Gods!—that's all."

Notice how the following paraphrase of this text robs it of the salty flavor and zest so important to its meaning:

"Now take my counsel, and avoid all trouble. Do you understand, salute whenever an officer speaks to you. And no matter how much they whip you, keep your lips sealed; for you should know they have no use for philosophers; and when it's your turn for punishment, take it like a man; it could be worse."

The meanings of words employed in social communication are subject to three varieties of alterations: alterations owing to time, alterations owing to place, and alterations owing to circumstances.

Chronological Changes

Language changes as people change. Only dead languages—languages no longer used for communication—remain static. Words employed in the dynamic affairs of social activity are alive. "All language is vehicular and transitive," said Emerson, "and is good, as ferries and horses are, for conveyance, not as farms and houses are, for homestead." There is no telling what the words we speak today will mean tomorrow, but whatever meanings they acquire we will ourselves supply. The following account by George H. McKnight calls attention to differences in meaning accounted for by time:

"Sir James Barrie in 'When a Man's Single,' published about 1900, records a price scale announced by a London grocer as follows: 'Eggs, new-laid 1s.3d; eggs, fresh, 1s.2d.; eggs, warranted, 1s.; eggs, 10d.' About fourteen years later in May, 1914, the present writer observed in a London grocer's stall the following price scale: new-laid eggs, 10d.; Selected, 12d.; Warranted, 16d. In the period preceding the war the value of eggs had not greatly changed, but the value of words had. The superlative *new-laid* of 1900 had become degraded to the bottom of the scale."[4]

We might observe the same sort of change in the word *large* as used to designate size of packages of breakfast food, soap flakes, and tooth paste. One manufacturer of dental cream prints *large* on the smallest package of the product offered for sale. With the introduction of *super, extra large*, and *giant economy size*, the once superlative *large* is greatly diminished.

The alterations of language directly responsible to changing times include: alterations in spelling and punctuation, alterations in meaning, alterations in pronunciation, alterations in sentence structure and syntax, alterations in sentence length, alterations in arrangement of words, and alterations in idioms and word choices.

Regional Differences

The dynamic forces which control approval or disapproval of specific language forms are the natural, uninhibited, free forces of society. Usage is decided by community agreement, not by regulations imposed by scholars, dictionary makers, or divines. For this reason, language is no more uniform than custom and tradition are uniform throughout a large geographic area.

In the United States, three principal dialects have been defined: New England, Southern, and General American, but linguistic geographers, sampling the speech habits of people in small communities and plotting these usages on a map, find many variations of speech behavior within the large dialect areas. The territorial boundaries of a given location are shown on maps included in the *Linguistic Atlas*. Because people do not stay put but are constantly moving from one community to another, there is a process of continual and progressive differentiation affecting language all the time.

[4] George H. McKnight, *English Words and Their Background*, New York, 1923, p. 280.

A single example of the regional variations in usage will serve to explain this type of linguistic change:

Three expressions for eating something between meals are widely used: *bite* in the New England settlement area, *snack* in the Southern area and the South Midland, *piece* in the North Midland. The areas of these three terms overlap a great deal, especially in the thickly populated tract extending from Greater New York City to Baltimore.

Although *bite* is predominantly a New England term, it occurs beside *snack* or *piece* or both all the way from the Hudson Valley to the Potomac. In similar fashion, *snack* is not confined to the South and the South Midland but is used also in Philadelphia and enjoys a great popularity in Greater New York City and the Hudson Valley.

Piece is in general use in all of Pennsylvania except for Philadelphia and its immediate vicinity, in Northern West Virginia, and in the Ohio Valley. It is less common in the Shenandoah Valley and rather rare on the Kanawha, where the Southern *snack* has become established. The Kanawha Valley has also the two local expressions *check* and *jack-bite* beside *snack* and *piece*. Neither of these terms has been noted elsewhere in the Eastern States.

Scattered instances of *piece meal*, in this sense have been recorded in the Blue Ridge and on the Kanawha.

Piece is not uncommon in the New England counties of Pennsylvania, in parts of Upstate New York, and on the Jersey side of the upper Delaware. Since Pennsylvania expressions rarely spread to these sections and since the word is not current in New England, *piece* may have a Dutch background.[5]

Semantic Differences

Just as the precise value of coins and bank notes varies with each transaction into which they are introduced, so do words have different meanings or values at different times, in different places, and under different circumstances. *Baste* means one thing to a cook and something quite different to a tailor. *Morgue* means one thing to an undertaker, something else to a newspaper-

[5] Hans Kurath, *A Word Geography of the Eastern United States*, Ann Arbor, Michigan, 1949, pp. 71–72.

man. Meaning of any word is determined by the context in which it is employed. It is also dependent, as we showed in Chapter 1, upon the experience of the person who employs it. And since the total experiences of any two individuals are never identical, words can never mean exactly the same thing to both parties in communication, or on any two separate occasions.

Semantic differences in meaning of words is the source of much difficulty and misunderstanding. This fact is clarified in the following excerpt from an editorial:

. . . A friend suggested that it might be well if Americans talked less about *democracy* and more about *human freedom*—particularly for propaganda purposes. He quoted to us the opinion of a Frenchman who said that the word *democracy* is no good in Soviet territory: the Russians use it all the time, and a lot of captive and neutral people don't care much for what the word connotes after seeing the Red concept of "democracy" in action.

No doubt our friend has a point which the American Government's bringers-of-light-to-benighted-lands might ponder seriously. For it is true that the Soviets have stolen and poisoned some of our most cherished words in what might be called a semantic germ warfare. Russian "democracy" is to American democracy as illiteracy is to literacy or no is to yes. But the Reds have hollered the word so loudly at so many people that maybe half the world now has the wrong definition.

This semantic warfare isn't confined to the international theater, either. Here at home such words as liberal and progressive certainly don't mean what they did 25 years ago. Come to think of it, even the cool, precise and scholarly word investigation has lately come to take on a rather sinister sound and meaning.[6]

3.3   Words as Symbols

As symbols, words replace things; that is, they stand for something other than themselves. A child, not understanding the relation between words and things, when asked whether the moon

[6] *Collier's*, May 2, 1953, p. 70.

could have been called "the sun" and the sun "moon," said: "No, because the sun makes it warm and the moon gives light."

The word *symbol* comes to us from the Greek *symbololon* meaning "mark, token, or ticket." When words are used as tokens, they enable us to condense experience and reality in such a way as to make abstract thought possible. The story is told of a little girl whose parents sent her to a potato field to count the sacks of potatoes which had been harvested. When she arrived at the field, she suddenly realized that she didn't know how to count. But rather than fail in her mission, she took one potato out of each sack and delivered them to her parents. What the girl in this story had done, of course, was to let a potato stand for, or symbolize, a whole sack of potatoes. Had she been able to count, she could have employed a mathematical symbol to represent the total number of sacks.

A large number of things quite familiar to us have assigned symbolic values: insignia, uniforms, flags, monetary currency, jewelry, and a host of other things. "There are," as S. I. Hayakawa has pointed out, "few things that men do or want to do, possess or want to possess, that have not, in addition to their mechanical or biological value, a symbolic value."

But our concern here is with words as symbols, and with our capacity to create, manipulate, and assign values to them as we please. When we speak of words, sounds, and gestures as tools of communication, we use the word *tool* symbolically. *Bridge*, in the sense of bridging gaps between speakers and listeners, is also symbolic. When we say prices "soar," or the value of the dollar "dipped," we are symbolizing experience with words borrowed from other experiences. When we use the word *heart* to express the idea of sympathetic understanding, or the word *head* to represent clear thinking, or *muscle* to denote strength, we are exercising our ability to use words in the creation of thoughts and ideas.

Not only do symbols give human beings the supreme power of abstract thought, but symbolic language exerts a powerful influence on man's thoughts. Many a symbol is an image imprinted in our minds by unsatisfied or repressed drives or desires. J. A. M. Meerloo, instructor in psychiatry at Columbia University, points out that words such as *Fatherland, Cowardice, Honor, Old Glory* lure the soul of mankind. We react, he says, without volition, for archaic feelings are touched and drag us away. When symbolic words are abused by overuse, their potency diminishes and they become banal slogans which influence behavior while failing to engage the intellect.

C. S. Forester, in the following passage, explains how personal experiences may be exploited in the symbolic process:

"No writer—at least no writer such as myself—ever quite escapes his own childhood. He returns to it again and again, with affection and with longing and with increasing accuracy of recollection and detail, for this is personal history that has been experienced. And this is the stuff that stories and books are made of."[7]

EXERCISES

1. Point out examples in the following passage of abstract words which must be defined as you see fit:

Movies were nothing new in 1912, and though they were looked on darkly as promoters of juvenile delinquency by clergymen, whose congregations and collections they seemed to be stealing, they were not taken seriously by those who concerned themselves with the niceties of taste. The nickelodeon, which had been the inspiration of two Pittsburgh showmen, John P. Harris and Harry Davis, in 1905 had spread across the country, a wildfire of tricked-up elegance and the forerunner of today's movie palace. A nickelodeon was simply a converted store, ornamented with cast-off opera and theater props, sometimes seating as many as ninety customers. It offered a movie show that ran anywhere from twenty minutes to an hour. The usual fare was a one-reel melodrama, a comedy of even shorter length, and a "song slide" which projected popular

[7] "Hornblower's London," *Holiday*, August, 1955.

lyrics on the screen to encourage the customers to sing along with a paid crooner and pianist. There were between eight and ten thousand nickelodeons in America by 1908, with electric signs and fancy names—"Bijou Dream," "Pictorium," "Dreamland," "Theatorium," and "Jewell"—and a major attraction of the day was a thriller called *The Great Train Robbery*.

—Russell Lynes, *The Tastemakers*, pp. 226–227

2. Mention other senses than those defined in the passage above in which *nickelodeon* and *thriller* are currently employed. What is a movie palace? Can you think of other words which have changed their meanings over a period of years?

3. Read Herman Melville's "The Whiteness of the Whale," *Moby Dick*, Chapter 42. Write a paper in which you explain the author's use of symbolic values of the color white. What symbolic values are commonly attached to the following colors: green, purple, red, blue, yellow, black, pink?

4. According to Hans Kurath in *A Word Geography of the Eastern United States*, regional variations of pancake include *hot cake, griddle cake, fritter, flannel cake, batter cake, batty cake*. Can you list other variations you have heard?

5. Think of symbolic values traditionally attached to the following words: *goat, wolf, bear, squirrel, cat, whale, snake, elephant, wildcat, cow, rabbit, fox, tiger*. Explain the symbolism in a literary work, such as Jack London's *The Sea Wolf*, Herman Melville's *Moby Dick*, Edgar Allan Poe's "The Black Cat," or Thomas Wolfe's *You Can't Go Home Again*.

6. Read a portion of "The Massachusetts School Law of 1647," as presented in Henry S. Commager's *Living Ideas in America*. Point out as many usages—diction, spelling, punctuation, structure, etc.—as you can which are no longer current.

7. Notice by reading the following passage how words change their meanings because of accumulated experiences:

An author re-reading his philosophical juvenalia is apt to say "I wonder what I meant when I wrote that." But another curious thing can happen. He finds that he agrees with his younger self, but now means by the words he uses something very different from what he meant before. This latter is what has happened in the case of my paper on "Representation and Expression." I would even now try to defend most of what I wrote in that paper, but what I should be defending would differ from what I think I thought I was defending in 1914.

—C. A. Mace

List five words which have come to mean something different for you in the past five years because of your education.

8. What is the relationship between the words *universe* and *university*? How are these words self-explanatory?

9. What words in the following passage describing a supersonic air flight are not defined in the dictionary in the sense employed here:

The airplane began to nose over. It is a characteristic of airplanes going through the transonic speed to nose down slightly as they exceed Mach 1 (the speed of sound). But when Smith tried to pull the ship up, he found that the control stick was stuck fast. He could not budge it. The plane continued to steepen its dive and gain speed. As it neared 20 degrees Smith radioed the company that he was having trouble with the hydraulic system. He grabbed the stick with both hands and pulled with all his strength. No response. By this time the dive had steepened to an 80 degree angle. His wingman gave the orders to bail out. The orders weren't needed. Smith was already making his preparations as fast as he could move; stopcocked the engine, opened the speed brake, pulled his helmet visor down over his eyes. With his right hand he pulled up on the armrest of the seat, ejecting the canopy. From the dead silence of the closed cockpit to the open rush of air going by at more than 700 miles an hour, a tremendous noise like a long continuous explosion filled his ears.

"I don't actually remember pulling the trigger to eject the seat," Smith says. "The last thing I remember was seeing the Mach meter in front of my face, reading 1.05. The next thing, I woke up in the hospital five days later!"

—Al Beers, "Two Seconds to Live,"
Spartan Engineer, January, 1956

FOR FURTHER READING

Black, Max, "The Uses of Language," *Critical Thinking*, New York, 1946.

Chase, Stuart, "Five Roads to Agreement," *The Rotarian*, February, 1954.

Chase, Stuart, "How Language Shapes Our Thoughts," *Harper's Magazine*, April, 1954.

Chase, Stuart, *The Power of Words*, New York, 1955.

Friedman, Norman, "Faith, Reason, and the Symbol," *The Reconstructionist*, May 15, 1953.

Goldberg, Isaac, *The Wonder of Words*, New York, 1938.

Hayakawa, S. I., *Language in Thought and Action*, New York, 1949.

Hepp, Maylon H. "Signs, Meanings, and Language," chap. 2 of *Thinking Things Through*, New York, 1956.

Langer, Susanne K., "The Lord of Creation," *Fortune*, January, 1944.

MacLeish, Archibald, "The Language of Poetry," *Saturday Review of Literature*, March 5, 1955.

Morris, Charles W., "Signs! Signs! Signs!" in *The Open Self*, New York, 1948.

Rowan, Carl T., "A Symbol by the Sea," from *South of Freedom*, New York, 1952.

Sapir, Edward, *Language*, New York, 1921, 1949.

Sapir, Edward, "The Social Functions of Language," from "Language," in *Encyclopedia of the Social Sciences*, Vol. IX.

II

FOCUS YOUR ATTENTION

4

FOCUS ATTENTION ON IDEAS

COMMUNICATION STARTS WITH AN IDEA AND the urge to share it with others. As E. S. Martin once said, "It is a great advantage to a writer to have sense. . . . It is an advantage to him to have learning. . . . But the thing he *must* have is ideas . . . he must have bubbles in his mind." Far too many speeches and essays consist of words strung together in arbitrary arrangements without ever approaching an idea. Before you begin to speak or write, you must have something to say. Otherwise all the techniques in the world will prove as useless as an empty rifle on a battlefield. "Anyone can learn to write," says Stephen Leacock, "who has something to say and knows how to say it." This principle, of course, applies also to speaking. And, we might add, anyone can learn to read or listen who can detect ideas and recognize the methods by which they are clarified and developed.

4.1   The Nature of Ideas

An idea is a thought or perception which is created in the face of desire by intellect and emotion acting on the facts of experience. It is the conversion of nature into the "rhetoric of thought," in harmony with purpose and controlled by judgment. This rather abstract definition may be explained as follows:

Ideas as Products of Experience

An idea is the product of your own creative thinking, or reflection. An incident in Jack London's story "To Build a Fire" will illustrate: In the story, a tenderfoot in the Yukon found himself at the mercy of a 75-degree-below-zero temperature. His best efforts to build a fire and keep it going had failed. An inventory of his feelings and sensations told him he was freezing to death. He had gotten his feet wet and knew that no amount of running will stimulate circulation in wet feet at such temperatures. "The sight of his dog put a wild idea into his head. He remembered the tale of the man caught in a blizzard, who killed a steer and crawled inside the carcass, and so was saved. He would kill the dog and bury his hands in the warm body until the numbness went out of them. Then he would build another fire."

The last two sentences contain the idea in simple form. Notice that the man in the story employed past experience in the creation of his idea.

Ideas as Problem Solutions

Whenever you recognize a problem in your own environment and arrive at a solution to it, you have created an idea. The character in London's story recognized the problem of keeping alive at extremely frigid temperatures. The idea, pointed out, is a solution to this problem.

The simplest way to corner an idea is to recognize a problem and then look for a solution to it. Suppose you are asked to write a paper or give a talk on a subject of your own choice, and you select "college football" as your topic. Start by listing a number of problems connected with football in college; choose one of these problems for your topic; and arrive at a solution to the problem—through reading, personal experience, or conversation with others—before you begin to plan your paper or talk.

Ideas as Images of Reality

You act and feel in accord with your own mental images of real things (see p. 6). These images may or may not be adequate reflections or pictures of reality. The soundness and workability of your ideas will depend to a large extent on how closely your mind-pictures do resemble what actually exists. In London's story the tenderfoot's mental images were inadequate. He imagined that he could catch his dog, strangle it, and warm his hands inside the body. But when he tried to carry out his plan, he found that he had misjudged the dog. He couldn't catch it. A new look in his eye put the dog on guard. His idea proved unsatisfactory. His proposal failed to solve the problem. He ultimately froze to death.

Ideas as Original Creations

The creation of an idea is like the bursting of a rosebud. It develops, unfolds, blossoms in your own thinking. It is a personal matter governed almost entirely by internal urges. No one can accomplish the feat for you. You must think for yourself.

In speaking and writing, you formulate ideas from experience, express the thoughts in words, and then transmit them to others. In reading and listening, you re-create the author's idea by substituting his words for actual experience. You then gain insight from vicarious experience, just as the author gained insight from real experience. Communication is successfully established when your thought coincides with the author's thought. E. L. Thorndike, the famous educator, likened the comprehension of meaning to solving a problem in mathematics: "It consists of selecting the right elements of the situation and putting them together in the right relations, and also with the right amount of weight or influence or force for each."

Ideas as Unifying Agents in Communication

Once an idea is phrased in a clear-cut, well-defined, succinct statement of thesis—a topic sentence, a logical proposition, a legal brief, a scientific hypothesis, a discussion problem, a poetic theme—it functions as a unifying agent for all devices used to convey meaning. It is the focal point of the entire context in which it appears. Everything else hinges on it. It determines means of clarification, methods of development, modes of support, and types of exemplification. Such verbal factors as diction, style, tone, literary form, sentence arrangement, emphasis, choice of detail, and mechanical adjustments are all decided by the nature of the idea concerned. It unifies sentences, paragraphs, complete essays, books, or sets of books; talks, discussions, conversations, symposiums, or conferences.

4.2   Transmission of Ideas

Focusing Attention on an Idea You Really Want to Communicate

Much of the difficulty experienced by students in the communication of meaning results from poor selection of a subject or topic for writing or speaking. The things you are sincerely interested in or passionately curious about will furnish abundant ideas for practice in communication. Follow these suggestions:

a.   Select an idea connected with things familiar to you. There are countless opportunities for creating ideas right under your nose. One of Mark Twain's most famous stories was written about a frog. Walt Whitman found a bumper crop of ideas in a leaf of grass. King Solomon created a profound idea out of the habits of an ant. Exploit your hobbies, your vocational interests, your experiences, your personal problems.

b. Select an idea related to your personal experience. You must live a little before you can talk or write at all. Whenever people talk from ignorance rather than from knowledge, or parrot what others have already said, they communicate badly. Their inexperience gives them away. Herman Melville's sea tales— *Typee, Omoo, Mardi, Moby Dick,* and *Billy Budd*—were inspired by the author's personal experiences on a whaling ship. Ernie Pyle's ideas came out of his personal observations at the battle front. Betty MacDonald found material for *The Egg and I* in her personal experiences on a chicken ranch.

c. Select an idea based on acquired knowledge. Knowledge comes from a burning curiosity about the world. Carl Sandburg became curious about Abraham Lincoln and produced a veritable library of books on Lincoln's life. H. L. Mencken became curious about American words and produced his *The American Language* in four editions and two supplements. André Maurois's curiosity about George Sand brought him in touch with "mountains of letters, records, and miscellaneous documents" about the French novelist, which supplied the necessary data for *Lelia: the Life of George Sand.*

d. Select an idea that defines a real need or solves a real problem in your life or in society. Recognition of a real need should not stump you. We are all pretty critical of the way things are run in this world. We go about asking why someone doesn't do something about traffic problems, about juvenile delinquency, about disturbances in the dormitory, and so on. If you feel there is a real need for something, you have hit upon a subject for communication.

e. Select an idea which lends itself to the specific assignment you want to accomplish. You may be asked to write a particular kind of paper or deliver a particular kind of talk. The nature of the assignment will help you determine which ideas to select. Here are some standard types of discourse: (1) observation and description of a person, place, object, or event, (2) explanation of a process, (3) recognition and solution of a problem, (4) statement of personal opinion or point of view, (5) report of investigated facts, (6) definition of a word or concept, (7) analysis of a subject, (8) definition of a thesis, hypothesis, or proposition, (9) criticism or evaluation of a book, essay, or lecture.

Translating Your Idea into Words

Words are signals invested with meanings by which ideas can be transferred from one person to another. Words are not the ideas themselves; they are the vehicle by which the thoughts are transported. The most intimate communication between people extends far beyond mere words to depths of understanding which defy verbalization and can only be approached by techniques of free association. The loftiest thoughts in either poetry or prose are not found in words but in the interaction of mental images which words create. Words set the machinery of mind in motion.

When an idea takes form in your mind, it grows out of, or develops from, specific facts or mental images of specific facts. In translating the idea into words, you simply reverse the order of progression. You start with the solution, the crux of the matter, and then proceed to supply the facts from which it was derived and by which it can be supported. The following directions will help you to state the central idea of a talk or paper.

a. Phrase the idea in one complete, declarative sentence, if possible:

General education is basic to the proper development of man's total capacities.

Herman Melville was the first important naturalist in the mainstream of American fiction.

Society has robbed man of his economic independence.

b. State the central idea, or thesis, so that your meaning will be perfectly clear. The title of an essay or talk is usually much too condensed and abbreviated for this purpose. One of Stephen Leacock's well-known essays is titled "Education Is Eating Up Life." Now this statement is perfectly satisfactory as a title, but as a thesis it leaves too much to random interpretation. A thesis would read something like this: "General education and the liberal arts take up about twenty years of the life of most college students."

c. Make the thesis statement as specific as your purpose requires. It makes a difference whether you are going to write a full-length book or a 500-word paper on your chosen subject. An idea must be of manageable size, depending on the time and space at your disposal. Notice this statement: "Effective communication is important to successful human relations." This may appear to be a good idea for a 500-word paper or a four-minute talk, but it is too broad, too general, too all-inclusive. About this thesis you could write the history of the world. But the idea can be restricted and tailored for precise purposes in a number of ways. Notice what happens when we limit human relations to specific varieties of human relations: Effective communication is important in labor-management disputes. Effective communication is important in student-teacher relationships. Effective communication is important in maintaining family unity. Effective communication is important in seeking a job or position. Effective communication is important to the success of the United Nations. Other limitations of the idea can be made by (1) specifying the nature of *effective communication* or (2) defining the meaning of *important*.

d. State the thesis in a way that lends itself to adequate development. If you intend to develop a thesis by the presentation of verifiable facts, you must state it in such a way that it can be developed by facts. Compare these two statements:

California produces better oranges than does Texas.

California produces more oranges than does Texas.

The first statement cannot be developed or supported by factual data. The second statement does lend itself to factual development.

e. Make your thesis an adequate summary of all the evidence you intend to muster in its support. If you believe, for example, that the American way of life is the result of the interaction of both puritan and frontier influences, you will not phrase your idea thus: The American way of life is largely a result of frontier influence.

4.3 Reception and Comprehension of Ideas

Determining the exact meaning of a verbal context is a much more complex operation than putting together the parts of a jigsaw puzzle. In the case of the puzzle, you have clear-cut lines to guide you. By simple trial and error you can determine which pieces will fit where. But in the case of language, there are tints and shades of meaning, verbal blends that baffle even the most erudite scholars. Language is much too dynamic to be straitjacketed by prescriptive rules and dogmas. There are no foolproof formulas or theorems in verbal discourse. Your mind is assailed by every word in a passage, and it is your business to weigh such influences as tone, style, connotations, word order, emotional toning, and sentence complexity. You must consider every subtle distinction and every fleeting association in order to determine the precise intent.

Detecting an author's or speaker's meaning is not always as difficult as we have made it sound. Communication is not a game of hide and seek, or of charades. The communicator usually wants his reader or listener to grasp his idea and recognize his purpose. Because this is true he supplies hints, cues, and markers to point up his meaning.

The act of translating words into ideas is, as we have said, an act of re-creation. With the same elements the author employed in defining his meaning, you are asked to re-create it for yourself. The progression is from the whole context—the entire speech or essay—to the central thought—the idea. (See also Sections 1.2 and 3.2, and Reference Guides, D-5.4.)

Verbal Context in Which an Idea Is Placed

In Chapter 2 we discussed the process of perception, the method by which you interpret any unfamiliar phenomenon. With respect to reception of ideas, the steps may be interpreted as follows:

a. Read or listen to the entire passage or speech.

b. Separate the passage into logical, manageable, comprehensible elements.

c. Bring the elements together again in such a way as to clarify a central thought or idea.

Context of Situation in Which Meaning Is Defined

If you know something of the time and place and the occasion on which an idea is expressed, you have definite clues to the meaning. For example, if you are listening to a lecture in social science class, you have brought with you definite expectations concerning vocabulary, subject matter, and method of approach. If you are reading Francis Bacon's essay "Of Studies," you need just as definite an orientation. Seventeenth-century English differed somewhat from current English, and you will need to be aware of the differences. Notice this line from the essay: "Distilled books are like common distilled waters, flashy things." The word *flashy* in this context means "tasteless," a meaning current in Bacon's day but now quite obsolete.

Specific Clues to the Author's Meaning

Fortunately, most speakers and writers offer clues or signposts to direct you to their thoughts. Here are a number of them that you should be on the lookout for:

THE TITLE. Although a title of a speech or piece of writing seldom expresses the precise thesis or central idea to be communicated, it very often supplies a clue. Here are examples of various kinds of titles that suggest ideas and methods of development:

Why Johnny Can't Read and What You Can Do About it
(problem solution)
Colleges Don't Make Sense (thesis)
How to Write and Be Read (directions)
In Praise of Fireworks (eulogy)
Vocabulary and Success (cause-effect)
Art and Life (comparison and contrast)
For Whom the Bell Tolls (allusion)

INTRODUCTION, BODY, AND CONCLUSION. These three divisions of a talk or essay, if they can be identified, may offer valuable clues to the author's meaning. The introduction generally defines the limits of the topic, sets the tone, explains the author's purposes, establishes the method of development, and states the thesis. These items should be recognized as quickly as possible. Sometimes a speaker will begin his remarks with a story or anecdote which will offer a clue.

The body of a speech or article usually contains supporting evidence and argument for the thesis. Consideration of these data may lead you directly to the author's conviction, or help you verify your initial notion of what it is.

The conclusion may consist of a restatement of the thesis which can be used as a final check on your understanding.

TRANSITION MARKERS. If an extended context in either written or spoken English is reasonably coherent, it usually contains transition guideposts for the reader's or listener's direction. Paragraph indentations, punctuation points, and size of type are helpful in written contexts. Such cues as gestures, voice quality, facial features, and emphasis are helpful for talks or lectures. Poignant phrases such as the following should be unmisakable:

> My primary purpose is . . .
> This is my first point . . .
> In contrast to this idea . . .
> Furthermore, let it be said . . .
> In conclusion, let me say . . .
> There are three reasons why . . .

AUTHOR'S PURPOSE, TONE, AND EMOTIONAL MOOD. In straightforward prose contexts it is not difficult to ascertain what the author is up to. A speaker very often clearly announces his intentions. Written articles, essays, and reports usually specify what purpose is to be accomplished. Satire and criticism, however, offer various degrees of difficulty. It is hard to determine, for example, precisely what Mark Twain meant by his essay "Is Shakespeare Dead?" You may decide after a cursory reading that the essay is good evidence for the Baconian theory of Shakespearean authorship. If, however, you consider the essay in the total context of the author's works, you may decide the meaning is quite ironical, and that Mark Twain is actually ridiculing the Baconians rather than upholding them.

Poets, playwrights, and novelists usually do not announce their purposes, so that about all one has to guide him is character, plot, and imagery. The problem of meaning is often so baffling in literary works as to challenge the most experienced literary scholars and critics. This fact is effectively established by Theodore

Morrison's "Dover Beach Revisited" (*Harper's Magazine,* February, 1940).

Diction

If the language seems especially difficult, you should initially latch on to familiar expressions and then gradually increase comprehension of the passage by word associations, definitions in context, and plain common sense. You should learn to make a boon companion of your dictionary.

A competent vocabulary is a practical necessity for college students, especially if they are to accomplish anything scholastically. The tendency in recent years to substitute pictures for words by extensive use of audio-visual devices, motion pictures, and television in the communication of ideas does not make an adequate vocabulary a luxury. One of the important reasons for developing a large working vocabulary is to increase your ability to comprehend what you read and listen to. The best time to acquire new words is when you have a distinct need for them. Specific methods of vocabulary building are outlined in Reference Guides, D-6.

4.4 Evaluation of Ideas

The only real test of an idea is its achievement of purpose. Communication is directional in that it aims to solicit certain responses from specific people under specified circumstances. The following checks may be used to test the usefulness of an idea, either transmitted or received:

a. Is the idea appropriate for the purposes you have in mind?

b. Is the idea the most practical solution to the problem defined?

c. Is the idea properly restricted for the time or space allotted to its development?

d. Is the idea significant to and tailored for the persons who are to receive it?

e. Is the idea suited to your own knowledge and interests?

f. Is the idea suited to the occasion?

g. Is the idea important enough to warrant the attention you plan to give it?

h. Is the idea one that can be developed with the resources at your command?

EXERCISES

1. Read James Marshall's "Wars Are Made in Classrooms," *Saturday Review of Literature,* November 11, 1944. What is the problem Mr. Marshall has defined? What is his solution?

2. Mr. Harper, writing on the subject of jazz, in *Harper's Magazine,* June, 1955, pp. 81–83, states his idea as follows: "My contention . . . is that contemporary jazz is flourishing and that you owe yourself a chance to discover it." Select five of the following topics and formulate ideas concerning them in single sentences, using Mr. Harper's sentence as a model: juvenile delinquency, classical music, college football, extracurricular activity, required courses, general education, traffic congestion, freedom of the press, international language, censorship of movies, women in politics, wonder drugs, loyalty oaths, public opinion polls, commercial advertising, student government, the school paper, required attendance, scientific method, atomic energy, the United Nations, social security, nursery school, do-it-yourself, radio listening, lecture courses, baby sitting, library fines, television drama, teen-age slang.

3. Copy the thesis statement or central idea of five essays or articles appearing in the suggested readings to follow or in your reading anthology.

4. Select a personal problem with which you are faced. Follow the suggestions given in this chapter and in Chapter 1 and arrive at a solution to your problem. Write a paper in which you include the following items:

a. Definition of the problem.

b. Circumstances in which the problem developed.

c. Difficulties caused by the problem.

   d. Facts regarding the problem which can be verified.
   e. Trial solutions.
   f. Best solution.
5. Read H. I. Phillips' "Little Red Riding Hood," *Collier's,* June
   20, 1940, pp. 16 ff. The central idea of this article is implied
   rather than stated. State the idea as you understand it in a
   single declarative sentence.
6. Reduce the following statement to a single sentence which expresses in general terms the author's idea or thought:

   > Take a male, native-born American citizen; let him be be-
   > tween thirty-five and sixty-seven years old, of Anglo-German
   > stock, Protestant and white; let him come from one of about
   > seven major States, and let him have either a brief military or
   > a more extensive legal and administrative background; let him
   > be identified with small-town life and possess a perfect record
   > of marital fidelity; and let him have no definable record on
   > major issues of contention. This man—and only about a hun-
   > dred out of 160 million qualify at any given time—will be
   > "Presidential timber."
   >
   > > —From a review of Sidney
   > > Hyman's *The American Presi-
   > > dent,* in the *Economist* of No-
   > > vember 13, 1954

7. List eight to ten problems of current interest—local, national,
   or international—that society seeks solutions for. Select one of
   the problems and determine by library research what solutions
   have been proposed.
8. Goodman Ace in "Ad Nauseam, Ad Infinitum," *Saturday Review,* February 20, 1954, offers what he calls "an effective idea
   which will give fast relief to the pain being caused television
   viewers by the so-called irritating commercials." Formulate the
   implied idea in a single sentence:

   > Men! Do people leave the room when your commercials
   > appear on their television sets? Scientific lavatory tests prove
   > that commercials have absolutely no effect on people who
   > leave the room while commercials are on their sets.
   >
   > What you need is the "honor commerical."
   >
   > The "honor commercial" is the commercial which appears on

the television screen with the harsh, irritating hard sell faded completely out. Only the picture of the product is shown and from the speaker comes the subdued voice of an announcer almost whispering: "The sponsor has put you on your honor to buy the product which is shown here. Thank you. And now back to our program."

The "honor commercial" is not like a doctor's prescription which contains several ingredients. The "honor commercial" contains just one ingredient—gratitude. Television viewers by the million will gratefully buy your product if you use the "honor commercial."

Give the "honor commercial" the thirty-minute test. You will experience almost instant relief because the "honor commercial" glorifies your product instead of dulling it. . . .

9. Read "Huck and Jim on a Raft" in Mark Twain's *Huck Finn,* and explain why this chapter should be included in Henry Steele Commager's *Living Ideas in America.*

FOR FURTHER READING

Allen, Frederick Lewis, "The All-American Standard," in *The Big Change,* New York, 1952.

Baker, Newton D., "The Decay of Self-Reliance," *Atlantic Monthly,* December, 1934.

Boas, George, "In Defense of Machines," *Harper's Magazine,* June, 1932.

Commager, Henry Steele, *Living Ideas in America,* New York, 1951.

Eiseley, Loren C., "The Bird and the Machine," *Harper's Magazine,* January, 1956.

Emerson, Ralph Waldo, "Self Reliance," and "The American Scholar," in *Essays.*

Frank, Mrs. Glenn, "Heartache on the Campus," *Woman's Home Companion,* April, 1945.

James, William, "The Moral Equivalent of War," from *Memories and Studies.*

Jones, Howard Mumford, "Undergraduates on Apron Strings," *Atlantic Monthly,* October, 1955.

Kallen, H. M., "Democracy's True Religion," *Saturday Review of Literature*, July 28, 1951.

Lindbergh, Charles A., "The Fourth Dimension of Survival," address, *Saturday Review of Literature*, February 27, 1954.

Lippman, Walter, "Education Without Culture," address before the American Association for the Advancement of Science, December 29, 1940.

Maugham, W. Somerset, *Of Human Bondage*.

Nevins, Allan, and Josephson, Matthew, "Should American History be Rewritten?" debate, *Saturday Review of Literature*, February 6, 1954.

Thoreau, Henry D., "Civil Disobedience."

5

FOCUS ATTENTION ON FACTS

A FACT IS A QUALITY OF REALITY WHICH anyone can observe who is properly equipped to make the observation. That water boils at 212° F. is a fact. That George Washington was the first President of the United States is a fact. That Abraham Lincoln was our greatest President is not a fact, but an opinion. A fact is a datum of experience which can be verified by any number of qualified observers, either by direct sensual observation or by the use of extrasensory equipment. In the following passage from Thoreau's "Walden" the various thermometer readings are verbal representations of facts: "A thermometer thrust into the middle of Walden on the sixth of March, 1847, stood at 32°, or freezing point; near the shore at 33°; in the middle of Flint's pond, the same day, at 32½°; at a dozen rods from shore, in shallow water, under ice a foot thick, at 36°." In this brief report, the author has specified the time of observation, the place or places of observation, and the circumstances under which the observations were made.

5.1   Observation of Facts

Personal Observation

We are all equipped with a number of sense organs by which we are able to observe the facts around us directly. A few of us are incapacitated by color blindness, tone deafness, or some such limitation of the senses, but for the most part we are perfectly capable of making observations. Our trouble is that we don't make proper use of our powers. Too often we see and hear only what we need, and want, and desire to observe. The most obvious things in our environment completely escape our attention until we have some good reason to notice them. Even then we may experience difficulty in bringing them in focus.

Edgar Allan Poe, in "The Purloined Letter," tells a story of a diligent but vain search by the police for a valuable letter hidden in "plain sight." According to Poe, the letter was deposited "immediately beneath the nose of the whole world, by way of best preventing any portion of that world from perceiving it." Edna St. Vincent Millay found the secret of observation by looking at objects as though she were "seeing them for the first time."

Have you ever wondered why children are often able to discover things that completely escape the attention of adults? A plausible explanation is that children have not had time to form set habits of observation—habits that allow them to ignore a great portion of the whirling chaos in which they find themselves. They notice insignificant details in this chaos because they are still in the process of breaking up the blur of experience into manageable pieces which can be assembled into a unified picture of reality. You did the same thing yourself, but once you had decided how the overall view was to look, you quickly forgot the minor details of which it was made. As one author states it: "We go through each day like people in dark tunnels armed only with flashlights. We get through the tunnels fairly efficiently. But we've only seen the narrow paths illumined by our lights. . . . Except for objects and situations that demand our functional attention, we see the rest of life as a kind of panorama, a large pattern, with few details, vaguely understandable in the mass and almost unbearably complicated if we look closely."[1]

Mark Twain, in this passage from his *Autobiography,* has recalled the intensity of his childhood observations and the accompanying associations:

I spent some part of every year at the farm until I was twelve or thirteen years old. The life which I led there with my cousins was

[1] Roger H. Garrison, *A Creative Approach to Writing,* New York, 1951, p. 3.

full of charm, and so is the memory of it yet. I can call back the
solemn twilight and mystery of the deep woods, the earthy smells,
the faint odors of the wild flowers, the sheen of rainwashed foliage,
the rattling clatter of drops when the wind shook the trees, the far
off hammering of woodpeckers and the muffled snapshot glimpses of
disturbed wild creatures scurrying through the grass—I can call it all
back and make it as real as it ever was, and as blessed. I can call back
the prairie, and its loneliness and peace, and a vast hawk hanging
motionless in the sky, with his wings spread wide and the blue of the
vault showing through the fringe of their end feathers. I can see the
woods in their autumn dress, the oaks purple, the hickories washed
with gold, the maples and the sumachs luminous with crimson fires,
and I can hear the rustle made by the fallen leaves as we plowed
through them. I can see the blue clusters of grapes hanging among
the foliage of the saplings, and I remember the taste of them and the
smell. I know how the wild blackberries looked, and how they tasted;
and the same with the pawpaws, the hazelnuts, and the persimmons;
and I can feel the thumping rain, upon my head, of hickory nuts and
walnuts when we were out in the frosty dawn to scramble for them
with the pigs, and the gusts of wind loosed them and sent them
down.

Now observing facts just to be observing them is not a particularly fruitful exercise. It may increase your range of interests
and thereby enhance your ability to create ideas that would never
have occurred to you otherwise, but the piling up of facts for no
particular purpose is something of a pastime like collecting
stamps, old coins, or beer bottle caps. Henry Adams has it that
"nothing in education is so astonishing as the amount of ignorance it accumulates in the form of inert facts." Our concern
here, of course, is not with facts for the mere sake of facts, but
with facts for a purpose, and that purpose the clarification, illumination, and support of conceived ideas.

Scientific Observation

Scientists, whose primary aim is to discover the truth about
the material world in which we live, have long since learned that

the human senses are unreliable. What appears as a perfectly stable object to the naked eye is found to be a whirling mass of incessant activity when viewed under a powerful microscope. What appears to be an indivisible whole is found to be a constellation of many separate things. If you have exceptionally good vision you may be able to distinguish two points on a page $\frac{1}{250}$ of an inch apart. If the points were any closer together, let us say $\frac{1}{1000}$ of an inch, they would appear as a single point. By using an electronic eye, scientists can magnify objects to something over 100,000 diameters, which enables them to isolate the virus of dread diseases such as poliomyelitis. What we call a sharp razor blade, if so magnified, would look like a jagged mountain contour.

The chances are unlikely that you will have occasion in the communication of ideas to be nearly so precise, but you can learn a great deal from the methods of scientists that will assist you in communicating meaning accurately. The following principles of observation represent a sort of scientific code of ethics:

a. All facts are processes which cannot be arrested. There is no such thing as a static fact.

b. All measurement of these processes is partial and selective. One can never know all about anything.

c. Accuracy and precision in the measurement of natural processes is of primary importance. Guesswork is an unforgivable sin.

d. Accuracy of measurement is decreased by man's inability to control factors and conditions which affect an observed process.

e. Accuracy of measurement is decreased by limitations of the observer: his sensual incapacities, his expectations, his hopes, desires, motives.

f. Accuracy of measurement is decreased by limitations of the instruments employed.

g. Completeness of observation is essential in establishing the truth about anything.

h. Description of observed facts must be clear, accurate, and precise. Vagueness and ambiguity must not be tolerated.

5.2 The Nature of Reports

A statement of fact is called a report. Statements which express an observer's personal feelings or opinions about facts are variously called judgments, inferences, predictions, or conclusions. While there is no such thing as completely eliminating subjective elements from a report, they should be rigidly controlled. A report should correspond as nearly as possible with observed reality. The following qualities are characteristic of acceptable reports.

Verifiability

A report is verifiable when any number of qualified observers can confirm its accuracy. Whenever you find a number of people making contradictory statements about a given phenomenon, you can be certain that some of the statements are nonfactual. Even if you found perfect agreement among several observers you could not be sure of the accuracy of testimony. All of the observers might be wrong, as were the physicians Oliver Wendell Holmes tells about, who tried to diagnose a patient's ailment with a stethoscope in which a fly had become lodged. But the likelihood of error is greatly decreased by unanimous agreement among many observers. In the absence of better information, we are justified in accepting as facts the confirmed statements of people best qualified to make accurate observations.

Disparity among reports of a given set of facts is the rule rather than the exception. This is not surprising when we consider the varying capacities, interests, values, and points of view of people. "Reality is a dome of many-colored glass, and from his little corner each of us sees a different combination of colors in the kaleidoscope." Three principal reasons may be advanced in explanation of the variability of reports: (a) individual differences among observers, (b) multiple meanings of the words employed, (c) unstable character of the world of facts.

Probability

Probability is a measure of the degree of assurance or confidence you can place in an observation or statement of fact. When you look at your watch to find out what time it is, you doubtless make mental allowance for the fact that it may register a few seconds faster or slower than standard time. When you hear the time announced on the radio, television, or time-of-day service, you can be sure that it is not quite correct. A scientist recognizing the limitations of his measuring instruments calculates the degree of confidence he can place in any instrument and then makes necessary allowance for error.

Weather predictions, court decisions, public opinion polls are all based on probabilities. Truth is always relative to the amount of evidence available or at hand. The following statements represent various degrees of probability. None of them is absolutely true.

> A woman's work is never done.
> Nomination in Mississippi means election.
> Water freezes at 32° F.
> Light travels at 186,000 miles per second.

Scientists have just discovered an error of 140 yards in the calculation of the distance between the center of the earth and the equator. The circumference of the earth is now estimated at 24,902 miles at its widest point, nearly a half-mile smaller than the figure generally accepted since 1909.

Point of View

What you can observe in a given set of circumstances will depend to some extent on your point of observation. A mountain appears quite different at the summit and at a distance of twenty-five miles. Vision can be impaired by holding an object at close range as well as by viewing it at a great distance. To be overly precise and undeniably accurate about one or two observed facts is not to tell the truth about the whole. Emerson said, "If a man fasten his attention on a single aspect of truth and apply himself to that alone for a long time, the truth becomes distorted and not itself but falsehood." This was the difficulty with the legendary blind men who inspected the elephant. Their points of view were too close to the subject of observation and too narrow to give them an adequate idea of the total organization of observable facts.

Jonathan Swift in *Gulliver's Travels* offers an example of establishing perspective by altering his point of view, from a magnified close-up of the Brobdingnagians to a diminutive miniature of the Lilliputians. George R. Harrison in "Faith and the Scientist," *Atlantic Monthly*, December, 1953, shows that the phrase "You can't change human nature" springs from a short-range view. He explains how a scientist explodes the popular theory by focusing attention on pertinent facts: "The shape of the human jaw and the size of the human brainpan change quite markedly in a hundred thousand years. The speed with which a thoroughbred can run a mile has been dropped from two minutes to one minute and thirty-six seconds in less than fifty years, by selective breeding. The patterns governing a young man's operation of his mental switches can be changed quite markedly in a few months."

Your point of view in any particular act of communication will depend largely on your purpose. What you hope to accomplish will determine whether your observation should be casual, controlled, or scientifically precise. Some elements which go to make up a given point of view are: the time of observation, the position or positions of the observer, the distance of the observer from the object, the purpose of the observation.

Perspective

The ability to understand the relationships of parts to whole in an observed object, event, or process is called perspective. A balanced perspective is one which gives proper emphasis to all factors in a dynamic situation. In Chapter 1 we discussed the elements which make up a dynamic communication event: act, scene, agent, agency, and purpose. These terms may be called the what, when, where, who, how, and why of communication. An adequate report will include as many of these factors as are pertinent to your purpose.

Act, or *what,* designates an observed activity, process, happening, event, or incident.

Scene, or *when-where,* designates the place, setting, time, conditions, context, set of circumstances in which the act occurred.

Agent, or *who,* designates the person or persons, or elements, involved in the process or activity.

Agency, or *how,* designates the instrument, device, or implement by which the activity was accomplished.

Purpose, or *why,* designates the motives, reasons, aims which produced the activity or process change.

The following suggestions if followed will help you secure balanced perspective in your reports: (a) observe precisely what happened or what was said, (b) observe the conditions under which the event occurred or the statement was made, (c) recognize the characteristics, limitations, experiences, qualifications, and vested interests of the person making the affirmation, whether yourself or another, (d) consider the limitations of the instrument, or language, employed, (e) determine the purposes, motives, "angles," or reasons for the action or the assertion.

Objectivity

An acceptable report is objective; that is, it represents an observer's impersonal, unbiased, and unopinionated response to facts. Types of subjectivity which creep into even the most carefully prepared reports include personal bias or egocentricity, group bias or ethnocentricity, and purposeful manipulation of facts, or slanting.

Personal bias, or egocentricity, is that characteristic of an observer which makes it difficult, if not impossible, to observe facts without evaluating their comparative worth, importance, or significance. Motives, beliefs, interests, attitudes, and values restrict and limit one's capacity to make accurate observations. This human foible is well illustrated in the case of the driver of a Spring City, Tennessee, school bus which collided with a freight train on August 23, 1955, causing the death of ten children and serious injury of several others. The bus driver, because of his ego involvement, testified that the railroad signals were not working. But a number of bystanders, not so involved, reported that the signals were functioning properly. Subsequent investigation confirmed the bystanders' reports.

Ethnocentricity is bias shared by all members of a society or culture. The fact that we think of China and Japan as "the East," when they are geographically west of the United States, is proof, according to Bergen Evans, that "we are still Europe-minded." An excellent example of "cultural myopia" is brought to light in an illuminating passage pertaining to the Alamo near San Antonio, Texas: "This is the blood-splashed ruin which every Texan —little or big—venerates as his national shrine. Every year it is drenched with geysers of high-decible oratory—streamy, impassioned, and gloriously inaccurate. Indeed, such inaccuracy has now become a matter of self-defense; for on this subject—and a few others—the Texans have brainwashed themselves so thoroughly that any speakers who told the whole truth would invite a lynching. So no orator ever hints that the Alamo was, in fact, the worst military blooper in American history, short of Pearl Harbor."[2]

Slanting is manipulation of facts in a report to suit the observer's own purpose. Slanting can be accomplished by controlled selection of facts as well as by evaluation of the facts themselves. Notice how you could slant a report either for or against the use

[2] John Fischer, "Personal and Otherwise," *Harper's Magazine*, July, 1955, p. 16.

of penicillin by selecting evidence from one of the columns below:

For	Against
Penicillin fights bacteria.	Penicillin is ineffective in treatment of nonbacterial diseases.
97.2% of cases treated with penicillin were benefited.	2.8% of cases treated suffered skin irritation.
Penicillin has saved many lives.	Penicillin has caused the instant death of some patients.

What Hayakawa calls "slanting both ways at once" is characteristic of a report which presents the facts both favorable and unfavorable to the subject under consideration. Leonard Engel's "Do We Have to Give Up Smoking?" *Harper's Magazine,* December, 1954, is an excellent example of such objectivity.

5.3   Evaluation of Facts

The following questions may be used as a guide for checking the adequacy of statements of fact.

The Observer

Is the observer physically, intellectually, and emotionally qualified to make accurate and impersonal observations? What is the observer's personal interest in the facts? Was the observer in a position to observe the facts accurately? Are the facts honestly reported?

The Facts

Can the facts be verified? Are the facts consistent with what people know to be true by experience? Are the facts consistent with each other? What is the margin of probability that the facts are true?

The Purpose

Are the facts appropriate to the purpose for which they are used? Are the facts sufficiently precise to satisfy this purpose? Are the facts dishonestly slanted or manipulated in order to achieve the purpose? Are the facts sufficiently complete to satisfy the purpose for which they are collected? Is the language in which the facts are reported unmistakably clear?

EXERCISES

1. Read the passage quoted here and then answer the questions which follow.

> Most Americans would probably be surprised to discover that productivity in the United States is growing faster now than it was a century ago. They have uncritically gained the impression that our economy was more dynamic when it was young and that, as it has been getting older, it is decaying, and many conservatives gloomily assert that it is being ruined by bad public policies. Both the radicals and the conservatives are wrong.
>
> Output per man-hour is growing more than *three times* as fast today as a hundred years ago. The increase in the rate of growth has been fairly steady. Between 1850 and 1880, output per man-hour increased 28 per cent; between 1890 and 1910, about 74 per cent; between 1910 and 1940, about 83 per cent. Between 1940 and 1950, the annual rate of increase was one fourth faster than between 1910 and 1940—large enough to double output per man-hour in thirty years.
>
> —Summer H. Slichter, "Productivity: Still Going Up," *Atlantic Monthly*, July, 1952

   a. Which of the author's statements are opinions or judgments?
   b. Which statements are factual?
   c. How precise are the facts?
   d. What words in the text show a recognition of probability?

e. What statement is a thesis supported by the factual statements?

f. What words are emotionally toned or opinionated?

g. What words in the text are high-order abstractions that might have various meanings for different people?

h. How does the author avoid the either-or, or black and white, fallacy?

2. Analyze the following passage for facts, judgments, opinions, predictions, and assumptions:

> Some 7,400,000 youngsters will joyfully empty public high schools when vacation begins this month. Nearly a quarter of a million more will fill them up again when school resumes in the fall. By 1960, secondary school enrollments will jump to more than 9,000,000. By 1965, the number will be 12,-000,000.
>
> This oncoming tidal wave of high school boys and girls will begin to hit the classrooms with increasing force in about three years—only three short years from now. That can mean a real problem for you and your community if you and your community have not kept up on high school construction or if your facilities are barely adequate.
>
> —*Changing Times*, June, 1955, p. 43

3. Study the news stories of several different newspapers. Bring to class four or five examples of stories that go beyond the facts by editorializing the news or offering opinion, judgment, or predictions. Find examples of loaded or emotionally toned words.

4. Consider the so-called "facts" in the following quotations, and rate them for their probability on this scale:

    A—Positive certainty

    B—Highly probable

    C—Occasionally true

    C—Highly improbable

a. The magnetism on Venus is estimated, by Dr. J. Houtgast of Utrecht, Netherlands, to be five times as great as on Earth.

b. Ancient archaeological specimens can now be dated through the use of radio carbon to over 20,000 years' antiquity.

c. One in ten people in the United States, according to a public opinion poll, believe that throwing spilled salt over one's shoulder circumvents bad luck.

d. The 1950 federal census reveals that there are 98.1 men for every 100 women in the United States.

e. A good paint job delights the eye and renews the home-owner's pride in his property.

f. A Philadelphia heart specialist says that women can drive cars better, stand shock better, and lose more blood without serious effects than men.

g. Colleges today are bursting at the seams with more students than they have facilities to handle.

h. Williams College and Princeton are both small schools.

i. To a woman, an automobile is just a wheeled vehicle used for transportation; to a man it is alive, miraculous, and sacred.

j. A nation-wide survey showed men patients outnumbered women patients in hospitals in 1953 by 77,720.

k. The secret of education lies in respecting the pupil.

l. Farmers gain $10 for every $1 spent by using phenothiazine to control internal parasites plaguing farm animals.

5. Rewrite each of the following neutral statements first in positively or favorably toned language, then in negatively or unfavorably toned language.

a. Professor Butt assigned his students 1000 pages of outside reading for next week.

b. My brother seems to win every game of snooker he plays.

c. Mr. Brown is no longer employed by the Ace Mercantile Company.

d. Some people do not attend church regularly.

e. I get frightened every time I get up in class to give a speech.

6. Explain a principle regarding facts that is supported by the following paragraph:

The heat of a human body anywhere near the master scales of the National Bureau of Standards causes an error in weight. This is the scales used to check the master weight, a metal cylinder of platinum and iridium, against duplicate cylinders. The weighing is done by remote control to prevent the body heat error.

7. Read Leonard Engel's "Do We Have to Give Up Smoking?" *Harper's Magazine,* December, 1954, and evaluate the facts presented on the following bases: objectivity, probability, point of view, perspective, verifiability.

8. Discuss the meaning of the word *scientific* in the following passage:

> Strict honesty is strictly scientific. Psychiatrists have discovered that they are able to help people only when they are strictly honest. If the patient is inclined to conceal the facts, if he undertakes to cover up something in his experience which he believes to be discreditable, the psychological counselor finds himself stymied immediately. It often happens that the sufferer's unwillingness or inability to look facts squarely in the face constitutes a barrier that even the most skillful scientist cannot surmount.
>
> —Roy L. Smith

Comment on the specific meaning of *science* and its derivitives in the following sentences:

a. Clean your teeth the scientific way: Use GL-70.
b. It is a scientific fact that dinosaurs once roamed the earth.
c. The struggle between science and religion has been a hard and bitter one.
d. Scientific tests prove that filter tip cigarettes are milder than other brands.
e. What we need is a scientific understanding of the problems of humanity.

9. Make careful observation of some person, place, or event connected with your life at college and acquaint the class with the results of your observation. Describe exactly and precisely what you have observed. Leave out no essential details. Keep your own feelings, attitudes, and opinions out of your account.

10. Listen to members of the class report on observations made for problem 9. Evaluate the facts presented by answering these questions.
    a. Are the facts presented consistent with what you know to be true by experience?
    b. Are the facts consistent with each other?
    c. Are the facts verifiable?

    d. Are the facts precise enough to be useful for the speaker's purpose?

    e. What evidence do you find of personal opinion, judgment, or evaluation of the facts presented?

    f. Did the observer get a balanced perspective about the facts?

FOR FURTHER READING

Benjamin, A. C., "The Philosophy of Science: The Problem of Factual Truth," in *American Philosophy*, edited by Ralph B. Winn, New York, 1955.

Bourne, Randolph, "What Is Opinion?" *The New Yorker*, September 11, 1915.

Chase, Stuart, "Get the Facts First," *Reader's Digest*, September, 1953.

Davis, W. M., "The Method of Science," *Scientific Monthly*, September, 1922.

Galsworthy, John, "Facts," in *A Commentary*, 1920.

Goldsmith, Oliver, "On National Prejudices," *The British Magazine*, August, 1760.

Hayakawa, S. I., "The Language of Reports," in *Language in Thought and Action*, New York, 1949.

Kluckhohn, Clyde, "Snapshot of America," in *Mirror for Man*, New York, 1949.

Smith, Lillian, "When I Was a Child," in *Killers of the Dream*, New York, 1949.

6

FOCUS ATTENTION ON PURPOSE

WITHOUT A DEFINITE PURPOSE FOR COM-
municating an idea, you would be like the character in the story
who "jumped on his horse and rode off in all directions." You
must know where you are going if you hope to arrive. If you aim
at nothing, you are, as Daniel O'Connor once said, "sure to hit
it." Effective communication is purposeful communication. The
following episode from William Saroyan's story "The Circus"
will illustrate: "One day Joey came tearing into the classroom of
the fifth grade at Emerson school ten minutes late, and without
so much as removing his hat or trying to explain his being late,
shouted, Hey Aram, what the hell are you doing here? The
circus is in town." Joey's remarks are definitely purposeful—
direct, sincere, and stimulating. If you could take an assignment
in speaking or writing as seriously as Joey took the arrival of the
circus in town, there would be little question of your acquiring
skill. Simulated or fake purposes put a damper on spontaneity
and turn honest expression into mere word-spinning. No matter
what the occasion, you must speak and write for reasons that are
honest and sincere, not trumped up to please the instructor.

6.1 Controlling Purpose

A controlling purpose in communication determines what attitude you will take toward your subject, what details you will
select to support your idea, and what language you will use in
transmitting the idea to others. A controlling purpose quite ob-

93

viously has little or nothing to do with your desire to get a good grade, to see your name in print, to satisfy the expectations of your parents, or to win a wager with your roommate. Such secondary matters are properly called ulterior purposes. Your central or primary purpose, that is, your controlling purpose, answers such questions as these: What exactly are you trying to say? What is the reader or listener expected to accept, believe, or do?

These are the questions you should ask yourself while speaking and writing, and the questions you should ask of an author or speaker while reading or listening.

6.2   Statement of Purpose

A controlling purpose should be clearly defined in your mind before you attempt to express your idea in words. You need to formulate it in a clear-cut statement, such as these:

> To convince my classmates that they should support Mr. X for president of the Student Council.
> To explain to employees of industrial firms how to go about getting a raise in pay.
> To point out to taxpayers how to reduce their income tax.
> To report to the police the results of observations made at the scene of an accident.

In preparing a paper or talk for class assignment, you should write your purpose on a card and refer to it at every stage of your preparation. This should help you discipline your thoughts and keep them from wandering off the subject and going astray.

It is not necessary to state your purpose in the text of your paper or talk, but it should be perfectly clear, whether stated or implied.

6.3   Ulterior Purposes

Ulterior or covert purposes are concealed purposes. Every verbal expression, no matter how frank it may be, tends to conceal as well as to reveal what is in the author's mind. Most people are cagy with words and use them to justify, rationalize, and defend cherished points of view, to take advantage of the ignorance of others, to hypnotize, to seduce, and to mislead. Modern advertising offers endless examples of communication regulated by ulterior purposes.

6.4   General and Specific Purposes

The common purpose of all communication is to solicit response. Responses may be actions, ideas, moods and feelings, evaluations and judgments, and attitudes or dispositions. Such typical responses to language suggest six general purposes for communication: to inform, to create, to evaluate, to direct, to divert, and to persuade.

Specific purposes are general purposes reduced to specific cases. Here is an example of a general purpose applied to a specific subject: "This paper will make no attempt to treat the subject exhaustively; its aim is simply to call attention to the frontier as a fertile field for investigation, and to suggest some of the problems which arise in connection with it."[1] Mr. Turner, in this statement, has set limits for the essay and outlined a plan for treating the subject.

Notice that the following statement of purpose is directed to specific people: "My purpose here is to show the American a phase of the frontier which he has not yet considered, and show the European that the frontier has for more than four centuries affected his life and well-being most profoundly."[2]

Reporting

A report, as explained in Chapter 5, is discourse designed to give an accurate, precise, clear, complete, and unbiased account of observed facts.

---

[1] Frederick J. Turner, "The Significance of the Frontier in American History."
[2] Walter Prescott Webb, "Ended: 400 Year Boom."

The following characteristics of bona-fide reports may be used as a check list for both transmission and reception of factual information.

ADHERENCE TO THE FACTS.   Since the purpose of a report is to supply information and nothing more, any evaluation of the information is out of order. Avoid personal judgments, exaggerations, unrestrained superlatives and overstatements, such as are apparent in the following italicized words: Last year 2,382,-712 visitors attended the Texas State Fair and *enjoyed* its sixteen-day *spectacle* of *lavish* entertainment.

IMPARTIALITY.   This means simply that the facts are not juggled, manipulated, or in any way misrepresented. Notice the extreme partiality, prejudice, and subjectivity of the following non-report: "For a *magnificent* mile the street is lined with a *fabulous, high-fashion* shopping section. It has many office structures, such as the beacon-topped Palmolive building, whose flashing light is a *welcome* sight to travelers, flying across Lake Michigan on stormy nights. There is also the vine-covered Fourth Presbyterian church, an *oasis of quiet and beauty*. . . . It all adds up to a *grand* street, a truly *fabulous* avenue."

TIMELINESS.   An out-of-date report is about as useless as a last year's ticket to a football game. The world simply does not sit still for its portrait. If your report is to be even remotely accurate, you must secure the very latest information on your subject. Make sure the reports you read or listen to are up to date.

COMPLETENESS.   We have already established that all observation is selective, that we can never know all about anything, that precision is a relative matter. Completeness here means inclusion of all essential information on the subject as regulated by purpose. Because we usually see things as we want to see them rather than as they are, we are prone to leave out of our accounts any facts that will mar the idealized picture we have painted of reality. In the following "report" of the accuracy of weather predictions made by the *Farmer's Almanac,* the evidence is quite obviously selective and incomplete: "The Almanac's weather predictions, made from 12 to 16 months in advance, are amazingly accurate. For instance, the editor predicted the big snow of 1948 which paralyzed the Eastern states, though the weather bureau missed it. Again, the Bureau predicted the Eastern summer of '49 would be hot, but the Almanac forecast correctly it would be cool and wet."

CLARITY. Ambiguity has no proper place in communication, and especially no place in a report. Since the purpose of a report is to supply information, the facts must be presented in a way that will make them immediately useful. No one wants to spend time translating turgid language into understandable terms, even though he must often do this very thing in listening to and reading the reports of others.

RELIABILITY. The reliability of a report depends upon the qualifications of the person who observed the facts. The world is full of people who lack the professional knowledge essential to making accurate observations of facts they wish to report. A published report is not necessarily a reliable report. You should apply the same tests to reporters that you use for checking the acceptability of an authority. See Section 8.3.

Problem Solving

When your purpose is to create ideas, you are concerned with problem solving. This subject is fully treated in Chapter 4. We usually classify problems under two headings: (a) personal problems and (b) social problems. Personal problems are problems of health, vocation, personality, education, recreation, religion, and personal finance. Social problems are problems that involve two or more people in a community or group.

Here is an example of a statement of purpose which lends itself to creative development: "It is the purpose of this book in the chapters that follow to discuss this discrepancy between education and life. The field of education here discussed is that of 'general education' and the liberal arts which occupy about twenty years of the life of the great majority of college students. The work of technical and professional schools . . . is sufficiently direct to lessen the danger of wandering into the wilderness as liberal arts has done. This wandering into the wilderness has made the journey of education too long, too cumbersome, and too expensive."[3]

The problem in this statement is quite obviously a social problem, since it concerns many people. The last sentence in the statement contains the idea. Notice how carefully and definitely the author limits the subject area.

The following rules of problem solving, proposed by Professor Wallace Brett Dorham of Harvard and his associates from other universities, can be applied for exercises in both the transmission and reception of meaning:

TEN SIMPLE RULES

1. Learn all about a problem before trying to solve it. Listen a lot. Talk a little.
2. See the *total situation*. Don't act on just a part of it.
3. Don't be deceived by *logic*. Most problems are full of emotion. Emotions aren't "logical."
4. Watch the meaning of words. Look behind words to get their full impact.
5. No moral judgments, please. Until you have diagnosed a problem don't leap to conclusions about what's *right* and what's *wrong*.
6. Imagine yourself in the other fellow's shoes. See how the problem looks from where he sits.
7. When a problem gets you down, get away from it. Put it in the back of your mind for a week. When you approach it again the solution may be obvious.
8. Ask yourself, "What are the forces acting upon the other fellow? Why does he behave as he does?"
9. *Diagnosis* must come before *action*. Use the doctor's approach. Don't prescribe until you're sure what is wrong.

[3] Stephen Leacock, *Too Much College*, New York, 1940, pp. 19–20.

10. Easy does it. Quick solutions are often the quick route to trouble. Take your time.[4]

Criticism

When you make a report, you deal in facts; when you solve a problem, you deal in ideas; when you evaluate or criticize something, you deal in judgments or values. Values are personal and subjective, and for this reason they are often stigmatized. They usually present a clearer picture of the observer than they do of the thing observed. But values are not always "valueless" in communication. On some occasions you gladly dispense with facts and settle for expert judgment about facts. When you need advice about legal affairs, you trust the judgment of a lawyer. When you want advice about your health, you seek the trained judgment of a physician. When you want to ascertain the authenticity of a Rembrandt painting, you trust the opinion of an art specialist. We depend upon the educated tastes and judgments of experts because we believe that such persons are thoroughly acquainted with the facts and are thereby in a better position to evaluate them properly than is the average layman.

The very trust we place in professionally competent persons may, however, make us easy marks for quacks, charlatans, and con men. The important question becomes: How can one separate the genuine from the spurious in matters of taste, judgment, and criticism? Three simple tests of validity may be applied: Is the criticism based on careful observation or investigation of facts? Is the criticism impartial or fair to all persons involved? Is the criticism based on an appropriate standard of judgment?

CRITICISM BASED ON FACT. Wishful thinking which is grounded in desire, feeling, and vested interest is quite different from sound criticism based on verifiable facts. Walter Blair's "Six Davy Crocketts" is an example of sound criticism. Here is

[4] Howard Whitman, "How to Keep Out of Trouble," *Collier's*, September 25, 1948, p. 28. Reprinted by special permission of the author, Howard Whitman.

the author's statement of purpose: "It has seemed worth while to examine the documents about this man to find out the reason for these contradictory versions." Examination of documents is, of course, a legitimate means of getting at the truth.

CRITICISM AS OBJECTIVE EVALUATION. Criticism which is divorced as nearly as possible from bias and vested interest is preferable to that designed for personal profit. An independent research agency is more likely to respect consumers' interests with regard to household commodities than is a commercial firm which manufactures the articles. A professor's judgment of a college dictionary is likely to be more valid than the publisher's appraisal.

CRITICISM BASED ON STANDARDS. Three kinds of critical standards or criteria are used for evaluation: impressionistic, intrinsic, and extrinsic.

When the standard is impressionistic, the critic's judgment is a matter of taste, personal preference, common sense, or inclination. Of the three types mentioned, it is the most unstandard and unreliable, but it is the most widely employed. This is the standard Mark Twain referred to when he said: "There are no standards of taste in wine, cigars, poetry, prose, etc. Each man's own taste is the standard and a majority vote cannot decide for him or in any slightest degree affect the supremacy of his own standard." Mark Twain's works are replete with criticism based on his personal standard of judgment. For example, after hearing *Lohengrin,* he commented: "The banging and slamming and booming and crashing were something beyond belief. The racking and pitiless pain of it remains stored up in my memory along side the memory of the time I had my teeth fixed."

Charles Dickens employed an impressionistic standard in his judgment of American Indians: "To come to the point at once, I beg to say that I have not the least belief in the Noble Savage. I consider him a prodigious nuisance, and an enormous superstition. His calling rum firewater, and me a paleface, wholly fail

to reconcile me to him. I don't care what he calls me. I call him
a savage, and I call a savage a something highly desirable to be
civilized off the face of the earth."

When the standard of judgment is intrinsic, a subject is evaluated in its own terms. When, for example, literature is appraised
by this method, attention is focused on the *text* of a poem, story,
or play. The problem is one of internal consistency of the work
itself. No outside authorities are introduced. No comparisons
with other texts are made. If the parts of the work being appraised fit together to form and function as a perfect whole, the
work is judged to have merit. The important questions in this
type of criticism are: What is the author trying to accomplish?
How does he accomplish it? How successfully does he accomplish it?

Here is a significant passage from De Quincey's "On the
Knocking at the Gate in 'Macbeth' " which illustrates this type
of criticism:

The murderers and the murder must be insulated—put off by an
immeasurable gulf from the ordinary tide and succession of human
affairs—locked up and sequestered in some deep recess; we must be
made sensible that the world of ordinary life is suddenly arrested,
laid asleep, tranced, racked into a dread armistice; time must be
annihilated, relation to things without abolished; and all must pass
self-withdrawn into a deep syncope and suspension of earthly passion.
Hence it is that, when the deed is done, when the work of darkness
is perfect, then the world of darkness passes away like a pageantry in
the clouds: the knocking at the gate is heard, and it makes known
audibly that the reaction has commenced. . . .

When the standard is extrinsic, an appeal is made to authority.
Conventional rules are established by men of intellectual distinction and educated tastes. These rules are then employed as yard-
sticks for measuring the comparative worth of anything to which
the rules pertain. This technique is exemplified in Mark Twain's
well-known essay "Fenimore Cooper's Literary Offences," in
which nineteen rules governing literary art are borrowed from the

eminent critics of the day and then applied to the works of Cooper, notably *Deerslayer*. Another instance of extrinsic criticism may be found in Aldous Huxley's "Vulgarity in Literature," in which the author painstakingly defines *vulgarity* and then applies the formula to the works of Edgar Allan Poe.

SUGGESTIONS FOR CRITICAL EVALUATION

a. Focus your attention on the thing you want to criticize. Keep other matters out of your mind.

b. Avoid expressing your personal feelings, preferences, or biases as the sole basis of your criticism.

c. Study the facts diligently before making an interpretation of them.

d. Use a standard of judgment if possible.

e. Adapt the method and tone of criticism to readers and listeners.

Explanations and Directions

In addition to depending on facts, ideas, and judgments for getting along in the world, we also depend on explanations and directions. Following directions is one of the most important skills you can acquire for getting an education. Learning to solve problems in mathematics, to perform experiments in science courses, or to work out assignments in practically any course you take in college requires the ability to follow directions. The emphasis is on performance, activity, and manipulation of actual objects. The important question which becomes the focal point of this type of discourse is: *How?* Whenever we successfully perform a task, solve a problem, accomplish an assignment, or realize an objective, other people want to know *how* we did it.

Mortimer J. Adler's essay "How to Mark a Book" is an excellent example of directions. In the essay, Mr. Adler identifies the particular types of marks he makes in a book while reading it, and he explains how the marks are to be used and interpreted. Specific directions are arranged in outline form, plainly numbered for the convenience of the reader. The "Ten Simple Rules" we quoted a few pages back is another good example of directions.

Often it is necessary to accompany directions and explanations with charts, diagrams, maps, pictures, illustrations, to supplement or make up for deficiencies and limitations of language. Speakers have a slight advantage over writers in this respect. Gestures, bodily movements, voice inflections, and actual demonstrations of a process or activity are valuable aids to understanding.

Here are some suggestions for making explanations and giving directions: (a) Make all explanations perfectly clear and unambiguous. (b) Be simple, concrete, and direct. (c) Make directions accurate, precise, and vivid. (d) Use any visual aids which will help put over the idea. (e) Arrange instructions in a logical order, from simple to complex, familiar to unfamiliar, or in chronological, spatial, or analytical fashion, in harmony with the subject matter.

Entertainment

Every act of communication depends to some extent on interest. One of the principal aims of conversation is to find diversion from serious things. Conversation has been called the "joyous art of doing nothing." It may also be called "communication for communication's sake." By verbal exchange we release pent-up emotional tensions. Psychologists have discovered that we satisfy many hidden needs and counteract frustrations in the normal processes of communication. Joking, storytelling, repartee, satire, burlesque are verbal cathartics that are more valuable than a doctor's prescription.

Everybody likes to hear a good joke, but nothing is more deadly to good rapport in communication than a story that falls flat on its face. It is dangerous to make any generalizations about what is, or what is not, entertaining, because people differ widely in their responses to so-called humor. What will bring hysterical tears of laughter into the eyes of one person may thoroughly disgust another. W. C. Fields, famous Hollywood comedian, used to ask his directors: "Who decides what is funny?" No standard rules can be set forth. What will work magic for one speaker or writer will fizzle for another. The best asset you can have for this sort of thing is knack, and you can't buy that at the bookstore.

Special devices for making words entertaining and diverting include exaggeration, imitation, mistranslation, dialect, satire, irony, sarcasm, equivocation, reverse English, limericks, anecdotes, puns, Wellerisms, Malapropisms, Spoonerisms, children's sayings, pantomimes, etc.

Suggestions for creating diversion are: (a) Be sure the joke, story, anecdote, or humorous device is entertaining to you. (b) Focus attention on a punch line if there is one. Don't muff it. (c) Prepare your reader or listener for what is to come. Tension has to be built up and then released. (d) Tell the joke right; don't miss any of the key words; don't hesitate. If you can't quite remember how it goes, don't tell it. (e) Tell it loud enough so everyone can hear. Don't mumble. (f) Don't try a dialect unless you've mastered it. (g) Insure your success with sure-fire delivery. Don't expect the words alone to turn the trick. (h) Make your entertainment appropriate to the subject and occasion.

Persuasion

The important thing in persuasion is appropriateness of response from readers and listeners. What a speaker or writer says, or how he says it, is important only in producing desired results. A man selling automobiles may be able to make ever so pretty a speech, wrapped up in most delightful words, but if he can't make a sale he has not succeeded. Competence or skill in persuasion should always be measured by the effects on those to whom it is directed. Desirable effects are not solely the result of words. Who you are may have as much influence as what you say, or even more. Your own personality is an instrument for transmitting thoughts and securing desired responses.

Persuasion may be said to appeal to every human faculty: sensual, intellectual, and emotional. An effective communicator employs whatever devices and techniques work to his own advantage as long as they are honest and in the best interests of his audience or readers. Some people respond to logic and reason; others are more easily persuaded by sentiment and emotion. A successful insurance salesman will probably use both logical and emotional appeals in his attempt to convince a prospect of the value of a policy. The salesman will present statistical facts about death rates, financial reports of the company's assets, case histories of people who profited by insurance, as well as predictions of the plight a family would be in should the breadwinner suddenly die.

Analysis of persuasion reveals three principal varieties; inspiration, conversion, and activation.

Inspiration, or stimulation, is the reinforcement of ideas and beliefs already held by the audience or reader. Many sermons, newspaper editorials, and platform speeches are of this variety. These lines from an editorial published in the *New York Times* on Washington's Birthday, 1955, are illustrative: "On this birthday we can well honor George Washington for what he did. It is even more important that we honor him for what he was, and that in so doing, we recognize the truth of the declaration that those who are great among their fellow-men are first of all the servants of those whom they lead. Humility makes that possible and that is one of the touchstones to Washington's greatness."

Conversion is a type of persuasion that alters or changes existing beliefs and substitutes new convictions for old. A good example is Dr. Frederic Wertham's essay "The Comics—Very Funny!" in which the author refutes seventeen arguments which favor comic books and makes a strong plea for a conversion of public attitude. Thoreau's "Civil Disobedience" is another excellent example of this type of persuasion, as is Norman Cousins' "Modern Man Is Obsolete," Bergen Evans' "A Tale of a Tub," and Erich Fromm's "The Illusion of Individuality." The following lines are quoted from Erich Fromm's essay: "I want to mention briefly some of the educational methods used today which in effect . . . discourage original thinking. One is the emphasis on knowledge of facts, or I should rather say on information. The pathetic superstition prevails that by knowing more and more facts one arrives at knowledge of reality. Hundreds of scattered and unrelated facts are dumped into the heads of students; their time and energy are taken up by learning more and more facts so that there is little left for thinking. . . ."[5]

Activation, or inducement, not only stimulates and converts, but also promotes overt activity or behavior. Examples of such persuasion are found in political propaganda, commercial advertising and solicitations for financial support. Robert M. Hutchins' "Gate Receipts and Glory" is a good example of this type of persuasion.

6.5   Check List for Purposeful Communication

We have discussed six major purposes for cummunicating: to inform, to create, to direct, to criticize, to divert, and to persuade. Consider the following points in determining the adequacy of your own purposes in writing or speaking, or the purposes of authors and speakers to whom you attend.

Clarity of Purpose

Vagueness may indicate the lack of a clearly discernible purpose. It may also mean that you or your author have been overpowered by words. Notice the blurred effect of this statement of purpose: "To attempt in the light of our findings to make a significant contribution to the philosophy of American education,

[5] *Escape from Freedom*, New York, 1941.

to improve its quality, and to define more clearly the role of modern languages and literatures in American education at all levels." Such a statement is likely to be misunderstood by many people who are not familiar with pedagogical jargon. Statements of purpose should be clear, concise, and meaningful: "To show how the study of languages and literature may help to achieve the aims and goals of American education whether in the elementary school or in college."

Restriction of Purpose

You will do well to confine your efforts to a single purpose. Such a matter depends on the length and thoroughness of your concentration. For average assignments in communication, singleness of purpose is better than dissipation of effort. The following purpose should be limited to one of the specific items: "To show the causes, conflicts, engagements, results, and implications of the Civil War."

Realistic Purpose

This is the same as asking: Are you sincerely interested in accomplishing this purpose? If your heart is not in it, the whole project may get out of hand. Far too many students in communication skills courses adopt purposes that can be scarcely understood, let alone achieved. Don't let this happen to you! If you are vitally interested in changing styles in women's clothing, or polling public opinion, or finding a satisfactory therapy for paranoia, then let your interest or curiosity guide you. If you have no interest in these topics, leave them alone.

EXERCISES

1. Determine the author's purpose in each of the following passages.
    Newspaper circulation is now at all-time peaks. Advertising volume is incredible; the goose hangs high. Profits in spite of

costs and taxes are pretty good. We in our business are well fed, well clothed, well sheltered, and anxious to let well enough alone. We think we are good, because business and circulation are good. In the last decades the phenomena of science have thrown multiple competition at us; not only are we surviving but we are expanding almost everywhere and in some places fabulously. It is quite true that over the years there has been a high mortality rate among newspapers, but even that, at least for the moment, appears to be suspended.

Despite all the happy omens, however, it may be useful to step out of the sunshine for a few minutes in order to observe some scattered clouds.

—Louis B. Seltzer

Statistics, for us, fall naturally into various colors. For instance, 7,377,777, whether it stands for imports or exports, is undoubtedly red. But 1,019,901 is a pale, light, cool, grayish blue. And can any one doubt that 525,555,555,555 is of a bright aggressive yellow color, and gives off a high pitched note from the rapid motion of its myriad pinions? There is something querulous and peevish and impatient about 525,555,555,555, too; we shall not admit it into the volume of statistics which we are compiling.

Hitherto there has been a science of statistics, but no art. That is, no avowed art. We suspect that certain advanced statisticians really approach the subject as we do, joyfully and all unshackled. But they pretend to be staid and dry and sober. They have respectable positions in the community to maintain. After compiling several pages of statistics full of sound and color, just for the sheer glee of reveling in sensation, they become cowards and conceal their glee; they write industrial and financial and sociological articles around their lovely tables and twist them into proving something important. They conceal their art, they muffle and smother their finer impulses beneath a repellent cloak of science. They are afraid that their toys will be taken away from them if they play with them frankly, so they affect some sort of useful employment.

—Don Marquis

Dialog writing has become a matter as ceremonious as Japanese drama. We had better codify these things so that everyone knows what to expect in given situations. Following are the proper lines for given situations. I've omitted some of the situations since we all know them well:

"Doctor, you've got to pull her through. You've got to. She's all I have."

"Son . . . you'd better get some rest.". . .

"Inspector, I never saw this man before in my life."

—John Crosby

Scientific method, as we understand it, comes into the world full-fledged with Galileo (1564–1642), and, to a somewhat lesser degree, in his contemporary, Kepler (1571–1630). Kepler is known to fame through his three laws: he first discovered that the planets move round the sun in ellipses, not in circles. To the modern mind there is nothing astonishing in the fact that the earth's orbit is an ellipse, but to minds trained on antiquity anything except a circle, or some complication of circles, seemed almost incredible for a heavenly body.

—Bertrand Russell

Dr. George Gallup and his American Institute of Public Opinion conducted surveys for two years on the reading habits of Americans in all walks of life and different sections of the land; one of the striking facts "that is scored and underscored in these studies is the tremendous influence of Hollywood on reading tastes." Gallup points out that Hollywood boosts the classics of literature into new and extraordinary popularity. When the movie *David Copperfield* was being publicized, the Cleveland Public Library ordered over 125 extra copies of the book to meet the probable rise in demand; and although the library had over five hundred copies of the book, the shelves were bare of *David Copperfield* and other Dickens novels for weeks.

—Leo C. Rosten

No civilization can live without ideals, or to put it in another way, without a firm faith in moral ideas. Our ideals and moral ideas have in the past been rooted in religion. But the religious basis of our ideals has been undermined, and the superstructure of ideals is plainly tottering. None of the commonly suggested remedies on examination seems likely to succeed. It would therefore look as if the early death of our civilization were inevitable.

—W. T. Stace

2. Read three assigned essays in your anthology of readings, and state the author's purpose or purposes in your own words, preferably in a single sentence.

3. Find two essays written on the same subject by different authors. Subjects might include football, segregation of races, subversive influences in democracy, education, religion, etc. Compare the purposes of the two authors and their methods of development.

4. Look at a number of published speeches in *Vital Speeches of the Day*, or in the *New York Times*, and copy down the speakers' direct statements of purpose.

5. As early as 1829, Catherine Beecher wrote, "The time *may* come when the world will look back with wonder to behold how much time and effort have been given to the mere cultivation of the memory, and how little mankind have been aware of what every teacher, parent, and friend could accomplish in forming the social, intellectual, and moral character of those by whom they are surrounded." What theory of education does this statement represent? According to this theory, what is the aim and purpose of education? What educational leaders in our day would agree to this purpose? Who would disagree?

6. Focus your attention on an idea you would like to communicate to others. Write a 350-word paper and give a three-minute talk on the subject. Select one of the following purposes: (a) Support your idea with verifiable facts. (b) State your personal opinions on the subject. (c) Give directions about how to accomplish what you propose. (d) Persuade your listeners or readers that they should accept your proposal.

7. Listen to a public address on radio or television and determine what the speaker is attempting to accomplish. State his central purpose in your own words. How well does he accomplish his purpose?

FOR FURTHER READING

The following essays are examples of writing regulated by purpose.

TO INFORM:

Clemens, Samuel L., "Past and Present," from *Life on the Mississippi*, chap. LIV.

Franklin, Benjamin, "Writing and Reading," from *The Autobiography of Benjamin Franklin*.

Mencken, H. L., "Larval Stage of a Bookworm," from *Happy Days*, New York, 1939, 1940.

Whyte, William H., Jr., "The Language of Advertising," *Fortune*, September, 1952.

TO CREATE:

Atkinson, Brooks, "In Defense of American 'Materialism,'" from *Once Around the Sun*, New York, 1951.

Hodnett, Edward, *The Art of Problem Solving*, New York, 1954.

King, Albion Roy, "Alcohol in the Colleges," *The Christian Century*, July 11, 1951.

Mead, Margaret, "Can Marriage Be for Life?" from *Male and Female*, New York, 1949.

Van Horne, Harriet, "Are We a Nation of Morons?" *Theatre Arts*, June, 1952.

TO CRITICIZE:

Clemens, Samuel L., "Fenimore Cooper's Literary Offences," from *Harriet Shelley and Other Essays*.

De Quincey, Thomas, "On the Knocking at the Gate in 'Macbeth.'"

McCord, David, "An Anatomy of Confusion," *Saturday Review*, December 5, 1953.

Marquis, Don, "Preface to a Book of Statistics," in *Prefaces*, New York, 1929.

Williamson, Samuel T., "How to Write Like a Social Scientist," *Saturday Review*, October 4, 1942.

TO DIRECT:

Dempsey, David, "How to Get Published, More or Less," *Harper's Magazine*, July, 1955.

Macrorie, Ken, "World's Best Directions Writer," *College English,* February, 1952.

Montague, C. E., "Three Ways of Saying Things," *Century Magazine,* April, 1929.

Whyte, William H., Jr., "You, Too, Can Write the Casual Style," *Harper's Magazine,* October, 1953.

TO DIVERT:

Cerf, Bennett, "How Not to Tell a Story," *Saturday Evening Post,* March 6, 1948.

Johnson, Burges, "The Jokes That Last," *Atlantic Monthly,* July, 1952.

Parker, Dorothy, "Arrangement in Black and White," in *The Portable Dorothy Parker,* New York, 1944.

TO PERSUADE:

Bryan, William Jennings, "Speech at Chicago, 1896," in Carl Niemeyer and William M. Murphy, *Challenges to Thought,* Harrisburg, Pennsylvania, 1952, pp. 438–442.

Highet, Gilbert, "The Art of Persuasion," *Vogue,* January, 1951.

Shakespeare, William, "Marc Antony Speaks to the Citizens of Rome," from *Julius Caesar,* Act III, Scene 2.

III

ORDER YOUR THOUGHT

7

EXPLAIN YOUR IDEA

LITTLE IS ACCOMPLISHED WHEN COM-
municated messages are misunderstood or misinterpreted, when
thoughts are twisted, words misconstrued, and meanings compromised. In order to eliminate all possibility of error (or noise),
we must make ideas vivid, sharply focused, and clear. This can
be accomplished by translating abstract statements into concrete facts and experiences, using any of the following devices.

7.1   Illustration

Illustrating an idea is painting a word picture of it for others
to see. Simple narratives, detailed descriptions, personal experiences, dramatic episodes (either true or fictional) involving human acts and motives are good insurance against vagueness
and ambiguity. The parables of Jesus—The Lost Sheep, The
Pearl of Great Price, The Grain of Mustard Seed—are excellent
examples of highly abstract ideas simplified dramatically so that
even a child can comprehend them.

The following guides should help you select illustrations by
which to clarify your thoughts:

a. Select illustrations which are representative cases, not rare
exceptions, of a general principle. Avoid far-fetched, unrealistic,
and preposterous illustrations.

b. Use sufficient illustrations to make your meaning perfectly
clear, but don't overdo it by presenting more than are necessary.

c. Select illustrations that are clearly related to the thesis you wish to defend.

d. Make illustrations vivid and illuminating by careful choice of words.

e. Select illustrations which will appeal to the audience or readers you want to reach. If possible, choose material from your own experiences.

f. If you use fictional or simulated illustrations, make them plausible and reasonable.

Notice the various uses of illustration in the following quoted passages. The first one shows how episodes from history, literature, or mythology may be employed:

Idea: Without the rich heart, wealth is an ugly beggar.

Illustration: "The King of Schiraz could not afford to be so bountiful as the poor Osmon who dwelt at his gate. Osmon had a humanity so broad and deep that although his speech was so bold and free with the Koran as to disgust all the dervishes, yet was there never a poor outcast, eccentric, or insane man, some fool who had cut off his beard, or who had been mutilated under a vow, or had a pet madness in his brain, but fled at once to him; that great heart lay there so sunny and hospitable in the centre of the country, that it seemed as if the instinct of all sufferers drew them to his side. And the madness which he harbored he did not share. Is not this to be rich? This only to be rightly rich?"[1]

Mark Twain, in discussing his attitude toward Negro slaves, illustrated his idea by using personal experience:

We had a little slave boy whom we had hired from someone, there in Hannibal. He was from the eastern shore of Maryland, and had been brought away from his family and his friends, halfway across the American continent, and sold. He was a cheery spirit, innocent and gentle, and the noisiest creature that ever was, perhaps. All day long he was singing, whispering, yelling, whooping, laughing—it was maddening, devastating, unendurable. At last one day, I lost all my temper, and went raging to my mother and said Sandy had been singing

[1] Ralph Waldo Emerson, "Manners."

for an hour without a single break and I couldn't stand it and wouldn't she please shut him up. The tears came into her eyes and her lip trembled, and she said something like this: "Poor thing, when he sings it shows that he is not remembering, and that comforts me, but when he is still I am afraid he is thinking, and I cannot bear it. He will never see his mother again; if he can sing, I must not hinder it, but be thankful for it. If you were older, you would understand me; then that friendless child's noise would make you glad."

It was a simple speech and made up of small words, but it went home, and Sandy's noise was not a trouble to me any more.[2]

Here is how a famous American humorist used an anecdote to clarify his idea:

Mathematics is always, for most of us, a sort of mystery which we don't even expect to understand. Let me illustrate the attitude by recalling a joke of a stage "review" of a few years ago. Some boys are seen coming out of school, comically overgrown and comically underdressed, grown too long and dressed too short, to make them look funny.

"Well, my little man," says a stock stage gentleman, in the stock voice of a stage question, "and what are you learning at school?"

"Reading and writing," says one of the comedian boys, his immobile face a marvel of wooden imbecility, blank as the alphabet.

"Reading and writing," repeats the stock gentleman, so as to let the audience get it, "and anything else?"

The "boy" answers, with no facial movement, "We learn gazinta."

"You learn what?"

"Gazinta."

"But what is gazinta?"

"Why," explains the boy, "like two gazinta four and five gazinta ten."[3]

7.2 Examples, or Specific Instances

Language has a way of condensing many experiences into single words. Examples, like illustrations, specify which experi-

[2] Mark Twain, *Autobiography*.
[3] Stephen Leacock, *Too Much College*, New York, 1940, p. 73.

ences you are talking about. They reduce abstract ideas to particular cases. In the passage quoted below, the precise meaning of *bad assumptions* is spelled out by citing examples: "Vacation time is accident time. Most accidents result from bad assumptions, such as: That nobody is coming over the brow of the hill; that a child isn't going to spring from between two parked cars; that the car ahead will pursue the even tenor of its way, and not jerk to a stop; that one more for the road will brighten the trip; that brakes, engine, and tires are all shipshape; that accidents are for others—you bear a charmed life."[4]

Frequently examples are introduced by the phrase *for example:* "Yet even our everyday speech includes high-flying metaphors and beautiful, if irresponsible fancies. For example, when confronted with something unusual we rarely say we are surprised or excited or startled. No, that would be too dull. We say, 'My heart stood still.' "

Often a single instance or example serves as a representative case: "The abilities of ingenious men were directed to make further improvements in the art of destroying an enemy. Among these, David Bushnell of Connecticut invented a machine for submarine navigation, which was found to answer the purpose of rowing horizontally, at any given depth under water, and of rising or sinking at pleasure. To this was attached a magazine of powder, and the whole was contrived in such a manner, as to make it practicable to blow up vessels by machinery under them."[6]

"Once in a sorority or fraternity, a student is compelled to conform to a caste system whether he approves it or not. If he doesn't join one, on the other hand, he is apt to find himself excluded from leadership in many college activities. Greek-letter students are a minority on most campuses but are so tightly knit and politically organized that they generally control elections.

[4] *Collier's,* June 24, 1955, p. 102.
[5] Louis Untermeyer, "Poets and Peasants," *Woman's Home Companion,* April, 1948, p. 12.
[6] David Ramsay, *History of the American Revolution,* Philadelphia, 1789.

"At Wisconsin, for example, which is typical of most state universities, the highest social honor obtainable is that of being chosen king or queen of the junior prom, but only once since 1925 has a nonfraternity man been elected prom king, and there has been only one prom queen who was not in a sorority."[7]

Some of the best examples for clarifying ideas may be found in personal experience:

"Birds, I know, are supposed to go south for the winter; but in Maine all they ask is a room with a southern exposure. I'll never forget the morning my brother found a barn owl in the bathroom. Our bathroom is as cold as a barn, but otherwise it is more like a telephone booth. My brother is very near-sighted and he went to the bathroom that morning without his glasses. The big owl just sat there, staring angrily at him, and my brother said, *'Oh, excuse me!'* and backed out as fast as he could."[8]

7.3   Reasons

Sound reasons go a long way toward making ideas, proposals, and suggestions clear. They tell *why* an idea or proposition has any merit.

In an attempt to answer the question "Why study English?" one naturally thinks of reasons. In a four-page leaflet published by the General Electric Corporation this question was answered. Here is a paragraph from the leaflet that points out reasons why language skill is important: "Tell them that English is important to them—and to us—because very soon their ability to read and to know and to remember what they have read, and to speak and to write well, will make all the difference, whether they and we or some other company of their career choice will succeed together. . . . As you move up the success ladder, what you write and what you say will determine in part your rate of climb."

---

[7] Mrs. Glenn Frank, "Heartache on the Campus," *Woman's Home Companion*, April, 1945.

[8] David L. Graham, "Scratch an Author," *Yankee*, October, 1955, p. 41.

Many times reasons are listed or enumerated. One writer, discussing state governments, lists five reasons for their decline:

(1) The part-time status and negligible salaries of state legislators and most state district attorneys. . . .

(2) The inability to reapportion legislatures so they will represent a state's population as it exists today, not as it did in the frontier past. . . .

(3) Detailed and cluttered state constitutions that lace state governments in a rigid straitjacket. . . .

(4) The one-party political domination which prevails in at least half the states. . . .

(5) The fact that state elections are held simultaneously with Presidential elections and congressional elections.[9]

7.4   Comparison and Contrast

Some ideas by their very nature lend themselves to contrast or comparison. The merits of a particular college dictionary, for example, can best be shown by comparing it with other college dictionaries. Advertisements of shoe polish or diet pills or spark plugs often contrast the effects of the advertised product with the effects of so-called inferior brands. Just as sharp color contrasts direct attention to poster ads, so do verbal contrasts accentuate ideas.

Joseph Wood Krutch in the following passage compares education and propaganda:

Nothing more clearly distinguishes a method of education from a technique of indoctrination than the fact that education demands from the subject some effort, especially some effort of attention, while propaganda does not. The advertiser will go to any length to make everything easy. The educator will see to it that something is expected of his pupil. He knows that no one can learn anything worth knowing unless he is willing to learn, as well as willing to be taught. He knows that learning how to learn is more important than any specific

---

[9] Richard L. Neuberger, "The Decay of State Governments," *Harper's Magazine*, October, 1953, pp. 36–37.

thing he can "communicate." And the grand question has now become whether or not the new techniques of mass communication inevitably and by their very nature weaken the power to learn at the same time that they make being taught so easy.[10]

Statistical and mathematical comparison is a common method of clarifying ideas, as the following passage shows:

Here in America last year we spent $10,000,000,000 for cocktails and other spirituous liquors. We spent $5,000,000,000 for tobacco. We spent $264,000,000, for chewing gum. But when I advocated on the floor of the United States Senate that we spend an extra $200,-000,000 a year for the next five years on the better care of our health, some people were shocked.

"How could you possibly spend that much money?" these people have asked. "Why $200,000,000 a year for five years is $1,000,000,-000!" Indeed it is. One billion. Forty-nine billions less than our drinking bill during those same five years. Twenty-four billions less than our smoking bill. More than $250,000,000 less than our bill for chewing gum.[11]

7.5 Analogy or Other Figures of Speech

Analogy is a special form of comparison, usually figurative, which explains unfamiliar concepts by relating them to familiar ones—that is, by pointing out similarities between what is already known and what is to be explained. Here are some examples:

"Language is a system of movements like figure dancing—but the most complicated system under human control. If two similar steps in a dance can condition each other so that both are confused or so that the dancer must exercise special care to keep them apart, imagine what happens when the steps are increased from the possible hundred or two in the dance to the

[10] Joseph Wood Krutch, "What We Say," *The American Scholar*, Summer, 1955.

[11] Margaret Chase Smith, "Billion-Dollar Prescription," *Saturday Review*, April 21, 1956, p. 43.

eight or ten thousand that constitute the stock of verbal movements at a speaker's command."[12]

A professional writer explains a short story by comparing it to a painting: "A story is to a full-length novel what a Rembrandt etching, with its lights and shadows concentrating on a single object, is to a vast Venetian canvas of Veronese or Tintoretto representing the work of a squad of junior artisans under a driving foreman. From their picaresque beginnings novels have wandered aimlessly over highways and byways looking for adventure. . . . A story, on the other hand, is a watch in the night, a slice of life. It is like a deathbed confession, when there is little time and breath to waste on long speeches, embroidery, and trivialities."[13]

The language of science, while rigidly controlled and extremely precise, is often so technical that its meanings are lost on the average reader or listener. For this reason, scientists frequently employ figurative and analogical expressions to make their meanings clear. Notice the figurative expressions in italics in the following passage written by a medical doctor: "Life for every individual is a *one-way street*; there are no *U-turns*. Birth, youth, maturity, senescence, and death are an inevitable biologic sequence, an inviolate law of living nature. . . . A very few only are willing to follow Huxley's advice to '*sit down* before a fact as a little child, be prepared to give up every preconceived notion, *follow* humbly wherever and to whatever *abyss* nature *leads*, else you shall learn nothing.' This humble *pursuit* of truth, this *spirit* of science, can become *as international as sunlight*. Only then will we have the *master key* to survival."[14]

Here is how a scientific writer describes the sun, by using figurative language: "If the solar surface and not the center were as hot as this, the radiation emitted into space would be so great that the whole Earth would be vaporized within a few minutes.

[12] Dwight L. Bolinger, "The Life and Death of Words," *The American Scholar*, Summer, 1953.

[13] Robert Moses, "Short Stories as I Like Them," *Saturday Review*, December 19, 1953, p. 10.

[14] R. R. Spencer, M.D., "Staying Alive," *Saturday Review*, October 27, 1951.

Indeed, this is just what would happen if some cosmic giant were to peel off the outer layers of the Sun like skinning an orange, for the tremendously hot inner regions would then be exposed. Fortunately, no such circumstance is possible, and the outer layers of the Sun provide a sort of blanket that protects us from its inner fires."[15]

Special qualities of personal experience may also be expressed metaphorically:

The stabler of the iron horse was up early this morning by the light of the stars amid the mountains, to fodder and harness his steed. Fire, too was awakened thus early to put the vital heat in him and get him off. . . . If the snow lies deep, they strap on his snowshoes, and, with the giant plow, plow a furrow from the mountains to the seaboard, in which the cars, like a following drill-barrow, sprinkle all the restless men and floating merchandise in the country for seed. All day the fire-steed flies over the country, stopping only that his master may rest, and I am awakened by his tramp and defiant snort at midnight, when in some remote glen in the woods he fronts the elements encased in ice and snow; and he will reach his stall only with the morning star, to start once more on his travels without rest or slumber.[16]

Suggestions for using figures of speech are as follows:

a. Use figures of speech to clarify and illuminate ideas, not to prove the soundness of them.

b. In factual reports, keep figurative expressions to a minimum.

c. Avoid using mixed, confused, or outlandish figures.

d. Employ figures of speech which are appropriate to the subject area under consideration, if possible.

e. Avoid trite, hackneyed, overworked figures of speech. Be original.

7.6   Analysis

Analysis is the breaking up or separation of anything into its component parts in order to show their interrelationships. We an-

[15] Fred Hoyle, *The Nature of the Universe*, New York, 1951.
[16] Henry David Thoreau, *Walden*.

alyze the spectrum into six major colors, the day into twenty-four hours, the year into four seasons, and society into a number of levels or classes.

There are several ways of analyzing a concept or idea. Structural analysis isolates various parts of a total organization: *The university is made up of a number of separate colleges*. Chronological analysis separates an idea into units of time: *The history of the English language includes Old English, Middle English, and Modern English*. Functional analysis shows the relative functions of different parts in a total operation: *The eight parts of speech all perform different functions in a sentence*.

In the following passage, these three types of analysis are combined:

> The Atlantic frontier was compounded of fisherman, fur-trader, miner, cattle-raiser, and farmer. Excepting the fisherman, each type of industry was on the march toward the West, impelled by an irresistible attraction. Each passed in successive waves across the continent. Stand at Cumberland Gap and watch the procession of civilization, marching single file—the buffalo following the trail to the salt springs, the Indian, the fur-trader and hunter, the cattle-raiser, the pioneer farmer—and the frontier has passed by. Stand at South Pass in the Rockies a century later and see the same procession with wider intervals between. The unequal rate of advance compels us to distinguish the frontier into the trader's frontier, the rancher's frontier, or the miner's frontier, and the farmer's frontier.[17]

The types of analysis just illustrated may be specified as follows:

Chronological analysis: units of time pointed out in the phrase "a century later."

Structural analysis: the "successive waves across the continent," made up of fisherman, fur-trader, miner, cattle-raiser, and farmer.

Functional analysis: the separation of the frontier into trader's

[17] F. J. Turner, "The Significance of the Frontier in American History."

frontier, rancher's frontier, miner's frontier, and farmer's frontier.

Russell Lynes' analysis of society into *highbrows,* or the elite; *middlebrows,* or the bourgeoisie; and *lowbrows,* or *hoi polloi,* is an example of structural analysis.

7.7 Definition and Explication

Definition is a means of bridging the gaps between words and the objects and experiences they signify. It is also a means of bridging gaps between people who want to exchange ideas. Definitions which explain and clarify your own unique meanings of words may have entirely escaped the dictionary. Lexicography cannot possibly keep pace with the multifarious uses to which language is put. Dictionary definitions are necessarily abstract, since they are *not,* as Wendell Johnson has pointed out, "statements about the non-verbal world of fact and experience, but words about words." They distill or condense an infinite number of specific usages to which a word has been put. They are usually much too general to clarify adequately an individual's creative thought. A dictionary merely substitutes one word for another, much as a bank exchanges one type of promissory note for another when you cash a check. Definition, to have any real value in communication, must get at the bullion in the vaults, must reduce abstraction to specific cases and relate words to concrete, observable facts. This can be accomplished in a number of ways: by examples, illustrations, reasons, directions, analogies, analyses, and any of the specific devices employed in the development of ideas. For example, one might define *communication* by contrasting it with *expression,* by analyzing its facets or skills, by giving directions about how it can be made effective, by giving reasons for its importance in democratic society, or by citing case histories of both effective and ineffective attempts to transfer meaning between people.

Unlike logical and formal definitions, personal, rhetorical, or extended definitions are not regulated by prescribed rules. Many words may be adequately defined by answering such simple questions as What? Who? When? Where? How? and Why? You might define *communism* by answering any or all of these questions:

a. What are the tenets of the communist belief?

b. Who originated the doctrines on which these beliefs are based?

c. When were the ideas conceived?

d. Where are the theories practiced and to what extent?

e. How are the doctrines implemented and the goals achieved?

f. What are the ultimate aims and objectives of the people who cherish the ideas?

The clarification of a particularly difficult passage or phrase in an otherwise quite understandable context is usually called *explication*. It may consist of translating a foreign idiom into simple English, of explaining an allusion to classical mythology, or of supplying clues to ambiguous terminology. Thomas De Quincey's "On the Knocking at the Gate in 'Macbeth' " is one of the most effective examples of explication ever written.

Following is an explication of a phrase from the writings of Emerson: "When Emerson uttered his famous phrase: 'Trust thyself—every heart vibrates to that iron string,' he makes, if I may say so, the whole iron curtain vibrate. He did not speak to the sentimental, the lazy, the superficial men, the men who are content to get by with the aid of a tutor and skillful appeals to the dean's office. What he had in mind is the stark truth that we brought nothing into this world and it is certain we can carry nothing out, and that therefore between these poles of time lies our only opportunity to develop character."[18]

[18] Howard Mumford Jones, "The Iron String," an address given at The Leverett House Junior-Senior Dinner, 1950.

Here is an example of explication of a familiar folk expression: "We look out the window on a stormy night when rain pours down the pane. 'It's raining cats and dogs,' we say. But why 'cats and dogs,' rather than 'mice and sheep' or some other animal team? This phrase goes back to pagan times. In certain mythologies cats controlled the weather and witches who rode on rainy nights were thought to take the form of cats. Dogs were pets of Odin, the Scandinavian stormy war god. Therefore, when the wind howled and the rain scratched its long claws upon the window, superstitious ancients spoke breathlessly of 'a rain of cats and dogs.' "[19]

7.8 Suggestion, Association, and Imagery

Impressionistic description, which makes use of free association of verbal images, is sometimes the most appropriate way of developing a thought, and depends for its effectiveness upon connotations rather than denotations of words, upon suggestion rather than logic. Details unified by a dominant impression are set forth in the order that they impress the observer. The thought process by which ideas are developed in this fashion is called *reverie*.

The kaleidoscopic mental images that accompany reverie are clearly illustrated in this passage:

I lay there pondering my situation, lost in the desert sand in danger, naked between sky and sand, withdrawn by too much silence from the poles of my life. I knew that I should wear out days and weeks returning to them if I were not sighted by some plane, or if next day the Moors did not find and murder me. Here I possessed nothing in the world. I was no more than a mortal strayed between

---

[19] Louis Untermeyer, "Poets and Peasants," *Woman's Home Companion,* April, 1948, p. 12.

sand and stars, conscious of the single blessing of breathing. And yet, I discovered myself filled with dreams.

They came to me soundlessly, like the waters of a spring, and in the beginning I could not understand the sweetness that was invading me. There was neither voice nor vision, but the presentiment of a presence, of a warmth very close and already half guessed. Then I began to grasp what was going on, and shutting my eyes I gave myself up to the enchantments of my memory.

Somewhere there was a park dark with firs and linden-trees and an old house that I loved. It mattered little that it was far away, that it could not warm me in my flesh, nor shelter me, reduced here to the role of dream. It was enough that it existed to fill my night with its presence. I was no longer this body flung up on a strand; I oriented myself; I was the child of this house, filled with the memory of its odors, with the cool breath of its vestibules, with the voices that had animated it, even to the very frogs in the pools that came here to be with me. I needed these thousand landmarks to identify myself, to discover of what absences the savor of this desert was composed, to find a meaning in this silence made of a thousand silences, where the very frogs were silent.[20]

Imagery is employed in the following passage to create a proper atmosphere for the author's thought:

The far summit [of Woedolor mountain] fairly smoked with frost; white vapors curled up from its white-wooded top, as from a chimney. The intense congelation made the whole country look like one petrifaction. The steel shoes of my pung craunched and gritted over the vitreous, chippy snow, as if it had been broken glass. The forests here and there skirting the route, feeling the same all-stiffening influence, their inmost fibres penetrated with the cold, strangely groaned—not in the swaying branches merely, but likewise in the vertical trunk—as the fitful gusts remorselessly swept through them. Brittle with excessive frost, many colossal tough-grained maples, snapped in twain like pipe-stems, cumbered the unfeeling earth.[21]

[20] Antoine de Saint-Exupéry, Wind, Sand, and Stars, New York, 1939, pp. 106–107.

[21] Herman Melville, "Tartarus of Maids."

7.9 Instructions, Explanations, and Directions

A very necessary and highly practical form of communication is the giving and receiving of directions. We depend upon directions when we take a dose of medicine, bake a cake, assemble a piece of furniture, perform an experiment in the laboratory, or locate the post office. Effective directions depend upon accuracy, simplicity, clarity, brevity, and completeness. Diagrams, maps, pictures, or graphs often help to make ideas clear and comprehensible.

In offering parents a solution to the problem of finding sufficient funds to finance their child's college education, one writer has listed seven ways of investigating scholarship awards; they are presented as directions:

1. Consult the principal of your child's high school.
2. Write to colleges of your child's choice, asking what scholarships they award. Ask about loan funds and campus job opportunities, too.
3. Consult books on scholarships available.
4. Ask your clergyman about scholarships to colleges affiliated with your church.
5. If your work is for a large company, ask if it has company-sponsored scholarships for children of employees.
6. If you are a member of a labor union, check on its activities. It may have a scholarship program.
7. If you belong to a national organization of any kind, find out whether or not it awards scholarships.[22]

The idea proposed in the following passage is a solution to a recognized problem. The accompanying illustrations graphically explain the idea.

If you drive through Europe, as more Americans are doing each year, a new boundary every few hundred miles means a new set of signs—and, for you, utter confusion.

[22] John W. Alexander, "Where's the Money Coming From for College?" *Woman's Day*, October, 1955, p. 30.

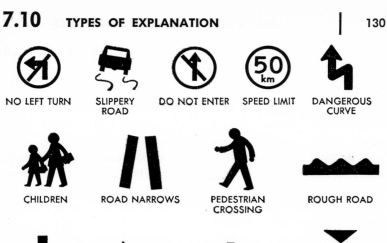

| NO LEFT TURN | SLIPPERY ROAD | DO NOT ENTER | SPEED LIMIT | DANGEROUS CURVE |

| CHILDREN | ROAD NARROWS | PEDESTRIAN CROSSING | ROUGH ROAD |

| INTERSECTION | DANGEROUS HILL | STOP SIGN AHEAD | LOW CLEARANCE |

The solution? Signs that mean the same thing everywhere in the world (even if it's kilometers instead of miles, as in the "speed limit" sign above). Just as everywhere a red light means "Stop," and a green light, "Go."

United Nations experts have drawn up a set of such signs—and we're showing you the most common ones. Eight countries have adopted them, and if more follow suit, you'll soon be able to drive anywhere without having to take a dictionary out of your pocket at every intersection.[23]

7.10 Types of Explanation in Combination

The following portion of a speech by a famous author demonstrates how a number of explanatory devices may be combined in communicating an idea:

One of the roads to agreement which particularly   DEFINITION
fascinated me was group dynamics—a study of the

[23] Gardner Soule, "Universal Traffic Signs," *Household*, August, 1955, p. 7.

energy locked up in people which can be released only through appropriate group action.

The Quakers in their business meetings have amply verified the value of group study—a verification extending over three centuries. They know how to pool the experience of members, study solutions of a problem which no individual member had previously thought of, and reach unanimous agreement. They avoid voting, so there is no majority to crow and no minority to feel sore. — ILLUSTRATION

I factored out nine principles from a Quaker meeting. Some tie into modern studies of group behavior, and all bear on classroom education. Besides unanimity, the Quaker principles include: participation and involvement of members in problems and solutions; careful listening—a technique alien to most Americans; periods of silence to delay emotional responses; "permissive" leaders; equality of status for all members; priority of facts over opinions; a moratorium for questions which stir emotions and cause sides to form. The question whether members of the Philadelphia Meeting should own slaves came up for decades. The unanimous answer was no, in 1776—85 years before the Civil War! — ANALYSIS

Here is a case from England. After World War II so many returned officers stormed Oxford and Cambridge that the ancient tutorial system broke down. Tutors, instead of taking one boy at a time, were forced to take on five or six. To everyone's surprise, it was found that students learned more by group study than alone. "There is a distinct gain in meeting more than one student," says a Rockefeller Foundation report by Robert T. Crane. "Students engage in mutual discussion, often continued beyond the session with the tutor." In group discussion the subject has a better chance of coming alive.[24] — SPECIFIC INSTANCE / TESTIMONY

[24] Stuart Chase, "Roads to Agreement," address, Chicago, Illinois, November 6, 1952.

EXERCISES

1. Read any essay or magazine article, assigned by your instructor, and analyze it for methods of clarification and types of support of the idea proposed. List all the devices you can identify.

2. Identify the devices used in the following paragraphs to explain and clarify the author's thought.

All reading experts agree that a poor vocabulary is a drawback to rapid reading. But don't stop to look up every new word in a dictionary. Keep going, at least to the end of the paragraph. Often the meaning of the word is made clear by the way it is used. If not, it may become clear if you try to figure it out before looking it up. "A large vocabulary," says Norman Lewis, "does not come from looking up long lists of words in a dictionary. It comes from wide reading, from being alert and curious."

—Ruth McCoy Harris

We must—all of us, men, women, and children—reorient ourselves with relation to the world in which we live. We must learn to weigh the daily news in terms of man's subsistence. We must come to understand our past, our history, in terms of the soil and water and forests and grasses that have made it what it is. We must see the years to come in the frame that makes space and time one, that will keep us strong only as, like Antaeus, we draw our strength from the earth. Our education must be reshaped, as the story of our existence in an environment as completely subjected to physical laws as is a ball we let drop from our hands. Our philosophies must be rewritten to remove them from the domain of words and "ideas," and to plant their roots firmly in the earth. Above all, we must weigh our place in the society of nations and our future through the decades to come in the scale of our total environment.

—William Vogt

In the Pacific off Vancouver Island, there is a stretch of water known as "The Zone of Silence." Because this area is acoustically dead, no sound can penetrate it. And since no bell or siren can warn ships of dangerous reefs, the ocean floor is studded with wrecks.

The world of ideas and events also has its "Zone of Silence." Here, too, everything is hushed, and unknown dangers lurk beneath the surface. This region, too, is generally shunned, and most publications steer clear of it—but not THE REPORTER. THE REPORTER explores it as fully as possible, and then reports on its dangers and tells you how they may affect you.

—George Hinckley, Circulation
Manager of *The Reporter*

Indian officials think the elephant can be used to pull plows cheaper and better than tractors. Recently they opened a campaign to test this. Jagmohan Singh Negi, forest minister of the state of Uttar Pradesh, made the following points in championing the cause of elephant against tractor:

1. A good elephant in his prime costs $600 to $800 against about $1,600 for a tractor of like horsepower.
2. An average elephant puts out the same effort as a 30-horsepower tractor.
3. Life span of an elephant is about 50 to 60 years—much longer than the mechanical device.
4. Daily upkeep of an elephant is only $3, while a tractor costs $10 to $12.
5. An elephant is more maneuverable than a tractor and can go places a tractor can't.
6. Elephant waste can be used as fertilizer.
7. An elephant can do other odd jobs around the house.
8. Mechanics are short in India, and whoever heard of removing the transmission of an elephant.

Critics of the plan point out these two main objections:

1. A tractor can plow 10 to 12 acres a day, while an elephant can only do about 5.
2. An elephant is temperamental.

—*The State Journal* (Lansing,
Michigan), December 11, 1955,
p. 57

A dictionary explains *inflation* as a "disproportionate and relatively sharp and sudden increase in the quantity of money or credit, or both, relative to the amount of exchange business."

This means, in effect, that as money increases in quantity it suffers in quality, in a manner of speaking. The prime effect of inflation is to make it harder for consumers to get the things they want and need because their money will buy less. This can happen even when consumer goods are plentiful, inflation through wage and other increases having put costs of production at high levels, with resulting higher prices.

—Editorial in *The State Journal*
(Lansing, Michigan) November
17, 1952.

3. Look up a topic in the *Reader's Guide to Periodical Literature,* and select two articles for reading. Compare the methods employed by the two authors in making their ideas clear. Explain which article is most easily comprehended.

4. Select an abstract word, such as *loyalty, patriotism, good will,* or *charity,* and write a 200-word definition of it, using several types of explanation.

5. Point out the analogy in the following passage. How is it used to slant facts to the author's purpose?

No question is more earnestly discussed these days among people interested in the future of American education than the prospect and consequences of what has been called "the tidal wave" of students which will flood our schools and colleges in the next ten to twenty years. . . .

The phrase "tidal wave" is not wholly appropriate. Tidal waves are misfortunes. They are frequently destructive, and sometimes catastrophic. Notice of their imminence is always cause for alarm. There are those who fear that the massive pressure of numbers will progressively lower the quality of American education. These forebodings are not lightly to be dismissed. The facts indicate that there is ample cause for concern. But the quality of American education need not, and must not, deteriorate.

—Clarence H. Faust, *Teachers for
Tomorrow,* Bulletin No. 2, The
Fund for the Advancement of
Education, 1956, pp. 4–5

6. Write a 350-word paper in which you explain and develop an idea in three separate ways. Identify in the margin of your paper what devices you have employed.
7. Give a three- to five-minute talk in which you explain and develop an idea in three separate ways.
8. Listen to speeches made by your classmates in fulfilling exercise 7. Identify the methods used to clarify ideas and explain meanings.
9. Write an extended definition of some abstract term that is likely to be easily misinterpreted, such as *communism, sportsmanship, devotion, success,* or *Christianity.*

FOR FURTHER READING

Blair, Walter, and Gerber, John, *Factual Prose*, Chicago, 3rd ed., 1955.

Bloomfield, Morton W., and Robbins, Edwin W., *Form and Idea: Thirty Essays for College Study*, New York, 1953.

Canby, Henry S., *Better Writing*, New York, 1926.

Lee, Irving J., *Customs and Crises in Communication*, New York, 1954.

8

DEFEND YOUR CONVICTION

ESTABLISHING A DEFENSE FOR YOUR IDEAS, theses, solutions, or beliefs is a matter of preparing a case for them, somewhat as an attorney prepares a case for a court trial. You want to convince readers or listeners of the soundness of your position. In order to succeed in this, you need a well-defined method of procedure which coincides as nearly as possible with the way people reason or think. The mere presentation of unorganized evidence will accomplish nothing. Facts in isolation have little value. Furthermore, when you read or listen to others, you need to understand how to determine the efficacy and soundness of ideas proposed. Four frequently employed methods of argument useful in communication are: induction, deduction, appeals to authority, and appeals to emotion.

8.1 Induction

Induction is the process by which we arrive at general conclusions after examining specific facts, isolated cases, or particular qualities of experience. It is not only one of the principal methods by which scientists unriddle the mysteries of the universe but also one of the most frequently employed means by which laymen discover "truth" in everyday affairs. Here is a down-to-earth explanation of the process:

Suppose you go into a fruiterer's shop, wanting an apple—you take up one, and, on biting it, you find it sour; you look at it, and see that

136

it is hard and green. You take up another one, and that too is hard, green and sour. The shopman offers you a third; but, before biting it you examine it, and find that it is hard and green, and you immediately say that you will not have it, as it must be sour, like those you have already tasted.

Nothing can be more simple than that, you think; but if you will take the trouble to analyze and trace out into its logical elements what has been done by the mind, you will be greatly surprised. In the first place, you have performed the operation of Induction. You found that, in two experiences, hardness and greenness in apples went together with sourness. It was so in the first place, and it was confirmed by the second. True, it is a very small basis, but still it is enough to make an induction from; you generalize the facts, and you expect to find sourness in apples where you get hardness and greenness. You found upon that a general law, that all hard and green apples are sour; and that so far as it goes, is a perfect induction.[1]

The net result or outcome of this type of reasoning is variously called a *generalization, conclusion, inference, hypothesis, prediction, principle,* or *law*. If such outcome is consistently confirmed by rigidly controlled experiments, it is called a *principle* or *law*. If the outcome is derived from a few hastily observed instances, as in Huxley's illustration of the apples, it is usually called an *inference* or a *hypothesis*. All generalizations are in a sense predictions, since they affirm the truth about something which has not been actually inspected or observed.

Dangers of Induction (see also Reference Guides, L. 1)

THE INDUCTIVE LEAP. The possibility of error is ever present in all induction. While you may never find an exception to Newton's law of gravity, you might easily find exceptions to the "rules of thumb" that control many casual decisions. The risk involved in generalization, whether slight or great, stems from what is called the *inductive leap*. When you pass from what is known to what is unknown, you take a "leap in the

[1] T. H. Huxley, "The Method of Scientific Investigation," in *Man's Place in Nature and Other Essays.*

dark." The fewer specific facts, experiences, or observations involved in your induction, the greater the leap.

Assuming the regularity and uniformity of nature, we predict
that spring will follow winter, that the North Star will always
be in the north heavens, that rabbits will be prolific, and that
sub-zero temperatures will freeze water. Sometimes we muster up
courage enough to predict the weather, although the weatherman
has an uncanny way of frustrating our best efforts to anticipate
his projected movements. The United States Weather Bureau
with the most scientific equipment available is often as mistaken as a New England farmer with his kit of folkloristic formulas for predicting a storm. For example, the big snow of 1948
came as a complete surprise to the Weather Bureau.

Human beings are even less predictable. When we make
sweeping generalizations about people, we walk on very thin ice.
In 1938 the National Resources Committee predicted that the
population of the United States—then about 130,000,000—
would soon level off. Sixteen trial predictions were made using
various combinations of fertility, mortality, and immigration as
bases. Not one of the sixteen estimates predicted that the population would reach 155,000,000 by 1951 or even by 1955. Six of
the predictions held the population below 155,000,000 for 1980,
one as low as 127,947,000. The only reasonable explanation for
such miscalculations is that people refuse to be resolved into a
formula or explained by a theorem.

A case study from American history further supports the idea
that predictions about people are risky. In 1867 the Republican
leaders in Washington predicted that Senator Edmund G. Ross
of Kansas would join the movement to impeach President
Johnson. Their hopes were based as follows:

There could be no doubt as to where Ross's sympathies lay; his
entire career was one of determined opposition to the slave states
of the South, their practices, and their friends. In 1854, when he was
only twenty-eight, he had taken part in the mob rescue of a fugitive
slave in Milwaukee. In 1856, he had joined the flood of anti-slavery

immigrants to "bleeding" Kansas who intended to keep it a free territory. Disgusted with the Democratic party of his youth, he had left that party and volunteered in the Kansas Free State Army to drive back a force of pro-slavery men invading the territory. In 1862, he had given up his newspaper work to enlist in the Union Army, from which he emerged a Major. Radical Republican leaders were sure that in Ross they had a solid member of that vital two-thirds.[2]

But they were wrong. Ross's relentless refusal to take dictation from the Republican leaders, or to vote in favor of impeachment, thwarted the determined efforts of the President's political enemies to unseat him in the White House.

SAMPLING.   One might by direct observation find that all the students in a particular college class are boys. If every member of the class is accounted for, no prediction is involved and no inductive leap is made. This would be an infallible induction. But if we observe two or three classes of students and find them made up solely of boys, and then infer that all the classes in the school are composed of boys, we have made an inductive leap, from a small sample to the total aggregate from which the sample is derived.

Most of the conclusions we draw about the world in which we live are of necessity inferred from selected samples. We are, for this reason, always in danger of making hasty generalizations— generalizations based on insufficient data, such as the following: speed is the major cause of automobile accidents; men can drive better than women; raisins are effective in the cure of boils; all politicians are grafters; all English teachers are cranks about language usage; the appearance of sea gulls precedes a storm; bad money drives out good; comic books are a major factor in juvenile delinquency; to spare the rod will spoil a child.

The following tests should help you to determine the adequacy of a generalization.

a. Have sufficient cases been examined to establish the truth?

[2] Senator John F. Kennedy, "Ross of Kansas," *Harper's Magazine*, December, 1955, p. 41.

b. Are the individual cases typical, or representative, of the total population from which they are drawn?

c. Is the observer sincerely trying to establish the truth?

d. Is the language employed precise and clear?

e. Are all extenuating factors which might affect the sample controlled or considered?

Uses of Induction

Induction is used in communication (a) to support conceived ideas or (b) to test the adequacy and acceptability of proposed ideas. Kinds of evidence which may be used to support ideas by this method include scientific facts, case histories, statistical data, analogy, and causal argument.

VERIFIABLE FACTS. Not all ideas lend themselves to factual support. That synthetic rubber will outwear natural rubber in automobile tires, or that deep-freezing will preserve foods indefinitely, may be supported by factual data; but that jazz music appeals to primitive instincts in human nature, or that all human beings have the capacity to develop a love of freedom and a desire for equality, depends on other forms of evidence.

An excellent example of how facts may be used to clear up popular fallacies or folk explanations of nature's riddles may be found in the following passage:

From start to finish, the entire visible discharge lasts anywhere from $\frac{1}{500}$ of a second to 1.6 seconds, depending roughly on the number of return strokes involved.

Besides making a bright flash, the lightning causes a tremendous bang. The noise level has been estimated at up to 120 decibels, which is considerably more than the 112 decibels produced by the Air Force's new F-100 fighter revving up its jet engine on the ground 100 feet away. . . .

What causes thunder? A number of folk explanations are popular. One says it's the noise produced when two thunderclouds bump into each other. Another, which sounds altogether plausible but is wrong nevertheless, says that thunder is produced when air rushes back into the semivacuum left in the wake of a lightning bolt after it has burned through the air.

Actually, thunder is simply the electrical rending of the air—the sound produced when the zillions of electrons which comprise lightning crash into other electrons in the atmosphere during a lightning stroke. The same sort of action accounts for the noise of an atomic bomb.[3]

Here is an account of a scientist's use of observed facts to verify a hypothesis concerning natural phenomena:

But the best evidence, known to me, of worms subsisting for at least considerable periods of time solely on the organic matter contained in earth, is afforded by some facts communicated to me by Dr. King. Nice large castings abound in extraordinary numbers, so that 5 or 6 were often found within the space of a square foot. They consist of fine, pale-colored earth, containing calcareous matter, which after having passed through the bodies of worms and being dried, coheres with considerable force. . . . Dr. King, who looked carefully, never saw even a fragment of a leaf thus drawn in.[4]

CASE HISTORIES.   The familiar expression "Let's get down to cases" suggests a type of support that involves people doing things, or acting in certain ways, under specific circumstances, for particular reasons. In other words, a case history, or a case study, is a dramatic episode, either factual or fictional, which answers the questions What? Who? When? Where? How? and Why? Usually a case history is cited in support or clarification of an abstract theory, principle, or idea.

Bernard De Voto, criticizing the United States security system, naturally turned to specific cases which had been tried by the Supreme Court:

Our security system has an inherent tendency to constantly erode away more of the free system which it was designed to preserve. As I write this, the Supreme Court has just shown how this tendency has

[3] Alfred M. Lansing, "Lightning," *Collier's*, July 8, 1955.
[4] Charles Darwin, "The Utility of Earthworms."

been operating in a whole category of cases, exemplified by that of Dr. John P. Peters, professor of medicine at Yale.

Dr. Peters was a part-time employee of the U.S. Public Health Service. His job was to advise the Surgeon General about the worth of applications for financial aid to medical researches. It did not involve any classified or confidential information and no question of security was involved. The Federal Security Administration had twice investigated his loyalty and had twice found that no evidence justified doubt of it. Nevertheless, the Review Board of the Civil Service Commission, on its own initiative, decided to reopen the case and notified Dr. Peters that it had "derogatory information" about him. At the hearing it held, no witness testified against Dr. Peters, he was not told who had provided the "derogatory information," and of course, he had no opportunity to cross-examine the anonymous informants. As the Supreme Court has observed, the Review Board did not itself know the identity of some of them, and some of them had not testified on oath. But it found against Dr. Peters and he was discharged from the Public Health Service.

Of the Supreme Court's opinion I mention here only its finding that the Review Board had no power or authority to reopen the case. It was, in fact, seeking "to do by (its own) regulation what it was not permitted to do under the order" that created it. That is one manifestation of the inherent tendency of the security system to encroach always farther on the free system. . . .[5]

Notice in this passage that Mr. De Voto has made a point regarding the security system by citing a representative case. His article makes other points which are argued by additional case studies.

The use of case studies in medical science is a standard method of procuring evidence:

Though Evans made no claims for the vitamin E potency in humans, Dr. P. Vogt-Moller, of the County Hospital at Odense, Denmark, tried vitamin E therapy on a group of cows known to be chronic aborters, and obtained favorable results. Then on July 25,

[5] "Spread of an Infection" from "The Easy Chair," *Harper's Magazine,* August, 1955, p. 12.

1931, he reported to the English medical journal, *Lancet,* the results of his next step. Case No. 1 was that of a twenty-four-year-old woman, who after four miscarriages, was given Evans' wheat oil orally. Her next pregnancy followed a normal course and a healthy baby was born. Case No. 2 was that of a twenty-nine-year-old woman who, after the birth of her first child, miscarried four times in succession. This woman was given about two tablespoons of wheat oil each week, and responded as successfully as the first case. Others, too, believe that vitamin E is necessary for the human mother, but the medical world still awaits more conclusive testimony. . . .[6]

MATHEMATICAL AND STATISTICAL DATA. If we want to know how many students are enrolled in a class, we take the roll. If we want to know how many cows there are in the pasture, we count noses. Since *enumeration* takes all the cases in an aggregate into consideration, possibility of error is restricted to errors of observation or errors of calculation. Here is an example of the use of numerical data:

In 1900, the college enrollment of some 238,000 students amounted to 4% of the college-age population 18–21 years of age. Today, our college enrollment of 2,500,000 is close to 30% of the college-age population. Through the years a larger and larger population of our young people have gone to college: 8% by 1920, 12% by 1930, 18% by 1940. Granted that there are distortions today produced by the vagaries of military service and the peculiarities of educational statistics, we nonetheless have a fairly accurate picture of what happens to the youth of college age. About three out of every five 18 years olds today graduate from high school. About one out of every five 18 year olds today goes to a four-year college. About one out of every eight obtains a college degree.[7]

Statistical methods are used for making meaningful generalizations from samples selected from large masses or quantities of numerical data. Statistics deal with probabilities rather than with certainties. The accuracy of a defended generalization depends to

[6] Bernard Jaffe, *Men of Science in America,* New York, 1944.
[7] John D. Millett, "The Impinding Crisis in Higher Education," *School and Society,* June 25, 1955, p. 194.

THE NUMBER OF YOUNG PEOPLE REACHING SCHOOL AND COLLEGE AGE WILL INCREASE FOR YEARS TO COME

During the past 50 years there has been a steady increase in the proportion of young people going to school and college. The ratio of high school enrollments to the size of the 14-17 age group rose from 11 per cent in 1900 to 80 per cent in 1954. The ratio of college enrollments to the size of the 18-21 age group rose from 4 per cent to nearly 30 per cent. While the size of these two age groups increased by less than half, high school and college enrollments rose nearly tenfold.

Statistics in Textual Form. Source: *Teachers for Tomorrow*, The Fund for the Advancement of Education, Bulletin No. 2, 1955.

a great extent upon the quality and quantity of the sample used. Deriving I.Q. scores, predicting presidential elections by public opinion polls, and determining the effectiveness of medical vaccines are activities that make good use of statistics. No attempt is made here to explain the intricacies of statistical calculation. The following outline shows some of the principal types or varieties of such calculations.

1. Measures of central tendency.
   a. Mean: the arithmetical average of all items included in a sample.

Average annual earnings
in various occupations, 1953

Non-teaching		**Teaching**	
Railroad engineers	$7,352	Professors in large state universities	$7,000
Railroad firemen	6,180	Associate professors in large state universities	5,600
Railroad conductors	6,676	Assistant professors in large state universities	4,600
Railroad switchtenders	4,697	Instructors in large state universities	3,700
Workers in automobile manufacturing industry	4,947	Teachers in big city high schools	5,526
Workers in bituminous coal mining industry	4,198	Teachers in small city high schools	4,292
Workers in electrical machinery manufacturing industry	4,133	Teachers in big city elementary schools	4,817
Workers in stone, clay, and glass manufacturing industry	3,956	Teachers in small city elementary schools	3,682
Telephone operators of the New York Telephone Co.	3,224	Teachers in small town elementary schools	3,190

Statistics in Tabular Form. Source: *Teachers for Tomorrow,* The Fund for the Advancement of Education, Bulletin No. 2, 1955.

  b. Median: the middle item, score, or response, when all data are placed in rank order (from highest to lowest).
  c. Mode: the item, score, or response which occurs most frequently in a selected sample.
2. Measures of dispersion.
  a. Range: the numerical difference between the highest and lowest item, score, or response.
  b. Standard deviation: a measure of the difference between a particular item in the sample and the mean of the sample.
  c. Normal distribution: the characteristic differences among a large number of items selected at random from a total population or aggregate.
3. Measures of probability.
  a. Standard error: a measure of the mathematical limits within

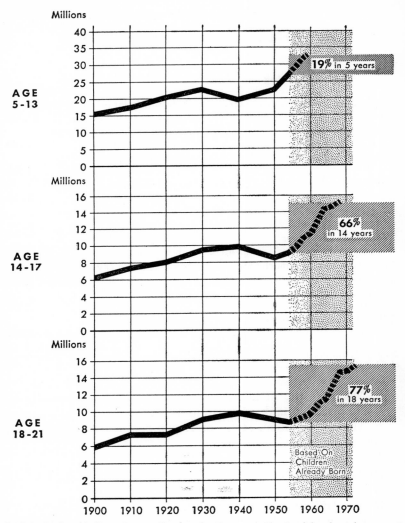

Statistics in Graphic Form. Source: *Teachers for Tomorrow,* The Fund for the Advancement of Education, Bulletin No. 2, 1955.

which a true score, or response, can be safely established.
b. Level of confidence: a measure of the mathematical probability that a statistical calculation is a true indication of reality.
4. Measures of relationship.
a. Correlation coefficient: a measure of the degree of correspondence between two selected items, scores, responses.
b. Significance of difference: a measure of the probability that
derived differences among selected items are real differences,
that is, differences not due to mere chance.

Three forms of presenting statistical data are commonly used:
textual, tabular, and graphic. These forms are shown in the accompanying illustrations.

ANALOGY.   Analogy is a form of induction by which one reasons that if two objects, situations, or arrangements are similar
in some respects, they are similar in all respects. The risk taken
in this type of reasoning is usually very great. Analogous objects
or situations have differences as well as similarities, and, more
likely than not, the existing differences outnumber the observed
similarities.

A public service television commercial, designed to persuade
people to support public education in America, presented the
following argument: "If we want to insure a good crop of corn,
we plant the kernels in the ground rather than grind them into
feed. So, if we want to insure a good crop of students in our
schools, we must pay adequate wages to teachers." The connections between raising corn and educating children, pointed out in
this argument, are so vague as to establish nothing, and so far-
fetched as to do the argument more harm than good. But sometimes the connections in analogy seem close enough to actually
prove a relationship. This is the real danger. Analogy clarifies
thought rather than proves a thesis. Whenever analogy is used as
proof, it should be reinforced by other types of evidence, such
as verifiable facts or recognized authority.

In an attempt to show that verbal skill cannot be acquired by following the codified rules of a handbook, one writer draws an analogy between English instruction and the game of football:

Let us compare the English class with the football team, the English teacher with the coach, and the grammar book with the football rule book.

The coach's job, of course, is to teach the team how to become expert in playing the game of football so that the team may give a good account of itself when pitted against other teams of experts.

Now then, does the coach present the players with the rule book and tell them to study it diligently for a while and then get out there on the field and die for dear old Hemandhaw? Certainly not. There is nothing in the rule book about how to kick a field goal, how to shoot a long, true, spiraling pass, how to punt, tackle, block, and plunge through the line. The team could study the rule book until judgment day and not be able to tell a football from a watermelon. And to send such youngsters out to play against a tough, experienced opponent would be equivalent to sending them to the hospital.

The competent coach leaves the rule book in the locker room, and he escorts his young stalwarts to the gridiron. And it is there that they learn to play football by playing football. The few rules they need to know are absorbed naturally and casually as they give themselves heart and soul to the magnificent fun of learning the fine points of playing an extremely difficult and strenuous game. They learn by doing, and they let the referees worry over the rule book.[8]

CAUSE-EFFECT RELATIONSHIPS. Reasoning from an observed activity, process, or event to its probable cause or to its probable consequences is a form of induction called causal argument. Thus, when we put a kettle of water on the fire, we predict that when the temperature of the water reaches 212° F. it will boil. When we hear a child scream, we reason that physical injury of one kind or another has caused the outcry. When a medical doctor diagnoses a patient's illness, he reasons from effects to causes. When he prescribes a remedy, he reasons from cause to effect.

As with other forms of induction, causal argument is accom-

[8] Frank Colby, "Grammar Without Groans," *The Practical Handbook of Better English*, New York, 1947, p. 6.

panied by certain risks or dangers. Principally they are as follows:

a. The assumption of causal relations between any two events separated in time may be unfounded. If A occurs prior to B, it does not necessarily follow that A causes B. The fact that you see lightning before you hear the thunder does not mean that lightning causes thunder. Yet many people accept arguments just as flimsy and illogical: that walking under a ladder will cause disaster, that three on a match portends evil consequences, that Monday's child works for a living, that impure blood produces boils.

b. It is often impossible to distinguish causes and effects. Does the sun rise because the rooster crows, or does the rooster crow because the sun rises? Which came first, the chicken or the egg? Does whiskey, when you are well, make you sick; or does whiskey make you well when you're sick? Do you attend the movies to escape boredom, or are you bored because you attend the movies? Do people stutter because they are frustrated, or are they frustrated because they stutter? Do delinquent children read comic books, or do comic books make delinquent children? Many people are firmly convinced that a college education guarantees vocational success. Actually, success in college and success in a career may both be outcomes or effects of the same personality factors, or causes.

c. The dynamic complexity of causal relations may be ignored. Events occur in dynamic settings: multiple causes produce multiple effects. In other words,

Effects result from many causes,

and
Every cause has many effects.

A child runs into the street from behind a parked car and is struck by an oncoming vehicle. What was the cause of the accident? The mother of the child may blame her own carelessness in letting the child run free to play in the street. The driver of the vehicle may blame the accident on the fact that his vision was obstructed. An investigating officer may blame the driver for breaking the speed limit. The child may say that he was chasing a butterfly which led him astray. All of these causes and many more may have been operative, so that assigning a single cause for the disaster is certainly partial and unsatisfactory.

Bergen Evans in "Look Out, Here I Come," discusses the multiple causation responsible for automobile accidents:

Most "causes" of accidents are only contributory factors. They are merely the conditions under which if you behave in a certain way you are likely to have an accident. (The experts compute that "on the average a person violates a safe practice three hundred times before he is injured in consequence.") But the behavior is the thing and much of the behavior seems to be motivated by what De Quincey called "the glory of motion." People collide at intersections not out of carelessness so much as out of resentment at the other fellow's daring to cross their path. Drivers get out of their lanes and race to death at the summit of hills because they are furiously determined to put an end to the "persecution" of the cars dawdling in front of them. Autoists speed as much to save face as time and frequently and literally lose both.[9]

An example which further argues the complexity of causal relations follows:

. . . We must beware of assuming that the prime *causes* of the decline of attention are to be found in such symptoms as *Quick*, advertising, the radio, television, the gossip column, the picture magazine, the soap opera, the mass-newspaper, the comic book, the pulps, the mammary-glandular "historical" works of fiction, the inspirational best seller, the cinema, the jukebox, the monosyllabic

[9] *Atlantic Monthly*, December, 1946.

novel. They aid in the relaxation of attention, but they do not cause it. They are merely carriers of the germ. . . .

For the fundamental causes of the decline of attention, we shall have to go back to our quotation from Wordsworth. They lie deep in the history of the last 300 years and are almost surely connected with the rise of aggressive nationalism and the victory of the industrial revolution.[10]

Notice the thoughtful analysis of causal factors in human warfare as presented by a philosopher:

The causes of war are psychological, biological, economic, and political—that is, they lie in the impulses of men, the competition of groups, the material needs of societies, and fluctuations of national power.

The basic causes are in ourselves, for the state is an enlarged picture of the soul. The five major instincts of mankind—food-getting, mating, parental love, fighting, and association—are the ultimate sources of war.[11]

The following passage demonstrates how easy it is for people to ignore the real, operative causes of human behavior:

Is your voice flat because of listlessness; shrill through ragged nerves? You may plead guilty but without seeing how that will affect your child's speech.

Here's how. Not long ago a woman brought her husky-voiced ten-year-old to the Queen's Speech and Hearing Center at Queen's College in New York City. Dr. Jon Elsenson, the clinic's director, gave her a jolt. "Take the boy home," he said. "Let me work with you." For the boy's voice was husky for one reason only—because his mother's was husky and he had imitated her. When the mother's huskiness was cured, the boy's cleared up naturally and quickly.[12]

---

[10] Clifton Fadiman, "The Decline of Attention," *Saturday Review of Literature,* August 6, 1949.

[11] Will Durant, "Why Fight Men?" *Saturday Evening Post,* July 10, 1937.

[12] Flora Rheta Schreiber, "Think! Before You Speak . . . Before Your Child," *Everywoman's,* May, 1955, p. 11.

Results or effects of proposed action are sometimes predicted on the basis of casual factors:

Today the high cost of living is due to two mutually dependent factors—the high cost of labor and the high cost of goods. Military demands—for both men and equipment—have reduced both the working force and production of civilian supplies and so raised the cost of both. If workers were allowed, if they wanted, to keep on at their jobs from the age of sixty-five to seventy-five, the labor force would increase by five to ten million workers and the growth in production would overcome to a considerable extent the shortage in goods. Prices might come down, if not to "normal," at least to a level that would not inspire profanity.[13]

8.2 Deduction

Deduction is a logical process by which we arrive at specific conclusions about unobserved facts by the application of general principles. This type of reasoning is made clear in T. H. Huxley's example of the hard, green, sour apples, mentioned in Section 8.1. You will remember that an observer, after sampling two hard, green apples, refused a third on the basis of a generalization, derived by induction, that "all green, hard apples are sour." Huxley's explanation of deduction follows:

Well, having got your natural law in this way, when you are offered another apple which you find is hard and green, you say, "all hard and green apples are sour; this apple is hard and green, therefore, this apple is sour." That train of reasoning is what logicians call a syllogism, and has all its various parts and terms—its major premise, its minor premise, and its conclusion. . . . So that, you see, you have, in the first place, established a law by induction, and upon that you have founded a deduction, and reasoned out the special conclusion of the particular case.

[13] Henry S. Curtis, "Why Retire at Sixty-five?" *Harper's Magazine*, April, 1952, p. 94.

The principal device of deductive reasoning, as Huxley explains, is the syllogism, which contains two statements believed to be true, followed by a conclusion deduced from the two statements of belief: All right angles are 90° angles: major premise. ABC is a right angle: minor premise. Therefore, ABC is a 90° angle: conclusion.

The Major Premise

The first statement in a syllogism is a generalization, or universally accepted truth. It asserts a relationship between two classes of objects, persons, or processes in the form of a rule to which no exceptions are admitted. A major premise may be derived in any one of the following ways: (a) It may be arbitrarily defined: A straight line is a 180° angle. (b) It may be derived by induction, in which case it is a generalization from observed phenomena, or verifiable facts: Water freezes at 32° F. (c) It may be the assertion of an authority: All Nazis are Aryans. (Hitler.) (d) It may be an unverified assumption: All lions are man-eaters. (e) It may be derived from another deductive argument:

First Syllogism

All Indians are warriors.
The Iroquois are Indians.
Therefore, the Iroquois are warriors.

Second Syllogism

The Iroquois are warriors.
You are an Iroquois.
Therefore, you are a warrior.

Deductive argument gets no nearer to truth than does the major premise. And the only major premises that can be certainly true are made so by definition, as in the case of 90° angles.

The Minor Premise

The second statement in a syllogism shows the relationship between one of the classes mentioned in the major premise and a third class. The minor premise is an assertion that an individual, or a smaller class, belongs to or may be identified with a larger class in the major premise. Thus, in the syllogism above relating to Indians, *Iroquois* is the small class included in *Indians*, the large class.

The Conclusion

The third statement in a syllogism is a logical deduction from the two premises which precede it. It affirms the identity of the particular case in the minor premise with the second, larger class in the major premise: All whales are *mammals*. The *porpoise* is a whale. Therefore, the porpoise is a mammal.

Validity and Truth

The principal usefulness of deductive reasoning is that it supplies a handy way of testing the validity of an argument. But it must be clearly understood that a valid argument is not necessarily true: All horses are cows. Betsy is a horse. Therefore, Betsy is a cow. The validity of a syllogism depends on the proper arrangement and control of the elements in the syllogism. The truth or probability of the conclusion depends entirely on the varifiability of the premises. Deduction may take any of the following forms:

a. Both premises may be true, the conclusion true, and the argument valid (the right-angle syllogism).

b. Either or both of the premises may be false and the conclusion true: All Koreans are Orientals. All Japanese are Koreans. Therefore, all Japanese are Orientals.

c. The premises may be false, the conclusion false, and the argument valid: All birds are fish. A whale is a bird. Therefore, a whale is a fish.

d. The premises may be true, the conclusion false, and the argument invalid: All whales are mammals. A horse is a mammal. Therefore, a whale is a horse.

8.3 Appeal to Authority

Whenever you find yourself in the position of defending an idea without first-hand information, you usually appeal to some well-known authority. This can be one of the most acceptable and effective ways of clinching an argument or of persuading readers or listeners to accept your proposals. It is far from a fool-proof method of reasoning, however, and should be employed with caution. Testimony, as we have already pointed out, varies from idle whim to expert judgment.

Often so-called authoritative statements are nothing more than expressions of personal opinion. Sometimes, as in the case of many paid commercials, they are nothing more than blind endorsement. Robert M. Hutchins ridicules the manipulated use of authority and testimony in his essay on collegiate football: "Athletics, we are told, produces well-rounded men, filled with the spirit of fair play. Athletics is good for the health of the players; it is also good for the morals of the spectators. Leadership on the playing fields means leadership in life. The Duke of Wellington said so. Athletes are red-blooded Americans, and athletic colleges are bulwarks against Communism. Gate receipts are used to build laboratories and to pay for those sports that can't pay for themselves. Football is purely a supplement to study. And without a winning team a college cannot hope to attract the students or the gifts which its work requires."[14] The point is that all too often authority is used merely to rationalize what people already believe to be true.

Here is an example of the use of authority to support an idea concerning language:

The terminology of grammar is obscure and misleading because it is not English at all, but Latin, and not a very good grade of Latin at that.

[14] Robert M. Hutchins, "Gate Receipts and Glory," *Saturday Evening Post*, December 3, 1938.

Richard Grant White, in *Words and Their Uses*, states, "When at last it dawned upon the pedagogues that English was a language—and they set themselves to giving rules for the art of writing and speaking it correctly—they attempted to form these rules upon the models furnished by the Latin language. From this heterogeneous union sprang that hybrid monster known as English grammar, before whose fruitless loins we have sacrificed, for nearly three hundred years, our children and the strangers within our gates. How preposterous, how impossible, for us to measure our English corn in Latin bushels."[15]

In order to insure the validity and truthfulness of an idea supported by authority, you need to apply the following tests of adequacy:

a. Does the authority actually exist? Is he accesible? Or is he an abstraction, like "reliable sources," or "informed opinion"?

b. Is the authority qualified to report accurately and to draw valid conclusions? Is he a specialist in the subject under consideration?

c. Is the authority conversant with the most recent discoveries in the field of investigation?

d. Does the authority present an objective, impartial, unbiased, unprejudiced opinion about his subject? Is the information intended to advance the self-interest of an individual or a group?

e. Does the authority deal with a real problem and does he get at the basis of the problem? Or does he present false alternatives and expect you to choose between two possible solutions to a problem, one of which he defends?

f. Does the authority express facts and opinions in language that is clear and understandable? Are any terms in the text of discourse used without adequate definition?

g. Is the authority using words to manipulate your thinking and influence your own judgment of the facts presented?

[15] Frank Colby, *Better English*, New York, 1947, pp. 2–3.

h. Does the authority ignore or suppress essential facts or arguments which seriously affect the conclusions drawn?

i. Does the authority supply information or ideas for the purpose you have in mind?

j. Does the authority make his fundamental position clear? Do the facts add up to a significant generalization? Do the facts justify the generalization?

8.4   Appeals to Emotion

Appeals to reason and appeals to emotion are like two sides of a single coin. "You can't have one without the other." They operate in unison like the harmonized voices of a duet. We think and feel simultaneously about a given problem. Thinking is always done in some kind of emotional setting or context. Emotional tension, like a power current, sets the wheels of intellect in motion. Ideas are born of need, and of pressures that first produce emotional feelings. If an idea once created is to be successfully transmitted to others, emotional experiences which gave it birth must be simulated in order to set the stage for recreation of the idea in the minds of listeners or readers.

Although we often think of emotional appeals as instruments of deception, or as verbal snares, they can be perfectly respectable devices for defending convictions and for promoting ideas. In fact, too much attention to logic and reason may rob an idea of its true value. Thoughts bogged down in a morass of facts and figures may win a hypocritical nod of the head, but natural, spontaneous, unshackled, and sincere expressions of feeling will produce more lasting results. Emotions lie deeper in the heart of man than reason, and persuasion is most effective which recognizes this fact.

The difference in attitude between a rational point of view and an emotional point of view is apparent in the following passage:

Gardeners are really disguised engineers who have no idea of the real function of a piece of ground behind the house. When I tell visitors my husband is in the garden, they go there, knowing pretty much what to expect. He's usually busy transporting a wheelbarrow of manure, spraying a bush, or tearing violently at the sod. Hot, calloused of hand, and dirty of hide, he welcomes guests with delight as new victims for the "grand tour." . . .

I don't mean to sound unsympathetic, but the conviction has been growing on me that a garden is not a factory. I don't like the labor of gardening; but, apart from that, I don't think it should be labor. My idea of a garden is a green place full of unkempt perennials and, prominently displayed, a hammock—a place of peace, with the humming of bees and the lush smell of sun-warmed grass. I like to go there and dream in the hammock and be sublimely idle. Among true gardeners, this is heresy. They admit a garden should be a delightful nook of restfulness, but they're too busy to sit down and absorb it. They are eternally transplanting, training vines, fiddling with borders. They cannot see a seed catalogue without wanting to tear out everything and plant something else.[16]

Language is so intimately related to human emotion that it is virtually impossible to find vocabulary items that are devoid of emotional appeal. Some words, of course, have a greater emotional potential than others. Folk idioms, figurative expressions, words which appeal to the physical senses, verbal images, analogical extensions, words with high-voltage connotations, concrete words, and specific words have a stronger emotional appeal than do abstract, technical, and scientific words. Successful communication appeals to emotions through vicarious experiences, through the use of such rhetorical devices as verbal imagery, symbolism, irony and satire, humor, suggestion, association, repetition, or through basic human motives, popular beliefs, traditions, and folkways.

Appeal to Emotions Through Vicarious Experience

Words in suitable contexts create psychological tensions that seek outlet in expressions of joy, laughter, sorrow, anxiety, de-

[16] Sylvia Angus, "A Garden Is to Sleep In," *Woman's Day*, May, 1955, p. 156.

spair, love, devotion, fear, shame, hate, anger, or pity. Case histories, illustrations, examples, or dramatic episodes which focus on gripping human experiences are almost certain to create emotional tension. Shakespeare offers two brilliant examples of this kind of discourse. One of them is the play within a play in *Hamlet*, in which the events connected with the death of Hamlet's father are simulated on the stage so that Hamlet can study the reactions of his uncle to the scenes. The other is Mark Antony's speech in *Julius Caesar*, Act III, Scene ii, in which the speaker completely reverses the attitudes of a mob toward Caesar by making a direct appeal to the emotions of his listeners. The secret of his success is contained in these lines: "I tell you that which you yourselves do know; show you sweet Caesar's wounds, poor, poor dumb mouths."

In the following passage, words are designed to make a direct appeal to the emotions:

An anxious mother consulted me some time ago. Her four-year-old daughter is the only girl in the apartment house where they live. The boys in the building, from about three to nine years old, hit her, beat her with guns, tie her up with rope whenever they get a chance. They hit her with whips which they buy at the circus. They push her off her bicycle and take her toys away. They handcuff her with handcuffs bought with coupons from comic books. They take her to a vacant lot and use her as a target for bow and arrow. They make a spearhead and scare her. Once, surrounding her in this way, they pulled off her panties to torture her (as they put it). Now her mother has fastened the child's panties with a string around her neck so the boys can't pull them down.[17]

Appeal to Emotions by the Use of Images and Symbols

Abstract concepts such as devotion, patriotism, happiness, and coöperation are much easier to grasp, appreciate, and react to when they are presented as images or symbols. The wedding

[17] Frederic Wertham, M.D., "The Comics . . . Very Funny!" *Saturday Review of Literature*, May 29, 1948.

ring, for example, is a symbol of eternal devotion and undying love. Old Glory is a symbol of American independence and unity. The bluebird is a symbol of happiness in Count Maurice Maeterlinck's famous play.

Stephen Leacock, in denouncing written examinations, uses images which stir up feelings as well as stimulate thoughts:

> All that is best in what we call the liberal arts—all the flowers of poetry and drama, literature and history, imagination and inspiration —becomes distorted and disturbed by the system of examinations and credits which deflect it from its proper semblance, like the comic face in a convex mirror. Literature looks in the mirror and reflects back as a "credit"—a comic credit with a wide grinning mouth, hair stuck out sideways and a brain-pan down to an inch and a half. But this credit is the real master for the student, controlling degrees, the entry to professions, jobs—all that he came to college for. No wonder the figure is grim—the joke on literature is so rich. The fellow is like those malicious evil spirits that carry on our humour in the next world, as malevolent buffoonery. He says to the student, "Divide the beauty of poetry into six elements and say them over to me, and I'll give you a degree as a horse-doctor." Or he says, "Name the six excellencies of Shakespeare that your professor told you out of his notes last October!"—and he roars with laughter. "If you can't," he says, "I won't let you out of college; you'll just stay shut up there till you do. No law for you!"
>
> The key to salvation is found by admitting once and for all that a large part of knowledge cannot be tested by written examinations, except to its own harm.[18]

Appeal to Emotions by Use of Colloquial Speech Patterns

The language of the folk has about it a sorcery that defies all analysis. The impact of localisms, colloquialisms, and folk expressions in extended contexts is greater than the force of their individual meanings and connotations. Here is an example of the use of colloquial expressions for emotional effects:

[18] "The Machine at Work," from *Too Much College*, New York, 1940, p. 34.

The man who must put on spats before he can talk with a friend is goofy. . . . "Lousy" was good enough for Shakespeare and it's good enough for a Professor of Education. If the Professor means "lousy" and refrains from writing it, he is the kind of person who would say "lady dog" and there is no place for him in hell, heaven, or *The Saturday Review*. . . . Ever hear of poetic license, gents? Don't get the idea that it is something issued by the Department of Public Safety.[19]

Notice the emotional impact of the colloquial speech idioms in this passage from the pen of Ernie Pyle:

We drove into the tiny town of La Detinais, a sweet old stone village. ● . . As we stood there talking in the lonely field, a soldier in coveralls ran up breathlessly and almost shouted: "Hey, there's a man alive in one of those planes across the road! He's been trapped there for days." . . .

We ran to the wrecked British plane, lying there upside down, and dropped on our hands and knees and peeked through a tiny hole in the side. A man lay on his back in the small space of the upside-down cockpit. He turned his eyes toward me when I peeked in, and he said in a typical British manner of offhand friendliness, "Oh, hello."

"Are you all right?" I asked, stupidly.

He answered, "Yes, quite, now that you chaps are here."

I asked him how long he had been trapped in the wrecked plane. He told me, and I said out loud. "Good God!" For, wounded and trapped he had been lying there for eight days.

His left leg was broken and punctured by an ack-ack burst. His back was terribly burned by raw gasoline. . . . He was in agony, yet in his correct Oxford accent he even apologized for taking up our time to get him out. The American soldiers of our rescue party cussed with open admiration. . . . One of them said, "God, but these Limies have guts!" It took us almost an hour. We don't know whether he will live or not, but he has a chance. . . .

When they finally laid him tenderly onto the canvas litter and

---

[19] Bernard De Voto, "Grammarian's Funeral," *Saturday Review of Literature*, October 9, 1937.

straightened his left leg, you could see the tendons relax and his facial muscles subside, and he gave a long half-groan, half-sigh of relief. And that was the one sound of human weakness uttered by that man of great courage in his hour of liberation.[20]

Notice the emotional overtones produced in this passage by sprinkling the text with folk expressions:

Our pampered tyrant, the American farmer, is about to get his boots licked again by both political parties.

Before next November's elections, Democrats and Republicans alike will be groveling all over the barnyard as they court the country vote—but the Democratic antics will be the most embarrassing. Nearly all Democratic politicians are now convinced that the farmers offer the largest single block of detachable votes—and many seem willing to use almost any tool of demagoguery which promises to pry it loose from the Republican grasp.

So when Congress opens up for business next month, the Democrats will set up a pious, baritone moan about the wretched plight of American agriculture. They will pass a farm-relief bill, loaded till its axles creak with rigid price supports, loans, "conservation" payments, and other shabbily-disguised subsidies. Then they will pray for the President to veto it. Quite possibly he will have the courage and honesty to do just that—and Democratic Congressmen will then be sure that they have the farm vote in a gunny sack.[21]

Appeal to Emotions by Use of Satire, Ridicule, and Humor

Such rhetorical devices as sarcasm, satire, ridicule, and humor also have strong emotional appeal. Notice how these devices argue that a liberal arts curriculum is an unsatisfactory preparation for domestic life in the following passage:

. . . When I was in college I was exposed to one year of zoology. The class spent the first six weeks dissecting pickled frogs. The class did—I didn't. I spent my time on the fire escape trying to keep from losing my lunch. From there we progressed to the amoeba, the crayfish,

[20] Ernie Pyle, *Brave Men*, New York, 1944, pp. 452–455.
[21] "The Country Slickers Take Us Again," in "Personal and Otherwise," *Harper's Magazine*, December, 1955, p. 21.

and the earthworm. We studied them all in detail. We dissected, we drew diagrams, we squinted into microscopes, we peered into test tubes—for two long laboratory and three lecture periods every week. For the one member the class who studied medicine this undoubtedly proved useful. The majority of us could have done with less concentration on lowly creatures and far more information about pregnancy, childbirth, prenatal care, the menopause, and sex. These matters were taken care of in a one-semester, one-hour-a-week hygiene course consisting of some sketchy lectures by the college physician (unmarried) and an embarrassed physical education instructor (also unmarried). . . .[22]

Appeal to Emotions Through Basic Human Motives

Emotional appeals may also be made to basic human motives, wants, needs, and goals. A large percentage of commercial advertisements are purposefully designed to make this type of appeal. The passage quoted attempts to capitalize on a woman's desire to be beautiful:

We have forgotten the blessings of walking and its many benefits to body and soul. We have forgotten the fluid, limber, long-legged physique that endless walking moulds, and the rose-suffused complexion. Now perhaps women can be persuaded to become walkers— that is to say, to walk three or four miles a day and occasionally twenty-five or thirty miles—if they knew how beautiful it would make them. And after a year or two of this—just as you were congratulating yourself on your astonishing rejuvenation and comeliness—you might find that you had also acquired iron health. . . . And most important of all, you may find that the walking has brought about an alchemy, a transfiguration of soul. . . .[23]

Appeal to Emotions Through Verbal Association and Suggestion

Transfer of value from one thing to another by association, juxtaposition, analogy, or suggestion is not an unusual type of

[22] Marion Walker Alcaro, "Colleges Don't Make Sense," *Woman's Day*, May, 1946.
[23] Brenda Ueland, "Walk a Thousand Miles This Year," *Vogue*, January, 1951, p. 181.

persuasive appeal. Identifying an idea with the cherished beliefs of a folk hero or the doctrines contained in the Holy Scriptures, as in the following passages, creates favorable emotional responses to the proposals: "Perhaps our rallying cry is to be found in the words of Abraham Lincoln who said: 'Let reverence for the laws be breathed by every American mother to the lisping babe that prattles on her lap; let it be taught in the schools, in seminaries, and in colleges; let it be written in primers, spelling-books, and in almanacs; let it be preached from the pulpit, proclaimed in legislative halls, and enforced in courts of justice. And, in short, let it become the political religion of the nation; and let the old and young, the rich and poor, the grave and the gay of all sexes and tongues and colors and conditions, sacrifice unceasingly upon its altars.' "[24]

"The Bible is still the best text-book on democracy, and Christianity the most effective guardian of our liberties. Men who lose the conviction that they are 'endowed by their Creator' are easy marks for enslavement by totalitarian rulers. A people who seek freedom some other way sooner or later not only lose their freedom, but lose their souls."[25]

The following suggestions should help you employ emotional appeals effectively:

a. Set the stage for the proper reception of your idea. Prepare the soil before you plant the seed. Create an atmosphere that will put your listeners and readers in the mood to accept your proposal. No pat formula for accomplishing this feat has been found. Perhaps your best qualification is knowledge of the ABC's of human motivation.

b. Adapt your methods to the people you hope to reach. Keep your eye on the target. Different people respond differently to verbal stimuli. Anticipate what devices will best serve your pur-

[24] Herbert Brownell, Jr., "Citizenship Education," speech delivered at the NEA annual convention, Miami Beach, Florida, July 3, 1953.

[25] Dr. Carl F. H. Henry, "Christianity and the American Heritage," address, Bellflower, California, July 4, 1953, broadcast over station KPOL (Los Angeles).

poses. Gilbert Highet reminds us that "a hook baited with clam will catch a sea bass, but if you drop it into a trout-stream you will get no trout."

c. Establish a common ground between your audience and yourself. All communication depends on mutual agreements. Identify yourself, if possible, with your listeners and readers before you try to manipulate them. A soldier willingly fights *with* his commanding officer, reluctantly *for* him.

d. Have something to offer. Few ideas are accepted without some kind of inducement. Antony dangled Caesar's will before his listeners. Crackerjacks conceal prizes in every package. Pill peddlers gain favor by offering slim figures, muscular superiority, controlled regularity, relief from pain. Cigarette advertisers offer pleasure and enjoyment. Many such inducements are properly called bribes and have a tendency to belittle the product they are designed to promote. The safest method is to make the idea itself as attractive as possible.

e. Let people know what you expect of them. Don't bury your light under a bushel. Bring it out in the open. A brush salesman would get nowhere if he offered his prospective customer no opportunity to purchase his product. If you offer your readers or listeners no solution to a defined problem, you may have created emotional tension for nothing.

f. Don't get in a hurry. Persuasion takes time. The people you want to influence have to have a chance to think things out for themselves. Move gradually from one stage to another, making sure your audience is with you at every stage: attention, interest, belief, desire, action.

EXERCISES

1. Clip several cartoons from current newspapers and judge the effectiveness and soundness of the analogies on which they are based.
2. Find several examples of analogy in commercial advertisements,

and try to determine how effective they are in winning desired responses.

3. Select three or more advertisements from recent magazines. Pick those which show a variety of appeals or which offer examples of specific types of reasoning. Analyze the advertisements for such matters as appeal to basic human motives, logic, and ability to engage the attention of the reader.

4. Discuss the validity of the reasoning apparent in the following statements. What is the nature of the argument in each case? What fallacy or fallacies do you detect?

   a. Americans should oppose socialized medicine because it proved unsuccessful in England.

   b. Dope addicts lack will power; that is why they are dope addicts.

   c. I don't trust that man; look at his sinister eyes and black mustache.

   d. There is a good movie at the Bijou; Marilyn Monroe is always good.

   e. If you really want to get sound advice about your problems, write to Dorothy Dix.

   f. Democracy has never succeeded in China; therefore, Chinese do not make good American citizens.

   g. Bill should win the essay contest without difficulty; he always was good in English.

   h. We can go fishing tomorrow; the weather bureau says it will be a good day.

   i. It is perfectly clear why the football team is losing this year; the new coach doesn't understand how to handle the men.

   j. I never saw two people more opposite in their likes and dislikes; they should have a very successful marriage.

   k. I don't trust a cop; they're all alike.

   l. Certainly Reno is east of Los Angeles; isn't California west of Nevada?

   m. World War II is to blame for the current crime wave; comic books have little if anything to do with it.

5. Find several examples in your reading of argument by authority, and test the validity of the arguments by finding out as much as you can about the authorities cited.

6. Study the arguments presented in a number of magazine adver-

tisements and point out the fallacies they contain. Compare the advertisers' claims for products with the facts presented in *Consumer Reports*.

7. Criticize the arguments presented in the following paragraphs:
   a. American bicycle manufacturers suffered a net loss of 1.9% on sales in 1954. Sales were 25% under the 1953 total. Last year 963,667 foreign-made bicycles entered the American market.
   b. George Stewart, whose birthday falls on Friday the thirteenth, plans to stay home from work that day.
   c. Maria Riva, beautiful daughter of an equally beautiful mother, Marlene Dietrich, said, "Life on the stage is not all glitter. It's not what it seems to be at first—not nearly as thrilling as being a wife and homemaker."
   d. William G. Leaman, Jr., Philadelphia heart specialist, says, "Women are smarter than men." The weaker sex myth, he said, just permits the ladies to live a less exerting life and outlive their male counterparts by an average of six to seven years. Added proofs to explode the age-old myth of female weakness are: women can lose more blood; women can stand more shock; they are far better drivers; they can go into a profession and hold their own provided men don't give them an inferiority complex. They can hold down a job, take care of a home, and family, and at the same time guard the supposedly stronger male.

8. Find an example of an argument presented in a newspaper editorial and rewrite the editorial, using a substitute argument of your own.

9. Select several examples of defended ideas and muster evidence to disprove the soundness of the arguments presented.

10. Check the results of a nation-wide opinion poll on some current problem. Do the findings agree with your opinions on the subject? Suggest ways in which the results of the poll may have been manipulated.

11. Write a 500-word paper on a subject about which you have strong convictions. Defend your idea logically.

12. Give a talk before the class on the same topic you used for exercise 11. Use the same arguments.

13. Criticize the argument apparent in the following news story.

A 60-pound Airedale dropped dead of a heart attack when two smaller dogs barked at him. His owners are suing the owners of the smaller dogs for $2,995. The smaller dogs were identified as a four-year-old terrier and a seven-month-old mixed breed. The owner of the Airedale contends that the two dogs were unleashed and began barking while the Airedale was being walked.

14. Explain the types of appeals made to prospective tourists in the following offer of "An Evening in Las Vegas, Nevada" for $25.

    Here is what you get: round-trip plane transportation from Los Angeles. Champagne in flight. Two cocktails at the hotel. Choice of a chicken or steak dinner. Motor tour of Las Vegas. Transportation to and from the airport. Plus ten dollars to spend at the hotel.

15. Discuss the validity of the following syllogism:

    Since the two methods are very different,
    And the scientific method is unmistakably practical,
    The humanities must be impractical.

FOR FURTHER READING

Altick, Richard, "Two Patterns of Thinking," in *Preface to Critical Reading*, New York, 1951.

Beardsley, Monroe C., *Practical Logic*, New York, 1950.

Bowen, Croswell, "Why They Go Wrong," *Saturday Review*, February 27, 1954.

Cannon, Walter B., *The Way of an Investigator*, New York, 1945.

Copi, Irving M., "Logic: The Problem of Reasoning," in *American Philosophy*, edited by Ralph B. Winn, New York, 1955.

Glazer, Nathan, "What Opinion Polls Can and Can't Do," *Commentary*, August, 1951.

Hodnett, Edward, *The Art of Problem Solving*, New York, 1955.

Huxley, T. H., "The Method of Scientific Investigation," in *Man's Place in Nature and Other Essays*.

Krutch, Joseph Wood, "How Probable Is Probability?" in *The Measure of Man*, New York, 1954.

Otto, M. C., "Scientific Method and the Good Life," in *The Human Experience*, New York, 1940.

Robinson, James H., "On Various Kinds of Thinking," from *The Mind in the Making*, New York, 1921.
Ruby, Lionel, *The Art of Making Sense*, Philadelphia, 1954.
Thouless, Robert H., *How to Think Straight*, New York, 1932.
Wallas, Graham, "The Four Stages of Thought," from *The Art of Thought*, New York, 1926.

9

ESTABLISH PERSPECTIVE

ONE OF THE PRIMARY REQUIREMENTS OF effective communication is order and arrangement of the elements or parts of a total discourse. If facts, ideas, and opinions are thrown together catch as catch can, in a kind of crazy-quilt pattern, meaning is likely to be disguised, concealed, or camouflaged. Many efforts to communicate ideas fail because no understandable structure is apparent. Too much attention to details and minutiae and too little attention to their function in clarifying thought impedes communication. A wise general briefs his soldiers on projected tactical operations so that every man can see his own assignment against the backdrop of the total maneuver.

Perspective in communication is established when the individual parts of a composition are ordered, structured, and arranged so that attention is clearly directed to the central idea to be transmitted or received. The qualities of composition which insure proper perspective among multifarious parts are: relevance, coherence, arrangement, and proportion.

9.1   Relevance

Relevance is belongingness. Any organization is made up of parts or elements which belong together, like the pieces of a jig-saw puzzle. The United States, for example, is a composite of forty-eight relevant units or states. The solar system is made up of an infinite number of corporate heavenly bodies. A university

170

is a plurality of colleges controlled by one administrative body. A family is a unity of individuals held together by ties of kinship, love, and devotion.

Just as the elements which make up a life cell are organized about a nucleus, so details of composition are organized with respect to a central idea or central purpose. All devices employed —facts, examples, testimonials, illustrations, anecdotes, statistics—should bear directly on the idea proposed and the purpose and intention of the author. Robert M. Hutchins, in his essay "Gate Receipts and Glory," says: "This article deals with athleticism, its cause, its symptoms, and its cure." By this announcement the author stakes out the limits of revelance. The central idea—athleticism has no proper place in American colleges and universities—is the focal point of the article. Every argument advanced by Professor Hutchins concerns this idea and helps to accomplish his purpose: to convince the American people that the aims of higher education are not being realized because of commercialized athletics.

The relevance of every detail employed in a given communication should be determined by asking such questions as: (a) Is the item directly related to the idea proposed? (b) Is the item in harmony with the purpose you have in mind? (c) Does the item call undue attention to itself at the expense of main ideas and established purpose? (d) Is the item necessary to a clear understanding of the idea you want to communicate? (e) Is the item merely included to pad the composition and make it longer than it would be otherwise?

9.2 Coherence

Coherence is the adhesive that glues or cements the various parts of a composition together. A given composition is made coherent by such devices as analogy, analysis, enumeration, parallel structure, paragraphing, transitional devices, statement and restatement, and consistency of tone and mood.

In the following passage the elements are tied together by analysis: "Today the population of cosmopolitan Singapore is predominantly Chinese—750 thousand out of a total of just over a million. The remainder is made up of 150,000 Malays, 100,-000 Indians, 10,000 Eurasians, and 15,000 Europeans, mostly British. . . ."[1]

Enumeration and parallel structure are apparent in the following code of precepts developed by Harry A. Bullis:

Bullis has developed a six-point code of precepts for the younger executives in General Mills:

1. Build men—big men.
2. Give everyone on the payroll an opportunity to advance if he is willing to pay the price of intelligent hard work.
3. Emphasize the human side of the organization and build morale.
4. Recognize that modern business is a responsible public service and that profit-making entails the developing of public good will and wider purchasing power with resulting general benefits.
5. Have a creative attitude of mind and use the research approach to every problem.
6. Have enthusiasm for change, courage for new ideas, and daring of imagination and sincerity of conviction.[2]

The use of parallel structure for making composition coherent is further demonstrated in the following paragraphs:

Considered among the most beautiful in the world, the Butchart Gardens in reality are four in one.

The Sunken Garden is perhaps the best known. One is unable to believe it was once a limestone quarry. Ivy and Virginia Creeper now completely cover the old quarry walls. Beautiful and rare flowers in intricately landscaped settings of small hills, streams, and ponds make the visitor catch his breath on first glimpse from the upper level.

The English Rose Garden has nearly every variety and shading of

[1] John Carlova, "Death of a Correspondent," *Harper's Magazine*, December, 1955, p. 53.
[2] Leo Cherne, "Harry A. Bullis: Portrait of the New Businessman," *Saturday Review of Literature*, January 23, 1954, pp. 57.

rose. Fountains, Florentine statuary and arbors are artistically displayed throughout the garden. One almost feels as if it were a gigantic rich, lovely tapestry.

The Japanese Garden includes an assortment of odd-shaped trees. Tiny bridges cross numerous little streams with covered branches along the shaded paths. The foliage is thick here, and very green. Even at midday the sun fails to penetrate its cool greenness.

The Italian Gardens are the most formal of all and are located nearest to the house. One exceptionally lovely arrangement is like a mammoth porch. The residence itself is now used as a restaurant, open during the tourist season. At the tea hour one can have English toasted scones and crumpets with fine weed honey and tea or coffee.

Near the entrance to the gardens are greenhouses and a small shop where seeds are sold.[3]

The relationship of parts to whole in this passage may be shown in outline form as follows:

I. The Butchart Gardens
   A. The Sunken Garden
   B. The English Rose Garden
   C. The Japanese Garden
   D. The Italian Gardens

Smooth continuity in composition is maintained by carefully chosen transitional words and phrases. In the essay "What's Happening to Prose?" by Mona Van Duyn, published in *College English*, October, 1954, you can find many transitional phrases used to tie together the ideas presented. Here are some of them:

The first thing I must do is to reassure you about . . .
I might start with . . .
This state of affairs is . . .
Furthermore . . .
But from the point of view of the writer . . .
The second state of affairs that I want to bring up . . .
Also, it seems to me that . . .
I must immediately make clear that I do not mean . . .

[3] "Gardens-within-a-Garden," *People and Places*, July, 1955, p. 19.

If I may quote Mr. Ransom again . . .
My third and final point can be summed up briefly.
This brings me to my conclusion and some parting wishes.

A brief summary at the end of a discourse, either written or spoken, helps to keep matters straight and coherent. Here is the summary of a commencement address:

In closing, let me return to those two important questions you are asking today.

Has all this been worth while? Your thorough grounding in the humanities, your rigorous training in the basic sciences, and your discipline in group-participation are all worth every bit of effort they have cost you. They are tools—indispensable for the work you are about to commence.

And what lies ahead? For *you* with ample courage ably proved, is a world waiting to have its boundaries pushed outward. A world still in the early stages of scientific progress. Progress that is *your* challenge and *your* privilege to help bring to pass. Horizons unlimited![4]

Maintaining a consistent attitude toward the subject matter is an excellent method of making a composition coherent. The amorous note in the following passage ties the separate parts into a single unity:

Gentle and unobtrusive as the river is, yet the tranquil woods seem hardly satisfied to allow its passage. The trees are rooted on the very verge of the water, and dip their pendent branches into it. At one spot there is a lofty bank, on the slope of which grow some hemlocks, declining across the stream with outstretched arms, as if resolute to take the plunge. In other places the banks are almost level with the water, so that the quiet congregation of trees set feet in the flood, and are fringed with foliage down to the surface. Cardinal flowers kindle their spiral flames and illuminate the dark nooks among the shrubbery. The pond-lily grows abundantly along the margin—that delicious flower, which . . . opens its virgin bosom to the first sun-

---

[4] Robert C. Sprague, "Horizons Unlimited," address delivered at Northeastern University, Boston, June 24, 1953.

light and perfects its being through the magic of that genial kiss. . . .
Grapevines here and there twine themselves around shrub and tree
and hang their clusters over the water within reach of the boatsman's
hand. Oftentimes they unite two trees of alien race in an inextricable
twine, marrying the hemlock and the maple against their will, and
enriching them with a purple offspring of which neither is the
parent.[5]

9.3   Arrangement

Effectiveness in communication demands that details which
elaborate, support, and defend ideas be arranged in some kind of
recognizable order. The suitability of a particular arrangement
may be determined by (a) the nature of the subject or idea, (b)
your purpose for communicating the idea, (c) the nature of the
defense you employ, and (d) the character of the details themselves.

Chronological Arrangement

Chronological arrangement is an arrangement of details in a
time sequence. Narrative by its very nature is a chronological
arrangement of facts. Here is an example:

In any case, the American colonies—while not entirely democratic
—had the seeds of democracy in them. The merchants who founded
Virginia provided in 1619 for a legislature to be elected by the
colonists, and on the boat coming over to Plymouth the Pilgrims
drew up an agreement among themselves, known as the Mayflower
Compact, which provided for a civil government with laws which
they could change whenever they thought best. Once our forefarthers
were located in this country the frontier conditions in which they
lived still further strengthened these democratic principles. . . . By
the time the colonies came to break away from the mother country
in 1776, democratic ideas were fully developed in this country. . . .[6]

[5] Nathaniel Hawthorne, "The Old Manse."
[6] Marshall M. Knappen, *Preserving Democracy*, Extension Bulletin, No. 243,
Michigan State University, East Lansing, 1945.

Notice the emphasis on time in this passage:

From the time of the spring equinox onward, as the sun's rays strike the earth more and more directly, the huge land mass of continental Asia begins to heat up. With growing intensity throughout the weeks that follow, the heat continues unrelieved. In late May and early June temperatures recorded in north India have reached as high as 126 degrees F. The capitol city, Delhi, has an average daytime temperature for May of 104 degrees. Then the Government offices and the foreign embassies switch to summer hours—the working day begins at 7:30 A.M. and finishes at 1:30 P.M. A large part of every day becomes devoted simply to avoiding the heat. Chics (the slatted, bamboo screens) are lowered all day over windows and verandas to keep the interiors of homes and offices cool and shaded from the sun and glare. Only after sunset are windows and houses opened up to the slightly cooler air of evening. Only in the late short twilight do people sit in their gardens or walk in the parks.[7]

Spatial or Geographical Arrangement

Whenever a body of facts is separated into parts like areas on a map, we call the arrangement spatial or geographical. The following are examples: "It is possible any day of the week to board an airplane and fly around the globe in a matter of hours. With only an overnight bag and a camera a modern Magellan can leave New York City in a giant clipper of the air which will touch him down in London, Rome, Istanbul, Beirut, Karachi, New Delhi, Hong Kong, Tokyo, Honolulu, and San Francisco in less than five days."[8]

"Proportionately, more old people live in New England than in any other part of the country. In Maine, New Hampshire, Vermont and Massachusetts, for example, the proportion is more than one third greater than in the country as a whole. Four states in the farm belt—Iowa, Kansas, Missouri and Nebraska—and

---

[7] Santha Rama Rau, "The Wind That Means Life to India," *New York Times Magazine,* June 8, 1952.

[8] W. D. Patterson, "E Pluribus Unum," *Saturday Review of Literature,* January 2, 1954, p. 16.

one mountain state, Montana, also have relatively high proportions of elderly people."[9]

Order of Importance

If you study the details of a conventional newspaper story, you will notice that as the story progresses the details become less and less important, although more and more concrete. This arrangement is called inverted order of importance and is so familiar as not to necessitate the citing of examples.

In novels, short stories, and dramas the order is reversed. As the action of the story proceeds the details become more and more significant until a climax is reached. In tragedy, this climax is often called the *catastrophe*. The climactic arrangement is not restricted to literature, however, and may be used effectively in any type of writing or speaking that depends for its success on the building up of suspense.

Just as progression may be demonstrated with full-length novels, it may also be shown in the arrangement of paragraphs or sentences: "The present method of teaching English is unrealistic, wasteful, and futile. The young student proceeds from bewilderment to prejudice, to antagonism, to complete uncertainty, to a disturbing sense of inferiority for not having learned to use his native tongue correctly."[10]

The language of the following paragraphs moves toward a climax:

Thursday, March 7, 1850, began like any other day in the dusty country village called Washington, D.C. Not that there was any lack of subjects for conversation: the Postmaster General had announced the establishment of a new post office in Wabashaw County—out in the wilds of the Minnesota Territory. Stevens, the haberdasher, advertising in that day's National Intelligencer, described his 1850 model hat as one to please "the most fastidious . . . at the price.

---

[9] ". . . 65 and Over," *Collier's*, December 9, 1955, p. 33.
[10] Frank Colby, *Better English*, New York, 1947, p. 7.

$4." A nearby Virginia plantation owner, James A. Reid, had posted a $50 reward for the return of his runaway slave, Issac. The National Temperance League was concluding its convention with a parade down Pennsylvania Avenue. Several F Street merchants swore at a luncheon meeting that they would give up newfangled gaslighting if it failed them once more. The sky was overcast, the air was muggy. In nearly every way, the 7th of March began much like innumerable other Washington days.

But there was something different, something else in the air. Perhaps it was the threat of national disunion. People gathered in little knots to talk about it—by the firehouse, in front of the White House, around open produce markets. Only three days earlier, Senator John C. Calhoun of South Carolina, leader of the South for more than 30 years, had told the world that "the South will be forced to choose between abolition and secession. . . . The Southern states . . . cannot remain, as things are now, consistently with honor and safety in the Union.["11]

9.4 Proportion: The Outline

Balance or proportion is achieved in communication by giving proper stress, emphasis, and weight to the elements which make up a unity or whole. The difference between main points or ideas in a composition and specific details which support main ideas must be kept clear.

Outlining is probably the simplest and most satisfactory way of regulating the relative prominence of the various parts of a talk or essay. An outline helps you avoid giving too much attention to some items and too little to others. It allows you to get an overview or bird's-eye view of the entire context which contains your idea. It helps you to gain perspective. Like a contractor's blueprint, it permits you to see at a glance the interrelationships of all the parts and to understand their proper functions. An outline has no merit in itself; its merit is determined solely by the

[11] John F. Kennedy, "A Great Day in American History," *Collier's*, November 25, 1955, p. 41.

amount of value it has for you for the particular purpose you have in mind.

Parallel Structure in Outlines

All communication in order to be effective must be structured or patterned. Words, sentences, paragraphs, and other units of discourse must perform a particular service in developing an idea or thought. To insure maximum efficiency, one must discipline words so that they will not get out of hand. Parallel structure is one method of keeping words in line. When elements of the same weight or rank are presented in the same form and given the same weight and prominence, we say the structure is parallel. Two basic relationships are concerned: coördination and subordination.

COÖRDINATION. Coördination is an order or arrangement which shows the equality or similarity of items of the same class by regulating their form and position in a verbal context. For example, the chapters of a book are coördinate to each other; therefore, they are set forth in language that is similar in form and structure. Notice that the chapter headings in this volume are all commands or imperative sentences:

1. Understand the Process.
2. Understand Yourself.
3. Understand the Uses of Language.
4. Focus Attention on Ideas.
5. Focus Attention on Facts.
6. Etc.

SUBORDINATION. Subordination is a way of showing the dependence of items of inferior or secondary rank to a larger or more inclusive class. The chapters in this volume are subordinate to the major divisions of the book, which in turn are all subordinate to the title of the book:

A. Get Your Bearings.
  1. Understand the Process.

      2. Understand Yourself.
      3. Understand the Uses of Language.
   B. Focus Your Attention.
      1. Focus Attention on Ideas.
      2. Focus Attention on Facts.
      3. Focus Attention on Purpose.
  Etc.

OUTLINE FORMS.   The coördinate and subordinate relationships of items in an outline are easily shown by using a consistent system of enumeration and indentation. Two common methods are illustrated:

Number-Letter System	Decimal System
I	1 . . . .
A	1.1 . . . .
1	1.11 . . . .
a	1.111 . . . .
(1)	1.1111 . . . .
(2)	1.1112 . . . .
b . . . . b	1.112 . . . .
2	1.12 . . . .
B	1.2 . . . .
II	2. . . . .

TYPES OF OUTLINES.   Two types of outlines are commonly employed: topic outlines and sentence outlines. In a topic outline, items included are not expressed as complete sentences, but rather as word labels, phrases, or clauses. In a sentence outline, the items included are put in complete sentences.
Here is an example of a topic outline:

Our Greatest Authors

  I. Novelists
    A. Theodore Dreiser
    B. Sinclair Lewis
    C. Ernest Hemingway
    D. John Dos Passos

    E. Upton Sinclair
    F. Ring Lardner
    G. Willa Cather
    H. Edith Wharton
    I. Evelyn Scott
    J. Elizabeth Madox Roberts
    K. Branch Cabell
    L. William Faulkner
 II. Dramatist
    A. Eugene O'Neill
III. Poets
    A. T. S. Eliot
    B. Robert Frost
    C. E. A. Robinson
    D. Hart Crane
    E. Robinson Jeffers
    F. Edna St. Vincent Millay
    G. Elinor Wylie
    H. Archibald MacLeish
    I. Leonie Adams
    J. Conrad Aiken
    K. Isidor Schneider
    L. Horace Gregory
    M. Stanley Kunitz
    N. Ezra Pound
 IV. Historians
    A. Charles A. Beard
    B. James Truslow Adams
  V. Biographer
    A. Lytton Strachey
 VI. Critics
    A. H. L. Mencken
    B. Van Wyck Brooks
    C. Lewis Mumford
    D. Paul Elmer More
    E. Irving Babbitt
    F. Edmund Wilson
    G. George Jean Nathan

H. Kenneth Burke
   I. Joseph Wood Krutch
VII. Philosopher
   A. George Santayana

Here is an example of a sentence outline:

Procedure for Creative Thinking

  I. Recognize a Problem.
    A. Recognize a need for some product.
    B. Recognize a puzzle to be solved.
  II. Prepare to meet the challenge of that recognition.
    A. Collect pertinent facts by engaging in careful research.
    B. Find out how similar problems have been solved.
  III. Do some mental coasting.
    A. Relax for a while.
    B. Let the subconscious mind work on the facts.
  IV. Arrive at a solution.
    A. Select the most feasible of several possible solutions.
    B. Select the solution that promises most for your effort.
  V. Verify the soundness of your solution.
    A. Take steps to make it operative.
    B. Try it out and assess the results.

The Major Divisions of Discourse

Three major divisions of all well-proportioned discourse are: introduction, body, and conclusion. An introduction directs attention to an idea to be communicated; the body supports, develops, clarifies, and defends the idea; the conclusion summarizes the argument presented in the body and points up the implications of the idea.

THE INTRODUCTION. Getting off to a good start is just as important in communication as it is in track. A weak or lame beginning might easily cause the breakdown of the communicative transaction. Psychologists argue that initial impressions are the most lasting. If this is true certainly the introduction of a talk or paper deserves careful thought and planning. Here are some of the functions which an introduction may be said to perform:

a. It establishes contact with audience or reader. The responsibility of tuning in each other's wave length belongs to both speaker and audience, and to writer and reader. Since the transmitter of an idea is the promoter, he must take special pains to make contact with the person or persons he wishes to influence, or from whom he wishes to get a response. It is up to him to engage the listener's or reader's interest and attention.

b. It maps out the sociocultural context in which the idea is to be defined. No idea exists in isolation. It has some sort of setting in place, time, and circumstance. It is the communicator's duty to inform his reader or listener about this setting. For example, Robert M. Hutchins in "Gate Receipts and Glory" is concerned with the American football scene in the late 1930's. Jonathan Swift's "A Modest Proposal" concerns Irish-English affairs during the eighteenth century. Emerson's "The American Scholar" concerns the state of higher education in America as of the year 1837.

c. It focuses attention on the idea proposed. Let the reader or audience know what you intend to accomplish. Certain reservations, of course, must be made for satirical discourse. If your plan of organization is such that the idea does not emerge until you are well along with a talk or paper, you would not want to commit yourself in the introduction. But for most exercises in prose writing, the introduction is the proper place for revealing the nature, extent, and scope of the idea.

d. It boosts the idea. If you are really interested in the success of your idea, you will give it every chance to produce the response you desire. Your reader or listener has a perfect right to know why you consider the idea important, why he should spend time listening to or reading about it.

e. It explains how you intend to proceed. This is an optional matter. You may get a better hearing for your idea if your readers or listeners know what to expect as you develop your thought.

An explanation of procedure, methods, degree of precision, difficult terms may well be included in an introduction.

Here is how these matters are treated in a speech made by Millicent C. McIntosh on the subject of "New Horizons for Women":

No subject has caused more controversy during the past half century than the status of women. No area of human relations is more fraught with disagreement, misunderstanding and prejudice. There are no final solutions to this problem, but I should like to make a few suggestions that can be applied in particular cases. My main point is that no new horizons for women can exist without new horizons for men also.

CONTEXT OF TIME

METHOD OF APPROACH

CENTRAL IDEA

Since the Second World War women have become increasingly important. In recent years many books and magazine articles have been written on both sides of the issue. In many instances there has been a new upsurge of anti-feminism; some people believe that women who seek horizons beyond their homes are harming their families. They insist that a woman's entire interest should be focused on the home. Let me point out that this attitude was shared by Hitler and Mussolini.[12]

SIGNIFICANCE OF THE SUBJECT

Although the nature of an introduction is relative to speaker's or author's purpose, the nature of the audience or readers, the complexity of the idea proposed, and the characteristics of the occasion, it should usually be brief, informal, engaging, and clear.

Specific devices for making an introduction to an idea are listed with examples taken from various printed essays:

[12] Delivered at Columbia University. Printed in *Vital Speeches of the Day*, March 1, 1953.

a. Specific incidents, examples, or anecdotes may be used.

"Walking abreast, 30 to 40 yards apart, five hunters moved through the woods in quest of deer. The fall day was clear and crisp, made to order for hunting. Suddenly one of the men spotted a movement in a clearing to the left; it looked like— yes, the shape was certainly that of a deer. He snapped his rifle to his shoulder, squeezed the trigger, and the target dropped. Elated, the hunter ran forward—and found a member of his own party on the ground, seriously wounded."[13]

b. A news event or story may be used.

"On February 3, 1955, a press conference was called at the Hotel Biltmore in New York City for the purpose of providing a young man named Harvey Matusow with an opportunity to make a public confession of fraud and perjury. . . ."[14]

c. A personal experience may be used.

"Every few weeks, a neighbor of mine steps across the lawn from his house and pokes his head into my window. He is a physician on the staff of a hospital, where a great deal of lung cancer surgery is done.

" 'Quit smoking yet?' he asks as he lights up.

" 'I'm waiting for you to stop,' I reply.

"And he says: 'Well, I think I'll wait a while yet.' "[15]

d. A quotation from literature may be used.

"Some months ago I was browsing through some old sheet music and came upon Irving Berlin's 'My Walking Stick.' Reading it through, I found the lines: 'I'd go insane without my cane.' And it struck me that there, in six words, was the thing we are in danger of losing in our musical theatre. . . ."[16]

" 'Heard melodies are sweet, but those unheard are,' the poet assures us, 'sweeter.' Something of the sort might well be said of

---

[13] Alfred M. Lansing, "Moose or Man," *Collier's*, October 29, 1954, p. 31.

[14] Richard H. Rovere, "The Kept Witnesses," *Harper's Magazine*, May, 1955, p. 25.

[15] Leonard Engel, "Do We Have to Give Up Smoking?" *Harper's Magazine*, December, 1954, p. 25.

[16] Fred Lounsberry, *New York Times*, June 22, 1952.

the Unreadable Great Books, the classics that one has resolved never to broach. . . ."[17]

"The celebrated French criminologist, Alphonse Bertillion, is supposed to have said that it is impossible for a bird to fly through a cloud without leaving traces. For thirty-six years it has been the unique function of Dr. Alexander O. Gettler to demonstrate that the actions of human beings are even less to be hidden than those of birds on the wing. . . ."[18]

e. A definition of a key word or phrase may be used.

" 'A university,' former President Robert M. Hutchins once said, 'is a community of scholars. It is not a kindergarten; it is not a club; it is not a reform school; it is not a political party. A university is a community of scholars.' By the same token, a college, if indeed the Hutchins-Barr-Adler concept is correct, must similarly be categorized as a community of scholars, some real, some potential; but nevertheless a group of persons who have elected to devote themselves to cultural and intellectual pursuits."[19]

f. A rhetorical question may be used.

"Would you entrust your life to a 'surgeon' who makes an incision with a pair of pruning shears? Would you defend yourself in court through a 'lawyer' who argues his case in Indian sign language? Would you take lessons on the violin from a 'musician' who plays a cowbell?"[20]

g. A slogan, truism, or terse statement may be used.

"One of the commonest slogans in strategic literature is the one inherited from Jomini, that 'methods change but principles are unchanging.' Until yesterday that thesis had much to justify

[17] Dudley Fitts, "On Unreading the Classics," *New York Times Book Review*, July 22, 1951.

[18] Robert Bendiner, "The Man Who Reads Corpses," *Harper's Magazine*, February, 1955, p. 62.

[19] John W. Parker, "The Place of the Teacher in American Higher Education," address delivered before the College Language Association, Nashville, Tennessee, April 24, 1953.

[20] Edwin V. Burkholder, "Don't Believe Astrologers!" *Redbook*, April, 1953, p. 28.

it, since methods changed on the whole not too abruptly and always within definite limits. . . ."[21]

h. An analogical comparison may be used.

"It is notoriously hard to tell what is really happening in American politics. Like the Missouri River in springtime, our political life is likely to baffle the casual observer. The surface is so covered with froth, floating brush, and cross riffles that it takes a lot of probing—and long experience of the channel—to guess where the main current is running."[22]

i. A startling or thought-provoking statement of fact or opinion may be used.

"There seem to be two kinds of places which attract tourists—the place everyone is going this year, and the place no one has ever been to."[23]

"There still are pioneers in our country. They don't travel in covered wagons anymore, but the stuff they're made of is just as sturdy, adventurous, and self-reliant as in the days our forefathers struck west and conquered a continent."[24]

"The wars of the future, if they take place, will not be fought with the ludicrous fire-crackers of World War II. They may not even be fought with the expensive nuclear bombs of the present. They are far more likely to be fought with a lethal material which, by 1985 at the latest, will exist in abundance. . . ."[25]

"All men are snobs about something. One is almost tempted to add: There is nothing about which men cannot feel snobbish. But this would doubtless be an exaggeration. There are certain disfiguring and mortal diseases about which there has probably

---

[21] Bernard Brodie, "Strategy Hits a Dead End," *Harper's Magazine*, October, 1955, p. 33.

[22] William G. Carleton, "The Triumph of the Moderates," *Harper's Magazine*, April, 1955, p. 31.

[23] Laurence Lafore, "The Forgotten Valley of the Dordogne," *Harper's Magazine*, May, 1955, p. 57.

[24] J. Vincent O'Ryan, "The Bravest Family in America," *Household*, November, 1955, p. 35.

[25] Hans Thirring, "The Noiseless Weapon," *Harper's Magazine*, October, 1955, p. 44.

never been any snobbery. I cannot imagine, for example, that there are any leprosy snobs. . . ."[26]

j. A purpose may be stated.

"What I want to talk about to you is just the general subject of how writing is written. . . ."[27]

In this paper I will discuss one communication channel and its specific use by a particular group of persons; a group, for example, such as you who comprise my audience this morning. I will talk about the preparation and the presentation of a talk that a key executive might be called upon to give; usually it would be an informative talk. The speaker that I have in mind is a high level person in the hierarchy of his company or organization. He is a successful man. None of his speech-making needs have to do with acquiring confidence or developing poise or preparing for leadership. He has none of these things. And I might add that I am NEVER concerned with any speaker's need to feel comfortable on his feet.[28]

k. A personal point of view may be expressed.

I am by profession an economist and economic historian. The bulk of my academic life has been taken up with studying the world's economic development during the nineteenth century. I have just ended three years' work on the Soviet Union and Communist China. The task there was not to study Communist economics but to discern, if possible, the shape and prospects for change in the whole societies now dominated from Moscow and Peking: their politics, social life, foreign policies, and their economies.

The title of this article reflects perhaps the most important single idea about Communism which I have acquired during these three years of study.[29]

[26] Aldous Huxley, "Selected Snobberies," from *Music at Night*, New York, 1930–1931.

[27] Gertrude Stein, "How Writing Is Written," from *How to Write*, 1931.

[28] Paul R. Beall, "Pass the Word Along," address delivered at the 6th Annual Conference on the Administration of Research held at Georgia Institute of Technology, Atlanta, September 8, 1952.

[29] W. W. Rostow, "Marx Was a City Boy," *Harper's Magazine*, February, 1955, p. 25.

1. A statement of fact may be made.

"The most important economic event of 1954 went almost unreported in the newspapers. It was the announcement that four million sixty thousand babies had been born in this country during the past year—the largest baby crop ever. . . ."[30]

"Last year more than two billion pounds of insecticide were manufactured in the United States. Some 30,000 registered formulas, containing some 100 pesticidal chemicals, have become virtual necessities to American agriculture."[31]

m. A problem may be defined.

"Many of us, of course, take new jobs because we are assigned them—or because the circumstances are so clear-cut that little choice is possible. But in this country in the immediate future, the opportunities for new positions are going to increase dramatically, so that for many Americans the question of when to change jobs will become more acute than it has ever been in the past."[32]

THE BODY. The body of composition or discourse is the proper place for support, clarification, and defense of the idea you wish to communicate. It should contain argument, reasons, proof, facts, and evidence, arranged and ordered in a way that will develop the idea you focused your attention on in the introduction. Chapters 5, 7, and 8 of this text are all concerned with the body of exposition. The following general suggestions apply to this part of your talk or essay:

a. The evidence presented must support the central idea you want to communicate.

b. The evidence must not betray anything included in the introduction.

c. The evidence should point directly to the conclusions.

d. The evidence should be consistent.

---

[30] Peter F. Drucker, "America's Next Twenty Years," *Harper's Magazine*, March, 1955, p. 27.

[31] Ralph G. Martin, "How Much Poison Are We Eating?" *Harper's Magazine*, April, 1955, p. 63.

[32] Alan Gregg, "When to Change Jobs—and Why," *Harper's Magazine*, August, 1955, p. 71.

e. The facts should be clearly presented, logically defended, and consistently arranged.

In order to insure the proper reception of thoughts, it is well to plan in advance the order of items, their relative positions, and the amount of attention to be given them. This can be done by constructing an outline plan. Here are some examples representing various purposes and types of support.

(1) Idea or thesis: Freedom must be shared by all nations, races, and people.
Purpose: To outline the problems facing the United Nations.
Method: Analysis of problems facing the United Nations.
Arrangement:
A. Problems of security.
B. Problems related to national aspirations.
C. Problems related to personal aspirations.
D. Problems of economic progress of both individuals and communities.

(2) Idea or thesis: Traffic accidents are caused by violation of the rights of others.
Purpose: To convince listeners or readers that so-called automobile "accidents" are not accidental.
Method: Analysis of causes:
A. Speeding.
B. Failure to yield right of way.
C. Improper turning from lanes.
D. Following too close.

(3) Idea or thesis: No single cause is responsible for teen-age crimes.
Purpose: To suggest a number of possible causes of juvenile delinquency.
Method: Analysis of causal factors:
A. Home influences.
1. Divorced parents.
2. Inadequate atmosphere.
3. Authoritarian discipline.
B. Educational practices and procedures.
1. Progressive education.
2. Authoritarian education.

C. Community influences.
   1. Lack of recreational facilities.
   2. Social and racial inequalities.
   3. Crowded tenement areas.
D. Influence of communication media.
   1. Comic books and paper backs.
   2. Motion pictures.
   3. Radio and television.
(4) Idea or thesis:
A. The extent of government control of the press in any age depends on the relationship of the government to its subjects. In other words, the more democracy, the less control.
B. The area of freedom contracts and the enforcement of restraints increases as the stresses on the stability of the government and the structure of society increase.
Purpose: To suggest the proper functions and controls of the mass media of communication.
Method: Analysis of theories:
A. The Authoritarian Theory: The Tudor-Stuart theory.
   1. The press in theory belonged to the office of the king.
   2. The press was obligated to support government policy.
B. The Libertarian Theory: a rationalistic philosophy.
   1. The purpose of the press is to participate in the search for truth by presenting all manner of evidence uncontrolled by authority.
   2. Man was considered to be a rational being endowed with ability to determine the truth when presented with conflicting evidence.
C. The Communist Theory: a Marxist philosophy.
   1. The function of the press is to strengthen the Communist social order.
   2. All instruments of communication are socialized and controlled by the state.
D. The Social Responsibility Theory: Hutchins Commission.
   1. The importance and prevalence of mass communications in democratic society impose an obligation or social responsibility.
   2. It may be necessary for some other agency than the man-

agers of the press themselves to see that the essential functions of the press are performed.

(Details for this outline were taken from "The Historical Pattern of Press Freedom," an address by Frederick S. Siefert at Iowa City, Iowa, May 18, 1953.) [Dean of Journalism Michigan State]

(5) Idea or thesis: Communism is a constant threat to democracy, and much too dangerous to be ignored.

Purpose: To convince listeners or readers that American attitudes toward communism are more defensible than characteristic European attitudes.

Method: Contrast and comparison of American and European assumptions regarding the effects of communism on society.

A. European assumptions.
  1. That communism is merely a political movement.
  2. That communism is greatly exaggerated as a threat.
  3. That communism has little appeal for average people.

B. American assumptions.
  1. That communism is a conspiracy for the seizure of power from capitalism.
  2. That communism has penetrated deep into American life.
  3. That communism has a real appeal for many idealistic young people.

(6) Idea or thesis: An "occasional talk" should be planned carefully before it is presented to an audience.

Purpose: To outline the steps appropriate to giving an effective five-minute talk.

Method: Directions which explain how to give an effective "occasional talk."

A. Choose a topic of strong personal interest.

B. Organize your talk under two or three principal headings.

C. Select examples or illustrations that are unusual, novel, striking, humorous, or timely.

D. Give adequate attention to your listeners.

E. Capitalize upon your anxiety during delivery by letting it help you make a speech that is alive and stimulating, rather than dull and mediocre.

(7) Idea or thesis: Coöperative, solidified public opinion is the most potent force of moderation and decency.

Purpose: To solve the problem of cheap and sensational television programs which masquerade as entertainment.

Method: Problem-solution argument culminating in a series of proposals.

A. Give the Federal Communications Commission power to levy fines for violations of certain minimal standards.

B. Form local citizens' listening councils empowered to report offensive programs to the Federal Commission.

C. Insist on collective responsibility of station managers.

D. Establish a presidential commission to study and report the situation.

(Adapted from a report of the Senate Juvenile Delinquency Subcommittee.)

(8) Idea or thesis: A number of places in the United States are brilliantly colored during the autumn months.

Purpose: To inform listeners or readers of the most beautiful places to tour in autumn.

Method: Spatial or geographical arrangement. Specification of most glamorous areas.

A. The Adirondack Mountains.

B. Lake Superior's North Shore.

C. Michigan's copper country.

D. Western North Carolina.

E. The Missouri Ozarks.

F. Southwestern Vermont.

G. Utah's Aquarius Plateau.

H. The White Mountains of New Hampshire.

(Adapted from "The Best Autumn Color Tours in America," *Better Homes and Gardens*, October, 1955.)

THE CONCLUSION. As with the introduction, no definite rules can be established for the conclusion. It should be a graceful rounding out of the total effort to communicate meaning. In the introduction, attention is directed to the whole concept or idea; in the body, the whole is treated in isolated parts; in the conclusion, the parts are reassembled into a whole concept.

A conclusion should not be merely tacked on to a composition, either written or spoken, just for the sake of having a conclusion.

When everything is said that needs to be said on a subject, it is time to stop. Long and rambling conclusions may destroy the effect of an otherwise effective composition. The stopping should be natural and graceful, not abrupt and disappointing. When the circle is complete and you have kept the promises made in the introduction and have brought your listener or reader to a full understanding of the idea proposed and of its implications, the transmission is completed.

A number of specific devices employed by public speakers for concluding talks are quoted:

a. A recap of ideas may be presented in the ~~body~~ *conclusions* with suggestions for further study.

"It is clear that we have dealt with only a few of the communication problems that arise in the initial experiences of the young manager. In considering these problems, we have discussed only the first steps of what is in reality a sequence of responsive interchanges. But early experiences are crucial in the proper shaping of human relationships. For a more detailed treatment of executive communications, and an analysis of the techniques for correlating oneself into the modern Management Team, I refer the reader to the author's forthcoming *Talking Upward Without Fear*."[33]

b. A set of directions related to the idea proposed may be given.

And now, having outlined only a few of the phenomena of changing one's job in the four periods of learning, doing, directing, and advising, I shall end with some concrete bits of advice.

Too many of the final decisions about changing one's job are made when one is too busy with other things. Take a week off. Get plenty of sleep and rest. . . .

Visit the place of your proposed position and take your wife with you. . . .

Define to yourself, and if possible, to some close personal friend,

[33] Alex Bavelas, "How to Talk to the Boss," *Harper's Magazine*, July, 1955, p. 32.

just what you are assuming as well as expecting more explicitly. . . .

Distinguish between decisions that are irrevocable and those that can be postponed or reversed. . . .

Find out if possible who wanted you, and who else has been chosen by him, and whether he is in a position—as well as of a character—to make good his promises.

These hints by no means cover all the contingencies, nor are they intended to. My essential thesis is that we shall see over the next decades an increase, both absolute and relative, in the number of positions offered and changes of positions made. . . .[34]

c. Points made in the body of composition may be summarized.

"I . . . will conclude with a summary: I have discussed two problems that high level executives have in making formal talk; the problem of preparation, and the problem of presentation. Under preparation I have talked about the menu, the factual lead-off, form, ghosts, teachers, and the discipline of writing. Under presentation I discussed visual aids, delivery, pace, and authority.

"The main point of all my remarks is a conclusion—(I think it *is* permissible to *lead up* to a conclusion). Any person at any time in his life can increase his skill and his art in passing the word along."[35]

d. There may be a graceful rounding off of the total effort to communicate meaning.

"The problem of why we are crazy is a *political* problem—a problem of rearranging the ways in which social power is now exercised. It needs the social inventiveness, the willingness to make choices, and the courage to take the risks that go with imaginative action. It does not need medicine, magic, or moonshine about the end of Rational Man. Perhaps if we spent less time in being fascinated by the spectacle of our lunacy, and more time thinking about how we now use—and could clearly better

[34] Alan Gregg, "When to Change Jobs—and Why," *Harper's Magazine,* August, 1955, p. 76.
[35] Paul R. Beall, "Pass the Word Along."

use—the common sense we have, we might find that there is still plenty of reason to believe in human reason."[36]

e. The idea proposed in the introduction may be restated.

"I would like now to return to the point from which I started. We have discussed at some length the material contributions which we can make one to the other, but the greatest contribution we can make, as partners in a chaotic world, is to keep alive that freedom without which life is meaningless. Working together, we can make this continent an inspiring example of what free men can accomplish. This will be a contribution, not only to the progress and advancement of our own people, but a contribution to the peace and progress of the world."[37]

f. A statement of belief may be made.

"I believe with all my heart that you and we must, no matter what happens, keep our faith in the democratic way of life, in the freedoms for which it stands and in the belief in the dignity of the individual and respect for his rights. To you all for whom I have come to have real affection, I want to say I have a deep and abiding faith in the future of my own country, in the future of your country and in the future of our steadfast partnership. Let us continue to work together to usher in a new era of peace and hope for humanity."[38]

g. An apt quotation may be used as a conclusion.

"All of these things that I have been talking about—death, tolls, the demon speed, highway congestion, the need for carrier coöperation, public apathy—your responsibility—and mine—lead me back to the conclusion of the Good Book (and that is not a bad place to go to occasionally): 'The race is not to the swift, nor the battle to the strong'—but to him that endureth to the end."[39]

[36] Charles Frankel, "Are We Really Crazy?" *Harper's Magazine*, June, 1955, p. 70.
[37] W. J. Sheridan, "Partners for Freedom," address, Hartford, Connecticut, September 25, 1952.
[38] Walter S. Gifford, "Ties That Bind," address, London, England, January 21, 1953.
[39] James K. Knudson, "The Auto Makers' Responsibility," address, Detroit, Michigan, January 19, 1953.

Other specific devices which can be used in the conclusion include: (a) application of the idea to specific problems; (b) appeal for specific action based on the idea presented; (c) personal evaluation of the facts presented; (d) listed proposals for approval of audience or readers.

EXERCISES

1. Arrange the following historical incidents in chronological order: discovery of gold in California, election of President Coolidge, opening of Panama Canal, discovery of America, opening of Oklahoma territory, Louisiana Purchase.

2. Arrange the following American cities in spatial order from east to west: Pittsburgh, Sioux Falls, Reno, Chicago, Kansas City, Minneapolis, Fort Worth, Los Angeles.

3. Rearrange the cities listed in exercise 2 according to population.

4. What order of details would you suggest for the following topics?
   a. Should social fraternities and sororities be eliminated?
   b. Should American Indians be given full civil rights?
   c. Is the United States developing a dangerous spirit of anti-intellectualism?
   d. Should the legal voting age be eighteen?
   e. Should statehood be granted to Hawaii and Alaska?

5. A teacher aide program has been instituted in the Bay City, Michigan, public school system. If you were the principal of a school, which of the following tasks would you assign to the teacher, and which to the teacher's aide?

   Lesson plans TA   T Group planning
   Counseling T   TA Dictation
   Taking roll T A   T Listing library books
   Helping absentees catch up T First aid to sick pupils T A
   Rearranging desks TA   T Making reports
   Correcting papers TA   T Teaching classes
   Supervising recess TA   T Conducting research

6. Determine the type of arrangement used in the following paragraphs.

Should parents make a determined effort to get schools to concentrate on penmanship?

Most schoolmen say the answer to this question is no. They agree that penmanship isn't given the attention it once was, but they say the hours saved are better spent on other subjects. And they insist that while the average student may not write a picture book hand, he does have a simple style useful enough for most purposes.

—Arthur Edson

Last November, having signed a customs form vouching that my baggage contained no antelope horns, Manchurian deer, hashish, "negatives or cliches," I entered Russia via Leningrad. A company of British actors, directed by Peter Brook, had been invited by the Ministry of Culture to perform "Hamlet" in Moscow; for the first time since the October Revolution English was to be spoken on a Russian stage; and I took advantage of the cultural thaw to ride in on the actors' wake and take a firsthand look at the Moscow theater.

—Kenneth Tynan, "Curtain Time in Moscow,"
Harper's Magazine, March, 1956

Behold the gem-strung towns and cities of the good, green East, flung like star-dust through the field of night. That spreading constellation to the north is called Chicago, and that giant wink that blazes in the moon is the pendant lake that it is built upon. Beyond, close-set and dense as a clenched-fist, are all the jeweled cities of the eastern seaboard. There's Boston, ringed with the bracelet of its shining little towns, and all the lights that sparkle on the rocky indentations of New England.

—Thomas Wolfe

7. Select a number of news stories from your local paper and study the order of importance of items included in the lead sentences. In which cases would you alter the arrangement?

8. Criticize the following outline of a student's paper.

    I. Introduction.

        A. To determine the requirements, qualifications, and opportunities of a home economist.

II. Body of Evidence.
  A. Who shall teach home economics?
    1. Legal requirements.
      a. Four-year college course.
      b. Teaching certificate.
      c. Advanced work.
    2. Personal Qualifications.
      a. Personality.
      b. Care of person and grooming habits.
      c. Physical fitness.
      d. Attitude.
      e. Behavior.
  B. Opportunities.
    1. Demand for teachers of Home Economics.
      a. Statistics of need.
      b. Home economics teacher opportunities as compared with other vocational interests in home economics.
    2. Salaries.
    3. Advancement.
    4. Satisfactions derived from teaching home economics.
      a. Personal.
      b. Helping others.
      c. Teacher-student relationship.
      d. Community interest.
III. Conclusion.

9. Make a detailed outline plan of a talk or paper you have been assigned to deliver or write. Pay special attention to the body of composition as explained in this chapter.

10. Make an outline of an essay assigned by your instructor.

11. Listen to a public lecture and make a detailed outline of the speaker's remarks. Compare your arrangement of ideas with your classmates' fulfillment of this assignment.

12. Use the following general outline for writing a process theme on a topic of your own choice:
  I. The Process.
    A. Definition of the process.
      1. Basic actions.
      2. Purposes.

    B. Explanation of the process.
        1. By whom carried out.
        2. Under what circumstances.
    C. The action.
        1. List of main steps.
        2. Special difficulties.
II. Materials required.
    A. Tools, apparatus, etc.
    B. Supplies.
    C. Conditions and circumstances.
III. The Procedure.
    A. Step 1.
    B. Step 2.
    C. Step 3.
    D. Etc.

IV

DIRECT YOUR EFFORTS

10

ADAPT TO YOUR SUBJECT AND PURPOSE

YOU WOULD HARDLY APPROVE OF WEARING chaps, spurs, and sombrero to a formal dance, or a tuxedo on a fishing trip. We have learned to adjust our clothing by a standard or criterion of appropriateness. And we need to employ just such a standard with our choice of language. The words used in discussing nuclear fission should be quite different from those used to narrate personal experiences on an all-night hike. Words are most suitable when they are selected for a particular subject and a particular purpose. When a spoken or written passage is made up of words which appear to be so perfectly appropriate as to be irreplaceable, communication becomes effective. This chapter concerns appropriateness of style and diction to specific subjects and purposes.

10.1 Style

Style is evident in *how* a thing is said rather than in *what* is said. It is a speaker's or writer's unmistakable signature or identifying mark. James Russell Lowell called it "the establishment of a perfect mutual understanding between the worker and his material." James Mason Brown called it "the means chosen or instinctive (doubtless both) by which a writer has his precise say." Style makes it possible to read between the lines what an

203

author or speaker is thinking but doesn't actually say in so many words.

Some stylistic devices interfere with effective transmission of thought. Walter Pater, for example, could not express a simple thought in simple language. The orchestration of his words drowns their meanings and wraps the reader in reverie. Ruskin's language, according to W. Somerset Maugham, has a tendency to lure the mind away from the idea expressed: "The rolling period, the stately epithet, the noun rich in poetic associations, the subordinate clauses that give the sentence weight and magnificence, the grandeur like that of wave following wave in the open sea; there is no doubt that in all this there is something inspiring. Words thus strung together fall on the ear like music. The appeal is sensuous rather than intellectual, and the beauty of the sound leads you easily to conclude that you need not bother about their meaning."[1]

Texts made up of long, involved sentences, heavy with allusions, abstract words, figures of speech, and rhetorical devices may cripple rather than expedite successful communication of ideas. The following discussion of the industrial revolution by Henry George is profound and fluent but puts a heavy tax on comprehension:

And, unpleasant as it may be to admit it, it is at last becoming evident that the enormous increase in productive power which has marked the present century and is still going on with accelerating ratio, has no tendency to extirpate poverty or to lighten the burdens of those compelled to toil. It simply widens the gulf between Dives and Lazarus, and makes the struggle for existence more intense. The march of invention has clothed mankind with powers of which a century ago the boldest imagination could not have dreamed. But in factories where labor-saving machinery has reached its most wonderful development, little children are at work; wherever the new forces are anything like fully utilized, large classes are maintained by charity or live on the verge of recourse to it; amid the greatest

[1] From *The Summing Up*, New York, 1938.

accumulations of wealth, men die of starvation, and puny infants suckle dry breasts; while everywhere the greed of gain, the worship of wealth, shows the force of the fear of want. The promised land flies before us like the mirage. The fruits of the tree of knowledge turn as we grasp them to apples of Sodom that crumble at the touch.[2]

Opposed to such erudite and slightly abstruse style is "shirt-tail English," or what Clifton Fadiman has called "Madison Avenue English." It is a language of revolt and innovation and makes use of exuberant verbal inventions after the manner of such undisciplined frontier expressions as *hornswoggle, splendiferous, sumtotalize,* and *teetotaciously.* Mr. Fadiman calls this style "a successful, technically admirable attempt to *attract* the attention without actually *engaging* it; to entertain rather than challenge; or, to use the editors' quite legitimate phrase, to be 'readable'—that is, to present material which can be read easily and forgotten quickly." Here is a parody of such a style which Mr. Fadiman quotes from *Variety,* the magazine of show business:

You will recall that we've been firming up this problem for some time, and just in the nature of pitching up a few mashie shots to see if we can come near the green, I'd like to express these angles:

First, I think we should take a reading of the whole general situation to see if it is being spitballed correctly so that we can eventually wham it through for approval or disapproval as the case might be. In other words, we've got to live with this for a long time, and there are certain rock bottom slants which we will have to try on for size.

Since this situation hits us where we live, and since it has to be geared in before we hit the stretch it is only logical that we throw in a few crossbucks before we take it off tackle. I can't help feeling that we're all soft as a grape at this stage of the game, and unless we want to get caught with our metaphors down, we'd better get the egg off our faces and the cablestitch sweaters off our teeth.

In other words, we might get caught off first base, and the whole thing might go over like a lead balloon. So let me urge that we all

2 From *Progress and Poverty,* 1879.

kick this around and put on our creative thinking caps so that all of us will profit in the final wrap-up.[3]

The tendency in American prose style in recent years, especially in such magazines as *Harper's Magazine, Atlantic Monthly,* and *The New Yorker,* is toward informal, casual, and familiar expression. There is, of course, nothing new about this style. William Hazlitt, over a century ago, anticipated the modern mode. He knew the value of frankness, sincerity, and brevity. "I hate anything," he said, "that occupies more space than it is worth. I hate to see a load of band-boxes go along the street, and I hate to see a parcel of big words without any meaning to them." Here is what he had to say about familiar style:

It is not easy to write a familiar style. Many people mistake a familiar for a vulgar style, and suppose that to write without affectation is to write at random. On the contrary, there is nothing that requires more precision, and, if I may say so, purity of expression, than the style I am speaking of. It utterly rejects not only all unmeaning pomp, but all low, cant phrases, and loose, unconnected, *slipshod* allusions. It is not to take the first word that offers, but the best word in common use; it is not to throw words together in any combinations we please, but to follow and avail ourselves of the true idiom of the language. To write a genuine familiar or truly English style is to write as one would speak in common conversation who had a thorough command and choice of words, or who could discourse with ease, force, and perspicuity, setting aside all pedantic and oratorical flourishes. Or, to give another illustration, to write naturally is the same thing in regard to common conversation as to read naturally is in regard to common speech. . . .[4]

The important thing in communication is adjustment of style to the author's subject and purpose. "Good writing," says Bernard De Voto, "is the adaptation of means to end, the adaptation of style to mood, the meaning, and the audience. Good writ-

[3] Quoted in "Some Plain Thoughts on Fancy Language," *Holiday,* September, 1952.
[4] William Hazlitt, "On Familiar Style."

ing is, especially, the use of words which have the emotional over-tone proper to the context."

Some important aspects of style for the purposes of effective and efficient communication of ideas are tone, complexity, and individuality.

Tone

The quality of style which reveals your own personal attitude toward your subject and audience and makes plain your opinions, judgments, and intentions is called *tone,* or *mood.* What you think, what you feel, and how you wish to be taken are clearly reflected in the words you employ and in how you put them together. When we express ourselves orally, our tone of voice gives us away: meaning of words is defined by pronunciation. In writing, tone is exhibited in choice of words, in the use of figurative and rhetorical devices, and in emotional toning which results from connotations which words have acquired by association. Seriousness, whimsicality, facetiousness, formality, informality, sarcasm, satire, approval, disapproval, straightforwardness, matter-of-factness, down-to-earthness, hypocrisy, superficiality, and sophistication are all matters of tone. How effective a given tone will be in producing the kind of effects intended depends on the consistency with which it is maintained throughout a context and upon its appropriateness to the subject, purpose, and occasion.

In the coronation address delivered by Queen Elizabeth II, the tone was at once dignified and disarming. It spoke clearly of the monarch's friendliness, humility, and good will:

"When I spoke to you last at Christmas, I asked you whatever your religion to pray for me on the day of my coronation —to pray God to give me wisdom and strength to carry out the promises I should then be making. Throughout this memorable day I have been uplifted and sustained by the knowledge your prayers and thoughts were with me. I have been aware all the time that my peoples spread far and wide throughout every continent and ocean in the world were united to support me in the task to which I have now been dedicated with such solemnity. . . ."

The effusive display of emotionally toned adjectives and conceited figures of speech in Mark Twain's description of the Cathedral of Milan reflects an attitude of spellbound stupefaction:

"What a wonder it is! So grand, so solemn, so vast! and yet so delicate, so airy, so graceful! A very world of solid weight, and yet it seems in the soft moonlight only a fairy delusion of frostwork that might vanish with a breath! A vision! a miracle! an anthem sung in stone, a poem wrought in marble. . . . They say that it is second only to St. Peter's at Rome. I cannot understand how it can be second to anything made by human hands. . . ."[5]

The grandeur of the Canadian Rockies is portrayed in the following description by effective choice of words:

First, it's the individual features: Jagged peaks reaching upward to the sky; Maligne Canyon opening at your feet like a weird gateway to hell; lakes now green now gray now blue, reflecting the moods of the sky; Takakkaw Falls leaping from the rim of a massive 1,800-foot-high rock wall; the wildlife in the forests along the highway, turning a curious eye to the tourist but without any fuss—like the bear that strolled by our cabin window. . . .

Then, as you go higher and get a wider perspective, it's the scale of this country that strikes you. Range after range, with pine-covered valleys in between where man seems never to have set foot—until you forget there are cities in the plains and feel you're back in pioneer days, pushing west through the wilderness. . . .[6]

By mixing abstract and concrete expressions in the following passage William Saroyan paints a verbal picture of the exciting conglomeration of events that make up a circus:

"The circus was everything everything else we knew wasn't. It was adventure, travel, danger, skill, grace, romance, comedy,

[5] Mark Twain, *Innocents Abroad*, Vol. 1.
[6] Albert Roland, "For 10 days, the Sky's the Limit!" *Household*, May, 1956.

peanuts, popcorn, chewing-gum and soda-water. We used to carry water to the elephants and stand around afterwards and try to seem associated with the whole magnificent affair, the putting up of the big tent, the getting everything in order, and the worldly-wise waiting for the people to come and spend their money."[7]

Eugene Field, while working on the *Denver Tribune*, hit upon the idea of using so-called "primer sentences" for giving vent to his attitudes about social inequality:

"The Mud is in the Street. The Lady has on a pair of Red Stockings. She is Trying to Cross the Street. Let us all give Three cheers for the Mud."[8]

Complexity

Complexity may be defined as the amount of information contained in a given set of words. Generally speaking, the more complex a passage is, the more difficult it is, and the more concentration is necessary for its comprehension. We think of extremely complex contexts as heavy or abstruse, as compared with simple contexts that make for easy listening or light reading. Compare the complexity of the following passages.

The first, while containing very few difficult words, is loaded with "information":

By definition, the amount of information in a language of independent and equally likely symbols is given by the logarithm of the number of alternatives: amount of information $= k \log an = nk \log p(x)$. In this expression I is the quantity of information; k is a constant of proportionality that determines the size of the unit of measurement; a is the number of different verbal units; n is the length of the sequence; $p(x)$ is the probability of occurrence of symbol x and is equal to $1/a$."[9]

---

[7] William Saroyan, *My Name Is Aram*, New York, 1937, pp. 133–134.

[8] Eugene Field, *The Tribune Primer*, originally published in the *Denver Tribune*, 1882.

[9] George A. Miller, *Language and Communication*, New York, 1951, pp. 101–102.

The second is much easier to read, partly because it contains less "information":

"Poor little Johnny gropes his way painfully through the labyrinth of his 'English' course. When his schooling is finished, whether it be grade school, high school, or college, he hasn't anything much to show for his years of grammatical travail but a lifetime conviction that 'English is simply too much for me.' "[10]

An effective communicator adjusts the complexity of language to the purposes he hopes to accomplish and to the nature of the subject he is treating.

Individuality

Even though language is a kind of community property that belongs to everyone, each person has his own way of using it. Since our attitudes, opinions, thoughts, goals, and interests are all reflected in the way we talk, our language habits constitute a reliable index of the kind of people we are. This is as it should be. Language is a means to an end, not an end in itself.

There is a sort of hypocrisy and dishonesty in attempting to imitate the style of others. Great writers such as Shakespeare, Dickens, Emerson, Thoreau, Hawthorne, Melville, Mark Twain, and Ernest Hemingway developed individual styles of writing that are unmistakable signatures to their works. We have no right to forge the signatures. And even if we should try, the deception would certainly give us away. According to Henry Seidel Canby, one's English should be "true, both to its great inheritance, and to the taste and sense and blood and rhythm of life that are his own."

Let your ideas, words, tone, and style reflect your own experience and your own personality. Effective communication is genuine, not spurious. A real meeting of minds between speaker and

---

[10] Frank Colby, *Practical Handbook of Better English*, New York, 1944, pp. 3–4.

listener or between writer and reader depends upon sincerity, originality, spontaneity, and freedom of expression. Mimicry, verbal forgery, plagiarism are the enemies of good communication. Hiding one's personality behind a highly conventional and standardized prose style can easily defeat one's purposes in transmitting ideas and convictions. The trouble with much current writing is that it could have been composed by almost anyone. It bears no marks of distinction, no clues to authorship, no individuality. Ghost writing accounts for the fact that many people do not even comprehend the words which appear under their own by-lines.

As Emerson has it: "The way to speak and write what shall not go out of fashion is to speak and write sincerely." Unfortunately, this is one of the most difficult lessons to learn. Even some of the so-called masters of literature insisted on clinging to an ostentatious instead of a simple, natural, and sincere style.

10.2 Vocabulary and Diction

Finding words which most clearly represent your ideas, your purposes, and your attitudes toward chosen subjects is what is meant by appropriateness of diction. Knowledge of facts is of vital importance in communication, but facts to be properly understood must be translated into words that accurately portray them. We have a way of covering up our insufficient vocabularies by calling things *doolollies, thingamajigs, whatchamacallits, gimmicks,* and *doodads.* The point is simply this: no matter what your subject—child psychology, football, photosynthesis, skin diving, or golf—use language appropriate to the subject. Physics has a special vocabulary. So do chemistry, mathematics, photography, religion, baseball, politics, literary criticism, philosophy, and logic. A person qualified to converse on any of these topics should have an adequate working vocabulary by which to express his thoughts.

Appropriateness

Whether a particular word is appropriate in a given context or not depends on the nature of the idea proposed and on the purpose of the speaker or writer. The precise meanings of words are decided by the persons who use them. *Gerrymander, filibuster, wheel horse, carpetbag, farm bloc, grass roots, steam roller,* and *standpatter* are all political terms which have gained currency through continued use by politicians. Many of these words were borrowed from other vocabularies: *wheel horse* from farming, *steam roller* from road construction. Thus it should be perfectly clear that words have different meanings for different purposes and under different circumstances.

Each of us has a general speaking and writing vocabulary made up of a large number of smaller specialized vocabularies. These specialized vocabularies are functional varieties of English. Thus we speak of the language of business, of advertising, of law, of politics, of medicine, of journalism, of literature, of literary criticism, of philosophy, of psychology, of cultural anthropology, of mathematics, of religious dogma, of logic, of semantics, and so on. There is some overlapping, to be sure, which simply means that some words do double duty.

The principal problem of appropriateness is the problem of finding words which will do most efficiently and effectively what we want them to do. To put the right words in the right places, so that listeners and readers will experience no difficulty in making out what we have in mind, is the secret of successful transmission of ideas. Understanding what others say and write certainly depends on acquaintance with the words they employ in expressing ideas. Whenever words are chosen with such care that no substitutes will quite do the job, communication is almost sure to succeed.

SUGGESTIONS FOR SELECTING WORDS APPROPRIATE TO SUBJECT AND PURPOSE.

a. Select words which direct attention to ideas. Words which call undue attention to themselves are likely to defeat the purposes you have in mind for them. Notice how the word *juxtaposition,* in the following context, destroys the central thought:

"The most dastardly gambit of the recipe-er is to get perfectly good food into such close juxtaposition that it loses all its edibility. This is best accomplished with a casserole. The beaming hostess brings out a deep dish, breaks the crust and a wonderful aroma of chicken pervades the dining room. But when you dip deeply, you find the chicken is in a two-inch layer and below that is six inches of broccoli or brussels sprouts."

b. Select words which fit the subject, purpose, and tone of communication. The italicized words in the following sentences are used loosely and might better be replaced by more suitable or definitive expressions:

"The *colossal* racket of their engine makes conversation impossible."

"Concentrate on devising any of these *gimmicks* which might make you your first million: a coffee grinding attachment for electric mixers . . . a telescopic shower that would allow the nozzle to be pulled down to shoulder height . . . disposable sun lenses for eye glasses."

"My roommate has a strong *phobia* for examinations."

"Some people dislike cooks; others have the same kind of *allergy* toward wireless operators."

"In the messroom the chef, while regaling himself with untidy forkfuls of spaghetti, will hold forth about the advantage of having cabins painted in *psychological* colors."

c. Employ figures of speech appropriate to the contexts in which they are placed. The simile in this passage might better have drawn on material or episodes connected with the life of a sailor:

"There is only one hope for heavenly justice as far as the mate is concerned: that the second mate may break a leg and the captain be forced to take over his watch. It is as good as an adolescent's night at the opera when the prima donna loses her bloomers in the high C."[11]

Forrester Blake in *Johnny Christmas*, a story of the Southwestern frontier, uses the following highly appropriate figures: "hotter'n a rope burn," "Silence fell like a folded wing," "Johnny's voice cracked like a quirt on the still air," "as tense as trigger springs," "Clay peaks burn at their tips as wood knots burn."

d. Avoid stilted, outlandish, freakish expressions, unless they fit your purposes exactly. Words like *colorama, guestimate, hooliganism, yesterlayed,* and other innovations in the Walter Winchell style, are show-off words. They are clever and cute but often out of tune with the ideas they are selected to enforce. Arthur H. Motley, president of Parade Publication, tells of a businessman who when addressing his plant personnel kept referring to the "Gargantuan problems of management." "I am sure," said Mr. Motley, "that most of the people who were listening expected to see a gorilla come down from the chandeliers. What he meant, of course, was that the problems of management are BIG problems."

Three months ago I subscribed to a lot of newspapers. I did not have time to read them myself, so I had them read for me. I was amazed at what I saw. One of those periodic flare-ups was going on in Iran. Over half of the newspapers which came to me had editorials referring to the fact that xenophobia was rampant in Iran. I have a hunch a lot of people thought that the hoof and mouth disease had struck the country. Actually xenophobia means a hatred or fear of strangers—any strangers. How much simpler it would have been to say that. . . .

Here's another typical example from an editorial page. I quote: "Mr. Acheson's apples, for all their polish, cannot conceal their vermiculated content." The writer meant the apples were wormy. . . .

[11] Jan De Hartog, "Ship's Company," *Harper's Magazine*, November, 1955, p. 36.

Here's one from a paper in Virginia. They were talking about a well known author and referred to him as a "lucid expositor." Why not say that he writes clearly.[12]

Precision

Language contains a large stock of words which may have a numerical value within a wide range of specific values. *Always, sometime,* and *several* are examples of such words, which when used promiscuously may easily cause communication to miss its target. Precision is a matter of certainty resulting from careful refinement of measurement. It is the difference between "In a few days" and "In five days." Lack of precision may be illustrated by the italicized words in this passage: "When he was an *old* man, Sequoia left the Cherokee Nation in what is now Oklahoma to go on a *long* journey to the *far* Southwest, seeking other Cherokees. On this *hard* journey, in August, 1843, *somewhere* in the mountains of Mexico, he died."

Notice the scientific precision of the language of George W. Gray:

When a leaf cell is examined microscopically, the eye sees at once that its green color is not diffused throughout the protoplasm but is concentrated in small floating bodies. These are called chloroplasts. Further dissection reveals that the chloroplasts are made up of still smaller bodies called grana, and it is these that contain the chlorophyll. A typical square inch of leaf surface has about a billion cells; there are, on the average, from 20 to 100 chloroplasts in each cell, about 100 grana to each chloroplast, and it is estimated that each grana holds about 10,000,000 chlorophyll molecules. One can extract the chlorophyll as a pure chemical, and chemists have found it possible to promote various photochemical reactions by exposing solutions of pure chlorophyll to light—but none has ever been able either to split water or to reduce carbon dioxide by this means.[13]

[12] Arthur H. Motley, "Can They Hear You?" address, Chicago, Illinois, December 5, 1952.
[13] George W. Gray, "Our Bridge from the Sun," *Harper's Magazine*, September, 1955, p. 71.

Precision can be insured by using specific examples to illustrate general principles. The two passages following are both concerned with the peculiarities of ship's officers. The first is a generalization from many instances. The second is a specific case and, therefore, much more precise.

Mates are basically the unhappiest people at sea, because they are busy becoming captains. As everyone who has been an adolescent knows, not to be something yet is a depressing situation. What's more, every mate is convinced that he is better than his captain, for his captain only tells him what to do, rarely does it himself. The happy mate, quite satisfied with his situation, is for some reason unsatisfactory. A man who wants to remain a mate is a bad mate and a man who is a mate and wants to become a captain is frustrated, so one can easily see that a mate's lot is a hard one.[14]

Stubb was the second mate. . . . A happy-go-lucky; neither craven nor valiant; taking perils as they came with an indifferent air; and while engaged in the most imminent crisis of the chase, toiling away, calm and collected as a journeyman joiner engaged for the year. Good-humored, easy, and careless, he presided over his whale-boat as if the most deadly encounter were but a dinner, and his crew all invited guests. He was as particular about the comfortable arrangement of his part of the boat, as an old stage-driver is about the snugness of his box. When close to the whale, in the very death-lock of the fight, he handled the unpitying lance coolly and offhandedly, as a whistling tinker his hammer. He would hum over his old rigadig tunes while flank and flank with the most exasperated monster. Long usage had, for this Stubb, converted the jaws of death into an easy chair. What he thought of death itself, there is no telling. . . .[15]

Economy

Statehouse custodians in Boise, Idaho, in order to keep people off a new asphalt surface of the government parking lot, recently put up signs—the only ones available—which read:

[14] Jan De Hartog, "Ship's Company," *Harper's Magazine*, November, 1955, p. 36.
[15] Herman Melville, *Moby Dick*, Chap. 27.

STATE LAND! KEEP OFF! REMOVE NO TIMBER!
GRAZE NO STOCK WITHOUT PERMIT! NO MINING!

Many of the words were quite obviously superfluous for the intended purpose. "Keep off!" would have done the job nicely and more effectively.

Effective writers and speakers are economical with words. Winston Churchill's speeches are excellent examples of economy in composition. Abraham Lincoln's "Gettysburg Address" is a classic of economy, precision, and directness.

It is possible, of course, to endanger proper reception of an idea by stripping it of all its accouterments. "Off agin, on agin, gone agin, Finnegan" is a pretty flimsy report, as is "I came, I saw, I conquered." But occasionally an entire sermon can be contained in a single sentence. Eugene Field is said to have haunted the declining years of Creston Clarke, a Shakespearean actor, with this capsule criticism of Clarke's *Lear:* "Mr. Clarke played the King all evening as though under constant fear that some one else was about to play the Ace."

Many beginners in communication skills courses feel obligated to fill up a specified number of pages with words on a given subject. Experienced writers, on the other hand, once they have finished an initial task of writing, go back and delete words, phrases, and sentences, sometimes whole paragraphs, that do not function as they should. Brevity is not only the soul of wit, but the soul of all varieties of communication.

Compare the following paragraphs or passages. Notice the economy of diction apparent in the first selection:

Any combat-ready SAC crew member . . . could tell you with closed eyes from what base he will depart, what course he will fly, at what altitude, and at what speed. He will know the time and location for each turn; the times, locations, and altitudes for the rendezvous with refueling tankers. He will know by heart the exact latitude and longitude at which he will make his penetration of the enemy radar screen, and what his courses and altitudes will be thereafter. Every man on the crew can draw on paper from memory what the target city will look like in the radar scope; and he can show you the pin-point in the city over which his bomb should explode and the off-set aiming point which is his guidepost. He can then tell you whether he is to turn right or left after the bomb run, what his course will be, the point at which he is to leave enemy territory, what his refueling points are, and the base for which he will head.[16]

Notice the verbal padding in the second:

If heart and mind be tuned to the poignant music of yesteryear, perhaps you can still hear them—hear the lonesome, high pitched train whistles that floated far across level fields and over rolling hills. No census will ever reveal how many millions of boys and girls in our nation have grown to manhood and womanhood within hearing distance of the whistles' half-sad, yet deeply appealing song.

Train whistles have been one of the intangible bonds that bound a vast sprawling nation together. For until the blatant, nerve-shattering raucous blasts of horns on diesel engines began splintering the quietness of rural areas, train whistles sang their pleasant and appealing "Whoo-whoo-who-who" over wide areas. In the nation's rich heartland, on the short grass prairies, among northeastern hills and valleys and in the pine lands of the south, men and women, boys and girls have listened to the whistles of the trains. . . .

There is something low-key and poignant about a long-drawn train whistle as it carries over the fields, echoes through the wood-lands, floats across a prairie or echoes among tree-clad hills. Many men and women can remember how the whistle sounded at night as the slow, sad, notes came through the darkness. Uncounted boys and girls, hearing those notes and perhaps seeing the night flyer gliding smoothly along through night's blackness like a jeweled snake, have resolved that someday they would be in a train like that, starting out on life's thrilling and lonesome adventure.[17]

Throwing words promiscuously around a half-conceived idea does not communicate thoughts to others. A good rule to follow is: Use words sparingly and make every one count.

[16] Richard S. Meryman, Jr., "The Guardians," *Harper's Magazine*, October, 1955, p. 39.
[17] *The State Journal* (Lansing, Michigan), August 21, 1955.

Clarity

An anecdote attributed to the dean of the Massachusetts Institute of Technology calls attention to the need for clarity of expression in the communication of ideas: A foreign plumber in New York City wrote to the Federal Bureau of Standards that he had found hydrochloric acid did a good job of cleaning out clogged drains. The bureau wrote: "The efficacy of hydrochloric acid is indisputable, but the corrosive residue is incompatible with metallic permanence." The plumber replied he was glad the bureau agreed. Again the bureau wrote: "We cannot assume responsibility for the production of toxic and noxious residue with hydrochloric acid and suggest you use an alternative procedure." The plumber was happy again at bureau agreement with his idea. Then the bureau wrote: "Don't use hydrochloric acid. It eats hell out of the pipes."

The pretentious language of many occupational and professional groups is properly criticized for its abstruseness and difficulty. But brevity, sincerity, and simplicity do not necessarily equate with clarity. A short word may be as ambiguous or even more ambiguous than a long word. The important question is not: Which word am I going to use? but Which word is essential to my meaning?

If a choice must be made between a popular expression and a so-called learned or erudite expression, it must be determined by suitability, clarity, and appropriateness.

Notice the unpretentious simplicity of this passage from the writings of Ernie Pyle: "Our fighters moved on after the enemy, and those who did not fight, but moved in the wake of the battles, would not catch up for hours. There was nothing left behind but the remains—the lifeless debris, the sunshine and the flowers, and utter silence. An amateur who wandered in this vacuum at the rear of a battle had a terrible sense of loneliness. Everything was dead—the men, the machines, the animals—and he alone was left alive."[18]

[18] Ernie Pyle, *The Nation*, March 19, 1945.

In sharp contrast to this language is the inflated diction so prevalent among certain journalists, platform speakers, government employees, and business and professional men: "We are peaking our program philosophically, but it is naïve to assume that the allotment program is an equity program unless the allotments are so abysmally low that the agency relaxes and allows the market determination."

Such a language of confusion, hypocrisy, and misunderstanding has been variously dubbed "avoirduprose," "bafflegab," "gobbledegook," and "desperanto." Here is how a member of the United States Chamber of Commerce simultaneously defines and illustrates it: "Multiloquence characterized by consummate interfusion of circumlocution or periphrasis, inscrutability, incognizability, and other familiar manifestations of abstruse expatriation commonly utilized for promulgations implementing procrustean determinations by government bodies."

Suggestions for regulating the relative simplicity of language are as follows:

a. Avoid unfamiliar, pompous, abstract, woolly, overelegant words, unless they serve your purpose best.

b. When technical words or foreign phrases must be used, define or translate them, unless they are well known.

c. Avoid padding your contexts with excessive words which can be deleted without altering your thought.

d. For most practical purposes, prefer concrete words to abstract generalizations, and direct to indirect discourse.

e. Pay no attention to the national origin of words; just be sure they are appropriate for your purposes and the meaning you want to convey.

f. Use short words if they accomplish your purpose, but don't be afraid of long words just because they are long.

g. Avoid stereotypes, clichés, and platitudes. Use live, original expressions.

h. Use finite verbs in the active voice whenever possible to do so without sounding awkward and clumsy.

i. Use concrete words which make a strong appeal to the senses.

EXERCISES

1. What is the author's attitude toward his subject in each of the following passages? How are you able to determine it? Which passage is most factual? Which most restrained? Which most emotionally toned, or slanted? In which passage does the author let the reader arrive at his own interpretation of the facts presented?

> Lying is universal—we all do it; we all *must* do it. Therefore, the wise thing is for us diligently to train ourselves to lie thoughtfully, judiciously; to lie with a good object, and not an evil one; to lie for others' advantage, and not our own; to lie healingly, charitably, humanely, not cruelly, hurtfully, maliciously; to lie gracefully and graciously, not awkwardly and clumsily; to lie firmly, frankly, squarely, with head erect, not haltingly, tortuously, with pusillanimous mien, as being ashamed of our high calling. Then shall we be rid of the rank and pestilent truth that is rotting the land; then shall we be great and good and beautiful, and worthy dwellers in a world where even benign Nature habitually lies, except when she promises execrable weather. Then— But I am but a new and feeble student in this gracious art; I cannot instruct *this* Club.
> —Mark Twain, "On the Decay of
> the Art of Lying," *Tom Sawyer
> Abroad*

> Nor can we rely on destructive atomic energy to take care of itself. Already there is the tempting but dangerous notion to the effect that the atomic bomb is so horrible and the terror of retaliation so great that we may have seen the last of war. This is quasi-logical, but war is no respecter of logic, relative or absolute. And if history teaches us anything, it is that the possibility of war increases in direct proportion to the effectiveness of the instruments of war.
> —Norman Cousins, "Modern Man
> Is Obsolete"

Some years ago when I was the dinner guest of a famous club in Boston, the chairman of the evening introduced me in the following words: "Our guest tonight is an economist. I need hardly remind you, gentlemen, of the large part played in our life of today by our economists. Indeed it has been calculated that if all the economists were laid out in a line, end to end, starting at the Mexican border, they would reach"— the orator paused impressively and added—"nowhere."

—Stephen Leacock, *Too Much College*

Every citizen of this great nation at some time or other probably has paused to ask himself: How much does my opinion count, anyway, in running the American government?

If he is a cynic, his answer may be: Nothing; realistically speaking, the common, ordinary citizen has no voice in government—it is the spokesman of industry or labor, of money or mass membership, who are heeded in high places.

Such an answer, of course, misses the mark. Wealth and concentrated voting power must be reckoned with in politics, but when you've said that you have told only part of the story. The rest of it—and the vital part—is that any time the common, ordinary citizens want to get action they can do so, because they actually hold the whip hand under our democratic form of government.

—Editorial in *The State Journal* (Lansing, Michigan), March 11, 1956

Douglas MacArthur is a man of vivid imagination. His island-hopping counter attack demoralized the Japanese. His Inchon landing won what biographer Gen. Cortney Whitney calls the military war in Korea. His method of dealing with the Japanese after V-J Day added a great Democracy to the free world.

—Bob Considine, "On the Line"

2. Read the following feature news story and suggest a number of ideas or theses that the facts presented support. What evidence would you use to defend one of the ideas you selected? What facts are irrelevant to this thesis?

For years penmanship flowered and prospered. Platt R. Spencer, who lived from 1800 to 1864, busily taught his system in a chain of business colleges, and thereby left his mark upon the American hand.

Long after Spencer, as handwriting styles changed from vertical to slanted letters, professors who could write in endless curlicues were highly respected.

Almost any adult over 35 can recall the hours spent at penmanship. Remember the endless lines of overlapping O's? Or the push-pull of the pen in an effort to form an unbroken picket line?

The date of the decline and fall of this type of penmanship varies with the school system.

Some, of course, still have it. But in most schools it faded fast in the 1920's and 1930's. In many schools depression delivered the knockout punch. Need to save money; let's fire the penmanship teacher!

Yet the real reason for changing the methods of teaching penmanship probably wasn't financial. It was a conviction on the part of many educators that penmanship, as then taught, wasted time.

Louis A. DiGesare of Scotia, New York, is a calligrapher and one of the pilgrims who visited Spencer's tomb. He hands you his hand-written card. The capitals are delicately shaded, the curls and curves of his name roll as rhythmically and relentlessly as the tide.

Many a businessman, no matter how much he deplores poor handwriting in others, has a signature that is indecipherable. And many a dainty woman writes a most unladylike scrawl.

—Arthur Edson, "Time Has Almost Blotted Out His Name"

3. The following essay concerning Paul Bunyan is an example of "thin" writing. How would you put more substance into the essay? Compare the complexity of this essay with one of the papers you have written to fulfill an assignment. Rewrite your paper, adding facts where your expression lacks substance.

Paul Bunyan, the legendary inventor of logging, weighed 70 pounds when he was born in Canada as Paul Bonjean. And he grew and grew and GREW.

He stepped across the St. Lawrence River in one step and became an American. He began cutting down forests so men could plant farm crops and build cities.

With Babe, his huge blue ox, he became a great logger. He opened the iron mines of Michigan to make shoes for Babe. He stood mountains on their heads and made the Bad Lands of the Dakotas.

Wading in a stream with his pickax dragging behind him, he made the Grand Canyon. He dug the Great Lakes as reservoirs for his men and animals and filled them with water from the Atlantic Ocean.

By and by the forests were cut, the mountains and lakes made, and there was no more work for Paul Bunyan. But his exploits were never forgotten and his name lives on.

—Violet Moore Higgins, "Paul Bunyan and the Logging Days"

4. Can you draw an analogy between the following discussion of photography and verbal communication? Rewrite the essay so that what it says applies directly to the communication of meaning with words.

Imagination in photography is that intangible asset which lifts a picture from the run-of-the-mill class and gives it personality. It can't be bought over the camera store counter like a roll of the newest film or a color film filter. It exists in the photographer's mind along with the exposure data knowledge . . . but can't be calculated by a mathematical guide or meter as an exposure can.

By using imagination, you get more than a photographic record of a person, place or event. You present a viewpoint that lends interest and captures attention.

Imagination can be exercised in the mental approach that leads up to taking a picture, in the technical aspects of shooting and in the final presentation of the finished print.

—Irving Desfor, "Imagination Can Make the Picture"

5. Analyze the language of a selected passage from one of your assigned readings. Answer the following questions:

a. To what extent is the language literal? To what extent figurative?
b. How long are the sentences?
c. How many of the words are unfamiliar to you? Are these words technical words associated with the subject matter? Does the context clarify its own meaning?
d. What is the author's attitude toward his subject? How do you know this?
e. How well does the author give you a picture of himself in the way he writes?

6. Repeat exercise 5 with some oral communication event.

FOR FURTHER READING

Barzun, Jacques, "English as She's Not Taught," *Atlantic Monthly,* December, 1953.

Barzun, Jacques, "How to Write and Be Read," from *Teacher in America,* Boston, 1946.

Brown, Ivor, "The Case for Greater Clarity in Writing," *New York Times Book Review,* July 30, 1950.

Burgess, Frank Gelett, *Short Words Are Words of Might.* In H. Blodgett and B. Johnson, *Readings for Our Times,* Boston, 1948.

Chase, Mary Ellen, "What Has Happened to Common Sense?" *Coronet,* May, 1950.

Dobree, Bonamy, "The New Way of Writing," from *Modern Prose Style,* New York, 1934.

Fadiman, Clifton, "Some Plain Thoughts on Fancy Language," *Holiday,* September, 1952. Also in *Reader's Digest,* December, 1932.

Flesch, Rudolf, "Live Words and Crowded Words," from *The Art of Plain Talk,* New York, 1946.

Lloyd, Donald J., "Snobs, Slobs, and the English Language," *The American Scholar,* Summer, 1951.

Nock, Albert J., *Free Speech and Plain Language,* New York, 1937.

Orwell, George, "Politics and the English Language," from *Shooting an Elephant,* New York, 1945.

Overstreet, Harry A., "The Psychology of Effective Writing," from *Influencing Human Behavior,* New York, 1925.

Panzer, Martin, "What's Wrong with English?" *Coronet*, March, 1954.

Quiller-Couch, Sir Arthur, "On Jargon," from *On the Art of Writing*.

Read, Allen Walker, "Corruption Words in American Politics," *Inside the ACD*, October, 1952.

Salomon, Louis B., "Whose Good English?" in *AAUP Bulletin*, Autumn, 1952.

White, E. B., "Calculating Machine" in *The Second Tree from the Corner*, New York, 1951.

Whyte, William H., Jr., "The Language of Advertising," *Fortune*, September, 1952.

Whyte, William H., Jr., "The Language of Business," *Fortune*, November, 1950.

Whyte, William H., Jr., "You, too, Can Write the Casual Style," *Harper's Magazine*, September, 1952.

ADAPT TO YOUR AUDIENCE AND THE OCCASION

ADAPTING TO YOUR SUBJECT IS NOT enough for successful communication of ideas. The ideas must be adapted also to specific readers or listeners and to specific occasions if meaning is to be comprehended by those for whom it is intended. Speaker and audience, or writer and reader, must be on the same wave length if meaning is to be successfully transmitted from one to the other.

11.1   Common Ground

"The fact narrated," said Emerson, "must correspond to something in me to be credible or intelligible. We as we read, must become Greeks, Romans, Turks, priest and king, martyr and executioner; must fasten these images to some reality in our

secret experience, or we shall learn nothing rightly." Similarity or coincidence of experiences between speaker and listener, or between writer and reader, is called common ground. If we let two overlapping circles represent the accumulative experiences

227

of two people who want to exchange ideas, the area of overlap will constitute the common ground between them.

By employing language symbols derived from common experiences, two individuals can exchange ideas successfully, but when either party makes use of experiential images not shared by the other, communication may easily break down. If a man in Texas, for example, has never seen snow, and you want to talk about snow, you will have to make use of his having seen cotton or confetti blown about by the wind in order to make your meaning clear.

Since the transmitter of a message is the person best able to make verbal adjustments, it becomes the responsibility of speakers and writers to adapt their thoughts to the people they want to reach or influence.

The principle of common ground, or the ability to assume another's point of view or frame of reference, is important in all stages of communication. It implies the following types of adjustment:

a. Choose ideas which are of mutual interest to both speaker and listener.

b. Support the idea with facts which are comprehensible to those who receive them.

c. Select illustrations, examples, definitions, testimonies, directions, and other methods of clarification and argument which are drawn from the experiences of readers and listeners.

d. Arrange the details of your presentation so that the pattern of thought can be easily recognized by those who receive it.

e. Employ speech idioms and diction which are familiar to those you address.

11.2   Role Playing in Communication

Whenever a speaker or writer confronts an audience or reader, he plays a dramatic role, as an actor does on a stage. During the course of a single day, we all play many different roles: student, friend, sweetheart, patient, teammate, counselor, roommate, employee, etc. Each person in our circle of acquaintances knows a different part of us.

As one writer says: ". . . We have as many sides to our character as we have friends to show them to. Quite unconsciously I find myself witty with one friend, large and magnanimous with another, petulant and stingy with another, wise and grave with another, and utterly frivolous with another. . . ."[1]

The matter of making adjustments to various people during a day's routine activities is something we seldom think about. It is automatic. "Put any company of people together with freedom for conversation," said Emerson, "and a rapid self-distribution takes place into sets and pairs. . . . All conversation is a magnetic experiment. I know that my friend can talk eloquently; you know that he cannot articulate a sentence; we have seen him in different company."

11.3 The Principle of Appropriateness

Appropriate diction is diction which is modified to suit the experience, limitations, and vocabulary of audiences or readers. As one writer has put it: "It would be ridiculous to address a group of soldiers in the same language you would employ in a council of war." Publishers, recognizing this, insist that contributors adapt their style to the tastes, habits, and attitudes of readers. There is probably no more effective way of gaining attention and of establishing belief than to speak and write in the language most appropriate to subject, audience, and occasion.

Suggestions for using appropriate diction follow:

a. Don't talk down to your audience or reader. Such a practice is insulting.

b. Try to determine what is expected of you. If you are supposed to be an authority on your subject, talk like an authority.

[1] R. Bourne, *Youth and Life*, Boston and New York, 1913, p. 144.

c. Don't let your adaptation of language deflate your idea. The idea is more important than the language in which it is couched.

d. Don't try to exhibit your prowess with words. No one cares that you have just made an addition to your vocabulary.

e. Be as natural as you can within the limits of your purpose. Some people sound like strangers the minute they address a public gathering. Be yourself.

11.4 Feedback, or Two-Way Communication

When we say that communication is a two-way process, we mean that ideas flow from speaker to listener and also from listener to speaker. Feedback is the echo or reaction a speaker or writer gets in the form of warmth, applause, and encouragement, or of doubt, denunciation, and resentment, to the idea he proposes. In the case of speaking, feedback may take a variety of forms: (a) laughter or absence of laughter at a joke or humorous story; (b) other emotional reactions including tears, anger, fear, pity, chagrin, exhibited in facial expressions of audience; (c) attitudes of listeners exhibited in gestures, attention or inattention, quiet or confusion, and poise or restlessness; (d) the raising of hands, to denote approval or disapproval, and applause or lack of applause; (e) participation of members of audience in the form of questions, challenging statements, or expressions of approval; (f) question and answer period or organized discussion following the presentation.

In the case of writing, feedback is of necessity delayed. It may be observed in overt reactions such as letters to the editor of a newspaper or magazine, personal letters to the writer or author, published acceptance or rejection of the idea proposed, or adoption of the idea in some plan of action.

Feedback is a kind of applause meter which registers the degree of correspondence between aim and achievement. If a speaker or writer overshoots or undershoots his mark, he can, by observing the nature of audience response, make adjustments that will bring a higher degree of success. If a speaker knows his audience and their characteristic reactions, he can operate more efficiently than if his listeners are complete strangers to him. If the audience knows the speaker and his usual modes of behavior, the making of appropriate responses will be comparatively easy.

The fact that reception of an idea can be greatly miscalculated is demonstrated by an advertising stunt in which a series of lovely poster girls was used to promote the sale of American merchandise in Italy. Here are some of the reported results: "An executive said: 'We can't waste time beating our heads against a stone wall. Those women just brought nothing but trouble, even if there wasn't anything indecent about them. The big complaint was that they were just too attractive.' A Milan department store which put the long-limbed girls in stockings stopped traffic. Twenty minutes later the manager was answering questions in the police station."[2]

Adam Smith, university lecturer of the eighteenth century, largely attributed his success as a speaker to the close attention he paid to his audience. "During one whole season," he said, "a certain student with a plain but expressive countenance was a great use to me in judging my success. . . . If he leant forward to listen, all was right; but if he leant back in an attitude of listlessness I felt at once that I was wrong, and that I must change either the subject or the style of my address."[3]

Professor Ray L. Birdwhistell, of the University of Louisville, has made a detailed study of gestures as indicators of audience reaction. He believes that the nose rub is as much a sign of rejection as "No!" that patting the hair means approval, and that a dead-pan look means disapproval.

It is doubtless true that gestures were used for communication long before words were invented, and that they still play an im-

---

[2] Norman J. Montellier, UP staff correspondent.
[3] Francis W. Hirst, *Adam Smith*, London, 1904, pp. 34–35.

portant role in the transfer of meaning from one person to another. We should learn to take the pulse of our audiences and readers in order to insure maximum reception of our ideas.

11.5   Analysis of Audiences and Readers

If we analyze audiences and readers in order to discover basic differences among people, it will be much easier to adapt to them than if we consider them simply as groups. A preliminary analysis such as is made here will help you determine (a) appropriateness of subject, (b) appropriateness of language, (c) appropriateness of appeals, (d) appropriateness of methods of clarification and defense.

Individual Differences

When a group of people assemble out of sheer curiosity or for reasons that have nothing to do with intellectual interests, they constitute a heterogeneous group or crowd. When, on the other hand, people assemble because of a common intellectual interest, they make an audience. It is difficult to adjust to a crowd because of the diversity of its members. It is much easier to adjust to people who have some common denominator that unites them. And yet, no audience is composed of precisely the same type of people. What are the differences among people that may be useful to a speaker or writer in adapting his ideas to them? Here are some of the very general differences:

a. Age: children, teen-agers, high-school youth, college students, adults.
b. Sex: men, women, mixed group.
c. Language: English as principal language, bilingual with English as secondary language.
d. Education: grade school, high school, college, technical training.
e. Race: average American, minority group, foreign born.
f. Occupation: farmers, laborers, business people, professional people, leisured class, retired people, unemployed.

g. Economic status: average incomes, wealthy, underprivileged.
h. Social status: community leaders, followers, average people, social registerites, suppressed people.
i. Political affiliation: strong political beliefs, indifferent attitudes toward politics, aggressive attitudes, self-conscious attitudes.
j. Religious affiliation: Protestant, Catholic, Jewish, no affiliation, agnostic, other.
k. Residence: country people, city people, small-town people.
l. Geographic area: North, South, East, Middle West, New England, etc.
m. Culture: reading and listening habits, entertainments preferred, extent of travel, membership in clubs, societies, etc.

Typical Audiences

The attitude of audiences and readers toward you, your idea, and your point of view should be carefully considered before you express your thoughts in language.

THE CAPTURED AUDIENCE.   When people come together because of the occasion rather than because they want to hear the speaker, the audience may be called a captured audience. Church congregations, conventions, commencement audiences, and classroom assemblies are captive audiences. Because such an audience may be completely indifferent about an idea to be proposed, the speaker must not assume audience interest in his topic. Interest must be created and maintained if it does not already exist. Here are some ways of soliciting audience attention and interest:

a. Vitalize the presentation. People are interested in people. Anything concerning the lives, struggles, hardships, accomplishments, headaches, or even toothaches, of people is bound to create interest. The liberal inclusion of case histories, examples, incidents, anecdotes will usually keep a reader or listener on your wave length.

b. Make your approach positive. Any negative, self-effacing, or apologetic suggestions you include in your talk will undermine your effectiveness. If you want to lose your audience, say something like this: "This is an opportunity I've been waiting for a long time. A captive audience and the greater part of an hour. I hope the operation is not too painful."

c. Enliven the presentation with physical activity. Think of the numerous ways the commercial advertiser capitalizes on the power of movement to attract attention: flickering lights, neon signs, animated figures, sky writing. A speaker who is not afraid to move will usually have better success than one who is rigid and immovable. The use of visual aids and the inclusion of dramatic stories which suggest action will pay rich dividends in audience interest.

d. Make your presentation novel. The same old routine of drab introductions and platitudinous courtesies is no good for an audience which needs to be charged with interest. Something rare, unusual, exotic, and different will break up the humdrum monotony of the average occasion.

e. Be specific, concrete, and familiar. If you attach your idea to a current event or local happening which has stimulated widespread interest or controversy, you are not in much danger of losing your audience.

THE EXPECTANT AUDIENCE. If you are an invited guest for an occasion and well sought after, you need not worry about stimulating interest. You should be careful not to betray the expectations of your solicitors. For an audience of this kind, you need careful preparation and good control of your physical and mental capacities. The one thing you must not forget is to make your remarks of personal concern to your audience. Don't be stand-offish and reserved.

THE CRITICAL AUDIENCE. A critical audience expects you not only to appear on the program but also to say something. It is made up of people qualified with open minds and willingness to learn or be convinced. Your emphasis with such people should be on the adequate, logical, and highly rational defense of your ideas. "To the young men and women of a generation trying to work these grim ingredients into a form that will have meaning and promise and a smidgen of hope, you don't talk platitudes. You talk straight across, and you talk realities, or you favor them by keeping a decent silence."[4]

THE HOSTILE AUDIENCE.   If an audience is likely to be antagonistic to you or your idea, the chances are strong that it is made up of people with confirmed prejudices, biases, and preconvictions. Some people are afflicted with a kind of intellectual blindness and will insist on the validity of their opinions in the face of irrefutable evidence. For such individuals logic and reasoning are of little avail. Your best chance of getting a hearing is to use emotional appeals. Avoid arguments, and don't expect to be 100 percent successful. Let your personality go to work for you, but do not compromise your convictions in order to get a hearing.

11.6   Factors Which Make an Occasion

An occasion is an environmental context or frame of reference in which communication occurs. The factors which operate in such a context affect the success or failure of the transfer of meaning. You need to know how to adapt to all types of conditions.

Physical Conditions

A good physical setting has a direct effect on transmission and reception of meaning, and also a psychological effect on speaker and listeners. If the acoustics of the room throw your voice about so as to produce unfortunate echoes, your effects will be likewise distorted. The temperature, lighting, interior decorating, color schemes, audio-visual equipment should all be adjusted for maximum efficiency. If the hall is large, you will need to adjust the quality and volume of your voice so that all can

[4] *Collier's*, June 10, 1955.

hear. The time of day can also affect your efficiency. It is usually more difficult to get a good audience right after lunch, for example, than it is in the morning. Distracting sounds such as those caused by heating systems should be eliminated if possible.

Mood of the Occasion

It will make a great deal of difference whether the circumstances under which you speak are formal or informal. When Lew Sarett went on lecture tours to read his poetry, he often appeared in the garb of an outdoorsman. This practice helped to create the kind of mood the poet wanted for proper reception of his verses. Many occasions in our day are informal, workshop-type arrangements. Often the speaker remains seated. The style of delivery and employment of language must be adjusted to the nature of the meeting.

Purpose of the Occasion

In the communication classroom, the purpose of an occasion is a matter settled by the instructor and the course of study. The more nearly a real communication event can be simulated the more likely will the effort expended result in acquired skill. Purpose in communication has been thoroughly treated elsewhere in this volume. We should merely remind ourselves here that delivering an after-dinner speech may require entirely different preparation from participation in group discussion, a keynote speech at a convention, or a sermon.

EXERCISES

1. Find examples from your reading of articles and essays adapted to specific types of people, such as college students, professional men and women, average readers, etc. Notice the differences in choice of words, style, sentence length, sentence structure, and types of argument.

2. What, would you say, are the basic assumptions of people who

are most likely to agree or disagree with the following statements.

In the notable reference book, "Who's Who in United States Politics," there is a dedication which ought to be immortalized in stone. Here it is: "To the American Politician . . . frequently abused . . . infrequently praised . . . but the *agree* backbone of the greatest nation on earth." *politicians are important*

And we ought to give him the credit that is his due.

Of course there are crooks and grafters among public officials—entirely too many of them. Too many who accept mink coats and refrigerators and cold, hard cash—but there are grafters and crooks among businessmen, and professional men, too—and among labor leaders,—even among men of the cloth.

> —William Harrison Fetridge, talk published in *Vital Speeches of the Day*, December 1, 1952

Mississippi will not abandon its 48th ranking among the states until it starts treating the Negro as a man instead of a second class citizen. . . .

The automatic inclusion of the tag-word—colored or Ne- *agree* gro—in every story concerning Negroes no matter what the story is, is as ridiculous as doing it also with everyone. How about . . . Harold Lee, Jew, was arrested . . . or James Watson, Polish-American, was charged . . . or Hiram Cavendish, Irish-English with a bit of French, was booked with . . .

> —Editorial in *The Chronicle Star*, Pascagoula, Mississippi, June 23, 1950

We are a deeply religious people whose institutions presuppose a Supreme Being. We have chaplains in congress and in the armed forces. Our coins bear the inscription "In God We *agree* Trust." . . .

Today we enjoy the blessings of freedom of religion in the fullest sense of the word. We also recognize the corresponding duty of not interfering with the rights of worship and freedom of conscience of others. We have learned how contagious the corroding effects of religious intolerance are. And we have learned from the experience in totalitarian countries that when a nation becomes contemptuous of religion and the rights of man, it is not long before all freedom is lost.

—Herbert Brownell, Jr.

A few hardy souls among us somehow get through school and college with barely passing grades in what we believe to be the subject of "English." But what we have achieved is not skill in writing and speaking—we have merely filed away in the bottom drawers of our minds a mass of undigested grammatical rules that are not rules, and obscure Anglo-Latin terms, and half-memorized snatches of passages from a few outmoded and extremely dull books of so-called "classic" literature.

—Frank Colby, *The Practical Handbook of Better English*

When an ad reads 'Earn Big Money at Home with Little or no Work"—Be On Guard. Too many people are misled by false promises of huge earnings to be made by sparetime work in the home.

—William S. Hill, Federal Trade Commission Investigation Bureau

3. Judging from the following sentences appearing in the prefaces of three handbooks of English composition, which one do you think would be most engaging for college students?

This book, then, has been written directly to students, with the idea of making them feel at home with the language, and of helping them to express their ideas in simple, clear, and well organized English.

—L. M. Myers, *Guide to American English*

The emphasis on purpose in this book attempts to give the student a point of view from which he can see his writing problems in perspective.

—James M. McCrimmon, *Writing with a Purpose*

Instead of pleasantly teaching us to drive the linguistic car comfortably, carefully, and skillfully, our schools waste many dreary years trying to turn us into automotive engineers. Small wonder then, . . . that we leave school knowing neither how the car is built nor how to drive it properly; and we spend the rest of our lives battering our poor fenders against the jagged rocks of syntax.

—Frank Colby, *Practical Hand-book of Better English*

4. Compare the language of the two people in the following dialogue. Explain the breakdown of communication between them. What was the nature of their conflict?

"Could I help you?" she asked in a businesslike tone.

"I hope so," I replied in all innocence. "I'm looking for an old-fashioned teddy bear."

"For a child?" she said.

"Well—yes," I confessed.

"I see. A teddy bear."

"Look, Miss, if you don't have teddy bears, just say so, and I'll—"

"Oh, we have—them—all right. Stuffed dogs, too, and cats and elephants and monkeys and lions. If that's the kind of thing you really want. For a child, I mean."

"OK," I sighed. "OK, I give up. I surrender. I'll ask the question you're dying to have me ask you: What is the matter with teddy bears?"

"Well, there's nothing really wrong with them—except that they don't teach anything."

"They don't teach anything! I see. And is this the New Order of Childhood—that a toy has got to educate some child in something? Are we so far along in civilization that a child no longer plays with a toy, he graduates in it?"

"The real function of a toy is to afford the child opportunity to develop coördination and ingenuity. Toys should be tools for learning, not trinkets. The trend now is toward toys which help kiddies adjust."

"Madame, when I was a kiddie I had a teddy bear named Theodore. He was at various stages of his life, white and soft, gray and lumpy, black and soggy—this taught me that love transcends physical characteristics. When I cried I dried my eyes with Theodore; when I was frustrated I chewed on Theodore; when I was dressed up, I combed Theodore until he eventually became bald as a bowling ball—all of which taught me the meaning of companionship. Whatever I ate or drank, Theodore ate and drank too, and so I learned to be unselfish. Because he could neither cry real tears nor walk by himself, I had to imagine things about Theodore, and so I learned the wonderful secret of making believe. I left him on the top of my sandbox slide one stormy night, and when I reached him in the morning, he was wrecked beyond repair. We buried him lovingly in the rock garden and that taught me the difference between being dead in 'that' world, and being alive in 'this' world. I have nothing against education and constructive play methods, but don't you think it's just possible our juvenile delinquency rate keeps rising because we try too early to teach our babies the meaning of words like 'realism'? Now, if you'll be good enough to show me where you have hidden the teddy bears. . . ."

—Martha Harris, "Teddy Bear Is Antidote for World's Woes," *The State Journal* (Lansing, Michigan), December 11, 1955

5. Rewrite the following definition of the purpose of government so that it may be understood by a child in the fifth or sixth grade.

We believe it is within the design and purpose of God that men should be free—free to think, believe and act as they wish, subject only to the equal rights of others. The primary purpose of government is to guarantee that men may so live.

To protect life, liberty and property men organize to prevent murder, spoliation, theft, fraud and injustice of all kinds, and to punish the perpetrators of such wrong-doing, governments are instituted among men.

Human experience clearly has indicated that certain things, such as the conduct of foreign affairs, providing for the common defense, instituting a uniform fiscal system based on money of intrinsic value and safeguarding the public health, can be done more effectively by government. Such things are its functions.

—H. E. Kershner (News columnist)

6. The next time you listen to a lecture, analyze the speaker's attitude toward his audience. What specific techniques does he employ that show he is seriously concerned with making his listeners understand his meaning?

FOR FURTHER READING

Bavelas, Alex, "How to Talk to the Boss," *Harper's Magazine*, July, 1955.

Dale, Edgar, "Clear Only If Known," *The News Letter*, Bureau of Educational Research, Ohio State University, January, 1952.

Fries, C. C., "Differences in Language Practice," *American English Grammar*, New York, 1940.

Greenough, J. B., and Kittredge, G. L., "Learned Words and Popular Words," in *Words and Their Ways in English Speech*, New York, 1901.

Hazlitt, William, "On Familiar Style."

Laird, Donald A., "Taste That Word," *The Rotarian*, January, 1954.

Marckwardt, Albert, "What Is Good English?" *Talks*, January, 1938.

Seldes, Gilbert, "A Nation of Teen-Agers," *The Great Audience*, New York, 1950.

Wilder, Thornton, "Toward an American Language," *Atlantic Monthly*, July, 1952.

Whyte, William H., Jr., "Cooperation—An Opportunity and a Challenge," *Fortune*, November, 1950.

V

ACQUIRE THE SKILLS

12

ACQUIRE PROFICIENCY IN LISTENING

LISTENING MAY BE DEFINED AS HEARING with comprehension. Many people confuse hearing with listening. You might audit an address uttered in a foreign tongue and, while hearing every word, understand and comprehend nothing. You might also hear the words of a language you do understand without comprehending the meaning and intent of the words. Effective listening is an active, not a passive, skill. It requires alertness and coöperation. An acquiescent and disinterested attitude toward the speaker is not enough. An effective listener is one who has developed the ability to attend thoughtfully to spoken discourse, to grasp the meaning intended by the speaker, and to respond critically to the total impact of the talk or address.

Since listening is an instantaneous activity, there can be no backtracking to check the exact phraseology of a passage once uttered. Conscious physical and mental alertness are required. A listener is a partner in the communicative act or experience. He must, therefore, keep his attention focused on what the speaker is saying, not allowing himself to be sidetracked by distractions of any kind.

Concentrated attention, however, is not all that is required. The speaker's message comes to you in the form of words. These words must be structured into ideas in your own mind. The speaker cannot do it for you. A few rare individuals in this world

245

can listen to a speech of extended length and then repeat verbatim the exact words employed by the speaker. But this ability does not necessarily make for effective listening. A good listener hears what a speaker says, comprehends the meaning of the words in context, identifies the central idea of the speech, and evaluates its merit by noting the adequacy or inadequacy of supporting details.

12.1 Requirements for Effective Listening

Maximum efficiency, or what is called optimum listening skill, demands, in addition to hearing capacity, the following essentials:

Sincere Interest in the Ideas Communicated

If you have a real stake, or vested interest, in what is being said, you will listen more attentively than if you have no clearcut motives to command your attention. Imagine yourself in any of the circumstances presented here, and you will understand that interest is probably the most important factor in listening skill.

> You are listening to a radio broadcast of a game in which your college team is vying for a chance at the Rose Bowl.
> You are listening to the winning numbers at a lottery drawing in which you have an entry.
> You are listening to your mother and father discuss plans for your college career.
> You are listening to the manager of a firm, which employs you, discuss company policy about pay raises.
> You are listening to a professor tell a class in which you are enrolled how to review for an examination.

The long and short of the matter is this: interest is a critical factor in effective listening. Lacking interest in a subject, you will do well to find out as much as you can about it before you listen. Knowledge creates interest.

A Definite Purpose for Listening

Effective listening is purposeful activity. You don't listen just to be listening. You must have a purpose which engages your attention and motivates your interest. If we consider the purposes discussed in Chapter 6, it would seem obvious that you listen for one of the following reasons:

To secure information.
To comprehend an idea.
To judge the adequacy of a criticism.
To understand how to perform a task.
To enjoy the experience of listening.
To escape boredom, monotony, and frustration.
To determine the suitability of a proposed course of action.

The nature of a communication event will partially determine your purpose. During a lecture in natural science you will probably listen for facts and ideas which you will want to retain. If a salesman is trying to sell you a set of brushes, you will listen critically to his methods of persuasion. If you are tuned in on a television variety program, you will listen for laughs. Without a definite purpose, your experience in any of these circumstances might prove unsatisfactory.

Undivided Attention to What Is Said

What Professor Ralph Nichols has called "hop-skip-and-jump listening" is like trying to listen to two football games broadcast at the same time over different radio stations. You switch your attention from one station to the other at various intervals and thus stand a good chance of missing important plays of both games. It is sufficiently difficult to keep your attention focused on one thing for any extended length of time. If you find yourself taking little mental excussions during a talk, you may wind up having tuned in on five or six exciting episodes, which the speaker mentioned, but which have little meaning for you because you failed to follow the line of thought that the speaker pursued. Notice what would happen if you were mentally absent when the italicized words, in the following speech at a freshman orientation meeting, were spoken:

> I have observed that good advice is so often conducive to contrary action . . . that I am tempted to resort to reverse English, to reach deep in the bag of personal experience and offer you some of the choicest bad advice that can be dished out in the few moments at my disposal. . . . About your courses of study. A few of you, possibly, have come here for the purpose of study. You are probably stuck with your program for the first semester and can't shift. You're probably saddled with a few tough courses. My earnest counsel is this. Just as soon as you get the chance hereafter, pick nothing but snap courses. . . . Discover them and seize upon them. . . . The less wear and tear on the brains now, the better. You must conserve what precious little you have. . . .[1]

You must take an active part at every stage of oral communication in which you are involved, if you hope to make the experience worth your time and effort.

Emotional Stability

If you bring a parcel of worries, troubles, aggravations, or emotional disturbances of any kind to a listening exercise, you may find it almost impossible to pay attention to the speaker. Also a speaker may get you in a nasty mood for listening by the mere mention of something that sets off a chain of distracting emotional responses. Psychological blocks to effective listening are preconditioned emotional sets which make you retreat from hearing about things associated with unpleasantness. You can actually become psychologically deaf to certain words and phrases. Even if you hear the words, your mind will refuse

[1] Harold O. Voorhis, "Advice to Freshmen," Remarks, freshman orientation meeting, Colgate University, September 18, 1953.

to remember them or their significance. If you can identify the words that thus bother you and try to counteract their pernicious effects by analyzing your own reactions, it may be that you can open your ears to topics to which your mind has hitherto been closed.

An Open Attitude

If your mind is completely made up about a topic before it is discussed, you will have less capacity to listen than if your mind is open and you want to learn. An individual with a closed mind and a negative attitude will spend his time, during a talk or lecture, rationalizing his own beliefs, criticizing the speaker's manner, or creating disturbances with other members of the audience. If you become offended because of something a speaker says that contradicts your preconvictions, you may find yourself devising a scathing renunciation of the speaker and his idea rather than properly evaluating what he says.

Ability to Analyze Discourse into Its Basic Elements

This entails the ability to recognize patterns of organization, of arrangement, of support, of clarification, and of defense. In other words, an effective listener is able to:

Distinguish between central ideas and supporting examples.
Recognize methods of argument both logical and psychological.
Recognize controlling and ulterior purposes of a speaker.
Recognize basic patterns of development.
Recognize various arrangements of details.
Recognize cues to meaning offered by speaker's vocal quality and physical activity.
Recognize meanings of words in new and unfamiliar contexts.

Ability to Evaluate Critically

To evaluate critically means to exercise sound judgment. It does not mean to oppose, to dispute, to disagree. If you have learned the three principal standards of evaluation—individual, intrinsic, and extrinsic—you will apply one or more of them to spoken discourse. Proper evaluation of spoken language assumes:

> Comprehension of what is said.
> Recognition of speaker's purposes.
> Ability to distinguish between statements of fact and of opinion.
> Ability to apply standards of criticism.

Much of what you listen to must be evaluated in terms of your own purposes. Such questions as these should act as guides:

Are the ideas useful for the purposes you have in mind?
Are the statements and ideas supported by personal experience or documentary evidence?
Is the speaker an authority on the subject?
Is the speaker unbiased and open-minded about the subject?
Is the subject one that can be properly developed by the method employed?
Are the details and examples sufficient in number to support the thesis?
Are the examples taken from the most recently discovered facts about the subject?
Are the facts verifiable, either by experience or by the findings of expert authority?
Are the supporting details such as to agree with what people know to be true by experience?
Are the words employed sufficiently exact, precise, and well defined as to leave no question about the intended meaning?
Are any techniques employed with obvious intent to deceive or mislead?

12.2   Barriers to Effective Listening

In Chapter 1 we spoke of disturbances, or "noise," which interferes with successful communication. Particular barriers which inhibit one's ability to listen effectively include the following:

Lack of Rapport Between Speaker and Audience

Lack of mutual respect, of coöperation, of common ground, between speaker and audience can cripple communication. Variance in social status, prestige, attitudes, interests, purposes, and experiences between speaker and audience may cause breakdown in understanding.

Inadequate Physical Conditions

Effective listening takes place in settings conducive to reception of ideas. Physical and psychological distractions may lure your mind away from the speaker and his subject: disturbing noises either in the audience or outside the room or building, glaring or depressing color schemes used in interior decoration, distance of listener from speaker, inadequacy of audio-visual equipment, excessively warm or cold temperatures, and offensive odors.

Physical condition of the listener also plays a part in effective listening. If you are feeling fatigue, bodily pain, or physical discomfort, you may miss much of what the speaker says. The time of day may make a great deal of difference in your receptivity. In an overheated room, for example, right after eating a hearty meal, you may find it almost impossible to keep awake.

Nonconducive Factors in the Occasion

How much you have to pay to get into the lecture hall may affect your ability to listen to what is said. If you happen to be a member of a captured audience and you merely submit to what you consider an imposition on your time, you may pose as an attentive listener but pay little if any real attention to the speaker's remarks.

Voluntary listening is almost always more effective than involuntary listening. Disciplined, coerced, and captured audiences are often hostile audiences. If you prejudge an occasion to be a very boring, dull, and repressing affair, the chances are good that you won't benefit much by attending—unless, of course, something happens to alter your attitude.

Inappropriate Language

If the language of the speaker is not adapted in any way to his audience, he may be wasting his time and breath. Several types of verbal misbehavior on the part of a speaker may isolate him from his audience:

a. The speaker may be a muddled thinker and unable to present his ideas in clear-cut, precise, comprehensible diction.

b. The speaker may be so accustomed to using professional jargon and "two-hundred-dollar words" that he imagines his thought cannot be translated into simpler terms.

c. The speaker may employ high-powered diction in order to impress the audience with his own importance or the importance of his subject.

d. The speaker may be deliberately trying to conceal his own ignorance of the subject, his lack of preparation, or his ulterior motives in speaking.

e. The speaker may insult the audience by "talking down" to them from a self-assumed pedestal.

f. The audience may be totally unequipped and unprepared to comprehend the ideas conveyed.

Listener's Lack of Perspective

We have established the fact that words are not ideas and that they have to be constructed into ideas by creative activity of listeners. To the extent that this is not accomplished communication fails. Unsatisfactory responses to verbal symbols are of two kinds: inadequate structure of ideas and irresponsible critical judgments.

Listeners who memorize verbatim concrete details of a speech, who depend solely on rote learning, may not understand at all the significance of the idea proposed or see how it can be applied in new and unique circumstances. The inability to comprehend part-whole relationships because of undue attention to parts is referred to as "the inability to see the forest for the trees." Listeners of this class may take voluminous notes on a lecture but at the same time be unable to make head or tail of the details they jot down.

Oversimplification of spoken discourse is another type of inadequate response. Listeners who suffer from this malady satisfy themselves with "a bird's-eye view of everything and a close-up of nothing." They are the kind of people who read only the headlines of a newspaper.

Some listeners are perpetually lost in a verbal fog. Because of inexperience, inadequate vocabulary, or bizarre word associations, they get a vague and hazy notion of communicated content but are unable to identify the speaker's conviction or the method by which it is developed.

The most hopeless of listeners are those who distort or misinterpret the speaker's words. They are simply incapable of understanding what is going on.

Irresponsible critical judgments, characteristic of individuals with inflexible standards of appraisal or highly subjective linguistic habits, include: impressionistic responses in which the listener's thought crowds out the speaker's idea; snap judgments; hasty generalizations; false identifications or transfers of meaning; reliance on rumor; wishful thinking; evaluation of factors unrelated to the idea presented; inflexible resistance to or blind acceptance of the speaker's idea.

12.3   Specific Types of Listening

Purposeful listening, like any other skill in communication, may be any one of the following types:

a. Informative: Listening for information, facts, directions, specific details. Emphasis is on reception.
b. Creative: Listening for ideas and problem solutions. Emphasis is on comprehension.

c. Critical: Listening in order to evaluate the validity and usefulness of a speaker's ideas and judgments. Emphasis is on sound reasoning.

d. Appreciative: Listening for pleasure and entertainment, for escape or relaxation. Emphasis is on appreciation.

Psychologists speak of other kinds of listening: unconscious listening, automatic listening, and listening with the "third ear" —a kind of extrasensory perception—but, since these types are not purposeful in a communicative sense, they are not discussed here.

Listening to Conversation

Conversation is the most common, the most intimate, the most promiscuous, the most interactive, and the most spontaneous form of listening experience we engage in. Conversation is a type of communication that most nearly accomplishes a fusion of two minds. Conversation creates conditions which guarantee its success: common ground, mutual respect, feedback, participation. It is self-initiating, self-adjustive, self-corrective, and self-controlled. Listening to conversation may satisfy a number of different purposes:

> To share the thoughts, feelings, and sensations of others.
> To overcome loneliness and depression.
> To test the mental acuity of another person: to act as a sounding board for his ideas.
> To submit to the wishes and desires of others.
> To flatter someone who wants to talk.
> To bring into focus ideas which are dormant in one's own mind.
> To echo the emotional feelings of another.
> To conform to another's wishes.
> To find flaws in another's argument.
> To receive information.
> To satisfy a craving for rumor, gossip, and slander.

It should be quite obvious that no one set of rules could insure listening effectiveness in all conversational events. Here, as with all other forms of communication, effectiveness is relative. There are, however, a few personality traits that seem appropriate for all varieties of conversation:

Open mind and objective attitude.
Sincere interest in people.
Social grace and diplomacy.
Responsiveness to suggestion.
Respect for others.
Social sensitivity and altruism.
Self-confidence.
Sense of humor.
Freedom of expression.
Spontaneity.

Listening to Classroom Lectures

Most classroom listening is one of two varieties: listening to instructions or directions for performing a given task or assignment; listening to ideas and supporting facts to be retained.

The following suggestions should aid you in comprehending the lecture content:

a. Identify the instructor's purpose. Ascertain what the instructor expects of you. Are you to be held accountable for the content of the lecture? Are you expected to understand main ideas and principles or to retain specific facts? How does the material to be presented fit into the overall organization of the course? If you can answer these questions you have established a purpose for listening. Without a purpose of your own the experience will profit you little.

b. Detect the main idea of the lecture as quickly as possible. Watch for significant cues in what the instructor says. Write down the central thesis to be supported.

c. Identify the pattern of organization used by the instructor.

In the case of directions, the pattern is very likely to be a series of parallel statements, such as the statements made right here in this section. If a problem is to be solved, or a hypothesis to be tested, or a thesis to be supported, watch for the organization of evidence: comparison and contrast, analogy, use of authority, examples, etc. Also detect the arrangement of details.

d. Analyze the content of the lecture. This means simply to break up the whole into recognizable parts that will, when put together, make a unified concept. Differentiate between introduction, body, and conclusion. Differentiate between main points and supporting details. Differentiate types of evidence as verifiable facts or personal judgments.

e. Ask questions if you fail to understand what the instructor is trying to accomplish. Be sure you understand the precise meaning of the words employed. Require the instructor to make the presentation clear to you. Make a definite attempt to clarify meanings in your own thinking and then check to determine how successful you have been.

f. Think for yourself. Listening is an active, not a passive, skill. Resist the idea that you are soaking up information. Given the facts and the clues, construct the ideas for yourself. Don't get the notion that they are prefabricated for you and all you have to do is accept them and put them on ice.

g. Take notes on what is said. There is no right or wrong way to do this. You should not take notes just for the sake of taking them, but as a means of retaining the ideas, directions, and information concerned. No one system of notetaking will work for all occasions. It is important that whatever you do make sense to you. Requiring yourself to take notes may act as a spur to keep your attention focused on what the instructor is saying. A good set of notes may also make it possible to reconstruct ideas at a later date when you might otherwise have forgotten them. Some lectures will lend themselves to an outline; others to a brief synopsis of the main idea.

Listening to Public Lectures

Assuming that you are an active, dynamic, purposeful, critical, and coöperative listener, the following suggestions should aid you in comprehending the meaning and intent of most public speeches, either formal or informal:

a. Make adequate physical preparation for listening. Control disturbing factors in the occasion. Sit where you can hear and see what is going on. Refuse to carry on a secondary communication with those about you. Assume a comfortable but alert posture.

b. Make adequate mental preparation for listening. Find out in advance what others have said on this subject so as to have some basis of comparison. Develop an interest in the subject by reading or talking with others. Come to the lecture with an open mind.

c. Make adequate psychological preparation for listening. Get rid of emotional tension, worry, and frustration. Leave your troubles at the door. Develop a positive attitude toward the speaker and his message. Control your prejudices and biases regarding the speaker, subject, and occasion.

d. Be ready to listen when the speaker starts talking. Don't miss the opening remarks. They may be clues to the entire talk. If you are engaged in conversation with a friend, cut it off.

e. Identify the central idea of the speech.

f. Determine the speaker's real as well as his ulterior purposes.

g. Identify the pattern of organization used by the speaker.

h. See the relationships of parts to the central idea.

i. Evaluate the speaker's statements.

j. Evaluate the speaker's total effectiveness.

k. Weigh and consider the arguments and evidence presented.

l. Determine what the speaker wants you to do.

m. Decide what use you can make of what you have heard.

EVALUATION CHART FOR LISTENERS

Speaker: .... Listener: ....

Subject: ....

Speaker's purpose: ....

Central idea: ....

I. Introduction: Check devices employed.

.......Humor   ....Statement of purpose
.......Announcement of topic   ....Recognition of sources
.......Significance of subject   ....Example of main idea
.......Definition of terms   ....Statement of method
.......Other

Evaluation: Check or circle appropriate
number: Poor Fair Good
Audience attitude established   1 2 3 4 5 6 7 8 9 0
Clarification of purpose   1 2 3 4 5 6 7 8 9 0

II. Body of Talk. Form of organization and support: ....
                   Types of reasoning: ....

Evaluation of effectiveness: 1 2 3 4 5 6 7 8 9 0

III. Conclusion: Check appropriate blanks:

.......Abrupt ending   ....Appeal to audience
.......Smooth ending   ....Summary of points
.......Restatement of idea   established
.......Example of idea   ....Admonition and advice
                                  ....Other

Evaluation of effectiveness: 1 2 3 4 5 6 7 8 9 0

Listening in Group Discussion

Group discussion is a form of coöperative problem solving.
If you are a member of a panel, forum, committee, or other
group which is organized with the idea of arriving at mutually

agreeable solutions to a common problem, you will need to know how to listen as well as to speak. Effective listening is just as important to successful discussion as is effective speaking. The outcome of discussion depends on the willingness of all members to objectify their personal attitudes and opinions and to focus on a most appropriate solution. Many people are incapable of crediting any ideas except their own. Here are some pertinent suggestions for listening in group discussion:

a. Listen to other members of the group. Don't monopolize the discussion yourself. While another member is talking, pay attention to what he is saying.

b. When you answer or challenge another's contribution, be sure you heard rightly what he said. Don't put words in his mouth.

c. Listen actively, not passively. Don't miss the significance of what other members are saying. You dare not get lost in a verbal shuffle.

d. Listen to learn and understand, not to criticize; but do not pass up irrelevancies, half-truths, unsound reasons without objection.

e. Listen to everything that is said so you can properly appraise its relative significance.

f. If you cannot understand one or more of the points proposed, call for clarification.

g. Meet the other speakers on their own ground. Don't isolate yourself from the group because of fixed attitudes, biases, and unwillingness to alter previous opinions. Give the other speakers the same break you demand for yourself.

h. Listen systematically. Keep close track of the progress of the discussion so that whatever contributions you make will properly fit into the total pattern.

i. Listen carefully to questions directed to you. Answer them honestly, but do not allow yourself to be tricked into saying something you don't mean. Questions may be intended to confuse you.

EVALUATION FORM FOR GROUP DISCUSSION

(Circle appropriate numbers to register your judgment of the effectiveness of the discussion)

Subject: ....

Listener: ....

Defined problem: ....

	Poor	Fair	Good
Adequacy of problem definition:	1 2 3	4 5 6	7 8 9 0
Clarification and definition of terms:	1 2 3	4 5 6	7 8 9 0
Group rapport or atmosphere:	1 2 3	4 5 6	7 8 9 0
Quality of leadership:	1 2 3	4 5 6	7 8 9 0
Spontaneity of participation:	1 2 3	4 5 6	7 8 9 0
Quality of argument:	1 2 3	4 5 6	7 8 9 0
Preparation of members:	1 2 3	4 5 6	7 8 9 0
Resolution of conflict between members:	1 2 3	4 5 6	7 8 9 0
Suitability of solution:	1 2 3	4 5 6	7 8 9 0
Handling of audience questions:	1 2 3	4 5 6	7 8 9 0

Check appropriate items below:

.... Some members monopolized the time.

.... Arguments were inconsistent.

.... Members became deadlocked in solution.

.... Leader was unable to control discussion.

.... Members were unable to think objectively.

.... Language was too vague or technical.

.... Discussion became a debate or bull session.

.... Solution seems unrealistic, impractical, or inconsistent with evidence.

.... Presentation seemed artificial.

.... Audience was not interested.

Listening and Mass Media of Communication

The audio-visual media of mass communication are radio, television, and motion pictures. The nature of the public services performed vary somewhat from medium to medium, but they may be generalized as follows: entertainment and amusement; information and education; announcements and messages of public interest; information about goods and services.

Like all the instruments and agencies of communication, the audio-visual media have great potentialities either for the good of society or for the exploitation of society. We must understand that the particular effects produced depend on numerous factors operating in a given situation among particular people. These factors include:

The circumstances under which a given communication is transmitted.

The circumstances under which the communication is received.

The purposes of the transmitter.

The purposes of the receiver.

The nature and character of the presentation or message.

The level of comprehension and appreciation of the receiver.

The emotional state, expectations, and social status of the receiver.

The values, tastes, and critical standards of the receiver.

The nature of social regulations and codes of censorship.

The fact that programs must be adjusted to audiences consisting of all varieties of listeners and viewers imposes great restrictions on the producer. Such restrictions have unfortunate effects on programming, evident in the use of stereotypes, sentimental plots, crude humor, and popular appeals. The basic assumption among people who control the mass media is that all people are essentially the same: that they have a collectivistic mentality.

A great deal of social research is carried on consistently in attempts to find out what the public taste will tolerate. How revealing the research is can only be estimated, but advertisers are always trying to find a workable formula that will ring the cash register. Albert E. Sindlinger, for example, working for Dr. Gallup of the Gallup Poll, was able by careful surveys of moviegoers to predict the gross receipts of any motion picture being produced in Hollywood. Mechanical devices have been devised to determine the language level of radio, television, and movie viewers and listeners; their tastes, values, interests, morals; and anything that will supply clues to listening behavior. Leo C. Rosten, arguing that Hollywood does not create its sterotypes out of the blue, said, "The movie makers are in many ways compelled to feed a popular diet to a public which is in firm possession of deplorable tastes—tastes derived from sources far older, deeper, and more potent than Hollywood."

George A. Miller has listed four conditions which determine the success of mass media. Mass media of communication succeed, he says: (a) if they urge people to do what the people already wanted to do; (b) if, as in the case of advertisements, they try to direct into a particular channel action that people were sure to take in some form or other anyhow; (c) if they are followed up by personal contacts and discussions held face to face; (d) if all channels are under the complete control of the propagandist and no counterarguments are ever presented in any media.

EVALUATION OF A RADIO, TELEVISION, OR MOTION-PICTURE PROGRAM

1. Purpose:
   Entertainment: Is the apparent purpose to supply relaxation and escape?
   Information: Is the apparent purpose to supply information and facts?
   Propaganda: Is the apparent purpose to influence or establish attitudes and values?
2. Audience: Determine the characteristics of the audience to which the program is directed.

Age and maturity	Education
Intellectual capacity	Social status
Artistic tastes	Economic status
Value system	Religion
Basic interests	Moral standards

3. Social responsibility:
   To what extent does the program foster, support, and create atti-

tudes, values, and convictions in the best interests of society? How? To what extent does the program try to eliminate class, group, and racial tension and contribute to the liberation of men's minds? To what extent does the program focus attention on important problems, issues, conflicts concerned with men's relation to society?

4. Popularity rating:

   How popular is this program with the public? Why? How long has the program been successful?

5. Critical estimate:

   What awards has the program won from outside agencies? What do the critics have to say of the program? What standards of judgment were employed?

6. Artistic value:

   Is the program adapted from a book or magazine story? To what extent has the author's version been changed? To what extent are you allowed to think for yourself and draw your own conclusions? Is there a consistent tone and dominant impression in the story?

7. Characterization:

   Do the characters conform to standardized types and conventional stereotypes? What stereotypes can you identify? What emotional appeals are utilized?

8. Realism:

   Does the program focus on important realities of living? Is the action characteristic of human beings, or is it exaggerated, exceptional, and far-fetched? Is the setting and atmosphere historically accurate? To what extent does the program document and dramatize life without falsifying it?

Evaluating Audio-Visual Advertising Propaganda

1. Method of attraction:

   What specific devices are employed to attract your attention?

Animation	Human interest
Novelty	Demonstration
Sound effects	Entertainment, burlesque,
Size	imitations
Motion	Curiosity

2. Dramatic situation:
   What specific dramatic incidents are depicted in which you can identify yourself?

   Eating or drinking
   Dressing and toilet preparation
   Interview

3. Associations:
   What devices are employed to associate a product with something you respect or admire?

   Prestige   Age and uniqueness
   Social status   Quality
   Belongingness   Health
   Popularity   Success
   Comfort and safety

4. Language:
   What language devices are employed to influence your thinking?

   Superlative statements   Equivocal words
   Repetitions   Vocal quality
   Pseudo-technical Jargon   Musical devices
   Puns, play on words   Casual style
   Rhymes and Jingles   Slogans
   Emotionally toned words

5. Evidence:
   What type of evidence is offered in support of assertions?

   Unsupported statements   Use of analogy
   Before and after comparisons Testimony and authority
   Either-or comparisons   Cause and effect
   Pseudo-scientific evidence   Statistical proof
   Direct demonstration   "Yes" technique

6. Special appeals:
   What direct appeals are made to your personal needs, motives, desires, or emotions?
   Basic physical needs—appetite, taste, sex, cleanliness, health, play
   Social needs or motives—wealth, independence, popularity, domi-

nation, submission, sociability, hospitality, conformity, distinction

Prestige and success factors—success, power, beauty, rivalry

Psychological needs—possession, comfort, fear, avoidance

Plain folks appeal

Band-wagon appeal—belongingness

7. The Bait:

What lure or come-on is offered to promote action on your part?

Bargain price	Something free
Special offer	Prizes for children
Limited supply	Gift offer
Something new	

EXERCISES

1. Listen to a lecture and make notes on the speaker's techniques by answering the following questions:

   a. What specific devices did the speaker employ to make contact with his audience? Did he make his listeners feel that his remarks were intended for them personally?

   b. What specific devices did the speaker employ to direct attention to the central idea he hoped to communicate?

   c. How many phases or subdivisions of this central idea did he discuss?

   d. What types of evidence did he employ to establish the validity of his claims?

   e. To what extent did he try to influence your thinking by appealing to your emotions?

   f. Could you detect any unethical verbal tricks by which he attempted to influence your thinking?

   g. To what extent was he able to engage the undivided attention of his listeners? Can you account for any breakdown which may have occurred in communication between the speaker and the audience?

   h. Was his language perfectly clear to you?

2. Take notes on a lecture or speech which you attend. Deliver

orally a brief summary of the speech, taking care not to leave out any of the main points made by the speaker.

3. Take notes on an assigned radio or television speech. Then write a brief evaluation of the author's ideas and his method of supporting them.

4. Test your ability to listen for information. Your instructor will read a passage from a current magazine—*Time, Newsweek,* or the *Reporter*—while you pay close attention to reported facts and details. Take no notes, but immediately afterward write a brief summary of the passage, stressing the items you consider most important.

5. While listening to the next round of class speeches, evaluate the individual speakers on the form provided in this chapter.

6. Write a paragraph criticizing the speech techniques of one of your classmates. Point out specific things that make you like his personality.

7. Listen to class speeches paying special attention to methods of slanting. Tell whether you think the devices you noted were used effectively or ineffectively.

8. Listen carefully to a group discussion in which you participate. What evidence do you find that members of the group are not really listening to or comprehending the ideas of others? Do you feel that the participants really understand each other any better at the end of the discussion than they did at the beginning?

9. Listen to a radio or television broadcast of a political speech and determine what essential values of the American way of life the speaker made use of in trying to influence the opinions of his listeners: the sanctity of the home, the right to personal opinion, etc.

10. Listen to a commercial advertisement on radio or television and analyze it by answering the following questions:
    a. What precisely are you expected to do as a result of hearing the advertisement?
    b. Can the claims presented be verified by personal experience?
    c. What specific techniques are employed to engage your attention, stimulate your interest, establish your belief, influence your judgment, and direct your action?

d. What verbal tricks are you able to identify, such as undefined words, unsupported statements, false alternatives, and misleading analogies?

FOR FURTHER READING

David, Harry, "Are You a Good Listener?" *The Pathfinder*, February 4, 1953.

Fulton, A. R., "It's Different from the Book," *Theatre Arts*, March, 1953.

Hummel, William, and Huntress, Keith, "The Media of Propaganda," from *The Analysis of Propaganda*, New York, 1949.

Hunt, Everett, "Modern Propaganda," *Quarterly Journal of Speech*, April, 1951.

Johnson, Wendell, "Do You Know How to Listen?" *ETC.*, Autumn, 1949.

Johnson, Wendell, *Your Most Enchanted Listener*, New York, 1956.

Klein, Alexander, "The Challenge of Mass Media: Movies, Radio, Television," *Yale Review*, Summer, 1950.

Kronenberger, Louis, "TV: A Prospectus," from *Company Manners*, New York, 1954.

Krutch, Joseph Wood, "What We Say," *The American Scholar*, Summer, 1955.

Lynes, Russell, *The Tastemakers*, New York, 1954.

McLuhan, Marshall, "Sight, Sound, and the Fury," *Commonweal*, April 9, 1954.

Mead, Margaret, "Sex and Censorship in Contemporary Society" in *New World Writing III*, issued May, 1953, by the New American Library of World Literature, Inc., New York.

Nichols, Ralph, and Stevens, Leonard A., "You Don't Know How to Listen," *Collier's*, July 25, 1953.

Overstreet, Harry A., "What We Hear," from *The Mature Mind*, New York, 1949.

Powdermaker, Hortense, *Hollywood the Dream Factory*, New York, 1950.

Rosten, Leo, *The Long Arm of Hollywood*, New York, 1941.

Schulberg, Budd, "Movies in America: After Fifty Years," *Atlantic Monthly*, November, 1947.

Seldes, Gilbert, *The Great Audience*, New York, 1950.

Seldes, Gilbert, "Radio, TV, and the Common Man," in *Is the Common Man Too Common*, edited by Joseph Wood Krutch, et al., Norman, Okla., 1954.

13

ACQUIRE PROFICIENCY IN READING

CONSERVATIVE ESTIMATES SHOW THAT during four years of college an average student will read above thirty million words. Faced with such an assignment, you should try to make the task as simple and time conserving as possible. Several reasons may be advanced to urge the importance of reading in the college curriculum:

a. Many students have not acquired the simple, basic, fundamental skills necessary for efficient reading.

b. Many students are unfamiliar with the areas of thought in which college reading is required.

c. Many students have insufficient vocabularies to cope with the content of college texts.

d. Many students have acquired habits of reading that hamper both speed and comprehension.

e. Many students have not learned how to evaluate the content of reading matter.

13.1 Diagnosis of Difficulties

Your first move in an attempt to improve your present reading habits is to ascertain what mistakes you now make. Answer the following questions honestly:

a. Do you read average subject matter at a rate slower than 200 words a minute?

b. Do you read one word at a time, stopping to ascertain its meaning before going on?

c. Do you often go back and reread words or phrases which you think you may have missed?

d. Do you move your head from left to right as you scan a printed page?

e. Do you move your lips to form the words you read?

f. Do you imagine you hear the words as you read silently?

g. Do you religiously fix your attention on every single word in a line of print?

h. Do you follow a line of printed matter with your finger while reading?

i. Do you stumble over difficult words without bothering to ascertain their meaning?

j. Does your mind wander to other matters while you are "engaged" in reading?

k. Do you avoid making pencil notations in a book you are reading?

l. Do you read all kinds of material—fiction, newspapers, textbooks—at the same rate?

m. Do you ignore clues to an author's meaning: chapters, titles, headlines, paragraph headings, footnotes, charts, diagrams, stylistic devices?

n. Do you read to absorb ideas and meanings without questioning their validity or usefulness?

o. Are you unable to explain in your own words the gist of meaning from reading matter?

p. Are you unable to determine the author's central idea in a passage?

If your answer is "yes" to any of these questions, you have room for improvement. The purpose of this chapter is to help you become an efficient reader.

13.2   The Dynamics of Effective Reading

To understand all of the factors that make for successful reading, it is profitable to see a particular reading exercise in total perspective. The following questions are designed to help you accomplish this:

a. What are you reading? How you will approach a given exercise in reading will depend a great deal on the nature of the reading matter. You can't expect to read a chemistry laboratory manual in the same way you read the newspaper. What you need to do initially is discover the type of discourse you are faced with. Find out if the assigned passage is a report, a critical evaluation, a problem solution, a satirical essay, a set of directions, a humorous sketch, or a persuasive appeal. When you have discovered this you have recognized the author's purpose.

Now discover the author's central idea. Get a quick overall view of the entire passage. Don't allow yourself to get lost in an undergrowth of minute details. If you get the main idea to start with, the details will fit into place as you move along. Keep the thesis, or central idea, in your mind all during the reading to aid you in comprehending the supporting material and interpreting the author's meaning. Don't be afraid to mark the place in your book where the thesis is stated.

b. What are the conditions and circumstances under which you are reading? You can't expect to keep your attention focused on a reading passage if the physical and emotional setting is all wrong. Reading under controlled laboratory conditions or in a study hall is usually more satisfactory than reading in a noisy dormitory room. If you want to get the most from a given assignment find a place most conducive to concentration. Don't allow distractions to lead your mind astray. Don't try to read when you are physically too tired to focus your attention on what you are doing. Don't allow worry, emotional tension, and social frustration to invade your thoughts while reading. Budget your activities so you can spend the necessary time on a given assignment.

c. What are your personal qualifications for reading the assigned passage? Two kinds of abilities are essential for maximum reading skill: the ability to comprehend what you read and the ability to evaluate what you read.

(1) In order to increase comprehension: Determine the author's purpose. (See Chapter 6.) Consider the entire verbal context in which an idea is placed (see pp. 69–70); consider the context of situation in which meaning is defined (see pp. 70–71); consider specific clues to the author's meaning—title, major headings, graphs and art work, transition markers, footnotes (see pp. 71–72). Consider the author's use of words. This is largely a matter of comprehending difficult or unusual language and of possessing an adequate vocabulary. Consider patterns of organization, support, and defense of ideas. (See Chapters 7 and 8.)

(2) In order to evaluate critically: Determine the author's qualifications for writing on the assigned topic. Recognize the author's characteristic style, tone, and mood. Read between the lines for possible hidden or covert meanings. Recognize the author's ulterior purposes or vested interests if any. Recognize verbal dishonesty and propagandistic devices. Recognize fallacies of language and logic. Recognize your own emotional blind spots. (See Chapter 2.)

d. How efficiently do you read? Efficiency is a matter of reading mechanics. The faster you can read without loss of comprehension and sound judgment, the more will be your intake. An average college student should be able to read average subject matter at 250 words a minute. Slow readers get through 165–200 words. Fast readers may exceed 375 words a minute. With easy materials such as short stories or fiction rates go up to 600 words per minute. Efficiency demands that you make the best use of your time. Follow these suggestions:

(1) Control your eyespan. Reading whole phrases or clauses at a single fixation of the eyes on a page is much more economical of time than focusing attention on single words. It also aids comprehension. Try reading the following passage pausing at each slant line.

Now, / in / the / dog / days / of / summer / when / pavements / buckle / and / cities / become / ovens, / let / us / think / of / cool / things / of / seascapes / and / ice-cold / watermelons, / of / polar / bears / and / tall / green / trees. / (Editorial in *Collier's*, August 19, 1955)

Now try reading the same passage, pausing at the slant lines as indicated here. Read each group of words at a single glance.

Now, / in the dog days / of summer / when pavements buckle / and cities become ovens, / let us think / of cool things / of seascapes / and ice-cold watermelons, / of polar bears / and tall green trees. /

(2) Separate the context into thought units, such as:
Subject—predicate—complement: A twenty-year-old youth / has just killed / a policeman. /
Subject—predicate: Fast readers / are good readers. /
Subject—modifier—predicate—modifier: A boy of thirteen / is a problem / at home and at school. /
Who—what—when—where—how—why: The other day / an Army general / asked me bluntly / what I thought was wrong / with us Americans. / In a day or so / Claudia had the yard / looking neat and clean / without a weed in sight. /

(3) Read a whole group of words without moving eyes, lips, or head. Seal your lips. Lock your head between your hands. Don't go back and reread what you have read. Keep going. Don't follow the lines with a finger or pencil. Don't pronounce the words in your mind. Picture them.

(4) Pace yourself on easy materials like fiction or news stories. Keep track of your rate and gradually increase the difficulty of the material. Don't expect to read all types of reading matter at the same rate of speed.

(5) Try skimming a passage hurriedly, looking only for key words and phrases, and see how well you can comprehend the meaning without fixing on every word.

e. What is your purpose in reading? All reading should be purposeful, even if only to kill time. Whatever reason you have for reading a particular book, essay, article, or newspaper will determine how you will go about it. If you are reading want ads in order to find out where you can get a job, you will certainly skip a lot of details in your perusal. Your focus on the sport page may be much different. Reviewing for examinations suggests a different type of concentration from an initial reading of an assigned chapter. Reading a set of directions which you must follow to achieve a goal is much different from reading to pass the time.

13.3   Reading for Understanding

There are several ways of attacking an assignment for a college course of study: the whole-part-whole method, the section by section method, and the analytical method. The most suitable method to follow will depend on the nature of the assignment.

The Whole-Part-Whole Method

This method of reading contains three principal stages: (a) a bird's-eye view of the whole assignment; (b) a close-up inspection of parts, sections, or divisions; and (c) a reassembling of the parts into an integrated whole. These stages coincide with the three stages of perception introduced on p. 23. Since the method follows exactly the process of mental activity in the search for meaning, it offers excellent opportunities for successful study. It should be especially useful in courses in the humanities, literature, psychology, education, social science, and to some extent in the natural and physical sciences. Follow these simple directions:

ONCE OVER LIGHTLY.   Read for main ideas, author's purpose, methods of development, and logical divisions. Read rapidly, skimming details and minutiae. Mark places in the text which you think deserve close scrutiny. Pay special attention to introduction and conclusion, title, and topic headings.

CAREFUL READING.   Note the sequence of ideas, methods of support, specific details, and definition of words. Follow the author's thinking step by step. Pay attention to transitional signposts designed to direct you. Notice illustrations, graphs, or whatever is included to clarify the thought. Focus attention on difficult passages. Slight nothing that will furnish a clue to the author's meaning.

REVIEW.   Put every part of the whole assignment into its proper slot or niche. See the author's idea as a unified whole made up of a complex arrangement of parts. Ask yourself these questions: Do I know what the author has established, or proposed? Do I know how his idea is supported? Do I know the significance or applicability of these ideas?

Section-by-Section Method

This method may be called a part-whole method and is especially useful for extremely long assignments that cannot be completed at one sitting. Follow these directions:

DIVISION OF ASSIGNMENT.   Notice the major divisions of the whole assignment and select a number of sections to complete at the first reading. Read each section carefully, as you did in step 2 of the whole-part-whole method.

COVERING WHOLE ASSIGNMENT.   Complete all sections of the assignment in the same manner, making note of the transition between sections or divisions. Keep the logical progression of ideas in mind. Notice how one part prepares you for the next part.

REVIEW.   When you have completed all sections, review the entire passage, as in step 3 of the whole-part-whole method. Make sure that your focus on parts has not obscured your view or understanding of the whole.

The Analytical Method

This method of reading is a magnified form of stage 2 of the whole-part-whole method. The technique, especially appropriate for problem solving, breaks an entity into its essential factors, recognizes the interrelationships of these factors, and fosters insights which yield hypotheses, solutions, or conclusions. This method is especially helpful in mathematics, science courses, and even literature. You might employ it with "whodunit" fiction, if you are interested in playing games with the author. Satire and allegory are especially susceptible to analysis. If your specific purpose in reading is to criticize an argument, or evaluate an opinion, you will probably want to carefully analyze the author's text.

What factors to consider in analysis depends almost solely on the nature of the subject matter, but to some extent on the qualifications of the reader: his sensitivity and understanding of the subject, his purpose in making the analysis, and his level of aspiration.

13.4   Reading for Pleasure and Appreciation

Pleasurable reading appeals to feelings and emotions of readers as well as to intellect. Actually mind and emotion cannot be separated. But, generally speaking, reports, histories, problem solutions, and analyses make a strong appeal to the intellect, whereas poetry, essays, fiction, drama, biography make a strong appeal to the emotions. The essential difference between these two major classes of discourse may be shown by paraphrasing one of Wordsworth's verses:

> A violet by a mossy stone
> Half hidden from the eye!—
> Fair as a star, when only one
> Is shining in the sky.[1]

These lines are beautiful and pleasing. The words are simple, everyday words—certainly not what one might call "poetic words." The beauty and delight which emanate from the lines

[1] Wordsworth, *Lucy: She Dwelt Among the Untrodden Ways.*

are accounted for by the simplicity of expression, the verbal imagery, figures of speech—personification and simile—the rhythm of the lines, and the rhyme scheme. All together they produce, in a sensitive reader, a feeling of emotional pleasure.

Notice, now, how the same thought loses its emotional appeal when translated into prose: A violet, barely visible, beside a weather-beaten rock, attracts my attention because of its singular comeliness.

Every piece of literature has some unique quality about it that makes for enjoyment. It would be unrealistic to contend that all readers enjoy the same characteristics or qualities, just as it would be wrong to insist that one must be able to recognize particular qualities of a literary work in order to enjoy it. Shakespeare designed his plays to appeal to all levels of intelligence and all varieties of taste. Such masterpieces of literature are a source of continual enjoyment. Subtleties of tone, characterization, and conflict come to light after many readings. John Keats has it that "A thing of beauty is a joy forever."

The public taste in literature has been jaded by too much escape literature. The public demand for superficial plots, vulgar language, stereotyped characters, cheap morality, violence, and sentimentality has made "philistines" of otherwise highly qualified writers. A *philistine* is one who sells his artistic birthright for gate receipts and royalties. People whose enjoyment of literature is restricted to naked plots miss some of the greatest pleasures to be derived from reading.

13.5 Reading Newspapers

Of all the mass media of communication, newspapers probably exert the greatest influence on the thinking of the American people. This is because we have learned to depend upon the printed word for "complete and reliable information" about the world, and what takes place in it from day to day. Despite the introduction of radio and television as means of spreading the news, newspaper circulation increased by over a million copies between 1954 and 1955.

Someone has compared the front page of a newspaper to a big window through which one may see many amazing and inspiring things, as well as a few dingy things, which help people to interpret life and to avoid its pitfalls. Norman Cousins has suggested that "newspapers are basic and important not only as a means of satisfying curiosity about what is happening, but as a means of supplying information essential to the making of decisions." "The climate of public opinion," he says, "is inevitably shaped in large part by the mechanism of communication—newspaper, radio, television, magazine, book, or whatever."

In America, there is an important relationship between public opinion and government. Common, ordinary citizens in a democracy theoretically hold a whip hand. It has become a kind of truism that the only way to make democracy work is to make facts available to the people. It is believed that we cannot make sound judgments unless we have an informed and alert public opinion, unless our information is correct. Limiting the people's right to know what is going on is usually equated with tyranny, and freedom of the press is generally considered one of the surest ways of safeguarding the nation against authoritarian rule.

Another popular belief about newspapers, as revealed by William Allen White, is "that the more definitely the business office dominates a newspaper and makes it conspicuously profitable, the less valuable the newspaper is to the community." "Like all simplifications, this one should be distrusted," he warns, "because it implies a connection between dishonesty and prosperity in a newspaper which is not always warranted by the facts." There is some evidence, however, that the newspaper does not fulfill its moral obligation to readers, because of the economic necessity for operating in the black.

It is quite apparent that some newspapers have become primarily media of entertainment rather than of information; that they have largely abandoned their responsibilities to society by catering to readers' desire for escape, sensationalism, and diversion. One writer has affirmed that the average newspaper contains: two pages of comics, one page of Hollywood gossip, another page of society news, three pages of sports, several pages of ads, and a dozen columns intended to cover everything that has happened locally, within the state, within the nation, and within the world in the previous twenty-four hours.

Oswald Spengler, in *The Decline of the West*, several years ago argued that the newspaper *creates* what people believe rather than *reports* what has occurred. "The press," he said, "keeps the waking consciousness of whole peoples and continents under a deafening drum-fire of theses, catch-words, standpoints, scenes, feelings, day by day and year by year, so that every Ego becomes a function of a monstrous intellectual Something." To the extent that this accusation is true, the newspaper requires a much more critical reading than does, let us say, a college textbook, or a novel.

If we can assume that the primary function of a newspaper is to communicate to society what its members do, feel, and think, recognition of various devices employed to manipulate interpretation of the text is of vital importance, especially in a country which is in great measure governed by public opinion.

How Newspapers Show Their Bias

A number of standard journalistic practices, when properly understood, exhibit a newspaper's bias, or subjectivity.

SLANTED HEADLINES. The function of a headline in a news story is to summarize the central idea of the story. If it is more than an impersonal summary—that is, if it interprets or evaluates the content of the story—it tells the reader how to judge the facts presented. People who skim-read a newspaper by glancing at the headlines are likely to get a distorted and manipulated version of the facts. Prefabricated ideas, points of view, attitudes, judgments, convictions are thus supplied to unwary and uncritical readers. The following news story will illustrate:

INDONESIAN HEAD CALM IN CRISIS

Jakarta, Indonesia, Aug. 5 (AP)—President Svekarno returned today from a pilgrimage to Mecca. Despite the two-week-old government crisis, the president said he would vacation until Aug. 15, to rest up from his trip.

The president made no mention of the cabinet crises in a brief statement at the airport. Stopping in New Delhi yesterday, he said he hoped to straighten out the situation "within a week or two after I get home."[2]

The word *calm* in the headline is certainly the editor's own opinion, and may not be at all reflective of how the president actually felt.

Notice the emotionally toned words or unsolicited opinion in the following headlines:

ICE SHOW CUTIES GIVE REDS A WARM AMERICAN RECEPTION

SLIPPING YANKS CAN BLAME SELVES FOR THEIR PLIGHT

POSITION OF STORY IN THE PAPER. Certain positions on the page of a newspaper are psychologically more attractive than other positions. Quite obviously, a story on the front page attracts

2	3	1
6	4	5

[2] *The State Journal* (Lansing, Michigan), August 5, 1955, p. 2, col. 2.

more attention than stories on succeeding pages of the newspaper. In some papers the back page is nearly as attractive as the front page. Page three has priority over page two. The top of a page carries more weight than the bottom. The relative importance of specific positions is roughly indicated by the priority numbers in the diagram. Number 1 is most important; 6 is least important. The make-up of a particular paper determines to some extent the position of greatest importance. The place marked 1 is almost universally reserved, however, for the "biggest" story of the day. The editor helps make a story "big," important, and vital by the mere act of placing it there.

SIZE OF HEADLINES AND LENGTH OF STORY. The relative importance of a given story, in the editor's opinion, can also be indicated by the size of type used in the headline and by the amount of space allotted to the story. Streamer headlines are employed to emphasize the high priority of the stories they summarize. Smaller headlines are reserved for stories of less importance.

The length of a story is adjusted in the same fashion. The following chart shows the varying amounts of space devoted to the story of Shirley Temple's divorce, in four leading newspapers. The stories appeared on December 6, 1949.

Paper	Position	Column Inches
New York Times	Inside page	4
New York Mirror	Page 1	75
Chicago Tribune	Page 1	46
Christian Science Monitor		0

SELECTION OF NEWS STORIES. A newspaper is of necessity selective. It would be quite impossible to report every incident that takes place in the world. What, then, is the basis of selection?

Without a doubt the actual criteria used by most newspapers in selecting stories for publication are somewhat as follows: Will the public read the story? Will the story produce desired responses among readers? Will the story sell newspapers? Will the story promote the vested interests of the newspaper and the advertisers?

Hundreds of dispatches come to the newspaper office daily from the news services—Associated Press, United Press, International News Service—from special correspondents, and from local reporters. Some of the stories must be eliminated, and by the selection of stories an editor can show his bias. Two principal considerations must influence the editor's selection of stories: (a) the avowed function of the paper; (b) the interests, wants, needs of the readers. A family newspaper in a small town will certainly make a different selection from that of a large metropolitan paper. A newspaper representing the voice of labor will not make the same selection as one affiliated with a church organization.

H. A. Overstreet, in *The Mature Mind,* has pointed out that "newspapers have developed what might be called *a vested interest in catastrophe.*" Because people demand a reading fare that includes murder, crime, scandal, and catastrophe, that is what they get. The reader's preoccupation with news of a sensational nature accounts for the omission in many newspapers of important and highly significant news stories. A breakdown of the amount of space devoted to various types of content in some American newspapers reveals that crime, divorce, and disaster stories occupy as much as 35 percent of a total edition.

SELECTION OF FACTS ON WHICH TO BASE A STORY.   Because of space limitations in a newspaper, stories must often be cut down and squeezed in slots much too small to do them justice. Often important phases of a story or pertinent facts are omitted —facts which might, if included, alter radically the reader's interpretation. Lifting quotations from a speech to be reported is particularly dangerous. An editor can quite easily turn the tide of public opinion either for or against a speaker by carefully selecting isolated passages of the speech for publication. An editor can also regulate the balance between pro and con arguments in a story so as to produce the effect he desires.

MANIPULATION OF LANGUAGE. Journalese is a form of jargon that aims to influence reader response without taking credit for the effects produced. Its principal earmarks include: (a) stereotyped phrases: *Latin dancer, Hollywood actress, American G.I., wealthy automobile dealer, unsuspecting victim, unidentified bystander;* (b) clichés: *trail of blood, widespread search, blood-spattered clothing, bond of discussion, temporary relief, lingering death, burst into flame, plunged over an embankment;* (c) loaded words: *Red, bureaucrat, striking beauty, skid row, topflight, juvenile mob, spectacular;* (d) rumor: *reliable sources, official sources, it was reported, witnesses testify, alleged, unknown source, on good authority;* (e) Passive voice or impersonal construction: *criminal charge was filed against* ———, *death has taken two, three men were wounded;* (f) deadwood: "Haled back before the jurist a short time later, Ward was asked if he *had the means to engage* an attorney." "*In the process of the repair work* it was discovered that the floor in one section of the gymnasium had rotted out."

DIRECT EXPRESSION OF BIAS. The editorial page is reserved for direct expression of a newspaper's bias and point of view. Besides the editorials themselves, there are letters from subscribers, cartoons, and syndicated columns—all of which make no bones about the particular stand taken on public affairs, political policy, and interpretation of the news. When editorial space is taken up with idle topics, such as "theories about the cause of Northern Lights," we suspect the editor's lack of firm convictions regarding social and economic rights or the struggle for freedom of enslaved peoples.

SPECIAL APPEALS. A large variety of special devices are employed with intent to lure, capture, and control newspaper readers. Some newspapers use colored paper to attract attention; others put headlines in glaring red type; still others use symbols and emblems, such as the American flag, to testify to their patriotic affiliation. The use of candid photography makes a strong appeal to nonreaders and citizens who haven't time to work out the details reported in fine type. Clifton Fadiman in "The Decline of Attention" listed a number of special devices of journalism used to attract attention and appeal to a large number of readers: "emphasis on timeliness; avoidance of abstract ideas; emphasis on personalities; exploitation of the 'column'; preference of wisecrack to wit; rapid alternation of appeals (known as 'balance,' or something for everybody); idolization of contemporary gods, such as cinema stars, sports heroes, and clean-faced, high-school girl graduates."

Judging the Social Functions of the Press

The American newspaper poses as an instrument by which to enlighten the minds of its readers; improve their social well-being; protect their interests; safeguard their liberties; and promote a form of government in which they can be happy, free, and secure. What better criteria can you ask for judging the character, content, and techniques of any newspaper which makes these claims?

OBJECTIVITY OR IMPARTIALITY.   A standard of objectivity maintains that news stories should be impersonal, non-evaluative, and unslanted. The existence of this standard has led, in this country, to a sharp distinction between news and editorials. The theory is based on the assumption that facts will speak for themselves and would probably be misinterpreted by editorial comment. The theory is criticized by people who maintain that often facts must be interpreted if the true meaning in social contexts is to be clarified.

SOCIAL RESPONSIBILITY.   This standard of legitimate journalism insists that instruments of communication must perform a public service in order to justify their existence. To the extent that a newspaper uses its power for selfish and unworthy purposes it is considered faithless to a high trust.

INDEPENDENCE. What were originally small communication enterprises, home-owned and regionally oriented, have in recent years become swallowed up or incorporated into huge communication empires with almost unlimited power to control public opinion. A good newspaper will exercise freedom from all obligations except that of fidelity to the public interest.

FREEDOM. Freedom of the press is a basic tenet of American democracy. The idea that only a free individual can develop his capacities to the fullest and at the same time benefit society was expressed by John Stuart Mill. Jefferson's version has it that "where the press is free, and every man able to read, all is safe." The ideal is a state of affairs in which the press preserves its own freedom and the freedom of its readers. Monopoly, consolidation, censorship, and suppression are the enemies of democracy and militate against realization of this ideal. Any device that has a tendency to cripple free thought and expression is a restriction of democratic rights.

ACCURACY. The tendency among the large majority of newspaper readers is to believe without question what they see in print. This fact places upon the press a heavy responsibility to maintain high standards of truth, accuracy, and thoroughness. Good faith with the reader has been called "the foundation of all journalism worthy of the name." It is the duty of an editor to make prompt and complete correction of errors which occur in the news.

MORALITY. Freedom of expression should never be construed to mean freedom to exploit the reader of the news. Certain moral standards must be maintained to protect individuals. A newspaper should certainly not publish unofficial charges against persons which might affect their reputation, social status, or moral character. Neither should it invade the privacy of individuals against their will. If featuring stories of crime, vice, and scandal is found to have a demoralizing effect on readers, these too might better be toned down, relegated to inferior positions of importance, or eliminated.

Evaluation of a Newspaper

The following suggestions for evaluating a newspaper will help you determine its policies, vested interests, and public services.

OWNERSHIP AND CONTROL OF THE NEWSPAPER.   Is it a member of a chain of newspapers, such as the Hearst, McCormick, Scripps-Howard, and Gannett chains? Is it owned by a wealthy businessman, as the *Chicago Sun-Times* is owned by Marshall Field III? Is the business management sound? Is it self-supporting? Does the newspaper have a competitor in the city or town where it is published? To what extent is the paper controlled by the advertisers?

PRINCIPAL TENETS OF THE EDITORIAL POLICY.   Is there evidence of political bias? What groups of individuals are likely to be benefited or harmed by this policy? Is there a consistent policy throughout the paper: editorials, news stories, cartoons, feature stories? Is this policy one which you honestly agree with? What is the editorial stand on key issues of the day: labor-management, government control, racial segregation, support of the schools, foreign policy? What points of view, business interests, or pressure groups does the newspaper defend? Does the newspaper point up reforms or changes needed in society? Would you call the paper "conservative" or "liberal" with respect to the interests, viewpoints, language, rights, and privileges of the common man? What community projects does the newspaper sponsor?

ACCURACY AND IMPARTIALITY OF THE NEWS REPORTS.   Are the headlines an accurate summary of the news stories? Are the news stories strictly factual? What evidence do you find of editorializing in the news? Are you allowed opportunity to think for yourself in reading the news? What specific devices do you find that slant the news for or against the subject of a report? Are important details omitted or suppressed in news accounts? What types of stories are suppressed? What is the ratio of local, national, and foreign news?

SOURCES OF NEWS REPORTS. Does the newspaper rely on few sources for the news? Are these sources reliable? To what extent are you left in doubt as to the real source of a story? What is the point of origin of specific foreign dispatches?

SENSATIONAL DEVICES EMPLOYED BY THE PAPER. Does the paper employ large streamer-type headlines? Is colored ink or colored paper used to attract attention? What is the ratio of space devoted to pictures and to printed stories? How sensational is the subject matter or content of the stories: crime, sex, rape, divorce, catastrophe? How much of the paper is devoted to amusements: cross-word puzzles, fiction stories, comics, special features? To what class of people does the language of headlines and stories appeal?

VALUE OF PUBLIC SERVICES OFFERED BY THE PAPER. Does the newspaper offer you the services you require? Do the advertisements help you get the most for your money? What use do you make of: sports news, society news, book reports, financial section, advertisements, do-it-yourself suggestions, home and garden information, critical discussion of the arts, indexes to radio, television, and motion-picture programs, children's pages? To what extent does the newspaper represent your own voice on matters of community interest: crime, justice, delinquency, city planning, education, traffic control? Does the newspaper solicit your opinion on any of these matters?

LANGUAGE OF THE NEWS. Do the headlines generalize from what is known to be true to what the editor wants you to believe to be true? To what extent are the statements in news stories confined to facts? To what extent do statements of opinion, judgment, prediction enter into news accounts? Do you detect any emotionally toned or charged words, slogans, or clichés in the stories?

13.6   Reading Magazines and Periodicals

Magazines, like newspapers, are sources of valuable information, education, pleasure, and entertainment, as well as instruments for forming public opinion and disseminating propaganda. The American people depend on magazines for interpretation of the news, for relaxation and pastime, for directions and advice on practical problems, for reports of what is going on in the world of science, of medicine, of education, of religion, of politics, of psychology, and of art. Nearly six thousand magazines, with a circulation of over 250,000,000, are published in this country. They constitute an invaluable index to the character, interests, and beliefs of the American people.

Classification of Magazines

The large variety of magazines published and circulated in this country presents a slightly different problem of classification from that used for newspapers. Magazines are more specialized and are adapted to various levels of reading ability, tastes, interests, and opinions. They include comic books and lurid love stories, popular magazines, which enjoy widest circulation, and sophisticated, quality, and highbrow journals which appeal to a cultural minority.

A widely employed way to classify magazines is to separate them into three groups: pulp, slick, and quality. Pulp magazines, named after the paper on which they are printed, include such periodicals as *Ranch Stories, Western Stories, True Story, Love Story, Detective Stories, Ghost Story,* and others of like caliber. Slick magazines, also named after the paper used in them, include *Collier's, Ladies' Home Journal, Good Housekeeping, Esquire, Saturday Evening Post, Better Homes and Gardens,* and such popular periodicals. Quality magazines, named after the nature of their content, include such periodicals as *Harper's Magazine, Atlantic Monthly,* the little magazines, and professional journals.

The pulp-slick-quality classification is unfortunate and inadequate for several reasons: It assumes that readers can be analyzed into three educational and cultural backgrounds. It ignores the fact that a writer will publish in any journal which accepts his material or pays his price. It allows no opportunity for classifying magazines according to the function they perform. It assumes an equality of merit among so-called professional journals. It stereotypes people, their interests and capacities. It is based on minority opinion of what is meritorious or unmeritorious in content, style, and vocabulary.

A functional classification might yield such types of magazines as the following:

News magazine and reports: *Time*
Pictorial magazines: *Life*
Women's magazines: *Ladies' Home Journal*
Men's magazines: *Esquire*
Sophisticated journals: *The New Yorker*
Youth's magazines: *Seventeen*
Digests: *Reader's Digest*
Professional journals: *School and Society*
Critical journals: *Saturday Review*
Politically slanted journals: *New Republic*
Travel magazines: *National Geographic*
Health magazines: *Health*
Sports magazines: *Field and Stream*
Scientific magazines: *Scientific Monthly*
Discussion magazines: *Forum*
Children's magazines: *Boy's Life*
Story magazines: *Argosy*
Style magazines: *Vogue*
Farmer's magazines: *Country Gentleman*
Home magazines: *House Beautiful*
Instruction-fiction combination: *Collier's*
Focus on ideas: *Harper's Magazine*
Movie magazines: *Photoplay*
Hobby magazines: *Popular Mechanics*

Cultural magazines: *Etude*

Religious journals: *The Watchtower*

Evaluation of a Magazine

The following questions may prove valuable in helping you to judge the comparative merits of any magazine.

OWNERSHIP AND CONTROL. Is the magazine published by a multiple-title publisher, like Crowell-Collier, Curtis, or Time, Inc.? Does the magazine voice the opinions and point of view of a pressure group which has an ax to grind?

EDITORIAL POLICY. Does the magazine have a stated policy regarding the nature and quality of its contents and services? Can you determine what the editorial policy is? Does the editor encourage unknown writers, or does it publish only well-known craftsmen? Does the magazine contain an editorial section, or any section devoted to statements of opinion and interpretation of current events? Have you ever heard of any of the contributing editors?

FEEDBACK. Is there a department in the magazine devoted to letters from subscribers? Are these letters answered or commented on by the editor? Are the letters all favorable to the magazine?

FUNCTION. What is the primary purpose of the magazine? Does it serve multiple purposes? How well do you think its purposes are realized?

CIRCULATION AND READERSHIP. Can you determine the approximate circulation of the magazine? What type of readers does it seem to be edited for? Are you among these readers? Do you find the language easy to read and understand?

FORMAT. What is the nature of the organization of the contents? Can you find what you are looking for without difficulty? Does the cover appeal to you? Is it in harmony with the purpose and nature of the magazine? Are the advertisements arranged so that they do not detract from your reading of articles and stories? Is the type easily readable and pleasing?

SPECIAL FEATURES. What special features does the magazine contain to lure you as one of its readers? Do these features perform a real service for you? Does the magazine, for example, contain book reviews, travel hints, film reviews, educational guides, science reports, news features, style hints, or purchasing guides?

SUBJECT MATTER. What proportion of the magazine is devoted to fiction? informative articles? criticism? poetry? amusements? explanations and directions? comments and opinions?

ADVERTISEMENTS. To what class of people are the advertisements directed? What percentage of the total space in the magazine is devoted to advertisements? What kind of appeals are made use of in the advertisements? Do the advertisements annoy you as you leaf through the magazine? Do you consider any of the advertisements of real service to you? What features do you consider especially attractive to you? What kind of language is employed in an attempt to win your confidence?

13.7   Evaluation of Books

Criteria for evaluating books vary with every school of criticism, and it would be impossible to list all the ones which have been proposed. The most appropriate method of evaluation relates the qualities of a particular book to its purpose. Thus, a detective story and a biography would be judged by entirely different standards. The following very general questions, however, may be asked of any book:

a. What is the author's purpose in writing?
b. Does the book make its point clear?
c. Is the language employed appropriate to the subject matter and the author's intent?

d. Is the book unified? Do the various parts fit together to make a recognizable whole?

e. How well does the author accomplish his apparent purpose?

f. Does the author's style contribute to the total effect he wants to produce?

g. What do the critics say of the book? Is there general agreement on its merits or defects? (Criticism may be found easily in the *Book Review Digest*. Ask your reference librarian where to find it.)

h. Has the book won popular acclaim, awards, prizes, or meritorious mention?

i. Does the book serve its purpose for you?

j. To what extent are you allowed to think for yourself while reading the book?

k. Has the book ever been censored? What is the basis of censorship? Do you agree with the censors?

EXERCISES

1. Read an article in a magazine of wide circulation, such as *Time, Reader's Digest,* or *Coronet.* Discover your reading rate as follows:
   a. Count the number of letters in a line and divide by five. This will give you the approximate number of words per line.
   b. Read the article at normal speed.
   c. Count the number of lines you have read in five minutes.
   d. Multiply the number of lines read by the number of words per line and divide by five. This will give you the number of words you read in one minute. You should be able to read 400 words a minute with reading matter of this kind.
2. Repeat exercise 1 with a professional magazine, or one of limited circulation, such as *Harper's Magazine, Atlantic Monthly,* or *The New Yorker.*
3. Examine a chapter in one of your textbooks used in another

course. Determine how long it takes you to discover what the main thought of the chapter is and into how many subordinate points it is divided.

4. Select an article or chapter from a book and determine what your purpose is in reading it and what method you will employ. Your instructor will give you a comprehension test on the chapter read.

5. Make a detailed outline of the chapter you read for exercise **4**.

6. Make a survey of current newspapers, magazines, and books for examples of these subjective devices:
   a. Loaded words.
   b. Use of authority.
   c. The "yes" technique.
   d. Propagandistic devices.

7. Make a collection of newspaper cartoons as examples of false or misleading analogies. What does the cartoonist imply by selecting the particular analogy in each instance?

8. Select a news event that is important enough to run for several days in the newspapers. Follow the story in two or three different newspapers. Make the following comparisons:
   a. What facts are included in one paper but left out of the others?
   b. What position is given to the story in each of the papers?
   c. What space and emphasis are given to the story in the several papers?
   d. What evidence do you find of editorializing in the news stories?
   e. Explain the differences in treatment of particular stories in the various papers.

9. Read a chapter in one of your textbooks assigned for reading in another class. Underline all the words of which you are not sure of the intended meaning. Look up these words in a dictionary. Reread the chapter and determine to what extent the exercise has helped you to comprehend the author's meaning.

10. Select an advertisement from a popular magazine. Analyze it for techniques of persuasion. What devices do you find that are intended to influence your thinking? How effective are these devices in influencing you?

FOR FURTHER READING

Adler, Mortimer J., "How to Mark a Book," *Saturday Review of Literature*, July 6, 1940.

Anderson, Russell F., "News from Nowhere," *Saturday Review of Literature*, May 29, 1948.

Bennett, Arnold, "Why a Classic Is a Classic," in *Literary Taste: How to Form It*, New York, 1918.

Cousins, Norman, "History is Made by Headlines," *Saturday Review*, July 25, 1954.

Dale, Edgar, *How to Read a Newspaper*, Chicago, 1941.

Davis, Elmer, "News and the Whole Truth," *Atlantic Monthly*, August, 1952.

Frohock, W. M., "The Menace of the Paperback," *Southwest Review*, Winter, 1954.

Graham, Robert, "Adman's Nightmare: Is the Prune a Witch?" The *Reporter*, October 13, 1953.

Griswold, A. W., "On Reading," *Harper's Magazine*, April, 1952.

Harris, Ruth McCoy, "How Well Do You Read?" *Liberty*, August 25, 1945.

Johnson, Gerald, "Great Newspapers, if Any," *Harper's Magazine*, June, 1948.

Kerfoot, J. B., *How to Read*, New York, 1916.

Mott, Frank Luther, "The Responsibility of the Newspaper Reader," in *The News in America*, Cambridge, 1952.

Mursell, James L., "The Miracle of Learning," *Atlantic Monthly*, June, 1935.

Perry, William G., Jr., and Whitlock, Charles P., "The Right to Think—Through Reading," *Atlantic Monthly*, November, 1952.

Shores, Louis, "Finding Time to Read," *Coronet*, January, 1954.

Smith, Elinor Goulding, "Story for the Slicks," in *The Pocket Atlantic*, New York, 1946.

Trilling, Lionel, "Manners, Morals, and the Novel," in *The Liberal Imagination*, New York, 1948, 1950.

White, William Allen, "Good Newspapers and Bad," *Atlantic Monthly*, May, 1934.

Woolf, Virginia, "How One Should Read a Book," in *The Second Common Reader*, New York, 1932. (Also in *Yale Review*, October, 1926.)

14

ACQUIRE PROFICIENCY IN SPEAKING

THE PURPOSES OF THIS CHAPTER ARE TO list the essential qualifications of an effective speaker and to discuss various types of oral communication.

14.1 Qualifications of an Effective Speaker

The basic qualifications of an effective speaker include engaging personal qualities, adequate preparation for the occasion, and skillful delivery.

Personal Qualities

An effective speaker must have an open personality. He must be able to sell himself in order to get acceptance of his ideas. Perhaps the most important personal assets to effective oral communication are emotional poise, honesty and integrity, and sincerity.

EMOTIONAL POISE. A poised speaker is able to control his own behavior in such a way as to invite appropriate responses from his audience. Quite often *how* an idea is expressed has greater influence than *what* is said. Listeners are affected by signs and mannerisms of which a speaker himself may be unaware. They know without being told that a speaker is friendly or hostile, natural or hypocritical, relaxed or frightened, sincere or affected.

A speaker needs a sense of security and self-confidence if he hopes to achieve his purpose and engage his audience. Stage fright can block all efforts to communicate meaning by interfering with both transmission and reception of thoughts. Stage fright is a kind of emotional panic which makes rational thinking all but impossible. It is usually caused by the speaker's giving too much attention to himself and not enough to his subject and his audience. Everyone has a desire for social approval, and this desire alone causes emotional tension, when personality is put on trial, which ironically enough may find release in modes of behavior which are anything but flattering. The most experienced speakers, as well as beginners, have moments of emotional panic before audiences. And apparently there is no sure cure for such difficulty. But it can be directed so as to produce positive rather than negative results.

Emotional tension, if not properly directed, results in nervousness, fidgeting, stuttering, stammering, forgetfulness, and mental panic—not to mention a number of accompanying physical and psychosomatic reactions. If the energy produced by the emotional tension can be directed to the speaker's advantage, stage fright can be an asset rather than a liability. Here are some suggestions that have proved helpful:

a. Make adequate preparation for the talk. Have all facts, illustrations, patterns of development well in mind before facing the audience. Don't expect to be able to figure out what to say after you are introduced as the speaker. Do not memorize the speech. If you memorize it and then forget one important cue, you may be thrown off completely.

b. Speak in a natural, conversational tone of voice. Don't try to emulate an orator. Remind yourself you are talking to people right in front of you. If you try to imitate someone else you have heard, you may become frightened at the sound of your own voice. Sincerity is the very essence of effective communication.

c. Warm up the audience before you present the main idea. If you can put your listeners at ease, you will feel at home in their company. Bring your audience to attention by saying something they will not want to miss. Exhibit enthusiasm for your subject and good will for your listeners. Open up your personality. Be natural. And remember, if you expect people to be interested in your subject, you must make them interested.

d. Avoid making apologies. Start off on the right foot by being positive with regard to yourself, your subject, and your listeners. Apologies create negative impressions and depreciate you almost instantly. Act as though you really have something important to say.

e. Look the audience in the eye and in the mind. Remember that communication is a two-way operation. You can't possibly know what your listeners are feeling and thinking or how they are reacting to your words unless you look at them. If you bury yourself in notes and address your remarks to the ceiling, the windows and doors, or the floor, the audience becomes for you some kind of monster which paralyzes you with fear. Take advantage of the good will, encouragement, and eagerness to listen displayed by the *people* you address. Direct your thoughts *to* these very people, not *at* them. Your audience is as much a part of your act as is your subject.

f. Don't be afraid to move. If you allow your physical body to become rigid and "freeze," the chill may transfer to your intellect. Let go. Relax both physical and emotional tension by moving about, by making gestures when appropriate, and by establishing a normal breathing pattern.

HONESTY AND INTEGRITY. The effectiveness of what you say is partly determined by what you are. "Instantly we know," says Emerson, "whose words are loaded with life, and whose not." "I learn immediately from any speaker," he says, "how much he has already lived, through the poverty or splendor of his speech." The attitude you assume while speaking is a reflection of your character. You can't expect an audience to accept ideas which you yourself do not understand or believe. Talk from your own experience and your words will fall on fertile ground. Say what you feel and think, and your "character will teach above your will."

SINCERITY. Sincerity, as we have said before, is the very essence of successful communication. Affectation pays small dividends in audience response. The important thing is to be yourself. Let the sparkle, the vitality, the spontaneity of normal conversation characterize all your attempts to communicate orally. Choose topics for speaking that you are sincerely interested in, not ones that you imagine might impress your instructor. One should never be allowed to talk about a subject which is of no real concern to him. Talk from the heart, not off the top of your head. Listeners know instantly when you are putting on something you don't really feel.

Preparing the Speech

Making adequate preparation for speaking will not guarantee success, but lack of preparation will almost surely result in failure. The following successive steps are suggested for preparing a brief, informal talk:

a. Choose a subject that interests you. Sometimes fear in oral communication is fear of the subject rather than fear of the audience. By all means avoid subjects that bore you, for they are certain to bore your audience.

b. Determine a specific purpose for speaking. Don't merely talk about a subject. Plan to accomplish some predetermined goal. Have a definite point to make or a definite response to solicit from your listeners. An effective speaker knows in advance what he wants his audience to know, feel, understand, believe, or do.

c. Organize the talk around a central purpose. Select a pattern of organization that fits your subject and idea and make an outline of how you intend to proceed. Memorize the outline. Carefully plan in advance each step of the way you intend to take your listeners: introduction, presentation of evidence, conclusion.

d. Obtain illustrations, facts, and evidence to support the main ideas of your talk. Do whatever research is necessary to find supporting material for the points you want to make. Try to think of personal experiences which will illustrate your thoughts.

e. Determine in advance the nature of the occasion, the characteristics of the audience, the physical limitations of the setting, and the amount of time at your disposal. Adapt your speech accordingly.

Delivering the Speech

Matters of delivery are discussed under the headings of physical qualities, audio-visual aids, and vocal qualities.

PHYSICAL QUALITIES. An effective speaker employs physical movement, gestures, and posture to assist him in communicating meaning. No hard and fast rules should be established about how one should stand or hold his arms and hands. It is more important for a speaker to feel at ease than it is for him to assume a so-called "correct" posture. But you must consider the audience as well as yourself. The eye is quicker than the ear, so that what you do may easily detract from what you say.

Mannerisms which have nothing to add to the subject of the talk should be avoided: shuffling of the feet, toying with a pencil, rubbing the nose, or scratching the head. In other words, movements should always direct attention to ideas, not to the speaker. Gestures are just as much a part of a communicator's equipment as are words. They often say much more than do words, and more effectively. A nod of the head, a look of surprise, a clenched fist are very useful in making meaning clear. But useless gestures—moving of the hand at frequent intervals, pounding the table—do no more than keep audience attention on the speaker. Gestures should never be awkward or forced. They should be natural and inevitable.

AUDIO-VISUAL AIDS.   Audio-visual aids or props are especially useful in explaining complex processes or points that are not easily clarified in language. Sometimes they are used to reinforce what is expressed in language. The old saying "A picture is worth a thousand words" is sometimes true. Audio-visual aids, however, are not always an asset to a speaker. They can, if not properly handled, distract the attention of listeners from an idea. Special precautions are necessary whenever you use such aids as charts, maps, diagrams, models, replicas, pictures, or graphs. Here are some suggestions for their use:

a. Use audio-visual aids only when they serve a definite purpose.

b. Make careful preparation for using such materials before you are ready to deliver a speech. If you are going to display intricate charts or diagrams on the blackboard, prepare the aids in advance.

c. Make the charts large enough so that they can be seen by everyone in the audience. Display them in such a fashion that sunlight, for example, does not obliterate the view. Make lines heavy and distinct. Use large block letters.

d. Make charts simple and clear. Do not crowd too much into a single diagram. Use several diagrams if necessary.

e. Coördinate the aids with the verbal explanation. Avoid long silences while you are arranging the samples, models, or displays. Do not talk to the blackboard or charts. Keep your attention directed at all times to the audience. Do not stand in front of the charts or in such a position that only some of your listeners and viewers can see what is going on. Move about if necessary.

f. Do not pass around hand-out materials for the audience to consider while you are talking, unless: everyone has a copy in his hand at the same time.

g. When you have finished with a particular aid, put it away, so that it will not distract attention.

h. Practice using the aids until you can handle them smoothly and efficiently. You can kill your presentation by letting the materials get the best of you during a speech.

i. In case of tape recordings, motion pictures, slide projections, and recorded materials, get someone to assist you. Make sure that the equipment is in working order before you begin. Nothing is more disconcerting than a mechanical breakdown during an otherwise effective talk.

VOCAL QUALITIES. The qualities of voice that are important in communication skill are volume, articulation, fluency, and variation of pitch and tempo.

The first requirement of voice is that it be audible to listeners. A speaker must adjust the volume of his voice to the circumstances under which he speaks. Every member of the audience has a right to hear what is said, not just those in the front row. Loudness and softness may be employed for special effects, for emphasis, or for the creation of atmosphere. Volume depends largely on breath control, and if you have difficulty projecting your voice or sustaining volume you should practice breathing exercises. The best voice for communication is relaxed and controlled, not tight, strained, or blusterous.

Articulation and fluency are matters of vocalization of words. Because pronunciation of words differs in different sections of the country, a speaker must make sure that his words can be understood by his listeners. Most people talk quite carelessly, not bothering to enunciate all the syllables of words. While there is probably no one "correct" way to speak the language, effective communication demands a reasonable amount of distinctness in word formation. "What are you going to do?" is preferable to "Whatcha gonna do?" Vocal mannerisms such as the static-like "er" "and uh" and other verbalized pauses are distracting. The function of words is to freight ideas. They cannot accomplish this unless they are understood. Over-precision, blurred syllabication, slurred consonants, flattened vowels, humming cadences, rumbling resonance, or drumbeat staccato may interfere with the

reception of meaning. The following types of sloppy pronunciation should be avoided:

> Sound additions: *often* for *of'n; lightening* for *lightning; heigth*
> for *height;* or *atheletic* for *athletic.*
> Sound omissions: *comin'* for *coming; pome* for *poem.*
> Sound reversals: *henious* for *heinous; larnyx* for *larynx.*
> Sound substitutions: *receipt* for *recipe; git* for *get.*
> Misplaced stress: *municip'le* for *munic'ipal.*
> Phonic pronunciation: *depot* for *de'po; forecastle* for *fo'c'sl.*

Monotone is characteristic of speech that offers no variety in
pitch, tone, volume, and rate. It is one of the commonest of
speech faults and one of the most difficult to correct. A speaker
who employs a monotone lulls his audience to sleep rather than
stimulates their thinking. A dead-level voice blurs the thought it
attempts to clarify. Very few people use a monotone in conversation, but a great many do when they get up in front of an audience, for a variety of causes: lack of self-confidence, lack of purpose, lack of interest in the topic, insincerity, or habit. The
easiest and surest way to get rid of a monotone is to eliminate
the causes:

a. Develop a sincere interest in the idea to be communicated.

b. Develop a wholesome attitude toward the audience.

c. Have a definite purpose for communicating an idea.

d. Have a genuine interest in getting people to comprehend
your meaning.

e. Be honest and sincere.

14.2 Conversation

Social conversation is the form of communication that comes
closest to reality. It is the very life of community activity, the
proving ground for thought creation, and the laboratory for communication skill. Our purpose here is not to learn *how* to converse with friends and associates, but rather to consider the char-

acteristics of satisfactory conversation in order to improve our abilities in other forms of oral communication. Following are important characteristics of free conversation.

a. Conversation is purposeful. Conversation is satisfactory when both parties in the act are sincerely motivated. Desire to make your thought known and understood is probably the most important factor in all communication. When you can engage in other types of oral communication with the same degree of seriousness which you employ in conversation, you will be on your way to attaining skill.

b. Conversation is two-way communication. It is a marriage of minds, a give-and-take relationship. One-way conversations soon wear themselves out. To converse is to participate.

c. Conversation is self-corrective. Misunderstandings are largely ruled out by free exchange of ideas. If you miss the point as first expressed, you can demand a translation into simpler language.

d. Conversation succeeds best when there is common ground between speaker and listener. As Emerson has it: "The fact narrated must correspond to something in me to be credible or intelligible." Shop talk repels an "outsider." Conversation is kept alive by its consistent focus on common interests and experiences.

e. Conversation is direct. The problem of eye contact is no problem in successful conversation and it owes much of its success to this directness.

f. Conversation is grounded in mutual respect. As one writer has explained, "Empathy is the most important creative act in the life of human beings." Empathy purges the raw emotions of their excessive self-concern. Without a genuine interpersonal relation, conversation would be meaningless. Without mutual assurance, understanding, confidence, trust, and loyalty, it would be impossible. Conversation dispels doubt. It equalizes and reconciles differences.

g. Conversation is spontaneous. It laughs at taboos. It breaks down lines of demarkation, repudiates social inhibitions, and unlocks prisons of dogma and regimentation.

h. Conversation is creative. Free association of ideas releases verbal images which may otherwise never come to light. You talk and suddenly become aware of new ideas, ideas which never before existed in your thinking. Conversation has brought them out.

i. Conversation makes people self-confident. When people hide their thoughts inside for fear of derision they prepare the way for feelings of inferiority. Free conversation destroys fear and self-depreciation.

j. Conversation is a cathartic. Emotional tension is released in the act of revealing hidden thoughts. Confessions, admissions, and revelations break down communication barriers, and persons with sick minds become well again.

14.3 Extemporaneous Speaking

An extemporaneous speech is one which is carefully planned, organized, and developed before it is delivered. It is not committed to memory; it is not read from a manuscript. It is purposeful and unified around a central idea. During delivery, the speaker makes use of a brief outline, if necessary. He selects language most appropriate for his subject, audience, and occasion. Most classroom speeches of this type are four or five minutes long. The following steps, if carefully considered, should insure success:

a. Choose a speech topic close to your heart. Talk about something you have experienced first-hand, or about which you have collected a good deal of information. If you are not personally interested in your subject, it is certain no one else will be (see pp. 66–67).

b. Have a definite purpose for speaking. Simply talking about the subject is not enough. You must know exactly what sort of response you expect from your audience. (See Chapter 6.)

c. Analyze the audience and occasion. Don't assume that all

people react exactly alike to verbal stimuli. If you must speak before your classmates, consider their interests, attitudes, goals, and language habits. Make your talk interesting and informative from their point of view. (See Chapter 11.)

d. Focus your attention on one controlling idea. Don't try to say everything you know about your subject. Limit your efforts to one well-defined phase or aspect of it (see pp. 106–107).

e. Develop your speech with illustrative examples, incidents, and experiences. Two or three examples will be sufficient for a short talk. (See Chapter 7.)

f. Develop your speech according to an established plan. Don't simply throw ideas together helter-skelter as they come to your mind. Present the talk point by point. Know what pattern of organization you are going to follow before you start. Don't make your audience have to guess your meaning. Keep your audience informed, not only of the ideas and evidence presented, but also of the method of development and plan of organization. Repeat main ideas from time to time so your listeners will not forget what you are doing. Make your transition from one point to another clear and easy to follow. Work from an outline. (See Chapters 8, 9, and 10.)

EVALUATION OF EXTEMPORANEOUS SPEECH

Speaker: .... Listener: ....

Subject: ....

Purpose: ....

Thesis or Central Idea: ....

I. The Speaker	Poor				Fair				Good	
A. Personal appeal	1	2	3	4	5	6	7	8	9	0
B. Poise	1	2	3	4	5	6	7	8	9	0
C. Audience contact	1	2	3	4	5	6	7	8	9	0
D. Physical activity	1	2	3	4	5	6	7	8	9	0
E. Fluency and spontaneity	1	2	3	4	5	6	7	8	9	0
F. Attitude	1	2	3	4	5	6	7	8	9	0
G. Vocal control	1	2	3	4	5	6	7	8	9	0
H. Manipulation of aids	1	2	3	4	5	6	7	8	9	0

Suggestions: ....

II. The Audience

	Hostile			Indifferent				Friendly		
A. Attitude toward subject	1	2	3	4	5	6	7	8	9	0
B. Attitude toward speaker	1	2	3	4	5	6	7	8	9	0
C. Attention and interest	1	2	3	4	5	6	7	8	9	0
D. Acceptance of idea	1	2	3	4	5	6	7	8	9	0

Suggestions: ....

III. The Topic

	Poor				Fair				Good		
A. Suitability to speaker	1	2	3	4	5	6	7	8	9	0
B. Suitability to audience	1	2	3	4	5	6	7	8	9	0
C. Clarity of purpose	1	2	3	4	5	6	7	8	9	0
D. Focus on idea	1	2	3	4	5	6	7	8	9	0
E. Clarity of organization	1	2	3	4	5	6	7	8	9	0
F. Adequacy of support	1	2	3	4	5	6	7	8	9	0
G. Effectiveness of examples	1	2	3	4	5	6	7	8	9	0
H. Validity of argument	1	2	3	4	5	6	7	8	9	0
I. Appropriateness of language	1	2	3	4	5	6	7	8	9	0

Suggestions: ....

IV. Final Estimate

A. Personality factors	1	2	3	4	5	6	7	8	9	0
B. Audience adjustment	1	2	3	4	5	6	7	8	9	0
C. Fluency and diction	1	2	3	4	5	6	7	8	9	0
D. Physical and vocal control	1	2	3	4	5	6	7	8	9	0
E. Content and organization	1	2	3	4	5	6	7	8	9	0

SCORE: ....

Persuasion

You might give out information, directions, explanations, and solutions to problems without being criticized for failing to impress an audience. But with persuasion, failure to solicit desired audience reaction is failure to succeed in your purpose. Persuasive speaking may be defined as discourse intended to influence or alter the thoughts, opinions, and actions of people. The etymological meaning of *persuasion* is "through sweetness." This suggests a diplomatic, tactful, and seductive form of discourse. In this type of communication it is imperative to know the characteristic make-up of the audience, their interests, beliefs, superstitions, attitudes, biases, and affiliations (see pp. 232–233).

Since an audience responds to a speaker as well as to a speech, personality traits are important factors in the success or failure of a persuasive speech (see pp. 25–27). A speaker who hopes to persuade others to his way of thinking must display intellectual integrity, sound judgment, knowledge of his subject, sense of fairness, impartiality, moderation, restraint, and good will.

SUCCESSIVE STEPS IN PERSUASION.   The varieties of persuasion suggest a progression from one state of mind to another: from stimulation to conversion to conviction to action. As has been suggested, a speaker's specific purpose may not necessarily include all of these stages. You may wish only to create atmosphere conducive to action, not to advocate a plan or to activate behavior. In any event, winning response may take place in a series of psychological steps or stages:

a. Attract attention. You dare not assume that listeners will give you undivided attention just because you have the floor. They won't. Their minds will wander if you don't keep them focused on your presentation. Psychological means of attracting attention include size, motion, variety, novelty, contrast, suspense, compactness, and repetition. You can make use of these devices in the following ways:

(1) Make your idea clear and vivid. Avoid every manner of ambiguity.
(2) Make your idea specific, in episodes and examples from human experience.
(3) Arrange ideas in simple, clear-cut, meaningful patterns of organization. Make use of contrast if possible.
(4) Keep the audience in suspense. Lure your listeners to follow your line of thought.
(5) Act alive by displaying physical activity that will keep attention focused on you.
(6) Use a novel approach that will maintain interest.

(7) Introduce enough humor or human interest into your talk to keep your listeners from becoming bored.

b. Stimulate interest. Make the most of your analysis of the audience. Adjust your talk to the character of the people you address. Pay especial attention to the appropriateness of language. Keep in mind that people are interested in people. Make use of case studies, specific examples, anecdotes, and humor. Other things that are almost sure to interest an audience are: secrets and revelations, confessions, rumors and tabooed information, inside stories, and sneak previews. Think of the devices used in the mass media to stimulate interest. Make use of whatever devices are most to your purpose.

c. Establish belief. The method of persuasive speaking consists of appeals to reason. Ideas must be supported by evidence and proof which an audience will accept and believe. There is, of course, little assurance that everyone will understand your logic, but people, no matter how illogical they may be themselves, will demand that you produce sound evidence to support your convictions and ideas. The specific devices of logic that may be used in persuasion are discussed in Chapter 8. Facts, testimony, authorities, causal relations, and generalizations are appropriate techniques of persuasion as well as of other types of communication. Statistical evidence may be very convincing. Be wary of analogy. Remember analogy clarifies meaning but proves nothing.

Some people will be converted more readily by logical appeals than by psychological or emotional ones. It is probably not generally true that man is an illogical, unreasoning animal who believes only what he wants to believe, even though only the most superficial levels of the mind are ever employed. It is true that logic is often a cold, sterile, and bleak form of discourse but it need not be. An effective speaker will bend the most unstimulating of facts to his purpose and turn them into inspiring, delightful, heart-warming, and engaging motives to action. The nature of the audience and the nature of the subject will partly determine to what extent logical arguments should be employed.

Too barren an attitude, too pretentious a display of evidence, too pompous an attitude may paralyze listeners.

d. Create desire. In addition to logical appeals, persuasion makes abundant use of psychological or emotional appeals. Because such appeals are employed by and associated with propaganda of an unsavory nature, they are quite often looked upon suspiciously. But how rarely are goals in communication ever achieved by logic alone. People resent being proved wrong, but they are flattered if a speaker's opinion agrees with theirs. Too much verbal proof is insulting. Persuasion must touch the heart.

An effective communicator will capitalize on his knowledge of human motivation. He will make strong appeals to his listeners' desire for security, community pride, ego fulfillment, patriotism, survival, recognition, self-respect, participation. A discussion of human motives may be found in Chapter 2 and on p. 163.

There are no rules whatever for psychological persuasion, and the techniques used by the greatest speaker can hardly be analyzed. Bismarck, Disraeli, Richelieu, Ben Franklin, Winston Churchill were eminent persuaders, but no one can tell how they achieved their success. What we said about the character of a speaker will doubtless offer a clue. Such qualities as personal integrity, will power, power of concentration, self-confidence, and sincerity are unquestionably powerful factors in persuasion. Certainly these great speakers were not always logical. Some of their methods were actually weird and incalculable.

e. Promote action. This is the stage in persuasion when the listener must turn indecision into decision. The speaker must help him cross the line. To accomplish this, he must employ some sort of lure or bait. He must have something definite and tangible to offer. Many persuasive speeches fail because the listeners don't quite know what they are expected to do. The inducement must, of course, be something that the listeners want or can be persuaded to want. What kind of lures can you offer?

Do you remember the Biblical tale of Christ's temptation? Satan made a persuasive speech in which he used desire for power and recognition as lures. Success, social prestige, happiness, financial gain, popularity, self-respect, pride are all lures which may turn the trick in persuasive attempts to promote action.

These, then, are five successive stages in the art of persuasion. But something more needs to be said. Persuasion is a process that works slowly and gradually. One dare not get in a hurry or all is lost. The audience must be in a receptive mood before anything can be accomplished, and then each step in the process requires time. Perhaps the creation of a conducive atmosphere is the most important essential of all.

THE ETHICS OF PERSUASION.   A speaker, like any other practitioner, should have a code of ethics by which to regulate his speech behavior. Here are some checks of honesty, integrity, and sincerity which may act as guides to your own behavior: Is the subject one that can be honestly developed by the method employed? Is the plea made in the best interests of the listeners? Were opposing arguments suppressed in order to convince the audience of the validity of your position? Are the facts verifiable, either by experience or by the findings of expert authorities? Are any techniques employed with purposeful intent to deceive and mislead? Are the words chosen to tell the truth, the whole truth, and nothing but the truth about the subject under consideration?

14.4   Group Discussion

Group discussion may be defined as coöperative problem solving. Discussion, in this sense, does not include aimless, unorganized, and uncontrolled group conversation, that may touch on a dozen or more topics and settle nothing. The principal characteristics of discussion as a technique of communication are these: Discussion is focused upon a central idea or problem.

Discussion members or participants are equally concerned with a feasible solution to the problem. Discussion aims to arrive at a solution which will satisfy all members. Discussion is democratically organized to give every member opportunity to participate. Discussion is controlled by principles of honesty, coöperation, mutual respect, and fair play.

Dimensions of Group Discussion

The principal dimensions of group discussion are: formal—informal; rigid—fluid; public—private. Discussions held before large nonparticipating audiences are very likely to become controlled exhibitions rather than sincere attempts to discover truth. Freedom of thought is imperative for successful problem solving. The more controls that are introduced, for no matter what reason, the less likely the discussion will be to prove successful. Problems are solved in fluid atmospheres where free association of ideas is uninhibited. Whatever forces operate to restrain freedom of thought work against successful discussion.

Essential Features of Discussion Method

Although there are many varieties of make-up and organization among discussion groups, certain essential features of method are common to all types:

DEFINITION AND LIMITATION OF THE PROBLEM. This includes bringing the problem into clear focus and staking out the ground or territory to be covered in the discussion. The problem should usually be phrased as a question, allowing more than a "yes" or "no" answer, in language which can be clearly understood (see pp. 97–99).

DEFINITION OF TERMS. Understanding the precise meaning attached to words is of basic importance in any form of communication. It is of utmost importance in discussion that all participants agree on meanings. Such abstractions as *communist, liberal, conservative, democratic* need careful defining if they are to play any part in problem solving. Often the simplest of words need to be defined. In a problem like "Should drinking be permitted among college students?" the word *drinking* must be limited to times, places, amounts, and beverages. (See pp. 125–127.)

ANALYSIS OF THE PROBLEM. Most problems can be analyzed into parts, phases, or aspects which can be assigned to individual members participating in discussion. There is, of course, no standard or arbitrary way of making an analysis. A problem concerned with segregation of races in American schools might be considered from political, social, economic, cultural, educational, and religious points of view. Or it might be analyzed spatially by geographic areas. Or it might be analyzed according to levels of education. There is practically no end to the number of separate analyses which could be made. The one selected for use should be determined by the nature of the problem and the goals of the participating members.

EVALUATION OF THE PROBLEM. The following questions may be used as criteria for judging the acceptability of the problem for discussion:

a. Does a problem really exist? For whom does it exist?

b. What observable phenomena call attention to the existence of a problem?

c. What are the causes of these phenomena?

d. Is the problem possible of solution?

e. What attempts have already been made to find a solution?

f. Why have these attempts failed?

g. Is the problem a problem of fact, or of policy?

ESTABLISHING A GOAL. Any number of solutions might be proposed for a given problem. How can one determine which one if any will be most acceptable? This can be accomplished by setting up minimum essentials or standards which must be satisfied. For example, suppose you were attempting to solve a problem concerned with increasing school enrollments. You might find all sorts of solutions to the problem of space if there were no limits placed on expenditure of money. A practical solution is always restricted by factors that cannot be readily controlled, and such factors must be considered. Within the limits of possibility a discussion group must settle on an attainable goal.

PRESENTING SOLUTIONS. Various possible solutions to the problem, within the limits established, may be presented by members of the discussion group. Such solutions would naturally be explained in detail, judged by the criteria agreed upon, and tested for possible consequences.

SELECTION OF MOST SUITABLE SOLUTION. This is a logical outcome of the preceding step or phase of discussion. Ideally, every member of the group would concur in the acceptance of the selected solution to the problem.

TESTING THE SOLUTION. As a final step, a discussion group might consider ways and means of testing the solution. This is identical with the verification of hypotheses in scientific method. (See also pp. 12–13 and 81–82.)

Preparation for Discussion

Making adequate preparation for discussion is of vital importance. Discussions engaged in by people lacking knowledge of their subject turn quickly into arguments based on private theories and personal opinions. The principal difference between a bull session and organized discussion concerns the matter of preparation. Here are some suggestions for study:

a. Review your own knowledge and experience of the problem.

b. Converse with others about the subject, especially people who are well informed.

c. Secure first-hand information by direct observation of the facts.

d. Secure testimony from recognized authorities, either by interview or by reading. Check the *Readers' Guide* in the library for a bibliography of literature on the subject.

e. Listen to radio and television discussions of the topic if available.

f. Collect as much data and information as you can find.

g. Arrange the data so as to suggest a possible solution to the problem.

h. Make a brief outline of what you have discovered:

(1) Problem:
(2) Your phase of the problem:
(3) Previous solutions:
(4) Definitions:
(5) Facts and data:
(6) Testimonials:
(7) Tentative solution:

Such an outline will help you keep your thinking straight when you are ready to discuss the problem.

Participation in Discussion

The qualifications for effective group discussion are really no different from those for other forms of communication. The qualifications discussed on pages 24–28 include: self-confidence, respect for others, emotional detachment, insatiable curiosity, and adaptability. There is, of course, a stronger need for cooperation in discussion than at other times. You must recognize the necessity for well-ordered, controlled, and self-adjusting group thinking. You must have a sincere desire to arrive at a solution to the defined problem. You must be able to make allowance for honest and sincere differences of opinion. You must be able to make objective evaluations.

The things you must do during discussion include the following:

a. Listen to what other members of the discussion group have to say (see pp. 258–259).

b. Assume your own share of the collective responsibility.

Don't be afraid to present the facts, evidence, and opinions you have collected. Don't remain silent for fear you will be criticized.

c. Keep your mind on the problem. Getting sidetracked from the main issue being discussed is fatal to successful communication. If other members digress, call attention to it.

d. Maintain a high degree of objectivity. Don't let your personal biases and preconvictions blind you to the true significance of the problem. Don't allow disagreements with your thought to silence you.

e. Don't monopolize the discussion. Give others a chance to present their views and findings. Saying too much is as bad as saying too little. Make your contributions brief, concise, and to the point.

f. Avoid fallacious reasoning or thinking. Don't be caught in verbal traps set by others. Keep your thinking straight.

g. Be honest, sincere, and accurate in what you say.

h. Control your emotions. Nothing can be gained by hostility, anger, and dogmatism.

Leadership in Discussion

Any effective communicator should be able to act as leader in group discussion. The qualities of leadership and the qualities of successful communication are the same. In discussion, a leader acts as monitor of the coöperative enterprise. These are some of his responsibilities:

a. Clarify the problem for all concerned, including the audience.

b. Establish friendly relations among the members of the group. Set the stage for discussion.

c. Make sure the discussion is well planned. Keep the members of the group on the problem.

d. Call attention to ambiguities of definition, clarification, and evidence.

e. Insure equal opportunity for all members to participate.

f. Keep the threads of discussion tied together so you can tell at all times what progress has been made toward solution.

g. Make transitions between phases of the problem smooth and meaningful.

h. Prevent confusion, antagonism, and violent disagreement by exercising diplomacy.

i. Keep the ball rolling. Don't allow the discussion to become dull and uninteresting.

j. Ask leading questions that will bring out ideas and facts from the members. Don't try to do everything yourself.

k. Take charge of the question-and-answer period between discussion group and audience.

l. Close the discussion by doing your best to bring members of the group to agreement on a solution to the problem.

Forms of Discussion

Various types of public and private discussion are in common use today. A brief description of some of these types will aid you in selecting the one most suitable to your specific purposes.

THE COMMITTEE.   A committee or conference is a private or closed form of discussion designed to fulfill a specific assignment. It is not always concerned with information, attitudes, and solutions. It usually has a definite function to perform in proposing a course of action. A chairman is the leader of a committee. Membership varies from two or three members to a very large number. Decisions are usually made by majority vote.

THE ROUND TABLE.   A group of experts or well-informed persons, usually four or five, meet to exchange viewpoints on a recognized problem. The tone is informal and conversational. No preplanning is engaged in. The leader is called a moderator. His duty is to allow every member opportunity to participate, to sift the various presented ideas, to challenge statements, to make opportunity for question-and-answer period, and to summarize the various points of view. The University of Chicago Round-table is an example.

THE PANEL. The panel is an informal type of discussion group which attempts to solve a particular problem before an audience. The number of participants varies from three to five or six. One member is elected as leader or chairman. The panel is usually seated in a semicircle before the audience. The members have made extensive plans for the discussion in advance, so they come prepared to present facts, arguments, and opinions which have been collected. The chairman remains largely in the background, not actually engaging in the discussion himself. One variety of panel discussion is coöperative investigation, in which a problem is analyzed into subtopics and assigned to individual members for study and presentation.

SYMPOSIUM. A symposium is a set of speeches of moderate length delivered by different speakers on the same subject before an audience. The purpose is to present a number of viewpoints on the subject, rather than to settle anything by arriving at a solution. The symposium is usually controlled by a chairman, who introduces the subject and the speakers and who takes charge of a question-answer period when all the speakers have finished. The Town Meeting of the Air is a symposium-type discussion.

LECTURE-FORUM. This type of discussion is like the symposium, except that a single speaker presents his views, followed by audience questions.

OPEN FORUM OR FREE DISCUSSION. In this type of discussion a chairman recognizes members of the audience who want to speak on a given problem. When time is called or when all who wish to have spoken, the chairman may summarize the points of view presented, or put the question to a popular vote.

MEET THE PRESS. In this type of discussion, no particular problem is defined. A panel of questioners interrogate an expert on a given subject with the idea of arriving at insights concerning various social or political problems.

BUZZ GROUPS. The buzz group is especially useful in getting a solution to a defined problem in a minimum of time with maximum audience participation. The audience is separated into small groups of five or six members each. Each of these small groups selects from its number a leader or representative. A chairman of the overall discussion presents a problem for consideration. The small groups discuss the problem freely, aiming at the most likely, feasible, and practical solution. At the end of a ten-minute period the representative of each small group submits the solution his group has agreed upon. The solutions are listed on a blackboard so that all can see them. A short question period is conducted, and then the matter is put to popular vote.

DEBATE. Formal debate is a form of restricted discussion controlled by rigid rules and procedures. It is a kind of verbal warfare in which two teams of speakers, having selected an affirmative or a negative point of view with respect to a defined problem, vie with each other in high-spirited exchange of wit and wisdom. A group of judges decides which team had the best argument. Debate is a game of skill; indeed, it is more a game than it is a search for truth. Practical discussion would never allow itself to become limited to one of two possible solutions.

EXERCISES

1. Observe some person, place, or event connected with your life on the college campus. Be prepared to share your observations with your classmates. Report exactly what you observed, being careful not to make personal judgments of your observations. Give a three-minute talk in which you attempt to give a faithful and complete picture of the facts.
2. Select a subject of personal interest to you and develop an idea which you would like to convey to others. Give a three- to five-minute talk in class in which you share your idea with others.

Develop the idea in three different ways or by using three different methods of clarification.

3. Select an abstract word which is often misunderstood or used loosely. Give a two- to three-minute talk in which you define a specific meaning for this word as you might use it in conversation or discourse.

4. Give a five-minute talk before the class in which you explain some process or give directions telling your classmates how to do something or perform a task. Use visual aids if you wish.

5. Your instructor will give you a topic of general interest for an assignment in extemporaneous speaking. Collect your thoughts about the subject for ten or fifteen minutes. Then deliver the speech in class.

6. Attend a motion picture or play of your own choice. Give a three-minute talk in which you criticize the production on the basis of some standard which you present.

7. Make a detailed report on a subject you have investigated thoroughly. If you were asked to write a research paper for a class assignment, use this subject for your talk. Stick as closely to the facts as possible. Defend your findings by presenting various kinds of evidence.

8. Engage in group discussion with other members of the class on a topic you have investigated at some length. Your instructor will tell you how to proceed with this assignment.

9. Give a three- to five-minute talk in which you try to persuade your audience to accept an idea you propose. Use whatever devices seem most appropriate under the circumstances: both logical and emotional appeals.

FOR FURTHER READING

Baker, Virgil, "The Art of Public Speaking," *Vital Speeches of the Day*, March 1, 1932.

Burgess, Gelett, "Conversation Is More Than Talk," *Your Life*, December, 1947.

Crocker, Lionel, "Good Speech Is Good Business," *Vital Speeches of the Day*, March 1, 1953.

Davenport, John, "Slurvian Self-Taught," *The New Yorker,* June 18, 1949.

Harding, Harold F., "The Principles of Poor Speaking," *The Scientific Monthly,* January, 1948.

Holliday, Robert C., "Caun't Speak the Language," from *Walking-Stick Papers,* New York, 1918.

Leighton, Ann, "Conversation," *Atlantic Monthly,* August, 1949.

Loomis, Charles B., "The Familiar Gusher," *Reader's Digest,* October, 1949.

Pei, Mario, "Non-Linguistic Systems of Communication," from *The Story of Language,* New York, 1949.

Potter, Russell, "Talking Things Over," *Saturday Review,* May 22, 1954.

Price, Stephen S., "Put Your Best Voice Forward," *American Magazine,* January, 1955.

Ruble, Besse Waynick, "So You're Going to Introduce the Speaker," *Family Circle,* October, 1954.

Stassen, Harold E., and Dewey, Thomas E., "Should the Communist Party in the United States Be Outlawed?" debate, in *Vital Speeches of the Day,* June 1, 1948.

Utterback, W. E., *Thinking and Conference Leadership: Techniques of Discussion,* New York, 1950.

15

ACQUIRE PROFICIENCY IN WRITING

THE PHYSICAL ABSENCE OF THE READER IN written communication creates a problem for a writer that is not easily surmounted. When you sit down to write a letter to your parents, or your brother or sister, you experience no particular difficulty. But when you prepare to set forth ideas on paper directed to everyone in general and no one in particular, the task becomes quite different. If writing were a purely mechanical matter, this absence of reader would cause no difficulty. But, as Wendell Johnson has said, "You can't write writing." You must write something for somebody to read. Perhaps the best way to explain this is to make a distinction between expression and communication. Expression is the transferral of thoughts to paper and ink with no thought of a reader in mind. Many student themes turn out to be mere expressions of thought. Communication is directed to an "audience" and makes adjustment to interests, attitudes, language habits, and vocabulary of actual people. The first requisite in effective writing, then, is to write with a definite reader in mind. Choose someone you know to write to, and much of what might be called drivel will disappear from your communicative efforts.

15.1 Essential Steps in Writing

While every task or assignment in writing has unique characteristics, a number of safe generalizations can be applied to all writing, whether formal or informal, objective or subjective, factual or nonfactual. Three things which every writer must be equipped with before he can transfer his thoughts to paper are: an idea (something to say), a purpose (some reason for saying it), and a medium (language forms which will represent the idea). If you are equipped with these minimum essentials, you can proceed on a given assignment as follows:

Focusing Attention on an Idea

If you start with an idea rather than with a subject or topic, you save yourself a lot of time and grief. An idea is a unity—a whole. It contains within itself the essence of everything you want to say. A subject or topic has to be reduced to an idea anyhow before it can be properly handled. Why not start with an idea, something you really believe, rather than something you merely decided to believe for the sake of the class assignment? In other words, instead of writing about "ice fishing," write about "ice fishing is great fun," or whatever you believe about "ice fishing." Instead of writing about "juvenile delinquency," write about "juvenile delinquency is on the increase," or "juvenile delinquency is the responsibility of parents," or "comic books are a major cause of juvenile delinquency." (See Chapter 4.) Once you have selected an idea, write it on a card or slip of paper and keep it in front of you while writing. Bad writing is far too often the result of failure to keep an idea-as-a-whole constantly in mind. Emerson's writing, although superior in many ways, suffers from failure to keep an idea in its entirety in mind during each stage of composition.

Deciding on a Definite Purpose for Writing

Student writing often suffers from lack of real purpose or direction. When purpose is ignored and attention is focused almost solely on sentence structure and grammatical correctness, the result is almost unreadable. A paper grammatically correct in every detail but without apparent purpose is unacceptable. Purpose suggests effects or results or responses you hope to achieve. It is not enough that you select a general purpose such as "to inform," "to amuse," or "to instruct." Your purpose must be to consider a potential reader whose behavior you want to influence. Instead of trying "to urge people to support charitable organizations," try "to persuade students in the class to donate blood to the Red Cross." On the card or paper slip which contains your idea, jot down your precise purpose in writing. These two essentials will then act as unifying devices for everything you include in your paper. (See Chapter 6.)

Collecting Facts, Data, Evidence Which Support Your Idea in Harmony with Your Purpose (see Chapter 5)

Four major sources of information may be used: (a) your own personal experiences and past observation; (b) additional observations made after deciding to write; (c) information from others acquired through interviews, information services, or conversations with people; (d) library references. The library is probably the best and most complete source of information. You should find out as soon as possible how particular types of materials are classified in the library and where you can find them.

Planning the Paper and Sifting the Material You Have Collected

This step requires the ability to think straight and to see the whole paper in perspective. An outline is a most practical device for planning a paper (see Chapter 9). If you make even a brief outline of relationship of main ideas and supporting facts, you should be able to determine which collected facts, data, and opinions will serve your purpose and which will not. The length of the paper you are to write will help you to determine how much may be included. Be sure to consider methods of clarification (Chapter 7), methods of defense (Chapter 8), and arrangement of details (Chapter 9).

The Rough Draft

Writing the rough draft is a matter of filling out the outline and supplying transition markers between the several parts of the paper. Begin at the beginning and stop when you are finished. Pay attention during this stage of composition to your point of view (objective or subjective). Keep the tone consistent. Don't allow yourself to get bogged down in trivial matters of style that can be straightened out later. Write without interruption straight through the paper. If you think of important facts while writing that are not in your outline, work them in as you go along. Aim at sincerity, simplicity, and clarity.

Revision of the Rough Draft

Revision is necessary for elimination of mechanical errors, improvement in organization, checking unity and consistency of development, elimination of ambiguity, and adjustment of length. Some writers revise and rewrite a manuscript a half-dozen times or more. You may not have time to do that, but you must plan for at least one careful revision. Read your paper aloud and listen to the sound of it. Make such alterations as you can by checking the following list.

Check List for Revision

1. Unity.   Are your thinking and writing centered in a single idea? Do all the facts included support this central idea? Is there any excess verbal padding? If the idea is a composite of several parts, is each part treated with equal care?

2. Consistency of purpose. Do the facts, opinions, evidence included in the paper achieve the purpose you have in mind? Is the tone of the paper consistent? Is the point of view of the paper consistently maintained?

3. Clarity and specificity.   Is the organization of the paper perfectly clear? Have you employed specific examples to support your ideas? Are the words employed properly chosen for clarity and precision? To what extent have you introduced involved or awkward sentences, deadwood, and jargon into your writing? Are your ideas vivid and original?

4. Accuracy and objectivity. Have you checked the accuracy of facts you employ? Are references and testimonies quoted exactly as you found them? Have you lifted passages out of context and bent them to purposes for which they were not intended? Have you kept personal bias and emotional feeling controlled? Have you supported opinions with factual information?

5. Organization. Is your method of development logically sound? Have you introduced any fallacies of word or thought into your paper? Are the transitions between paragraphs smooth and meaningful? Does the paper have balance, or is one part overemphasized? Is your paper structured in parallel fashion? Is your paper the right length for your purpose? What can be omitted without hurting your thought?

6. Appropriateness. Is the language appropriate to your subject and your readers? Is the style of writing smooth, natural, fluent, original, and informal? Is the usage socially acceptable? Is the paper interesting, stimulating, and easy to read?

7. Mechanics. Have you given careful thought to the following matters? Spelling and punctuation and capitalization; dangling and misplaced modifiers; reference of pronouns; agreement between subject and verb; parallelism in sentences; length of sentences; ineffective repetition; sentence fragments; use of numerals; words unwittingly left out; weak passive voice; tense of verbs; paragraph indentation.

15.2   Manuscript Form

Individual newspapers, magazines, and even college classes have sets of rules and regulations for the preparation of a paper or manuscript. Since there is no standard form that is universally acceptable, the stipulations set forth here are merely suggestive and may be altered by your instructor.

a. Use paper of standard quality and weight, 8½″ x 11″ in size, ruled for longhand, and unruled for typing. Ruled lines should be at least ⅜″ apart.

b. Write on one side of the paper only.

c. Leave generous margins: 1½″ at top and left side of paper;

1 inch at bottom and right side of paper. No paper should be accepted if these marginal restrictions are ignored.

d. Double-space the lines of a typewritten paper. Don't crowd words on a line if writing longhand.

e. Indent paragraphs one-half inch or five spaces on a typewriter.

f. For dividing words at the end of a line, consult a standard dictionary and divide between syllables.

g. Use a typewriter if you can afford one. Use pen and ink if you can't. Use pencil in cases of emergency, but never one with very soft or very hard lead.

h. Center the title of a paper about one inch from the first line of text. Capitalize every word in the title except articles, conjunctions, and prepositions of less than five letters. Always capitalize the first and last word of a title.

i. Number pages in upper right-hand corner in arabic numerals. Do not number the first page.

j. Endorse your paper with your name, class, section number, paper title, date, etc., as your instructor directs.

k. Distinguish clearly between small and capital letters.

l. In typing leave two spaces after end punctuation; one space after internal punctuation. Make a dash by using two hyphens. Remember the numeral 1 is the same as the small letter L (1).

m. Make minor corrections on a manuscript if necessary. Cross out a misspelled word and spell it correctly directly above. Insert punctuation marks where necessary. When words have been omitted place a caret ($_\wedge$) at the place of omission and write the word in above the place indicated. Draw a line through words you want to delete.

15.3 Specific Forms of Written Discourse

The traditional classification of discourse into four forms —exposition, description, argumentation, and narration—has been largely supplanted by a more precise specification of functional forms: stories, editorials, book reviews, informal and formal essays, short stories, personal letters, scientific reports, biographical sketches, and so on. Our concern here is with five types selected because of their practical value for college students: simple development of an idea; explanation of a process; critical appraisal of facts, persons, or events; and investigative report.

Development of an Idea

SPECIFICATIONS. Select a single idea you want to develop, a problem you want to solve, or a point of view you want to defend (see Chapter 4.) Pay particular attention to the thesis to be established. State the thesis in a single declarative sentence and keep it in mind constantly during the writing. Make certain that no ambiguous words appear in the statement of the thesis.

ORGANIZATION AND DEVELOPMENT. Clarify the idea by such devices as examples, comparison and contrast, analogy, specific cases, definition, or whatever seems most appropriate. Defend the idea with factual evidence, personal observations, testimony of authority and experts, statistical data. Arrange the details in a fashion which lends itself best to your purpose: cause and effect, spatial, chronological, analytical, or climactic. Make an outline of your paper before you begin writing. Maintain unity, coherence, and balance throughout.

STYLE. Write the paper in your own words. Don't try to imitate someone else. Be original, spontaneous, and natural. Make the paper interesting and readable by the use of specific details, vivid description, simple diction, and conversational tone. Avoid the use of ambiguous phrases, jargon, deadwood, and trite expressions. Read the paper aloud several times before submitting it to your instructor. Cut out all awkward sentences and pompous expressions which are unnatural for you. Be sure the words you employ are well defined.

TONE. Adjust the tone of your composition—that is, the attitude you assume toward the subject matter—to your purpose. For most assignments, maintain an informal, objective, positive, serious tone.

Explanation of a Process

SPECIFICATIONS. Use this form of discourse when you want to explain how to perform a task, accomplish an exercise, make something, find something, or manipulate something. Carefully define all difficult terms employed in explanation. Do not assume that your reader is already familiar with the process you attempt to explain. Unify the paper by focusing on directions and explanations, not facts and information or opinions and judgments about the process.

ORGANIZATION AND DEVELOPMENT. Probably the most common arrangement of details for this kind of writing is chronological. Begin with the first requirement and procede through successive stages or steps to the completion. If, however, the process is complicated, like the assembly of an airship, you may have to give an overall view of the process, analyze it into smaller units, explain minor operations in detail, and then discuss them in relation to the whole process. Use whatever method will insure understanding. Analogy is particularly useful in this type of writing. Since your purpose is to explain rather than to prove or convince, you need not hesitate to make maximum use of any device that achieves your purpose.

CLARITY AND PRECISION. Keep in mind that clarity is of utmost importance in explanation, that success depends on how well your readers understand what you have written. Identify clearly successive stages in the process. Number them—1, 2, 3, 4, etc.—in order to keep the explanation from getting out of hand. Be sure to keep the statements in parallel structure. Avoid shifts in point of view, that is, from the indicative to the imperative mood of the verb. Keep the sentences clear and simple. Use specific words. Avoid technical terms unless clearly defined.

VISUAL AIDS.   Use charts, graphs, diagrams, or pictures when words by themselves are hard pressed to clarify your meaning. Don't use visual aids just to exhibit your artistic talent, or to cover up your inability to clarify your thought in words. Make the visual aids simple, uninvolved, and vivid. Don't crowd too much in one diagram. Be sure the graphic illustrations clearly support your text and are comprehensible to your reader.

STYLE AND TONE.   Avoid the use of choppy sentences, elliptical constructions, and sentence fragments. Make the paper read easily and smoothly. Avoid all subjective evaluations of the process concerned. Be simple, direct, brief, and specific.

Critical Evaluation

SPECIFICATIONS.   Select a subject for evaluation that is related to the needs, interests, and welfare of your reader. Employ recognizable and approved standards of judgment. Unify the paper with reference to an adopted standard rather than to personal bias or prejudice. Make a fair, honest, reasonable, and sincere appraisal of facts, not fancies.

ORGANIZATION AND DEVELOPMENT.   There is no universally standard procedure for criticism. You may use the same procedure as you use for the development of an idea. Your critical appraisal of anything is in fact an idea. You may use the method employed in explanation and direction. This method is used for such subjects as "How to Ruin a Cup of Coffee," "How to Write Like a Social Scientist," or "The Principles of Poor Speaking." Study the methods employed in a number of newspaper editorials or magazine articles. Remember that criticism is not necessarily derogatory. You may want to praise the subject in question or show your appreciation. Irony, satire, sarcasm, ridicule are all common methods of criticism. Sometimes implied criticism is more effective than expressed criticism. The very arrangement of objective, verifiable facts may suggest criticism of those facts.

TONE AND POINT OF VIEW. Consistency of tone, point of view, attitude, style, and method is imperative in effective criticism. Make it clear what you want the reader to think about the subject. If your attitude is negative, don't allow approval of some aspects of the subject to neutralize your argument. If your attitude is neutral, balance merits and demerits so that your reader can make up his own mind about whatever you criticize. In any event, be perfectly fair in your appraisal.

Essay Examinations

SPECIFICATIONS. Bear in mind that the purpose of an examination is not simply to test your memory but, what is more important, to test your ability to muster facts and opinions in defense of a thesis or central idea. Make a compact unity of your answer to a given question. Avoid incomplete sentences, ellipses, and abbreviations. Make sure you understand exactly what is expected of you.

ANALYSIS. Determine what kind of answer your instructor expects of you. Pay special attention to the phrasing of the question:

Identify requires a simple answer to such questions as who? what? when? where? why? and how? Be sure to include any identifying features which will reflect your knowledge and understanding.

Define requires a brief statement which classifies and differentiates (see pp. 395–404). An extended definition may be clarified and supported by examples, analogy, contrast and comparison, and any devices mentioned in Chapter 7.

Explain requires a concise statement of the function, operation, or make-up of something specified. Words coupled with *explain* may give clues to appropriate methods of development:

explain how, explain why, explain uses, etc. (see pp. 102–103).

Analyze requires the breaking down of a whole into its essential elements or functional units. Employ a single method of analysis and keep your thoughts and statements parallel by listing them in sequence or numbering them. Explain each part of the analyzed whole if required.

Enumerate requires a listing of items in proper sequence. The most important thing to remember in this type of question is parallel form and structure.

Compare usually requires a listing of similarities and differences.

Contrast designates differences alone. Two methods of procedure are suggested: (a) Write a single paragraph in which you compare analyzed features, traits, aspects of two or more subjects; (b) write two paragraphs, one devoted to each of the things being compared.

Discuss or *criticize* requires an evaluation of the merits or demerits of the subject in question. Write a well-rounded statement of your opinion, basing your judgment on recognized standards.

Summarize requires a summary or précis of many facts and details related to the subject. Pick out the most essential items to be included and take care to make every word count. Don't indulge in a lot of useless repetition.

ORGANIZATION AND DEVELOPMENT. Use the same procedure for an examination question that you would for a simple paragraph. Focus your attention on a central thesis, employing the same language used in the question, and proceed to develop the thesis. The answer to any question should contain main idea and supporting details.

STYLE AND TONE. Use a direct, sincere, simple, and unassuming style of writing. Humor and pretension will probably annoy rather than impress your instructor. Avoid padding the paper with superfluous language on the false assumption that the more you write the better grade you will receive. If the subject matter is one which has a technical or special vocabulary, make intelligent use of such vocabulary, but don't employ a word unless you know what it means.

The Research Paper

A research paper is one which develops an idea, or solves a problem, by presenting factual evidence. It is variously called an "investigative paper," "term paper," "source paper," or "library paper." Students writing such papers for college credit are forced by circumstances to find most of their evidence in published books, periodicals, and reference works, so that, in reality, the kind of paper we are concerned about is a "report of reports." Controlled experiments, observations, and surveys conducted by specialists are employed in the solution of problems recognized, defined, and analyzed by students. The writing of a successful research paper depends on a number of preliminary steps: (a) recognizing problems suitable for research; (b) seeing the paper in total perspective; (c) outlining the major parts of the paper; (d) finding and evaluating suitable evidence; (e) documenting the evidence; (f) drawing sound conclusions from the evidence.

RECOGNIZING PROBLEMS SUITABLE FOR RESEARCH. Choose a problem that has not been solved for you. Some topics deserve no more treatment than they have already received. We know, for example, who won the Civil War, what the agreements were in the Treaty of Versailles, and how penicillin was discovered. What we don't know, until we investigate the ever changing facts, is: to what extent the North and South have become integrated, to what extent the Treaty of Versailles caused World War II, or what the dangers are in the promiscuous use of penicillin. You can be fairly safe in assuming that if all of the information necessary to complete your research may be found in one reference work, the topic is unsatisfactory.

Choose a problem that has some significance for you or for

society. Scientists engage in research because there is a need for the kind of solutions to recognized problems that research can supply. Going through the motions of research simply to satisfy idle curiosity hardly seems sufficient justification for the effort expended. For example, we need to know what solutions to the problem of highway accidents have proved effective, but we care little for information about the comparative number of college men who do or do not wear hats.

Limit your topic so that you can treat it properly in the space and time at your disposal. Some subjects can be treated fully in 1000 words or less. Any attempt to expand the research in order to produce 3000 or 5000 words results in ineffective writing: needless repetition, padding, and lack of unity. Some subjects would require several volumes for adequate treatment. Don't try to solve the problem of juvenile delinquency in 1500 words.

SEEING THE PAPER IN TOTAL PERSPECTIVE. Select a definite purpose for research. You must know exactly what you want to find out if you hope to discover anything. Too many students choose a broad topic and set to work writing about it in a rather uncontrolled and purposeless fashion. The result is not worth reading. If you start with a central purpose, idea, or thesis which you want to support, defend, or confirm, you should have little difficulty deciding which facts are pertinent to your paper and which facts irrelevant or unnecessary.

Analyze your problem so you will know what kind of facts to collect. Suppose that your purpose is to determine the merits and demerits of a progressive educational program. Your analysis is self-contained in the statement of purpose: you want to collect two varieties of facts—facts which argue in favor of progressive education and facts which argue against progressive education. If your purpose is to discover the existing varieties of mental retardation, you will make your analysis as you collect the evidence. Analysis consists of breaking a subject up into its related parts.

Determine a method by which your idea can best be developed. If you have given careful attention to analysis of the problem, a suitable method of development should become immediately apparent. The method to employ in the problem of progressive education (mentioned in the last paragraph) is contrast and comparison. The method to employ for the problem of mental retardation, mentioned above, is analysis of types.

OUTLINE THE MAJOR PARTS OF THE PAPER. A suggested form for your outline follows:

I. Introduction
   A. Significance of subject
      1.
      2.
   B. Statement of purpose
   C. Method of investigation
II. Body of Evidence
   A. Main division of evidence
      1. Subordinate details
      2. Subordinate details
      3. Subordinate details
   B. Main division of evidence
      1.
      2.
   C. Main division of evidence
      1.
      2.
   D. Main division of evidence
      1.
      2.
      3.
      4.
III. Conclusions
   A.
   B.

Not until you have investigated your subject thoroughly will you be able to make a detailed outline of it. But a preliminary outline will assist you in focusing on the purpose you have set out to achieve.

FINDING AND EVALUATING SUITABLE EVIDENCE. The evidence for the kind of research expected of you may be found in the college library. Before you can hope to get your hands on the kinds of evidence which the library contains pertinent to your purpose, you must learn something of the organization of the library itself. No two libraries are arranged in exactly the same way, but they all have some features in common. Here are some things you should know about the library in order to locate the information you need for developing and supporting your research thesis.

The card catalogue has a subject index which will be most useful to you in library research. Suppose your problem is "to discover the peacetime uses of atomic energy." Look up the general topic "atomic energy" in the card catalogue which classifies books according to subject. By looking at the titles of these books and noting the dates of publication, you should be able to determine a number of them which promise to be useful to you. Check these books out at the loan desk and find out how likely they are to supply the information you need.

General reference works may be found in the general reference room of the library, which contains hundreds of volumes full of information on many different subjects. A number of such works are listed here:

Encyclopedias
  Collier's Encyclopedia, 1950, 20 vols.
  Columbia Encyclopedia, 2nd ed., 1950, 1 vol.
  Encyclopedia Americana, 1948, 30 vols.
  Encyclopedia Britannica, 14th ed., 1929, 24 vols.
  New International Encyclopedia, 2nd ed., 1922, 23 vols.
Yearbooks
  American Yearbook: A Record of Events and Progress, 1910–19;
      1925 to date.
  Americana Annual, 1923 to date.

Britannica Book of the Year, 1938 to date.
Information Please Almanac, 1947 to date.
New International Yearbook, 1908 to date.
Social Work Yearbook, 1929 to date.
Statesman's Yearbook, 1864 to date.
Statistical Abstracts of the United States, 1878 to date.
United Nations Yearbook, 1948 to date.
World Almanac and Book of Facts, 1868 to 1876; 1886 to date.

Special reference works in the reference library contain compiled facts on specific subjects. Some of these are listed here:

Biography
Current Biography, monthly, 1940 to date.
Dictionary of American Biography, 20 vols., 1928 to 1937. Supplement 1944.
Dictionary of National Biography, 1885 to 1937.
International Who's Who, 1935 to date.
Who's Who, 1849 to date.
Who's Who in America, 1899 to date.
World Biography, 4th ed., 1948.
Education
A Guide to American Universities and Colleges, 1948.
Cyclopedia of Education, 1911–13, 5 vols.
Encyclopedia of Educational Research, 1941.
Encyclopedia and Dictionary of Education, 1921–22, 4 vols.
Engineering
Condensed Encyclopedia of Engineering, 1928.
Hutchinson's Technical and Scientific Encyclopedia, 1935, 4 vols.
Fine Arts
Bryan's Dictionary of Painters and Engravers, 1903–05, 5 vols.
Cyclopedia of Painters and Paintings, 1892, 4 vols.
Grove's Dictionary of Music and Musicians, 3rd ed., 1927–28, 5 vols.
Harper's Encyclopedia of Art, 1937.
History
Cambridge Ancient History, 1923–39, 12 vols.
Cambridge Medieval History, 1911–36, 8 vols.
Cambridge Modern History, 1902–26, 13 vols.

Dictionary of American History, 1940, 5 vols.
An Encyclopedia of World History, 1948.
Literature
Cambridge History of American Literature, 1917–21, 4 vols.
Cambridge History of English Literature, 1907–27, 15 vols.
Columbia Dictionary of Modern European Literature, 1947.
Handbook to Literature, 1936.
Harper's Dictionary of Classical Literature, 1897.
Library of Literary Criticism of English and American Authors, 1901–05, 8 vols.
Literary History of the United States, 1949, 3 vols.
Oxford Companion to American Literature, 2nd ed., 1948.
Oxford Companion to Classical Literature, 2nd ed., 1925.
Oxford Companion to English Literature, 3rd ed., 1948.
Philosophy and Psychology
Dictionary of Philosophy and Psychology, 1901–05, 3 vols. Revised 1938.
Handbook of Psychological Literature, 1932.
Dictionary of Psychology, 1934.
Religion
Catholic Encyclopedia, 1907–14, 16 vols.
Dictionary of the Bible, 1898–1904, 5 vols.
Encyclopedia of Religion and Ethics, 1911–27, 12 vols.
Jewish Encyclopedia, 1901–06, 12 vols.
Social Science
Encyclopedia of the Social Sciences, 1930–35, 15 vols.

Indexes to periodicals will help you locate facts and information about your subject published in magazines. You need to know where in your college library these indexes are located and how to use them.

General Indexes
The Reader's Guide to Periodical Literature, 1900 to date.
This is the one you will probably find most useful. It indexes articles from many important magazines, both popular and specialized.
Poole's Index to Periodical Literature, 1802–1906.
Indexed by subject only.

International Index to Periodicals, 1907 to date.
Especially useful for science and the humanities.
The New York Times Index, 1913 to date.
A guide to events of national importance by reference to date, page, and column.
Specialized Indexes
Agriculture Index, 1916 to date.
Lists special agricultural bulletins and periodicals.
Art Index, 1929 to date.
A cumulative author and subject index to periodicals dealing with the fine arts.
Book Review Digest, 1905 to date.
Book reviews on general subjects, arranged by author and title.
Education Index, 1929 to date.
Covers the entire field of education.
Engineering Index, 1884 to date.
Since 1928 this work lists by author and subject periodicals in all fields of engineering.
Facts on File, 1940 to date.
Weekly digest of world events.
Index Medicus, 1879–1926. *Quarterly Cumulative Index Medicus,* 1927 to date.
Lists significant articles in all fields of medicine.
Index to Legal Periodicals, 1908 to date.
Authoritative list of articles in legal journals.
Industrial Arts Index, 1913 to date.
A selected list of engineering, trade, and business periodicals.
Psychological Index, 1927 to date.
Summaries of current literature in the fields of psychology.
United States Document Catalog.
Lists titles and subjects of U.S. documents.

EVALUATING THE USEFULNESS OF SOURCES AND EVIDENCE. Once you have located books, references, and periodical articles pertaining to your topic, you must determine how well such material suits your specific needs. Everything you use for your research paper must be directly related to your purpose. Some books will prove valueless to you; some outdated. You must return the books you cannot use. Be sure not to include information in your paper, no matter how interesting, that does not help to achieve the purpose you have selected. If the authorities you find do not agree on the facts investigated, you may need to evaluate the sources of information. A scale for doing this may be found on pages 156–157.

PREPARING A PRELIMINARY BIBLIOGRAPHY. In order to keep track of the books and periodicals that prove useful to you in research, you should list each reference on a 3″ x 5″ card. These cards can be annotated with your judgment of their worth to you.

```
659.14
D921r
                    Dunlap, Orrin E. Jr.,

                    Radio in Advertising,

                    New York,

                    1950.
```

TAKING NOTES ON THE SELECTED REFERENCES. It is important to take notes on what you read so that you will be able to manage and control the evidence you collect and keep it in harmony with your outline. The following suggestions may be useful to you:

a. Write notes on 4″ x 6″ cards, not on sheets of notebook paper.

b. identify the source by putting a "slug" at the top or bottom on the card. Be sure to indicate page numbers.

330.5
B979

Stanton, John F.,

Radio Rates Start to Crack,

Business Week, April 28, 1951, 21.

c. Use quotation marks for matter which you quote exactly.

d. Summarize long quotations unless you intend to include the full text in your paper.

Fire Fighting Equipment for Rural Areas   Fire fighting Equipment

Page 6 Power pumps have been found to be of little use on running fires because of the time required to lay hose lines, and in many cases the absence of a readily available water supply. For mop up work in heavy fuels, however, they have proved to be invaluable. Heavy duty low-speed pumps have been found best suited for this purpose because of their ability to stand up under continuous use over long periods with a minimum of attention.

e. Indicate on the card the place in your outline the information may be used.

MAKING A DETAILED OUTLINE OF YOUR PAPER. To do this you merely fill in the details on the skeleton outline you made before investigating the facts. You may have to alter some of the divisions in this outline so as to conform with the evidence you were able to discover. See the outline of specimen paper on page 344.

DOCUMENTING THE EVIDENCE. Documenting the evidence is a method by which an investigator pins down the evidence submitted in support of his thesis. It is a way of answering such questions as: How do you know this is true? Who says so? Where did you get the information? The truth of an argument largely depends upon the reliability of the sources. If you state exactly what sources you have used, a reader will be able to determine how much faith he can put in your findings. The conventional way to document evidence is to employ footnotes. Footnotes should be used: (a) to give credit for direct quotations; (b) to indicate the source of graphs, charts, and tables; (c) to indicate the source of ideas you have not quoted directly. Footnotes have two parts: (a) the index number which indicates that a footnote is presented; (b) the footnote proper. The following abbreviations are in common use:

cf.—compare
chap.—chapter
col.—column
ed.—editor or edition
ff.—and the following pages
fig.—figure
Ibid.—the same as above
p. or pp.—page or pages
tr.—translator or translated
vol.—volume

Notice the composition and make-up of the following footnotes:

Books

Order of items: Author's first name or initials; author's last name; title of book in italics (underlined); place of publications; date of publication; page reference.

[1] Fairfax Downey, *American Dogs in the Second World War*, New York, 1955, p. 9.

[2] Delwin M. Campbell, *Veterinary Military History*, Chicago, 1935, p. 949.

[3] *Ibid.*   ·

[4] Downey, pp. 10–11.

Footnote 3 refers to the same source indicated in footnote 2. Footnote 4 refers to the same source indicated in footnote 1.

Magazines

Order of items: Author, if any; title of article, in quotation marks; name of periodical, in italics; volume number of periodical; date of periodical; page reference.

[1] R. C. Ruark, "Have the War Dogs Been Good Soldiers?" *Saturday Evening Post*, 217, November 25, 1944, 18.

[2] D. Richards and C. Gibson, "A New Proposal Concerning Beginning Readings," *Elementary English*, 26, 1949, 461.

[3] Ruark, p. 218.

[4] *Ibid.*

[5] Richards and Gibson, p. 462.

Footnotes 1, 3, and 4 refer to the same source; footnotes 2 and 5 also refer to a similar source.

Newspapers

Order of items: Name of article or story, in quotation marks; name of newspaper, in italics; date, page reference, column number.

[1] "Panama Police Post Defies Seizure Bid," *The New York Times*, October 22, 1940, p. 4, col. 7.

DRAWING SOUND CONCLUSIONS. The reason you investigate facts and bring them together in a research paper is that you want to prove a thesis, support an idea, or solve a problem. Nothing in research is more important than drawing sound and justifiable conclusions from the data or evidence. This is where your own reasoning powers are engaged. The conclusions are the result of your own thinking. They should be logically sound and reasonable. They should be directly related to your purpose and the data presented. They should be stated in clear, succinct language that leaves no doubt of what you have determined. They should summarize all the evidence you have brought together.

PROCEDURE FOR WRITING A RESEARCH PAPER.

a. Determine precisely what you hope to accomplish by research. State your purpose so you and your readers will know just what you want to find out.

b. Make a survey of material available on the chosen subject by getting acquainted with the resources of the library.

c. Make a tentative outline of the paper showing an analysis of the subject into main divisions of thought.

d. Select material from books and periodicals that are useful in supporting your thesis.

e. Make bibliography cards for the selected items.

f. Take notes on the material you intend to include in your paper.

g. Make a detailed outline of your paper.

h. Write a rough draft of your paper, following the scheme your outline suggests.

i. Revise the rough draft by cutting out superfluous material, checking transitional sentences, putting in footnotes where required, and challenging your choice of words. Make sure your purpose has determined your selection of evidence and is clearly reflected in your conclusions.

j. Prepare the final draft. Include the following items:

1. A title page.
2. An introduction.
3. A body of evidence properly documented.
4. A list of conclusions.
5. A bibliography of references.

A SAMPLE RESEARCH PAPER.

Teaching First Graders How to Read
by
Judy Jenks

I. Introduction
  A. Significance of the problem.
  B. Statement of purpose: To determine the best way of teaching first graders how to read.
  C. Definition.
II. Body of evidence
  A. Old methods.
    1. Mechanical method.
    2. Phonic method.
    3. Phonetic method.
  B. Modern method.
    1. Thought method.
      a. Systematic lessons.
    2. Sight vocabulary.
    3. Oral and silent reading.
III. Conclusion:
  A. Summary.

I. Introduction
  A. Significance of the problem.

The child who cannot read well cannot succeed in history, geography, science, or any other school subject that requires reading. Inadequate reading ability causes much discouragement and frustration throughout a child's life. Many children create disciplinary problems or even leave school because, not having acquired adequate ability to read well, they have no desire to learn.

Today's society requires a greater reading ability than was required a generation ago. If children fail to learn how to read at an early age they will run into the same problems that many college students now face: not knowing how to read and understand what has been read.

B. Statement of purpose.
The purpose of this paper is to determine
the best way of teaching first graders to read.
C. Definition of terms.
Many people do not know exactly what reading
is. It is not merely the pronunciation of printed
words on a page. It is possible to learn to pronounce the words of a foreign language and yet
have no understanding of their meanings. For this
reason, reading must be thought to include comprehension of meanings. It includes thinking and reasoning as well as seeing and recognizing. The
reader must challenge what he reads, on the basis
of what he already knows, and re-examine his present ideas in the light of new information.

II. Body of Evidence

Several methods have been used in trying to
find the best method to teach the child to translate unfamiliar printed symbols into thoughts. The
first methods used were known as mechanical
methods. Included in this group are the alphabetic
method, the phonic method, and the phonetic
method.[1]
The oldest of the mechanical methods was the alphabetic method, which was primarily the memoriza-
tion of the alphabet. This method was used in
America as early as 1860.[2] The child learned to
name and identify, in order, the individual letters; he also learned to sound certain two- and
three-letter combinations of nonsense syllables
such as sa, ba, ib, ob, pag, and glo.[3] Having
learned the name of each letter, he was supposed
to convert the word into its alphabetic name unit
and obtain a pronunciation or sound of the word as
a unit. This was supposed to give him the meaning

1. Paul Mc Kee, Reading and Literature in the
Elementary School, Boston, 1934, p. 141.
2. Ibid.
3. Ibid.

of the printed word. Educators believed that in
this process the ability to name the letters of a
word led to the correct pronunciation of the
word.[4]

In the phonic method the emphasis was placed
upon the memorizing of the elementary sounds of
the letters rather than their names. In attempting
to arrive at the correct sound or pronunciation of
a given word, the pupil was taught to blend the
sounds of the individual letters together.[5] It became clear that the sound of a word is not always
a combination of the sounds of individual letters
in the word. For one thing, a single letter often
has various sounds and many words have silent
letters.

The phonetic method was then introduced in an
attempt to overcome all the difficulties found in
the previous two. Recognizing the fact that there
are approximately forty-four sounds in the English
language and only twenty-six letters in the alphabet, theorists invented additional printed characters for the sounds not cared for by the elementary sounds of the twenty-six letters.[6] The
child was required to learn the sound of each of
the forty-four characters and to work out the
sound of a given word by blending the sounds of
each letter in the word.[7] A second plan used what
are commonly known as diacritical marks. With this
plan the pupil was required to learn each letter
in the alphabet and in addition the sound to be
employed when a given letter was accompanied by a
given diacritical mark.[8]

These three mechanical methods have at least
three characteristics in common. In the first

---

4. Ibid., p. 142.
5. Ibid.
6. Arthur Gates, Interest and Ability in Reading, New York, 1940, p. 201.
7. Ibid.
8. Ibid., p. 202.

place they are all synthetic in their procedure.[9]
They teach first the names or sounds of letters,
then two-letter combinations, three-letter combinations, one-syllable words, two-syllable words,
three-syllable words, phrases, and finally sentences.[10] In the second place it is apparent that
the three mechanical methods seek first to develop
effective oral reading through pronunciation
drill, which is not sufficient. Finally, none of
these methods introduce reading as thought-getting
processes.

The old semanticists were primarily concerned
with the historical development and classification
of meanings. The chief concerns of our present day
semanticists are to point out relationships between symbols and what they refer to.[11] There must
be interest and pleasure in learning how to read
or else the child will get frustrated and lose all
desire to learn. The child is entering a new world
which substitutes written symbols for things, persons, and actions.[12] The trend in reading instruction now is to dig down beneath the surface to
deeper meanings; to ask questions and to use
checks which will demand the use of the higher
thought process in getting the full sense of meanings from printed pages.[13]

Three examples of systematic informal lessons
are: (1) familiar rhymes or stories; (2) words
that represent familiar concepts; and (3) direct
or personal experiences in which the child has
participated.[14]

---

9. Mc Kee, p. 143.
10. Ibid.
11. Nila B. Smith, "Reading Readiness," Elementary English, 26, 1949, 425.
12. D. Richards and C. Gibson, "A New Proposal
Concerning Beginning Reading," Elementary English,
26, 1949, 461.
13. Smith, p. 430.
14. Gates, p. 150.

A game was used by one teacher to make the children familiar with the rhyme and its story.[15] Jack
jumping over the candlestick was used as the example. First the teacher brought into the room a
candle and had each student jump over the stick.
The second day she drew pictures on the board and
had the pupils dictate to her what she should
draw. After the rhyme had been made familiar to
the children, she began the first lesson by reading it to them. She again made charts and drawings
of the rhyme on the board and had different students read it out loud. In this procedure the
rhyme was made familiar before the actual reading
began.[16]

The second systematic lesson is one of familiar
words. This method selects the word as the first
unit of perception. The pupil first learns to
recognize several words and then gradually works
them into phrases and sentences.[17] In the first
lesson several important words are taught to the
children; this work is done by word-picture cards.
In the second lesson two new words are taught by
means of the word cards and the old ones are re-
viewed. In addition the pupils work through an
exercise in the workbook which requires them to
identify each word taught so far, by selecting
from among several pictures the one that tells
what the word says. This is then continued until
the child finally reads stories in which all the
words that he has been learning and practicing are
used.[18]

The third method made use of direct personal experiences of the child as a method of learning. In
this process the teacher decided to have the stu-

15. S. C. Parker and Alice Temple, Unified Kindergarten-First Teaching, New York, 1950, p. 455.
16. Ibid., p. 470.
17. A. I. Gates, New Methods in Primary Reading,
New York, 1941, p. 198.
18. Ibid., p. 199.

dents learn words by using the building of a house as an example. As they were building the house they wrote down the steps and what they used as they went along. Cards were made and hung over such objects as the door and windows. The cards were then all put together and a book was formed. Most of these objects were familiar to the students from their own past experiences at home.[19]

Each of these three procedures emphasizes three principles. In the first place they do not begin with the aims or sounds of letters, proceed through the pronunciation of syllables and phonograms to the reading of whole words, and finally emerge into the comprehension of sentences and paragraphs.[20] They begin rather with the larger units such as words and sentences. In the second place each of the three procedures is a thought-getting method rather than a mechanical method.[21] Their approach is distinctly through material which carries meaning for the child. In the third place, each of the three procedures recognizes the importance of developing a desire to read.[22]

Also very important in reading is the child's sight vocabulary. These are words of which the pupil has learned to take cognizance. He learns to recognize the word and associate it with a certain thing or object.[23] It is obvious that all words do not have equal value. The words of greatest importance should be those words most frequently used in reading material.[24] There are two main procedures to be followed in developing a sight vocabulary. The first of these teaches the words incidentally through repetition in connection with various reading activities, including the syste-

19. Mc Kee, p. 150.
20. Mc Kee, p. 163.
21. Ibid.
22. Ibid., p. 164.
23. A. I. Gates, p. 196.
24. Ibid., p. 197.

matic lessons.[25] The second involves the use of
definite vocabulary exercises.[26]

Another question arising is whether or not a
child should begin to read orally or silently.
There are four types of silent reading. The first
one is true silent reading.[27] This implies that the
eyes are swung rhythmically across the page and
back again to the next line, the mind getting
thoughts as they are met.[28] This means that the
child actually does his silent reading by swinging
his eyes back and forth across each page. Most
children, however, do not do this so they go to
one of two other methods. One of these is puz-
zling, in which they try to puzzle their way out
by either guessing from the content, sounding out
the word by a previously learned method, or just
crawling along and staying on that one word for
several minutes; or else guessing or just skipping
over the word completely.[29]

Oral reading gives the teacher a chance to check
on a child's ability to read silently, his understanding of the words, his pronunciation and the
use of punctuation to give meaning.[30] Oral reading
is also often used to get meaning from literature,
and to give the child a chance to share his experiences with others.[31]

III. Conclusion

After reading about the many methods available today by which a child may be taught to read,
I have concluded that reading material should deal
with items familiar and meaningful to the child.

---

25. Ibid.
26. Ibid., p. 198.
27. E. W. Dolch, "Should Children Read Silently
First?" Elementary English, 25, 1948, 279.
28. Ibid., p. 280.
29. Ibid.
30. Henry Smith, Psychology in Teaching, New
York, 1954, p. 316.
31. Ibid.

The material should not be arbitrarily imposed, but should be introduced in a meaningful manner so that the child will not feel he is being pushed. Sentence, word, and letter recognition should advance side by side instead of being taught as separate parts of the whole process. The values of the analytic method (word, sentence, story, and story pictures) and the synthetic method (alphabetic, phonic, and phonetic) should thus be combined to form a process of actuality and meaning.

It is the same with oral and silent reading; each one complements the other. Teaching the child oral reading is preparing him for better silent reading, and having him read aloud enables the teacher to detect the child's difficulties and correct them.

List of References

BOOKS

Gans, Roma, Reading Is Fun, New York, 1950.

Gates, Arthur, Interest and Ability in Reading, New York, 1940.

Gates, A. I., New Methods in Primary Reading, New York, 1941.

Mc Kee, Paul, Reading and Literature in the Elementary School, Boston, 1934.

Parker, S. C., and Temple, Alice, Unified Kindergarten-First Grade Teaching, New York, 1950.

Russell, David, and Karp, Etta, Reading Aids Through the Grades, New York, 1945.

Smith, Henry, Psychology in Teaching, New York, 1950.

MAGAZINE ARTICLES, SIGNED

Dolch, E. W., "Should Children Read Silently First?" Elementary English, 25, 1948, 279-284.

Richards, D., and Gibson, C., "A New Proposal Concerning Beginning Reading," Elementary English, 26, 1949, 461-469.

Smith, Nila B., "Reading Readiness," Elementary English, 26, 1949, 425-433.

EXERCISES

1. Write an editorial for your school paper in which you defend your personal opinion about a matter of concern on the campus.
2. Attend a campus event and jot down the facts you are able to observe. Write a short report in which you present the facts about the event. Avoid expressing your opinion of the facts.
3. Write a paper of 350–500 words in which you develop an idea, using at least three different methods of clarification and support.
4. Write a paper in which you explain how to accomplish a task or how a process works. Use visual aids if necessary. Be careful to make your meaning clear to whoever may read your paper.
5. Write a news story about some event to which you were an eyewitness. Follow the conventional style for news stories, being careful to include all appropriate information in the lead sentence. Avoid expressing your personal opinion about the facts you observed.
6. Select an abstract word that is used loosely by people in normal conversations. Write a 350-word definition of this word, assigning the meaning you select. Use whatever means of clarification seem most appropriate.
7. Write a research paper on a topic selected in conference with your instructor. Follow the directions for research writing set forth in this chapter. Restrict the length of the paper to about 1500 words.
8. Write a paper in which you evaluate a book you have read, a movie you have attended, a play you have seen, or a group discussion to which you have listened.
9. Select an advertisement from a current magazine and analyze it for techniques employed to influence your thinking. Write a paper in which you evaluate the effectiveness of the advertisement as far as you personally are concerned.
10. Write a paper in which you try to persuade your readers to your way of thinking about a subject of current interest. Use both logical and emotional appeals in dealing with the subject.

FOR FURTHER READING

Atkinson, Brooks, "In Praise of Plain Writing," *New York Times Book Review*, September 8, 1946.

Canby, Henry Seidel, *Better Writing*, New York, 1926.

Crocker, Lionel, "On Seas of Ink," *Vital Speeches of the Day*, December 6, 1946.

Graves, Robert, and Hodge, Alan, *The Reader Over Your Shoulder*, New York, 1943.

La Farge, Oliver, "The Art of Discontent," *Vogue*, 1952.

Lardner, Ring, *How to Write Short Stories*, New York, 1924.

Leacock, Stephen, *How to Write*, New York, 1945.

Lindey, Alexander, "Plagiarism and Originality," *Reader's Digest*, November, 1952.

Merrill, Paul W., "The Principles of Poor Writing," *Scientific Monthly*, January, 1947.

Sandburg, Carl, "Trying to Write," *Atlantic Monthly*, September, 1950.

REFERENCE
GUIDE

REFERENCE GUIDES

One of the most satisfactory methods of improving your ability to communicate ideas successfully is to learn to criticize your own efforts. In order to do this intelligently, you must have adequate standards by which to judge the adequacy of your vocabulary choices, arguments, support of ideas, arrangement of materials, and conformity to standard conventions of punctuation, spelling, syntax, and paragraph structure. The Reference Guides which follow are designed to make such self-criticism possible. The detailed suggestions which are offered should prove helpful whenever you are in doubt about a particular usage, or when you want to revise your initial attempts to communicate thoughts in either writing or speaking.

The guides are arranged as follows:

D—Diction
A—Affective Devices (propaganda techniques)
L—Logical Fallacies
P—Paragraphs
S—Sentences
G—Conventions of Grammar and Syntax
M—Mechanics (punctuation and spelling)

DICTION

Words can be both a medium of understanding and a barrier to understanding. They can promote understanding if and when (a) they convey an author's or speaker's thoughts exactly; (b) they are appropriate to subject, audience, and occasion; (c) they are simple, clear, and direct.

D-1 EXACTNESS (See also Section 10.2)

George Orwell once said, "The English language is becoming ugly and inaccurate because our thoughts are foolish, but the slovenliness of our language makes it easier for us to have foolish thoughts." Using words which do not adequately express thoughts intended can thwart the most sincere efforts to communicate meaning. Vagueness is usually a sign of muddled thinking, insufficient vocabulary, or slovenly verbal habits. Effective communication requires a keen sensitivity to words and their myriad shades of meaning. In each of the following sentences the intended thought is compromised by the inaccuracy of the italicized word: "I'd like to *renovate* in your mind the number of times that a radio is clicked on just to find out the correct time." "Two days after our arrival we were sent on a fifteen-mile field trip in the mountains where there were *assimilated* enemy troops in bivouac." "His major is music; he is *taking* five different instruments."

D-1.1   Words which accurately portray your thought

Say what you mean. Choose words whose meanings are sharp and clear, and appropriate in the contexts in which you place them.

The difficulty connected with inaccurate choice of words is emphasized in this passage from a newspaper column by John Crosby:

. . . That tireless investigator of other people's business, Allen Funt, took his "candid camera" and his concealed microphone out the other day to find out how many people knew what the word *retroactive* meant. He walked up to an elevator starter and declared belligerently: "Listen, I think you ought to know that the last elevator on the right is retroactive."

"Gee," said the starter, "haven't heard any complaints from the elevator man."

"It's dangerous."

"Gee, we'll have to look into it. You think it's very dangerous?"

"It certainly is dangerous. You can get into all kinds of trouble with that."

Mr. Funt then wandered out, smiling his sadistic smile, and accosted a young lady at a soda fountain. "Boy," he exclaimed, "isn't this weather retroactive though?" She agreed heartily that it was.

"Most retroactive day we've had," said Funt.

"Yes," said the girl. "Terrible."

"You know what retroactive weather is, don't you?" asked Funt.

"Very hot without stopping," said the girl firmly.

The next victim was a gentleman window shopping. "Hey, buddy," said Funt grimly. "If I were you I wouldn't go into that store."

"Why not?"

"Those people in there, they're very retroactive. . . ."[1]

D-1.2   Mistaking one word for another

Mrs. Malaprop, a character in Sheridan's comedy *The Rivals*, confused *alligator* with *allegory* in the famous remark: "As headstrong as an allegory on the banks of the Nile." Such confusions

[1] *New York Herald Tribune,* 1950.

in words are called *malapropisms*. They should be avoided, not only because they distort meaning, but also because they are a source of embarrassment to their author.

Words which are pronounced alike but spelled differently are responsible for many errors in writing. Such words are called *homonyms: to, too, two; weigh, way; principal, principle*; etc.

Other words, originating from the same root, slightly different in both spelling and pronunciation, are a source of error in both oral and written communication: *continual, continuous; respectful, respective*; etc.

Following is an alphabetically arranged list of words frequently confused for one reason or another:

About, around. *About* means "approximately"; *around* means "encompassing or encircling."

> *About* 150 people attended the lecture. He wore a beaded belt *around* his waist.

Accept, except. *Accept* means "to receive" or "to agree"; *except* means "to exclude" or "with the exception of."

> I *accept* your offer on the terms stipulated.
>
> All members of the committee were present *except* one.
>
> I *accept* the conditions of the contract, if I may *except* the third in the enumerated list.

Acquire, obtain. *Acquire* means "to accumulate bit by bit"; *obtain* means "to come into possession of."

> My brother has *acquired* a library of rare volumes.
>
> Permission may be *obtained* from the principal.

Adopt, adapt. *Adopt* means "to take as your own"; *adapt* means "to alter or change."

> You might *adopt* a child if you want someone to play with.
>
> I shall *adapt* your proposal to meet the needs of our special circumstances.

Advantage, merit, quality. *Advantage* suggests superiority of one thing over another.

> Your experience with people gives you an *advantage* over me.
>
> I think your proposal has certain *merits* even though I reject it.
>
> Your paper has many good *qualities*.

The *values* of a dictionary cannot be explained in the time available.

Affect, effect. *Affect* means "to produce an effect or change" or "to pretend or assume"; *effect* means "to cause" (as a verb) or "result" (as a noun).

Temperature *affects* water.

The sudden appearance of the disguised men *effected* a panic among the spectators.

Your remarks have had a profound *effect* on my thinking.

Aggravate, irritate. *Aggravate* means "to make worse or more severe"; *irritate* means "to excite to impatience or anger."

His heart trouble was *aggravated* by the strenuous exercise.

I am *irritated* by your snide remarks.

All right, alright. *Alright* is regarded as a misspelling of *all right.*

All together, altogether. *All together* means "all in one place" or "all at the same time"; *altogether* means "wholly."

All together now, let's go over the top.

I am not *altogether* satisfied with your story.

Allusion, illusion, delusion. An allusion is "an incidental, casual, or indirect reference to something"; an illusion is "a deceiving image or hallucination"; a delusion is "a false belief or opinion."

The speaker made an *allusion* to the writings of Milton.

Your eyes are deceived by *illusion.*

He is under the *delusion* that he passed the examination.

Already, all ready. *Already* means "by now" or "previously"; *all ready* means "everyone or everything is ready," or "completely ready."

It is *already* noon by my watch.

Are you *all ready* to go?

Amount, number. *Amount* is used for things measured in bulk; the *number* of things can be counted.

The *amount* of flour in the barrel can be measured.

A small *amount* of money was found in the safe.

The *number* of questions you can answer will depend on your willingness to budget your time.

And etc. *Etc.* is the abbreviation for et cetera, meaning "and so forth"; *and* in this construction is superfluous as well as redundant.

Anxious, eager. *Anxious* means "full of anxiety" or "greatly troubled"; *eager* means "ardent in desire or feeling."

Tom is *anxious* about his child's health.

My son is *eager* to join the Boy Scouts.

Any way, anyway, anyways. The first of these three locutions is two separate words; the second means "in any case"; the third is a variant form of anyway or anywise and is considered poor usage.

Any way is the right way.

You may have won the prize, but you'll have to pay tax on it *anyway*.

Apt, likely, liable. *Apt* means "inclined, disposed, or prone"; *likely* means "expected" or "probable"; *liable* means "exposed to something undesirable."

My sister is an *apt* student of composition.

You are *liable for* damages whether you report the incident or not.

He is the man voted most *likely* to succeed.

As, as if, like. Both *as* and *as if* are conjunctions used to introduce clauses. *Like* is a preposition and is followed by an object (noun or pronoun).

He looks *like* a scarecrow in this garb.

He is twice *as* old *as* his cousin is.

He acts *as if* he were afraid to express his mind.

My family is not so sophisticated *as* yours.

Awful, difficult, unfortunate. *Awful* means literally "full of awe" but is widely used in place of much milder expressions. Its tendency to exaggerate should be avoided. Instead of saying, "I have an awful headache," say, "I have a severe headache." Instead of saying, "You are awful late," say, "You are very late."

Beside, besides. *Beside* means "by the side of"; *besides* means "in addition to."

He is *beside* himself with glee.

You will have to take a course in gym *besides* your other studies.

Can, may. *Can* denotes ability; *may* denotes permission. The distinction between the two expressions is usually maintained by careful speakers and writers.

I doubt that you *can* win the race, but you *may* compete if you wish.

Common, mutual. Both words concern a shared experience, but *mutual* usually suggests reciprocation.

We have a *common* ally.

They have a *mutual* dislike for each other.

Complement, compliment. *Complement* means "that which makes up or supplies a deficiency" or "two things which mutually complete each other"; *compliment* means "praise, respect, or tribute."

Milady's gloves and shoes *complement* her dress.

I must *compliment* you on your ability to solve the problem.

Contemptible, Contemptuous. *Contemptible* means "deserving contempt"; *contemptuous* means "showing contempt."

A man who deserts his family is a *contemptible* cur.

She gave me a *contemptuous* look that froze my enthusiasm.

Continual, continuous. *Continual* means "intermittent" or "occurring at close intervals"; *continuous* means "without interruption."

Her *continual* complaints finally won her a hearing.

The hot weather was *continuous* all summer.

Council, counsel. A council is an administrative body; counsel means advice.

The City *Council* is now in session.

I need some *counsel* in planning my curriculum.

Disinterested, uninterested. *Disinterested* means "impartial" or "unbiased"; *uninterested* means "having no interest in a thing."

I am a casual, *disinterested* observer.

I am completely *uninterested* in what you have to sell.

Effect, affect. See *Affect.*

Elude, allude. *Elude* means "to evade"; *allude* means "to refer to."

My wife has *eluded* me all day.

In his paper he *alluded* to Hamlet.

Except, accept. See *Accept.*

Fine, good, splendid. Such words are vague synonyms of approval. Use a word that clearly defines your thought. Instead of saying, "It was a good movie," say, "The picture was gripping and full of suspense."

Former, first. *Former* is used when two things are mentioned; *first, second, third,* etc., when more than two are listed.

I am studying music and art; the *former* is my favorite.

Of the three subjects mentioned, the *first* is most difficult for me.

Healthy, healthful. *Healthy* means "possessing health"; *healthful* means "conducive to health."

My mother is a *healthy* woman.

Arizona has a *healthful* climate.

Incredible, incredulous. *Incredible* means "hard to believe"; *incredulous* means "unbelieving."

His account of his trip to Africa is *incredible*.

He was too *incredulous* to accept the facts which were shown to him.

Infer, imply. *Infer* means "to draw conclusions from facts, data, or evidence"; *imply* means "to suggest a meaning not actually stated."

The detective *inferred* from his observations that the killer was not human.

He *implied* that he knew more than he was willing to reveal.

Job, position. *Job* refers to an acceptable piece of work; *position* to employment to which a certain amount of dignity is attached.

My *job* is to wash the dishes and sweep the floors.

What *position* do you hold in the university?

Majority, plurality. *Majority* means "more than half," or a number of votes which exceeds all others cast; *plurality* means "an excess of votes over the nearest rival."

Percent, percentage. *Percent* is employed with actual numbers; *percentage* is not.

The bank note draws 6 *percent* interest.

A large *percentage* of students are freshmen.

Personal, personnel. *Personal* refers to one's private life and experience; *personnel* refers to the people in an organization.

My *personal* opinion did not sway him.

The office *personnel* have a day off today.

Practical, practicable. A practical thing is "capable of being turned to use"; *practicable* means "capable of being put into practice."

The idea seemed good for *practical* purposes.

Your suggestion is hardly *practicable*.

Principal, principle. *Principal* usually refers to a teacher or a sum of money; principle means "a governing rule or truth."

The *principal* is out of town until Tuesday.

The *principle* of fair play was a guide to all his actions.

Respectfully, respectively, respectably. *Respectfully* means "in a courteous manner"; *respectively* means "each in the order named"; *respectably* means "in a manner worthy of esteem."

I expect to be treated *respectfully*.

The first and second places were won by Jack and Jill *respectively*.

I hope you conduct yourself *respectably*.

D-1.3 Vagueness

Avoid vague, general words which make meaning "fuzzy" and inexact. Ineffective speakers and writers depend heavily on what H. L. Mencken has called "counter-words"—words which are employed promiscuously in all sorts of contexts and put to so many uses that they lose all meaning. Notice, for example, how the word *rare* alters its meaning in the following sentences:

Wild canaries come among us on a *rare* April day.

I had a *rare* experience this afternoon on the beach.

What is so *rare* as a day in June?

He has some *rare* disease which I never heard of.

Red Shoes is a *rare* movie; you ought to see it.

Overworked words such as the following, when used indiscriminately, communicate ideas badly:

analysis	dynamic	gismo
angle	element	grand
aspect	emerge	gripping
awful	enterprise	impressive
basically	factor	interesting
beautiful	feature	intrigue
complex	fine	item
cute	flair	jigger
definitely	foul	justice
dingus	function	lousy
doodad	gadget	lurid
doololly	gesture	material
dreamboat	gimmick	nice

object	quality	stuff
oomph	radical	swell
outlook	reaction	thing
outstanding	realistic	thingamajig
patriotic	resource	values
perfect	romantic	vital
phase	sentimental	warp
plus	situation	whatchamacallit
problem	specifically	wonderful
putrid	streamlined	

D-1.4 Distortion of the idea

Avoid words which either exaggerate or depreciate your idea. C. E. Montague has suggested three different ways of stating facts: "You may state them about twice as big as they are, or about half as big as they are, or, if you have skill and complete confidence in your skill, you may state them just as big as they are."

Effective communication depends on stating things "just as big as they are." Excessive use of superlatives and hyperbole is communicative extravagance, characteristic of immature and unskillful speakers and writers. Euphemistic dodges which "underrate" or "undersell" ideas are also characteristic of ineffective communication. The following description of a street in Miami, Florida, demonstrates uncontrolled choice of words: "Collins Avenue is a glittering 15-mile row of superlatives. Undoubtedly, the most luxurious street in the world today, it is a canyon of glamour, flanked on both sides by more than 260 impressive hostelries, several beaches and a few empty lots not yet absorbed in the beach-building craze."[2]

Advertising copy supplies innumerable examples of unrestrained superlatives:

> The greatest drop of whiskey in the world.
> The greatest name in rubber.
> The most beautiful buy of all.

[2] *People and Places,* December, 1955, p. 19.

The proudest achievement in fifty years.
First choice for flavor and energy.
Nothing measures up to wool.

The following words if used indiscriminately may easily distort facts:

amazing	gorgeous	prohibitive
awful	horrible	spectacular
cardinal	incomprehensible	staggering
cataclysmic	inimitable	stampede
catastrophic	innumerable	stratospheric
cinemascopic	jamboree	stupendous
colossal	lavish	super-
conclusive	marvelous	teetotally
critical	massacre	terrible
deplorable	memorable	terrific
distinguished	microscopic	thrilling
eminent	motorama	ultra-
engaging	nondescript	unbelievable
fantastic	notorious	unprecedented
gigantic	outlandish	vital
glamorous	phenomenal	whopper
glitter	prize-winning	

A euphemism is a word which "substitutes a mild, indirect, or vague expression for a harsh or blunt one." Since the purpose of communication is to transfer meanings exactly, most euphemisms should be avoided. Following is a list of examples:

ambulance for *hearse*
beautician for *hairdresser*
café for *eating house*
crematorium for *crematory*
custodian for *janitor*
ecdysiast for *strip-tease artist*
expectorate for *spit*
fountaineer for *soda jerk*
houseman for *hotel detective*

landscape architect for *gardener*
maid for *hired girl*
memorial park for *graveyard*
mortuary for *morgue*
obsequies for *funeral*
powder room for *lavatory*
publicity director for *press agent*
sanitary officer for *garbage collector*
shoetician for *cobbler*
slumber shirt for *shroud*
state hospital for *lunatic asylum*
supervisor for *boss*
tonsorial artist for *barber*

Fine writing is another variety of "tall talk" that testifies of its author's insincerity and lack of restraint. It is flowery, swollen, and emotionally toned. Here is an example, quoted by Henry Seidel Canby in *Better Writing*: "Her hair was like a shower of primrose petals falling, and her cheeks were finished with the artistic touches of Aurora's rosy hand. Her eyes were like the corolla leaves of the blue-veined violet, her nose was a posy to her face, and her pearly teeth sparkled with nectarean dew."

D-1.5   Specific and concrete words

Prefer specific to general words and concrete to abstract ones. The overuse of highly abstract and general terms is likely to defeat successful communication of ideas. (See also pp. 50–51.) Abstract words present a generalized rather than a concrete concept of a person, place, or thing. Abstract words are quite useful in summary statements, but unless care is taken to support them with specific details they become vague, hazy, pretentious, almost meaningless, and certainly lifeless and dull expressions. Notice how the italicized words in the following sentence depend upon the rest of the passage for precise meaning: "There it was, tossed on a pile of grass cuttings, two blue eggs broken in its depths, and the sides of the nest crushed—*a pitiful wreck of lovely hopes and artistic skill."*

George Orwell says, "When you think of a concrete object, you think wordlessly, and then, if you want to describe the thing you have been visualizing, you probably hunt about till you find the exact words that seem to fit it. When you think of something abstract you are more inclined to use words from the start, and unless you make a conscious effort to prevent it, the existing dialect will come rushing in and do the job for you, at the expense of blurring or even changing your meaning." The author suggests that we put off using words until the meaning has become clear through mental images or sensations.

Compare the two statements following. Both concern the education of children. Notice the abstractness of one and the specificity of the other.

"Unless due regard is given the development of the child, the result will be irresponsibility, moral laxness, and inability to cope with the complexities of life"—Robert Gunning.

"So I told you that I knew of a way to teach reading that was altogether different from what they do in schools or in remedial reading courses or anywhere else. . . . Today Johnny can read—not perfectly, to be sure, but anyone can see that in a few more months he will have caught up with other boys of his age. And he is happy again: You and I and everyone else can see that he is a changed person"—Rudolf Flesch.

D-2 CLARITY (See also pp. 219–221)

If words are chosen with proper care, there should be no mistaking the meaning you intend to convey. But the fact that communication among individuals constantly breaks down for one reason or another makes it imperative that you use language which is clear. When communication is effective, meaning is unmistakable.

D-2.1 Pretentious, eccentric, or "outlandish" words

Undue attention to words has a tendency to obscure thoughts and ideas and to block, clog, and obfuscate communication of meaning. "Big words," unless used with care, can easily frustrate the purpose they are mustered to achieve. There are times, of course, when a big word is the right word and indispensable to clarity of expression. Scientists refer to nerve-deadening novocaine as *aminobenzoyl-diethylamino-ethanol*. Merthiolate is *sodium ethylmercurithiosalicylate*. Such words clearly indicate the chemical structure of a compound and are much more exact and more appropriate for scientific purposes than the simpler words of a layman.

To insist on the simplest of diction for all subjects and purposes is to ignore the doctrine of appropriateness in language and to put an unnecessary tax on a speaker or writer. But pretentious language that calls attention to words rather than thoughts is to be avoided. Ben Franklin's advice is: "Never use a long word when a short one will do."

Some people who have acquired a new word in their vocabularies are like children with a new toy—they want to show it off. Notice the exhibition of the word *transcendent* in the following passage: "Learning never ceases from the moment a child is born until life has ended; what a man learns as he grows older is of *transcendent* importance to him and to society."

Notice how the thought contained in the following sentences becomes clear and comprehensible when the italicized words are replaced by the simpler expressions in parentheses:

> While the political *desideratum* (essentials or needs) of world order became clearer, there was reluctance to work in forthright fashion to *utilize* (use) education to promote world order.
>
> Asians are devious or *inscrutable* (mysterious or incomprehensible).
>
> The zoo has just acquired a new *pachyderm* (elephant).

Mr. Acheson's apples, for all their polish, cannot conceal their *vermiculated* (wormy) content.

Xenophobia (hatred or fear of strangers) is rampant in Iran.

Mr. Nye is a *lucid expositor* (clear writer).

Knowing right from wrong is *anthropomorphism* (assuming the attributes of God).

Simple words that reveal rather than conceal their author's thoughts may be found in this explanation of air mass analysis: "The air which was warm, moist, and gray last night is still warm, moist and gray this morning; but it has been pushed fifty or one hundred miles to the south and east of where you live, and has been replaced by a mass of cold, dry air coming from the north or west. It is as simple as that; there is no mysterious 'It' in it; just plain physical sense. It is called air mass analysis" —Wolfgang Langewiesche.

Following is a brief list of verbal equivalents which supplies simple, clear, understandable substitutes for abstruse words:

Pretentious	*Communicative*
advise	inform
alteration	change
alternative	other
ameliorate	improve
animosity	ill will
basically	essentially
categorical	logical
clandestine	secret or private
commiseration	pity
component	part
conservative	moderate
consolidate	combine
conspicuous	excellent
constitute	make up
data	information
effect (verb)	do
eliminate	do away with

Pretentious	*Communicative*
entity	thing
equitable	fair
esoteric	private or confidential
establish	make
eventuate	happen
exemplary	commendable
exhibit	show
expedite	speed up
expire	die
exploit	take advantage of
extirpate	destroy
extraneous	unnecessary
extricate	disentangle
identical	same
ilk	class, kind, or sort
impact	effect
implement (verb)	foster, endorse, or supplement
implicit	implied
incarnadine	red
incommensurate	inadequate
incommodious	inconvenient
individual	person
inexorable	unyielding
inherent	native
initial	first
initiate	begin
institute (verb)	set up
insular	narrow
integrate	write
interim	interval
intrigue	excite
intrinsic	belonging to
liquidate	do away with
objective	aim, goal, or purpose
overall	general
partial to	in favor of
peripheral	external

Pretentious	*Communicative*
portion	part
primary	first or original
prior to	before
probationary	conditional
promote	advance
protagonist	advocate
reaction	opinion
rehabilitate	repair
sedulous	persistent
semblance	likeness
subsequent to	after
sufficient	enough
terminate	end
unique	exceptional
utilize	use
veritable	genuine
vital	important

Other types of expression that tend to obscure thoughts include freak inventions, foreign borrowings, and new words formed from familiar elements. Here are some examples:

ad-libber
alrightski
breadery (bakery)
brisbanality (platitudinous utterance)
carniceria (butcher shop)
chiropract (verb)
debamboozle
deracinated
de-regionalize
do-gooder
electragist (electrician)
Fleschurize (simplify)

freewayitis (frustration on a freeway)
impermissible
lollapalooza
manhattanize
peacherino
pitilacker (one cruel to animals)
splendiferous
subaqueous
supergobsloptious
swatfest (baseball game)
uninterpenetratingly
whooptician (college cheer leader)

D-2.2   Confusion of meanings   (see also pp. 51–52)

An ambiguous or equivocal expression is one that has several different meanings. Of course, all words are to some extent ambivalent or multi-meaningful. For some of the simplest words in the language there are as many as 150 separate meanings recorded in the dictionary. These meanings can quite easily become confused, and care must be taken not to use a word in more than one sense in a given context, making allowance, of course, for puns and other such types of verbal chicanery. In the epitaph written by Melville—"Here lies the emptiest of mortals; he was full of himself"—the equivocal use of *full* is humorous and inoffensive. When, however, meaning is obscured by equivocation, the practice is properly called dishonest.

A newspaper editorial, discussing the Biblical statement that knowing the truth will keep men free, argues: "If people are to keep their freedom they must have access to the truth. A responsible press reports accurately what people say. But what people say is not always true." Two different meanings of *truth* are confused here. Biblical truth is for the most part intuitive or mystical truth, whereas truth about the government is factual, historical, or ideological truth.

Ralph Barton Perry, in his essay "What Does It Mean to Be Free?" shows that as regards censorship of literature a surprising number of Americans consecrated in the traditions of democracy do not understand the principle of freedom on which these traditions are based. "They still tend," he says, "to lapse into the primitive view that it means freedom to think and communicate *true* or *safe* opinions." The trouble with a word like *freedom* is that it means so many things to different people as to be almost worthless for the purpose of clarifying thought.

D-2.3   Trite words and clichés

Trite words and phrases are substitutes for thinking. They save a speaker or writer the trouble of deciding precisely what he means, and for this reason they sidetrack ideas and obscure clear-cut intentions. Such verbal dodges have been called "the rubber stamps or stereotyped plates of thought and expression." Dead metaphors are figurative expressions that have lost, by overuse, their original zest and communicativeness. They are used by people who are too lazy to think for themselves, who are incapable of creative thought, or who distrust their own verbal ingenuity. Following is a list of expressions which are worn out from too frequent use:

abreast of the times
aching void
acid test
along the lines
apple of her eye
as luck would have it
at a loss for words
ax to grind
bitter end
brilliant performance
budding genius
cap the climax
captain of industry
clear as crystal
clear as mud
climate of opinion
do a tailspin
dodge the issue
doomed to disappointment
drastic action
eat crow
equal to the occasion
familiar landmark
fly in the ointment
force of circumstances
grist to the mill
hammer and anvil
have the floor

heartfelt thanks
heated argument
hit the ceiling
in the last analysis
iron resolution
irony of fate
it stands to reason
justice to the occasion
keep a stiff upper lip
kick in
know the ropes
muscle in
needs no introduction
no thinking man
ominous silence
on the order of the day
paramount issue
play into the hands of
powers that be
psychological moment
rising generation
ruling passion
run into the ground
shadow of a doubt
stand shoulder to shoulder
take my word for it
take up the cudgels
talk off the top of your head

think out loud
thunderous applause
toe the line

wheel of fortune
words fail me

Notice the stereotyped expressions in the following passage:

As I *stop to consider,* there are a lot of machines that *instill acute apprehension within my breast.* A vacuum cleaner *scares the living daylights out of me.* . . .

. . . *Little did I realize* that it was my subconscious protecting me from the psychic trauma of operating a machine that frightens me.

By a *logical extension of thought,* no one should be forced to engage in any activity that frightens him. I really get scared, *cold sweat, palpitations of the heart,* acute nausea, *trembling fingers, rubbery knees,* when *I sit myself down* to work my income tax. . . .[3]

In direct contrast to this style of writing are the following passages which employ original and effective figures of speech to clarify rather than obscure thoughts and ideas:

Not only were city hotels such as the Palmer House in Chicago . . . heavens and havens for travelers, but resort hotels such as the United States and the Grand Union in Saratoga provided them with fairylands for their holidays. The United States, which opened the same year as the San Francisco Palace, was even bigger than the pride of the West Coast, and if the Palace was so colossal that guests were constantly getting lost in it, the United States was a magnificent wedding cake encrusted with ornament that might well have been squeezed out of a pastry cone.[4]

The moon was a round white eye, the desert dark space matching darker space when midnight fell. Lightly shifting airs had died. Trees stood sentry-still about the camp. The fire had burned far down, leaving only coals, like garnets in gray ash, to cast their banded tints upon the banded wall.[5]

[3] Edmund Arnold, "Lazy Husband Espies New Bill of Rights," *The State Journal* (Lansing, Michigan), February 5, 1956, p. 17.
[4] Russell Lynes, *The Tastemakers,* New York, 1954, p. 87.
[5] Forrester Blake, *Johnny Christmas,* New York, 1948, p. 39.

D-3   BREVITY AND DIRECTNESS

Efficiency in communication depends on economy of diction. Effective communication is not long-winded and wasteful, but brief and to the point. Wordiness and over-verbalization reduce the force of ideas and impede their transmission.

D-3.1   Unnecessary and meaningless words

Words or phrases which add nothing to a statement, and might better be omitted, are called *deadwood*. The italicized words in the following sentences are examples:

He is a specialist in *the area of* speech correction.
We have been discussing *the matter of* absences.
There were many *who* arrived early.
Every *thinking* person *seems inclined to* agree *with the notion* that the more expensive the product the greater the quality *will be.*
This is *far and away* the best program of the year.
By and large I agree with the negative *side of the argument.*
My sister was hired *in the capacity of* secretary.
The man *who was standing* at the speaker's stand made a few introductory remarks *by way of getting things started.*
The early bird, *as the fellow says*, gets the worm.
I am dubious *as to* whether our plan will succeed.
In order to succeed in *the* teaching *profession* one must be *of an* adaptable *nature.*
The building is large *in size*, rectangular *in shape*, and brown *in color.*
In some instances I have seen the dark horse come in first *place.*

The following sentences may be shortened and improved by substituting the words in parentheses for the italicized ones.

Comparative education is *that area of* (the) professional study *which centers on* (of) educational ideas and practices in different countries and *cultural areas* (cultures) *of the world.*
In spite of the fact that (although) you are tardy, you may come in.

I have judged him *in terms of* (by) his accomplishments.

In the majority of instances (most) students fail *in* their courses *as a result* (because) of poor study habits.

He *emerged from the encounter* (came off) without a scratch.

I am aware of the fact that (I realize) you are here.

Other such "verbal false limbs" include:

with reference to	be subjected to
in connection with	as means for the exercise of
relative to	on the occasion of
make contact with	an effective means of
have the effect of	being as how
in duration	in recognition of
in the process of	at the level of
if I am not mistaken	for the most part
by the way	by way of
in the manner of	on the assumption that
exhibit a tendency to	on the whole
serve the purpose of	

The italicized words in the following sentences are excessive, meaningless, or unnecessary.

I am *definitely* not interested.

I am *particularly* fond of apples.

My father is *basically* a nonconformist.

Your suggestion is under *active* consideration.

Smoking is *positively* forbidden.

He is *admittedly* too young to drink.

Jones gulped *down* a *full* meal in ten minutes.

I do not *personally* care what happens to him.

I *frankly* do not care for opera.

Grammar is not *too* difficult to understand.

Beside the river *there* is a footpath.

D-3.2 Wordiness, careless repetition, and padding (see also pp. 216–218)

The following expressions are redundant; that is, one of the words in each pair is superfluous:

yes, indeed
fine and dandy
free gratis
repeat again
return back
fellow classmates
each and every
no, not at all
yea, verily
pray and beseech
go forward
kit and caboodle
evening vespers
silently still

love and embrace
back behind
forefront
clearly obvious
investigative research
childish immaturity
foot pedal
time and tide
tooth dentist
same identical
that there
where at
refer back

The italicized parts of the following sentences point out need-less or ineffective repetition of words:

> Isn't it about time to *study* your *studies?*
> The *accident* was completely *accidental.*
> She *placed* her book in the same *place.*
> I *thought* others would *think* I invited myself.
> He is a *humanist* and devoted to *humanity* and *humane* values.
> You become aware of *ideas* you had no *idea* existed in your mind.
> Don't *poke* at me, cow*poke.*

D-3.3 Words with the same meaning

Avoid stringing several words together which have very simi-lar meanings. Notice that the italicized words in the following sentences accomplish no more than any one of them could. (See also pp. 216–218.)

> He held a *crimson red* apple.
> The expression is *trite, hackneyed, stereotyped,* and *outworn.*
> She is an *ardent, firm, fast,* and *devoted* Catholic.
> His argument smells of *judgment, opinion,* and *inference.*
> I am aware of the *conflicts, trials, tribulations, difficulties,* and *headaches* connected with your occupation.

A *dime, ten cents, the tenth part of a dollar* will get you in.
He was downright *furious, ferocious, angry,* and *mad.*

D-3.4 Excessive use of the passive voice

Overuse of the passive voice is a wasteful practice in the expression of thought. It may best be shown by contrasting sentences in both the active and passive voices:

Passive: At an early hour this morning the identity of the victim had not been established.
Active: Early this morning, no one had identified the body.

Passive: Interest in boxing is stimulated by television.
Active: Television stimulates interest in boxing.

Passive: The condition of Mr. X was reported still critical.
Active: The reporter says Mr. X is still in critical condition.

Passive: In the Iron Curtain countries tyranny has been established partly through the crude process of revolution by force and partly through the more subtle use of slogan and promulgation of half-truths and whole lies.
Active: Brute force and subtle propaganda, in the form of slogans, half-truths, and lies, have established tyranny in countries behind the Iron Curtain.

Passive: Little thought is given to the question whether the desired end cannot be achieved by utilizing the existing program of studies and by introducing a new emphasis.
Active: Educators have given little thought to whether desirable ends can best be achieved by existing methods or by a new emphasis.

Passive: There are many levels on which the contemporary attitudes to freedom are expressed.
Active: Individuals express their attitudes toward freedom in various ways.

Passive: Fourteen pilot interviews were conducted to determine the dimensions of the factors to be studied.

Active: The investigator conducted fourteen pilot interviews to determine the dimensions of the factors to be studied.

D-4 APPROPRIATENESS (See also Section 3.2 and pp. 212–215)

A word is appropriate when it is suitable to the time, place, purpose, and circumstances in which it is employed. Appropriateness ignores the time-honored notion that there is one approved way of saying something. It is based on the theory that times and circumstances change and that people in different places employ language in ways that are quite dissimilar. Paul Roberts in "The Future of Grammar" has this to say of the relativism of language forms:

Linguists have long argued that correctness is altogether relative, having nothing to do with logic or the order of the universe, but depending on such variables as time, place, circumstance, age, sex. The language forms used, correctly, in addressing an umpire may be incorrect in addressing a bishop. And vice versa. The sentence "We heard the sweetest little bird singing the dearest little song" is correct if you're a twelve-year-old girl but incorrect if you're a fifty-year-old bartender. In some circles, "Ain't you comin' back?" will get you blackballed; in others, "Shall you not return?" will get you tossed out on your ear.[6]

a. First we shall discuss appropriateness in time (see pp. 52–53).

That the meanings, forms, and pronunciation of words change as times change can be clearly shown. The word *prove* in the sentence "The exception proves the rule" means to test or to try. This was an acceptable meaning of the word in the year 1600 when the truism or aphorism was gaining currency. Today *prove* usually means to verify or to confirm, so that the original meaning of the statement is often distorted. The word *apron* was originally *napron*. *Bird* was spelled *brid* and designated "the

[6] *Inside the ACD*, February, 1954.

young or offspring of fowl." Many words have lost their etymological or original senses and have acquired entirely new meanings.

> *Pitiful* originally meant "full of pity."
> *Hydrophobia* originally meant "fear of water."
> *Fee* originally meant "cattle."
> *Chivalry* originally meant "horsemanship."
> *Bedstead* originally meant "bed place."
> *Frantic* originally meant "insane."
> *Imbecile* originally meant "weak."
> *Impertinent* originally meant "irrelevant."
> *Insulate* originally meant "isolate."
> *Nice* originally meant "precise."

Because times change and people change, the language of
communication must also change. Old words no longer useful
in transmitting meaning are dropped. New words are added.
And existing words are altered to fit new concepts and new situations that affect our lives. For example, we say "The sun
comes up in the east," but our notion of the movements of
planets in the solar system has altered greatly since we first
noticed the sunrise. What we really mean by our statement is
that the earth has revolved on its axis to a point where the sun
becomes visible.

The fact that we call native Americans *Indians*, that we refer
to China and Japan as the *Far East*, that we speak of people
boarding an *all-steel* ship, is evidence that the meanings of words
have changed to keep pace with our changing beliefs and points
of view. The following passage shows how the word *liberal* has
been compromised by political forces:

A new group called the American Liberal Association has been
formed, its leaders drawn from both major political parties, and its
inaugural press release warns that "the Communists may have tempo-
rarily ended the cold war, but we still have a lukewarm war which
must not be confused with a lasting peace." The statement also says:
" . . . the Communist bloc has not abandoned its long-range at-

tempt to conquer the free world. The manners of the Soviets have recently improved, but not their morals. . . ."

We welcome not only the sensible statement, but the formation of a group dedicated primarily to rescuing the word "liberal" from its miserable estate and restoring it to its proper place in the lexicon of democracy. Time was—and not too long back—when a "liberal" was a rugged individualist, an independent, a from Missouri type whose role was to challenge any or all orthodox tenets, to bedevil the black-and-white thinkers, to keep the body politic on its toes.

In the thirties, for whatever combination of reasons, the conscientious liberal fell down on his job. Preoccupied with fending off the spectacular assault by extremists of the right, he left himself wide open to subtle infiltration from the left. In so doing the liberal departed from his own first principle—and invited disaster. The passive liberal is the politically dead liberal. The Communists and their allies stole his banner, his reputation, his very name.[7]

The principal factors that alter word meanings are: (1) the subject of communication; (2) the person or persons involved in exchange of ideas; (3) the physical and social setting in which words are employed; (4) the verbal context in which the word appears; (5) the author's purpose in employing the word.

Semantic change (see also pp. 54–55), or alteration of the meaning of words, is accomplished in five principal ways: generalization, specialization, elevation, degeneration, and transfer. As long as language is employed by people for communicating ideas these types of change will automatically take place: extension of meaning from specific objects to classes of objects; restriction of meaning from classes of objects to specific objects; elevation of meaning from depreciatory to laudatory senses; degeneration of meaning from laudatory or neutral senses to depreciatory senses; transfer of meaning from one object to another.

GENERALIZATION.   Words whose meanings have been extended:

Aid. This shortened form of aide-de-camp was originally a military

[7] *Collier's*, December 9, 1955, p. 114.

term but has been extended to include the entire field of human relations.

Boat. Originally the word designated a small open vessel; now it may refer to any kind of craft including a battleship, or even an automobile.

Chance. Originally a term denoting the fall of dice; now refers to any kind of gamble.

Colossal. Originally referred to the Colossus of Rhodes, one of the Seven Wonders of the World; now means anything of large proportions.

Fellow. Originally meant "partner"; now refers to any chance acquaintance.

Mecca. The sacred city of Islam; now denotes any center of interest.

Paraphernalia. Originally denoted articles belonging to a wife besides her dowry; now suggests any collection of odds and ends.

The following words, derived from proper names, demonstrate a particular variety of generalization:

Ampere. From Andre Marie Ampere.
Bloomer. From Mrs. Amelia Bloomer.
Bowdlerization. From Thomas Bowdler.
Malapropism. From Mrs. Malaprop in *The Rivals.*
Ohm. From Georg Simon Ohm.
Quisling. From Major Vidkun Quisling, head of the Norwegian Nazi party during World War II.
Volt. From Alessandro Volta.
Watt. From James Watt.

SPECIALIZATION. Words whose meanings have been restricted:

Corn. Originally a generic word for small grain; now means a particular variety of grain.

Last. Originally meant "to extend continuously in space or time"; now is restricted to time.

Liquor. Originally any kind of liquid; now a particular kind of liquid.

Stare. Originally "to look"; now "to gaze."

Starve. Originally "to die"; now "to die for want of food."

AMELIORATION OR ELEVATION. Words whose meanings have become elevated:

Boudoir. Originally "sulking room"; now means "a small private room belonging to a lady."
Fame. Originally "common talk or report"; now means "lofty reputation or renown."
Lady. Originally "bread kneader"; now "a woman of distinction."
Prestige. Originally "magic"; now "renown."

PEJORATION OR DEGENERATION. Words whose meanings have degenerated:

Heathen. Originally "dwellers on a heath"; now a term of reproach.
Hussy. Originally "housewife"; now means a woman of ill repute.
Knave. Originally applied to Christ in the Scriptures; now a term of denunciation.
Peasant. Originally designated "a countryman"; now "a tiller of the soil of mean estate."
Reek. Originally "smoke"; now "a stench."

TRANSFER. Old words which have come to designate new objects:

Clock. Originally meant "bell."
Doll. Originally meant "puppet."
Ferment. Originally meant "to boil."
Plum pudding. Originally an edible pudding; now used by whalemen to denote "the fragmentary parts of a whale's flesh."
Skyscraper. Originally "a tall sail on a ship"; more recently applied to "a tall building."
Yarn. Originally "a gut or empty intestine."

b. Second, there is appropriateness in place (see also pp. 53–54).

Language is not uniformly spoken and written by all the people who use it for communication. Speech patterns differ from person to person, social group to social group, and community to community. There is no such thing as a completely standard English language. Instead, language is made up of several dialects or peculiar ways of expressing thoughts and of pronouncing words. The dialects of British English are much more pronounced than those of American English, partly because people in America move about more. The mass media of communication—newspapers, magazines, radio, television, and motion pictures—have a standardizing effect on the language. But we can still tell fairly well by a person's speech habits what part of the country he is from: New England, the Southwest, the deep South, the Midwest, etc. As we move about from one section of the country to another, our language changes accordingly. E. B. White once wrote: "I find that, whether I will or no, my speech is gradually changing to conform to the language of the country. The tongue spoken here in Maine is as different from the tongue spoken in New York as Dutch is from German. Part of this difference is in the meaning of words, part in the pronunciation, part in the grammar. But the difference is very great."

D-4 Language appropriate to the community with which audience or readers are identified

A speaker or writer must exercise sound judgment in the choice of words (see Chapter 11). Expressions which are perfectly appropriate on some occasions are most inappropriate on other occasions. Most guides to good usage maintain that words must be in national rather than sectional or local use. Such a principle makes little room for adapting language to specific audiences, in particular places, on unique occasions, and therefore should not be rigidly enforced. On the other hand, one should certainly not employ "hillbilly" speech forms as a matter of consistent practice.

D-4.2 Provincial expressions and dialect words in formal discourse

A number of localisms, appropriate in informal writing and conversation, should be carefully avoided, except for special effects, in formal compositions. Such localisms are of several varieties:

a. Substitution of strong for weak verbs: *gruv* for *grieved*, *snew* for *snowed*.
b. Substitution of weak for strong verbs: *drinked* for *drank*, *knowed* for *knew*, *winned* for *won*.
c. Making nouns out of verbs: *know-how, kickback, eats, build-up, showdown, shake-up.*
d. Making verbs out of nouns and adjectives: *hide-an'-seekin', breakfasted, back, bar, cite, net, score, to better, to little up.*
e. Folk inventions: *blackcaps* for *black raspberries, cackle-berries* for *eggs*, *tote* for *carry*, *poke* for *bag* or *sack*, *heft* for *lift*, *loco* for *crazy*, *spell* for *time*.
f. Clippings or abbreviations: *okay, snafu, divvy, cab, phone, taxi, movie, facial.*
g. Metaphorical inventions: *rubberneck, grass roots, hot dog, square deal, ace high, stuffed shirt, egghead, bump into.*
h. Mispronunciations: *nary* for *none*, *ary* for *any*, *agin* for *again* or *against*, *fotch* for *fetch* or *bring*, *rech* for *reach*, *jest* for *just*.
i. Errors in syntax: *us* for *we*, *we* for *us*.
j. Use of obsolete forms: *erster, foist, afeared, afore, lief.*

c. Finally, we must consider appropriateness to purpose and occasion (see Chapters 10 and 11).

A word which is highly appropriate in one set of circumstances may be equally inappropriate in others. The important thing in communication is to find expressions most suitable for the purposes you have in mind and the people to whom they are directed. Varieties of language not appropriate for all occasions include colloquialisms and slang expressions, professional jargon, and vulgarisms and improprieties.

Colloquialisms and slang have their place in the language. A word is classified as colloquial when it is more appropriate for familiar conversations than for formal discourse. Specific varieties of colloquial expression are classified as slang.

(1) Popular substitutes for conventional expressions: *doll* for *girl*, *cop* for *policeman*, *shindig* for *dance*, *grub* for *food*, *heel* for *objectionable person*.

(2) Cant terms borrowed from specific occupational or social groups: *moll* for *sweetheart*, *folding money* for *paper currency*, *touch* for *loan*, *dead soldier* for *empty whiskey bottle*.

(3) Figurative expressions, blended compounds, abbreviations, and other inventions: *pill pusher* for *medical doctor*, *egghead* for *intelligentsia*, *okay* for *all right*, *'snuff sed* for *enough said*, *spime* for *space-time*, *gobbledegook* for *pretentious language*, *set-to* for *argument*.

The social status of such words continually changes. Some colloquial and slang words become established usage: *skyscraper*, *pal*, *maudlin*, *gerrymander*, *carouse*, *hoax*, *to back out*, *blackleg*, *loony*, *piano*, *turnpike*, *awful*. Some established expressions which became obsolete are revived as slang: *decked out*, *learn* (in sense "to teach"), *sconce*, *slug*, *crazy*, *gab*, *ignoramus*, *padre*, *mess*.

The history of language is a record of compromises between old words and new words. Without the adoption of colloquial expressions, the written language would soon become obsolete and inexpressible. It derives new lifeblood from the ever increasing stock of slang expressions.

D-4.3 Slang and colloquial expressions in familiar discourse and on informal occasions

The following passage, quoted from a feature article in a newspaper, makes much use of slang and colloquial expressions:

Once I knew a guy who was a perfect husband. For 17 years he trimmed his toenails in the woodshed, gave his dough to the old lady, midwifed for her cat and never opened his trap. A real dreamboat.

Then one day she poled him with a rusty singletree and took up with a left-handed pig drover from Dipwick Corners.

"He sucked his teeth," she told the judge. "The man was the

tooth-suckinest critter I ever did see. Even after soup. I jist hadda belt 'im."

She copped a suspended sentence on an assault charge and the judge tossed in a divorce on the house. . . .[8]

Professional jargon (see also pp. 219–221), that is, technical words from the specialized vocabularies of occupational and professional groups, has a way of infiltrating the common language of a society. Because uninitiated persons are very likely to misuse the words, they come to have vague and loose interpretations. Such words as *neurosis, romance, intelligence quotient* (I.Q.), *ego, inhibition, compensation, schizophrenia, perception, and introversion* are quite often misleading because of the discrepancy between their popular meanings and their technical meanings.

D-4.4 Technical language

Avoid technical language when subject, purpose, audience, or occasion do not warrant it.

The specialized vocabularies of particular occupations and professions include what is called jargon or cant: *journalese, pedaguese, Federal prose,* and all varieties of language peculiar to select groups of people. Many professional men and women find it next to impossible to express their thoughts in simple, clear, straightforward English. University students who learn to pattern their expression on the models of their elders produce some almost unintelligible lingo in their master's theses or doctoral dissertations: "In the proposed study I wish to describe and evaluate representative programs in these fields as a means of documenting what seems to me a trend of increasing concern with the role of higher education in the improvement of interpersonal and intergroup relations and of calling attention in this way to outstanding contributions in practice."[9]

Occupational and professional jargon can be used to com-

[8] Knight D. McKesson, *The State Journal* (Lansing, Michigan), February 5, 1956, p. 17.

[9] Quoted by Jacques Barzun in "How to Write and Be Read," *Teacher in America*, Boston, 1946.

municate ideas clearly if a speaker or writer takes the trouble to explain how his words are to be interpreted and understood. The word *vulgarity* has entirely different meanings when used by literary critics and when used in connection with levels of language. In his essay "Vulgarity in Literature,"[10] Aldous Huxley uses the term to characterize the writings of Edgar Allan Poe, but only after carefully limiting its meaning for this purpose. Vulgarity and propriety are one aspect of appropriateness. Language propriety, like so many aspects of communication, is a relative matter. Words sanctioned by society today may be outlawed tomorrow, and words which were approved in past days may be stigmatized in our time. But in any age, some words are approved, some disapproved by conventional standards of usage. Albert Marckwardt states the doctrine of usage as follows: "The history of most modern languages shows that from generation to generation, and from century to century, there has been in existence an accepted and received standard form of that language— English, French, or whatever it may be; and that that standard form has been based upon the speech of the class and section of the country which was politically, economically, and culturally dominant at the time."

That the acceptability or appropriateness of specific words and expressions changes from time to time is to be expected rather than deplored. Ruth Mary Weeks has explained this attitude as follows: "Language is a living thing and the greatest law of life and growth is change. Dictionaries, grammars, books of rhetoric are not eternal statutes handed down from heaven like the tables of Mosaic law. They are history, not dogma; description, not command—description of the changing speech habits of the mass of men."

D-4.5 Unconventional expressions

Use unconventional language forms for special effects only. Vergil D. Reed, businessman, once delivered a lecture in which he applauded the cultural accomplishments of Americans. He

[10] Aldous Huxley, *Music at Night and Other Essays*, New York, 1931.

titled the lecture "Us Uncultured Americans," an obvious impropriety, in defense of people who have been labeled "uncultured."

A newspaper feature writer used a number of improprieties in the following passage in order to imitate the language of children. The improprieties are italicized. ". . . I like to help Daddy fix things and I like to make snow *mans*. I like to watch my baby sister when she's not sleeping too. . . . She can make funny faces real *good*. . . . Yesterday I went in Mommy's bedroom where Sandy sleeps in her little bed. . . . Sandy had her eyes open. I said real *soft*, 'Hi Sandy Jean, hi.' "[11]

The following expressions and words are not socially acceptable in all circumstances. Some are gradually winning approval; others are almost universally tabooed.

Ain't. *Ain't* is a contraction which is variously used for "am not," "are not," "is not," and "have not." It is usually considered illiterate or dialectal and for this reason is avoided by careful writers and speakers on most occasions. Will Rogers once said to his wife, who was trying to break him of the habit of saying *ain't*, "I know a lot of people who ain't eatin' because they ain't sayin' ain't." Some people argue that, since *ain't* appears in the dictionary, it must be a proper word. Such persons have not noticed that dictionaries brand the expression as vulgar, illiterate, or uneducated.

Bust, bursted. *Bust*, although labeled inelegant, dialectal, or slang in most dictionaries, is generally considered acceptable informal usage in such sentences as:

I *busted* my head wide open.

This depression will *bust* the bank.

I'll have to *bust* that bronc.

Bursted is an improper past tense of burst, the principal parts of which are *burst, burst, burst*.

Can't. A perfectly proper contraction of *cannot*. When coupled with certain other words it varies in acceptability:

You *can't* hardly get them any more. (Double negative. Avoided

[11] *The State Journal* (Lansing, Michigan), February 19, 1956, p. 21.

by careful speakers and writers. In very common currency in informal speaking and conversation.)

I *can't* help getting into trouble. (Standard usage.)

I *can't* help but like him. (Widely employed by educated people.)

I *can't* seem to solve this problem. (Perfectly appropriate for almost all occasions.)

Complected. Generally accepted usage for *complexioned* in such sentences as: My sister is dark-*complected*.

Could of. Mistaken form of *could have*. Not acceptable, unless used in reproducing dialect.

Different than. Colloquial alternative for *different from*. It is gaining in acceptability, especially in such sentences as: The movie was *different than* I expected.

Don't. A contraction of *do not*. Often used as a substitute for *doesn't* in sentences such as: He *don't* know any better. This usage is illogical and scarcely ever approved.

Dove, dived. *Dived* is the preferred past tense of *dive*, but *dove* is as often employed even though sometimes criticized.

Due to. This expression is recognized as an adjective but has been severely criticized when used as a connective or adverb. The latter function is approved by popular usage, and there is no point in resisting its evident acceptance.

Enthuse. A verb fashioned on the adjective *enthusiastic*. This word has been deplored by purists for many years, but an increasing number of people employ it without compunction, just as they use *better* and many other adjectives as verbs.

Every once in a while. Such expressions as this one and *every so often* are quite illogical but perfectly idiomatic. They make just as much sense as *center around*, or *children* as the plural of *child*.

Feel bad. "To feel bad" and "to feel good" refer to one's mental attitude; "to feel poorly" and "to feel well" refer to physical health.

Funny. A colloquial substitute for *odd*. It is proper for all types of communication except extremely formal ones.

Hanged, hung. In legal terminology a man is hanged when he is executed. But legal language resists change much more than the vocabulary of ordinary spoken and written English. *Hung* is employed in the sense of *hanged* without criticism, except from purists.

Haven't hardly. A double negative the same as *can't hardly, won't hardly,* etc. Prefer *have hardly, can hardly,* and *will hardly.* The double negative is not wrong but is likely to be criticized.

It is me. English teachers have fought violently against this usage for years. When Winston Churchill used the expression in one of his public addresses, there seemed little point in objecting further. Such other ungrammatical constructions as "it is her," "it is him," "it is them" are not so well established. Their use in spoken discourse is readily condoned.

Lay, lie. The present tense of the verb *lay* is the past tense of the verb *lie,* which causes some confusion. The principal parts of the two verbs are: *lie, lay, lain; lay, laid, laid.*

Learn, teach. *Learn* is improper in such sentences as: I'll *learn* you the trick, or My father *learned* me to read. From a historical standpoint there should be no objection to such usage, but social custom insists on *teach* or *instruct* in this sense.

Leave, let. *Leave* is considered illiterate usage in such sentences as: *Leave* us go to town. It is often used facetiously in imitation of the lingo of uneducated people. It should not appear in serious, formal discourse.

Like, as. Many instructors in composition argue that *like* is a preposition and should not be used to introduce a clause. For this reason you should prefer *as* or *as if* to *like* in formal discourse:

It looks *like* (as if) it might rain.

He acts *like* (as though) he were an officer.

Cut this out *like* (as) I told you to.

Loan. This word has been frequently considered improper as a verb meaning "to lend." Current usage has made the expression acceptable:

She *loaned* me her watch.

Mad. To most Americans, *mad* means "angry," and there is no reason to object to this meaning.

May, can. In formal English, *can* means "to be able," *may* means "to seek permission." In colloquial and informal discourse *can* is used in both senses.

Most. *Almost* is often shortened to *most* in informal discourse, but this practice is not advisable for formal discourse.

Muchly. This is a poor substitute for *much*.

Myself. The personal pronouns *myself, himself, yourself* should not be used to replace *I, he, you*.

Only. A great to-do has been made by teachers and grammarians about the position of *only* in a sentence. The most practical rule is: Place *only* where it sounds least awkward and makes best sense.

Proven, proved. Either is acceptable as the past tense or past participle of the verb *prove*. *Proven* is quite often used to modify nouns:

This is a *proven* fact.

Have I *proved* my point?

Public (is, are). Either verb is acceptable. *Public* may be considered either singular or plural.

Raise, rear. The notion that children are reared rather than raised is no longer cherished by educated people. Either form is acceptable.

Raise, Rise. *Raise* is a transitive verb; *rise* an intransitive one:

I *rise* from my seat.

I *raise* a question.

Real. Technically *real* should not modify adjectives, but informal usage permits it:

I think you look *real* nice.

Reason is because. This is an illogical construction since *reason* and *cause* mean the same thing:

The *reason* I am late *is because* I had an accident. Prefer the following:

I am late *because* I had an accident.

Set, sit. There is some stigma attached to such expressions as "why don't you set down and rest a while?" *Sit* is preferred in such contexts. You *set* the table. You *set* a chair in the middle of the room. But you *sit* on the chair.

Shall, Will. American usage permits the use of *shall* or *will* almost interchangeably:

Will you have dinner with me?

I *will* (shall) have dinner with you.

Shall I do this exercise again?

You *shall* (will) do this exercise again.

The armed services in America have adopted a usage that is contrary to the once rigid regulation. When a sergeant wants a "rookie" to dress in fatigues, he says: "You *will* (not shall) wear fatigues."

Slow, slowly. Either "drive slow" or "drive slowly" is acceptable. But you would hardly say "I *slow* retraced my steps."

These kind. Say *this kind* or *these kinds.*

Till, until. Either one is acceptable.

Transpire. In 1831 the *Boston Transcript* carried the following note with reference to *transpire:* "It is commonly adopted by incorrect writers—English as well as Americans—as a substitute for the phrases, to take place, to occur, to be transacted, etc. . . . Custom has made this intelligible." After more than 100 years there is surely no reason to oppose custom further.

Try and. Many educators prefer *try to* to *try and*, in such sentences as: *Try to* (and) understand me. There should be no great objection to this usage.

Used to. It is perfectly proper to say, "My brother used to live in the city."

Ways. You should prefer "The ship is a long way off" to "The ship is a long ways off," especially in writing.

When, where. The following usages are generally frowned upon:

I see *where* the major is to be married.

Cheating is *when* you copy someone's paper.

Who, whom. *Who* is the nominative form; *whom* is objective. The same principle applies in "It is I" or "It is me." Such expressions as "Who are you going to vote for?" are sanctioned by popular usage, although grammatically incorrect.

Idioms are characteristic ways of putting words together that have been established by usage. Such expressions as "Where at are you hiding?" are condemned by educated people even though frequently heard in conversation. "To center around" seems quite illogical but is employed by eminent speakers and writers. "To refer back" is objectionable because of its redundancy, the same as "go on ahead." The following idioms are acceptable in all types of discourse:

abide by (a decision); in (a place); for (a time); with (a person)

acquaint with

adequate for (purpose); to (demand)

adhere to

admit of (doubt) to, into (place, class)

agree in (opinion); to (proposal); with (person); on (plan)

analogous to

analogy to, with, between

antagonistic to, against

argue with, against, for, about

base on, upon

believe in, on

center in, on, upon, around

combine with, into

communicate to, with

compare with, to

concur with, in

contrast with, to

correspond with, to

impress on, upon, with, by

infer from

inform of, about, concerning

initiate into

insight into

insist on, upon

listen to, for

parallel to, with

participate in, with, of

prejudiced against

prevail on, upon, with

quarrel with, about, for

reconcile to, with

reflect on, upon

rely on, upon

significance of

similar to

skillful in, at

subordinate to

subscribe to, for

substitute for

sympathize with, for

translate from, into

D-5   DEFINITION   (See also Section 7.7)

Definition is the specification of the exact meaning of a word in a particular context. It is one of the most useful means we have of clarifying thought and insuring the proper reception of ideas. Meaning itself may be considered in two dimensions: connotation and denotation. Connotation refers to personal, private, associational, and emotional meanings of a word for an individual. Denotation refers to the meaning of a word established by usage, the unemotional sense recorded in the dictionary. "When I use a word," Humpty Dumpty said, in a rather scornful tone, "it means just what I choose it to mean—neither more nor less" (Lewis Carroll).

D-5.1 Definition to clarify thought

Clarity and specificity are the important factors to be considered in all definition. Defining terms is a useless exercise unless your meaning emerges clear and understandable. One writer defined *opinions* as "beliefs which may be valid so far as they go but which a man who cannot rise above them cannot rationally refine or test." The meaning of *opinion* here is no more certain than it was before the word was defined.

D-5.2 Connotative language in definitions

When you want to communicate feelings as well as thoughts, use connotative, suggestive expressions. The following definition of *Christmas* depends on connotations rather than denotations of words. It is not intended to inform readers but to reinforce what they already know: "Christmas is music—the sparkle of Jingle Bells, the calm beauty of Silent Night, the warm fellowship of God Rest Ye Merry Gentlemen! . . . songs sending merriment bounding through a snowy village square. . . ."[12]

D-5.3 Denotative words for definitions

When you want to focus attention on ideas, use denotative language. The following definition of *swing music* is descriptive and objective: it does not attempt to influence your attitude in one way or another. "Swing differs from other music in that in other musical forms the orchestra re-creates the composer's musical ideas just as the composer conceived them. The performer is in a secondary role. In swing the performer appears in a more creative role. Through improvisation . . . the performer transforms the composer's fundamental melodic idea into his own conception of the theme. In other words, the swing musician does not simply convey to the listener what was original with the

[12] *Collier's*, December 24, 1954, p. 110.

composer; he himself *creates* the musical substance his auditors hear" (from *The Music Lovers' Encyclopedia*).

D-5.4 Different meanings of words (see also pp. 54–55)

A survey conducted by Charles C. Fries reveals the curious fact that for the 500 most frequently used words in English the *Oxford English Dictionary* records 14,070 separate meanings. The word *set*, for example, has 154 separate meanings alone. Words in the language which are used in one sense only are usually scientific and technical terms not widely employed in communication. The following discussion of the word *air lift*, quoted from *Inside the ACD*, demonstrates how the meanings of a word are multiplied:

"There appear to be three senses in which *air lift* is currently used. The commonest is probably 'the system of air transport' as used in such a sentence as 'The hazards of the United States air lift increased considerably.' The other senses are 'the load carried' (as in 'The remainder of the day's air lift arrived on schedule') and 'the act or process of transporting such a load' (as in 'taken to their destination in one air lift'). . . . In addition, it was interesting to notice recently (1949) that the New York *Times* used the term to describe a system of air transport being planned by the Russian government to circumvent the Yugoslav blockade of Albania."

D-5.5 Words defined in context (see also Section 1.2)

Before words can have any meaning at all, they must be employed in sentences or contexts. The verbal contexts in which they are placed gives them meaning, which meaning, if it becomes common usage, is listed in a dictionary. In other words, we define words to suit our own convenience, and the dictionary—which is a history of the way language is employed—records our usages. Notice the word *liberal* in these sentences:

A *liberal* education prepares one's mind for truth.
The doctor gave me a *liberal* dose of medicine.

Here is a *liberal* translation of Plato.
The history teacher is a *liberal* minded professor.

It should be perfectly clear that in no two of these contexts is the meaning of the word identical. What *liberal* means in each case is determined by the other words with which it appears.

Notice how the context defines the words in this sentence: "Inspiration occurs when the first seed of a poem strikes root in him." Here are some of the meanings assigned to *inspiration* in the dictionary: (a) act of breathing—opposite of expiration; (b) act or state of being intellectually or emotionally inspired; (c) a supernatural influence which qualifies men to receive and communicate divine truth; (d) an inspiring influence: a person; (e) a result of inspiration.

The word *poem* in the above context is a clue to the fact that *inspiration* is used in dictionary sense b. The point is that this meaning would never have gotten into the dictionary unless someone, somewhere, sometime had used the word in this sense. Other words in the context—*seed* and *strike root*—are given very special meanings by the way they are used.

If there is any question about how a word is to be understood, it is the author's responsibility to clarify his meaning exactly. Notice how Aldous Huxley explains the use of *vulgar* in this passage: "Vulgarity is a lowness that proclaims itself—and the self-proclamation is also intrinsically a lowness. For pretentiousness in whatever field, unless more than justified by native capacity and demonstrable achievement, is low in itself. Moreover, it underlines all other deficiencies and, as a suitable chemical will reveal words written in invisible ink, calls out the latent lownesses in a character, so that they manifest themselves in the form of open vulgarities" (from "Vulgarity in Literature").

Robert M. Hutchins, in defining *athleticism*, leaves no room for doubt as to his precise meaning: "Athleticism is not athletics. Athletics is physical education. . . . Athleticism is not physical education but sports promotion, and it is carried on for the monetary profit of the colleges through the entertainment of the public" (from "Gate Receipts and Glory").

D-5.6 Derivation of dictionary definitions

Dictionary definitions are derived from the actual contexts in which words have been used. Whenever a word acquires a new sense that becomes established in the language, the dictionary must be revised to include the new meaning. Since people are constantly using words in new ways, adding words to the language, adopting foreign expressions, the dictionary cannot hope to keep up with language changes. It merely records the meanings we attach to words. For this reason, the dictionary should be used as a guide to meaning, not as a Bible or lawbook. Dictionary definitions are necessarily general and abstract, since they are derived from the thousands of contexts in which the words have been employed.

Lexicographers use the form shown in the accompanying illustration for keeping a permanent file of this information. (The illustration is a replica of an actual card used in the making of *The American College Dictionary.*)

---

stratovision   n.

"A special slow-speed plane, almost as large as the B-29, has been designed for the stratovision system."

Science News Letter 8/25/45   p. 121

LK
Television

A portion of the right-hand column of a sample page from A *Dictionary of Americanisms* shows how the meanings of words are supported by the actual dated contexts from which they were derived.

D-5.7 Uses of a dictionary

In spite of the limitations and deficiencies of dictionaries, they are invaluable tools of language study. Among the numerous types

HOOSIERINA

1826 in *Chi. Tribune* (1949) 2 June 20/3 The Indiana hoosiers that came out last fall is settled from 2 to 4 milds of us. **1831** in J. P. Dunn *Indiana* (1919) II. 1154 He [a horse] is stabled however in Indianapolis, the center of the race track, he has been corned, littered and kept in Indiana and may be called a 'Hoosher.' **1832** *Ind. Democrat,* Ask for our 'hoosiers' good plantations. **1885** *Outing* Nov. 152/2 Did you notice that young Hoosier and his bride who sat opposite me at breakfast? **1947** *Harper's Mag.* Jan. 67/2 Other Hoosiers ridicule them as hillbillies.

b. A big, burly, uncouth specimen or individual, a frontiersman, countryman, rustic. Cf. **mountain hoosier.**

1832 in J. P. Dunn *Indiana* (1919) II. 1153 A Real Hoosier.—A sturgeon, who, no doubt, left Lake Michigan on a trip of pleasure . . . being brought on terra firma, and cast into a balance, he was found to weigh 83 pounds. **1857** Godkin in R. Ogden *Life E. L. Godkin* I. 157 The mere 'cracker' or 'hoosier,' as the poor [southern] whites are termed. **1900** Flynt *Tramping* 304 *Hoosier,* a 'farmer.' **1948** Dick *Dixie Frontier* 310 Before it was used to designate the citizens of Indiana, the term 'Hoosier' was used in the South to describe a rough or uncouth person.

c. A way of speaking characteristic of Hoosiers. *Rare.* Cf. **Hoosierism.**

1871 Eggleston *Hoosier Schoolm.* iv. 41 The 'big road' (Hoosier for *highway*) ran along the north-west side.

d. (See quots.)

1926 *Amer. Mercury* Jan. 64/2 The word *hoosier* is applied to anyone who is incompetent. **1944** *N. & Q.* March 188 Its advertisements . . . were answered by a number of Indianans who knew little or nothing about the lumbering business; hence the word *hoosier* in the lumber trade came to mean 'a man who doesn't know his job.'

2. In combs.: (1) **Hoosier bait,** a kind of gingerbread (see quot. 1919 and cf. next), *obs.;* (2) **cake,** (see quot. and cf. prec.), *obs.;* (3) **dinner,** (see quot.); (4) **frog,** (see quot.); (5) **land,** Indiana, a nickname; (6) **Poet,** James Whitcomb Riley (1849–1916), a poet of Indiana; (7) **State,** a nickname for Indiana.

(1) **1833** in Dunn *Indiana* (1919) II. 1127 My pockets are so shrunk of late I can not nibble 'Hoosher bait.' **1919** J. P. Dunn II. 1141 The man said, 'I guess you want hoosier-bait,' and when he produced it I found that he had the right idea. . . . The gingerbread referred to was cooked in square pans—about fifteen inches across. . . . A quarter-section sold for a fip, which was 6¼ cents. — (2) **1859** Bartlett 202 Hoosier Cake, a Western name for a sort of coarse gingerbread, which, say the Kentuckians, is the best bait to catch a hoosier with, the biped being fond of it. — (3) **1856** Fergusson *America* 324 We reached Seymour about half-past twelve, and had a 'Hoosier' dinner at the M'Callum house . . . plenty of dishes, but miserably cooked, and worse served. — (4) **1883** *Amer. Naturalist* XVII. 945 The Mink or Hoosier Frog. . . . This frog (*Rana septentrionalis*) seems comparatively unknown, and is found in localities far apart.

Source: *A Dictionary of Americanisms,* Edited by Mitford M. Mathews, The University of Chicago Press.

of information supplied by a reputable college dictionary are the following:

a. Spelling. Both preferred and alternate spellings of words are included. The entry shows whether or not the word is capitalized, at what points it may be divided into syllables, and how the compound is formed (in the case of compound words).

b. Pronunciation. The approved pronunciation of a word is usually given in parentheses following the main entry. Special symbols, or diacritical marks, explained in the introduction to the dictionary, are used to indicate how the letters are properly sounded and which syllables receive stress.

c. Parts of speech. The dictionary indicates all the parts of speech by which the word may function, how the plural of nouns is formed, what the principal parts of verbs are, how the comparative and superlative degrees of adjectives and adverbs are formed, and in the case of some prepositions how they are used in idiomatic phrases.

d. Meanings and definitions. Most words have more than one meaning. A good dictionary lists a number of distinct meanings, including obsolete and highly specialized meanings, as well as the most current and usual meaning.

e. Status. The status of a word concerns its social acceptability, the place of its currency, its timeliness, etc. Foreign words and their meanings are indicated. Such labels as *Colloq., Slang, Dial., Brit., Obs., Poetic*, etc., indicate status.

f. Etymology. A dictionary etymology shows the original form of a word, the language from which it was derived, and the meaning it was originally given. Such labels as *L* (Latin), *G* (German), *OF* (Old French), *ME* (Middle English) indicate the derivation or etymology.

g. Synonyms and antonyms. Occasionally a word entry is followed by words roughly similar in meaning or words with opposite meanings.

h. Contexts. Historical dictionaries, that is, dictionaries based on historical principles, include dated passages or contexts which supply a brief history of a word's usage. A few contexts are included in unabridged dictionaries, usually without dates. Abridged dictionaries, including college diction-

beauty

Vocabulary Entry —————— **beau·ty** (bū'tǐ), *n.*, *pl.* **-ties.** **1.** that quality of any object or sense or thought whereby it excites an admiring pleasure; qualification of a high order for delighting the eye or the aesthetic, intellectual, or moral sense. **2.** something beautiful, esp. a woman. **3.** a grace, charm, or pleasing excellence. [ME *beute*, t. OF: m. *beaule*, der. *beau*. See BEAU] —**Syn. 1.** loveliness, pulchritude.

Syllabication Dots —————— **be·di·zen'** (bǐ dī'zən, -dǐz'ən), *v.t.* to dress or adorn
Pronunciation —————— gaudily. [t. BE- + DIZEN] —**be·di'zen·ment,** *n.*

Part of Speech and Inflected Forms —— **be·gin** (bǐ gǐn'), *v.*, **began, begun, beginning.** —*v.i.* **1.** to enter upon an action; take the first step; commence; start. **2.** to come into existence; arise; originate. —*v.t.* **3.** to take the first step in; set about; start; commence. **4.** to originate; be the originator of. [ME *beginne(n)*. OE *beginnan*] —**be·gin'ner,** *n.*
—**Syn. 3.** BEGIN; COMMENCE, INITIATE, START (when followed by noun or gerund) refer to setting into motion or progress something which continues for some time. BEGIN is the common term: *to begin knitting a sweater.* COMMENCE is a more formal word, often suggesting a more prolonged or elaborate beginning: *to commence proceedings in court.* INITIATE implies an active and often ingenious first act in a new field: *to initiate a new procedure.* START means to make a first move or to set out on a course of action: *to start paving a street.* **4.** institute, inaugurate, initiate. —**Ant. 1.** end.

Synonym Study ——————

Variant principal parts —————— **be·jew·el** (bǐ jōō'əl), *v.t.*, **-eled, -eling** or *esp. Brit.* **-elled, -elling,** to adorn with or as with jewels.

Variant spelling —————— **be·la·bor** (bǐ lā'bər), *v.t.* **1.** to beat vigorously; ply with heavy blows. **2.** to assail persistently, as with ridicule. **3.** *Obs.* to labor at. Also, *Brit.,* **be·la'bour.**

Hyphenated Entry —————— **belles-let·tres** (bĕl lĕt'r), *n.pl.* the finer or higher forms of literature; literature regarded as a fine art. [F] —**bel·let·rist** (bĕl lĕt'rĭst), *n.* —**bel·le·tris·tic** (bĕl'lĕ trǐs'tǐk), *adj.* —**Syn.** See **literature.**

Word Element —————— **bene-,** a word element meaning "well", as in *benediction.* [t. L, comb. form of *bene,* adv.]

Consecutive Definition Numbers —— **be·neath** (bǐ nēth', -nĕth'), *adv.* ① below; in a lower place, position, state, etc. ② underneath: *the heaven above and the earth beneath.* —*prep.* ③ below; under; *beneath the same roof.* ④ further down than; underneath; lower in place than. ⑤ lower down on a slope than: *beneath the crest of a hill.* ⑥ inferior in position, power, etc. to: *a captain is beneath a major.* ⑦ unworthy of; below the level or dignity of: *beneath contempt.* [ME *be nethe,* OE *beneothan,* t. *be* by + *neothan* below] —**Syn. 3.** See **below.** —**Ant. 1.** above.

Etymology ——————

Usage Notes —————— **bent**[1] (bĕnt), *adj.* **1.** curved; crooked: *a bent stick, bow, etc.* **2.** determined; set; resolved (fol. by *on*) —*n.* **3.** bent state or form. **4.** direction taken (usually figurative); inclination; leaning; bias: *a bent for painting.* **5.** capacity of endurance. **6.** *Civ. Eng.* a transverse frame of a bridge or a building, designed to support either vertical or horizontal loads. [pp. of BEND[1]] —**Syn. 4.** tendency, propensity, proclivity, predilection.

Synonym List —————— **bent**[2] (bĕnt), *n.* **1.** bent grass. **2.** a stalk of such grass. **3.** (formerly) any stiff grass or sedge. **4.** *Scot. and N. Eng.* a grassy tract, a moor, or a hillside. [ME; OE *beonet,* c. G *binse* rush]

bet·ter (bĕt'ər), *adj.* (*comparative of* **good**). **1.** of superior quality or excellence: *a better position.* **2.** of superior value, use, fitness, desirability, acceptableness, etc.: *a better time for action.* **3.** larger; greater: *the better part of a lifetime.* **4.** improved in health; healthier —*adv.* (*comparative of* **well**). **5.** in a more excellent way or manner: *to behave better.* **6.** in a superior degree: *to know a man better.* **7.** more: *better than a mile to town.*
Example Contexts ——————
8. had better, would be wiser, safer, etc., to. **9. better off,** in better circumstances. **10. think better of,** to reconsider and decide more favorably or wisely. —*v.t.*
Idiomatic Phrases —————— **11.** to make better; improve; increase the good qualities of. **12. better oneself,** to improve one's social standing, education, etc. **13.** to improve upon; surpass; exceed: *they bettered working conditions.* —*n.* **14.** that which has superior excellence, etc.: *the better of two choices.* **15.** (*usually pl.*) one's superior in wisdom, wealth, etc. **16.** superiority; mastery: *to get the better of someone.* [ME *bettre,* OE *betera,* c. Goth. *batiza*] —**Syn. 11.** See **improve.**
Antonyms —————— —**Ant. 1.** worse. **11.** worsen.

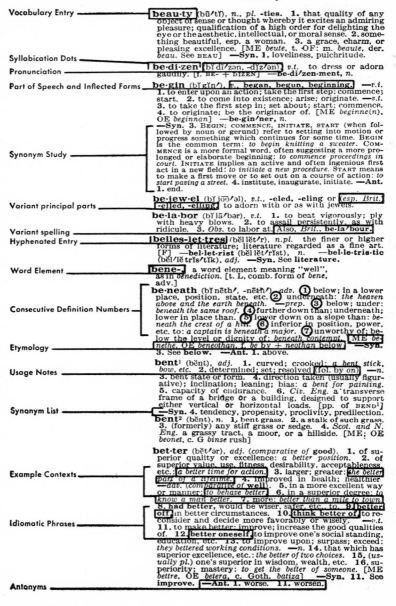

brunch

Prefix

bi-, a prefix meaning: **1.** twice, doubly, two, as in *bilateral, binocular, biweekly.* **2.** (in science) denoting in general two, as in *bicarbonate.* Also, **bin-.** [t. L, comb. form of *bis* twice, doubly, der. L *duo* two]

Abbreviation

Bi. *Chem.* bismuth.

B.I. British India.

bi·son (bī′sən, -zən), *n., pl.* **-son.** *Zool.* a large North American bovine ruminant, *Bison bison* (**American bison,** or buffalo), with high, well-haired shoulders. [t. L, t. Gmc.; cf. G *wisent*]

Illustration

American bison, *Bison bison*
(10 to 12 ft. long,
ab. 6 ft. high at the shoulder)

blood·mo·bile (blŭd′mə bēl′), *n.* a small truck with medical equipment for receiving blood donations.

Geographical Entry

Bos·ton (bôs′tən, bŏs′tən), *n.* **1.** the capital of Massachusetts, in the E part: the largest city and seaport in New England. 801,444; with suburbs, 2,354,507 (1950). **2.** (*l.c.*) a game of cards, played by four persons with two packs of cards. **3.** (*l.c.*) a social dance, a modification of the waltz. —**Bos·to·ni·an** (bôs tō′nī ən, bôs tō′-), *adj., n.*

Run-on Entry

bot·tle[1] (bŏt′əl), *n., v.,* **-tled, -tling.** —*n.* **1.** a portable vessel with a neck or mouth, now commonly made of glass, used for holding liquids. **2.** the contents of a bottle; as much as a bottle contains: *a bottle of wine.* **3.** the bottle, intoxicating liquor. **4.** bottled milk for babies: *raised on the bottle.* —*v.t.* **5.** to put into or seal in a bottle; esp. in England, to can or put up fruit or vegetables. **6.** bottle up, to shut in or restrain closely: *to bottle up one's feelings.* [ME *botel,* t. OF: *m. botele,* g. LL *butticula,* dim. of *buttis* BUTT⁴] —**bot′tle·like′,** *adj.* —**bot′tler,** *n.*

bot·tle[2] (bŏt′əl), *n.* *Brit. Dial.* a bundle, esp. of hay. [ME *botel,* t. OF, dim. of *botte* bundle]

Homograph Numbers

bouf·fant (boo fän′), *adj.* *French.* puffed out; full, as sleeves or draperies. —**bouf·fante** (boo fänt′), *adj. fem.*

Foreign word label

Brad·ley (brăd′lĭ), *n.* **1. Henry,** 1845–1923, British philologist and lexicographer. **2. Omar Nelson,** born 1893, U.S. general: Chief of Staff 1948–49; chairman, Joint Chiefs of Staff, 1949–1953.

Biographical Entry

brain washing, systematic indoctrination that changes or undermines one's political convictions. —**brain-wash,** *v.*

Two Word Entry

brain wave, 1. (*pl.*) *Med.* electroencephalogram. **2.** *Colloq.* a sudden idea or inspiration.

brass (brăs, bräs), *n.* **1.** a durable, malleable, and ductile yellow alloy, consisting essentially of copper and zinc. **2.** a utensil, ornament, or other article made of brass. **3.** *Mach.* a bearing, bush, or the like. **4.** *Music.* **a.** a musical instrument of the trumpet or horn families. **b.** such instruments collectively in a band or orchestra. **5.** *Brit.* a memorial tablet incised with an effigy, coat of arms or the like. **6.** metallic yellow; lemon, amber, or reddish yellow. **7.** *U.S. Slang.* **a.** high-ranking military officers. **b.** any important officials. **8.** *Colloq.* excessive assurance; impudence; effrontery. **9.** *Brit. Slang.* money. —*adj.* **10.** of brass. **11.** using musical instruments made of brass. [ME *bras,* OE *bræs*] —**brass′like′,** *adj.*

Subject Label

Geographic Label

Usage Label

brig·and·age (brĭg′əndĭj), *n.* the practice of brigands; plundering. Also, **brig·and·ism.**

Variant Form

brown·ie (brou′nĭ), *n.* **1.** (in folklore) a little brown goblin, esp. one who helps secretly in household work. **2.** *U.S.* a small, highly shortened chocolate cake, often containing nuts. **3.** (*cap.*) a trademark for a type of inexpensive box camera. **4.** any inexpensive box camera. **5.** (*cap.*) a member of the junior division (ages 8–11) of the Girl Scouts or (*Brit.*) the Girl Guides. —**Syn. 1.** See *fairy.*

Capitalization

Brum·mell (brŭm′əl), *n.* See Beau Brummell.

Cross Reference

brunch (brŭnch), *n.* a mid-morning meal that serves both as breakfast and lunch. [b. BREAKFAST and LUNCH] aries, supply an occasional context, especially with idiomatic expressions.

The accompanying pages from the *American College Dictionary* demonstrate the various services performed by a respectable college dictionary.

A CLASSIFIED LIST OF DICTIONARIES

Dictionaries on Historical Principles
A *Dictionary of American English* (DAE), 4 vols., 1938.
Dictionary of Americanisms (a supplement to DAE), 2 vols., 1951.
Oxford English Dictionary (OED), 10 vols. and Supplement, 1888–1933.
Unabridged Dictionaries
New Standard Dictionary of the English Language, 1941.
Webster's New International Dictionary of the English Language, Second Edition, 1934.
Smaller Dictionaries (suitable for college use)
The American College Dictionary, 1947.
Webster's New Collegiate Dictionary, 1949.
Webster's New World Dictionary, 1951.

D-6   VOCABULARY BUILDING

Because clarity and precision are so important in all varieties of communication, vocabulary building is essential for effective speaking, reading, writing, and listening.

Vocabulary building is necessary for transmission of meaning so that exact meanings may be communicated. An effective communicator chooses a word which clarifies his precise meaning under specific circumstances. Thus *beautiful* may mean vivacious, charming, lovely, engaging, graceful, elegant, delicate, comely, stylish, radiant, gorgeous, attractive, poised, or desirable. Anyone who summarizes all these shades of meaning in a single adjective is not very discriminating. The larger your active working vocabulary, the more surely can you express your thoughts so they can be understood.

Vocabulary building is even more important for reading and listening—the receptive skills. If you don't understand the meanings of an author's words, his thought is lost. Your recognition vocabulary for reading must be much larger than your active speaking and writing vocabulary. If a large percentage of the words that confront you in college textbooks are unfamiliar, you must take definite steps to increase your vocabulary. Here are some suggestions.

D-6.1 Acquiring words as you have need for them

The vocabulary which you possess right now and which you use every day in expressing your thoughts was acquired a word at a time, as you had use for it in conversation. Does a child depend on a dictionary and compiled word lists to pick up the native tongue? On the contrary, his need to make ideas clear to others helps him to acquire the right words. How do you suppose you can remember the sequence of numbers in your street address or on your automobile license plates? Your need for them reinforces the proper sequence in your mind. And how soon you forget them when you move to a new address or change your license plates. Working crossword puzzles does very little for the size of one's vocabulary. The need is too temporary, too short-lived. The best possible way to increase your vocabulary is to develop an active, sincere, and passionate interest in subject matter in which words are employed.

D-6.2 Acquiring words in context, not in isolation

Words don't really mean anything out of context. Suppose you are going to add the word *white* to your vocabulary. You look it up in the dictionary and find it means "reflecting to the eye all the rays of the spectrum." But of course it never actually means that, does it? It means something different every time it is used, as the following sentences testify:

My father was a *white* man, my mother an Indian.
It was mighty *white* of you to stick up for me.
In chess, the *whites* get the first move.
Though your sins be as scarlet, they shall be *whiter* than snow.
Macy's are having a *white* sale.
Your argument contains a black and *white* fallacy.

Now read the chapter in *Moby Dick* entitled "The Whiteness of the Whale" and make a list of the fine shades and gradations of meaning in the simple expression "the white whale."

If you run across a word like *isogloss* or *tangential* or *chi-square*, don't tear it apart from the context in which you find it. The words which come before and after the one in question give it meaning. Notice how the context following defines the word *polytone*. Incidentally, this meaning can be found in no dictionary. "Automobiles, skirting a village green, are like flies that have gained the inner ear—they buzz, cease, pause, start, shift, stop, halt, brake, and the whole effect is a nervous polytone curiously disturbing" (E. B. White).

D-6.3   Acquiring words by extensive reading in diversified fields

Every course of study you pursue has a specialized vocabulary which you must acquire in order to master the subject. But you need not stop with such acquisitions. Extend your reading interests beyond course work and be just as receptive of new words in extracurricular pursuits. Don't interrupt your reading by looking up every unfamiliar word as you come to it. Mark it with a pencil until you have finished the passage. If the meaning has not been deduced by that time, look it up in the dictionary. Determine which of the listed meanings most nearly apply, and read the context again to make sure the sense is clear.

D-6.4   Analyzing unfamiliar words into roots, prefixes, and suffixes

If you learn the meaning of frequently used Latin and Greek elements in words, you can decipher the meaning of unfamiliar words by analogy. Take the word *polytone,* mentioned above. You might think of other words beginning with *poly*—*polygon, polyglot, polygamy;* deduce that *poly* means "many," and decide that *polytone* means "many tones."

D-6.5 Putting the words to work

Keep a notebook in which you list unfamiliar words which you have acquired. Review them from time to time. Use the words in writing or speaking, until they become your own.

AFFECTIVE DEVICES

Affective uses of language, pitfalls of successful communication, are often employed in deliberate attempts to mislead and confuse. Every word has for each of us personal and private associations which affect its meaning. Some of these associations are pleasant, some painful, others fearful. When diction is employed for the purpose of setting off emotional reactions, communication is likely to be short-circuited and truth is likely to be compromised. Several devices are described and illustrated here which make up the propagandists' bag of verbal tricks.

A-1 EMOTIONALLY TONED OR LOADED WORDS (See also pp. 24–25 and Section 8.4)

Words which reflect an observer's personal opinion or value judgment of a subject rather than any discernible features of it are variously called loaded words, charged words, slanted expressions, or "snarl-words and purr-words." Emphasis is placed on their connotations rather than their denotations. They are almost always used to convince and influence readers and listeners —not to clarify ideas or establish the truth. Emotionally toned words may be used to glorify or to depreciate the subject they purportedly describe. The italicized words in the following passages are examples: "Deep in the *dim* and *dank* recesses of our

408

colleges . . . are men and women who are dedicated to the *frittering away* of public and private cash by carefully removing the front legs of flies." "Fellow Americans, there's a lot of *subversive* talk going around that $30 a week is not a living wage for teachers." "On my trip to Asia last fall I was *shocked*—even *frightened*—by what I learned. I am now prepared to speak in the House in behalf of any legislation I believe will strengthen the *free world* against the *Communist menace*." "The average cup of drugstore or cafeteria coffee is more likely to be nothing but *lukewarm*, gray *liquid fog* caught in crockery. It has the personality of *swamp mist*, strained through *sulphur*, and *bitter as an old regret*." "Even now we can picture you *savoring* that first bite of our *celebrated* apple pie ala mode . . . combining the *delectable* flavors of *succulent* slices of *winey-tart, tree-ripened* apples . . . of the spices with their sweet-sour *overtones* . . . of the *candied* crust—so light, so *flaky* yet with *delightful* "chewey" quality to it . . . of that *crowning* touch of *full-bodied, satin-smooth* ice cream." "Nothing can take the place of a daily newspaper as a medium for disseminating *complete* and *reliable* information about the happenings in a community." "An *unprecedented burst* of Christmas spending put *new life* in the business *boom* this week. Everybody, it seemed, was *in the chips*." "To the sensitive person the forty-five percent rise in juvenile delinquency in the last five years, the *staggering* increase in *violent* crimes, in the use of narcotics, in drunkenness, in broken homes, in *graft* and *corruption* in public affairs is *terrifying*." "For me the dictionary is neither a book of *curiosities* nor a *mausoleum* in which the *dead* are interred. Rather it is something *alive, vibrant, thrilling*."

A-2 SUGGESTION BY ASSOCIATION   (See also Section 7.8)

In commercial advertisements you can frequently find examples of the transfer of value by association of one object with another: The driver of an automobile is wearing a mink coat, thus suggesting that the car is luxurious; a Scotch terrier is pictured in the advertisement for a particular make of men's clothing, thus suggesting thrift; an American flag is pictured on the front page of a newspaper, suggesting that the editorial policy of the paper is true to American principles.

Words, as well as pictures, can transfer judgments from one object to another. Notice how the italicized words in the following passages communicate meaning by transfer: "The wars of the future, if they take place, will not be fought with the ludicrous *fire-crackers* of World War II." "This article deals with athleticism, its *cause*, its *symptoms* and its *cure*." "Bill Tilghman . . . said, 'I never shot a man in my life and missed him.' His *hardy pioneering spirit* and *resolute courage* are a legacy today's 160 million Americans are very proud to share." "I'm a *she-wolf* from Bitter Creek and it's my night to howl!" "Man can neither live nor lead by atoms, *bread*, and machines alone."

A large number of words in the language derive their meanings by association. Here are some examples:

long-hair culture	sneak preview
clocklike precision	bank nite
pioneer courage	flyte fuel
union made	grass-roots democracy
highbrow literature	bedrock
woolgathering	push-button driving
inside story	

A-3 THE "YES" TECHNIQUE

Initial impressions created by an author or speaker with his readers or audience exert a strong influence with respect to the acceptance or rejection of the ideas proposed. A clergyman, wishing to convert people living in nonurban areas, appeared in overalls to deliver his sermons, in an attempt to disarm his listeners and neutralize their suspicious attitudes toward "city slickers."

Ralph Waldo Emerson in his "The American Scholar" addressed his listeners as scholars, thus preparing the way for his "revolutionary" ideas. These are examples of the "yes" technique.

By starting out with a series of undeniable facts and statements, a speaker or writer can often gain a hearing for statements that are not easily verified and may be downright questionable. In the expression "First in war, first in peace, first in the hearts of his countrymen," there is a progression from what is easily confirmed to what is not so easily confirmed. A similar progression may be found in the following fictitious "facts" about a community social organization:

It's a Fact:
That the society was organized in 1937. That any taxpayer in the community is eligible for membership. That there are 714 members now enrolled. That many of the members are outstanding citizens. That the society is non-sectarian and non-political. That the membership dues are very small. That membership in the society is valuable in many ways. That the society is not run by a clique. That the society can and will do many things for you.

A-4 REPETITION AND RESTATEMENT

Repetition of words or ideas as a persuasive device is based on the theory that the oftener a thing is repeated the more likely it will be accepted and remembered. Advertisers make much use of this device in advertising copy and on radio and television commercials.

Notice the effect produced by the repetition of the word *fear* in the following context: "There is elation in the world today because of victory. But there is also fear. It is a primitive fear, the fear of the unknown, the fear of forces man can neither channel nor comprehend. This fear is not new; in its classical form it is the fear of irrational death. But overnight it has become intensified, magnified. . . . Where man can find no answer, he will find fear . . ." (Norman Cousins).

Repetition of sounds in such alliterative expressions as these are also affective devices: "not a cough in a carload"; "drives like a dream"; "top touch tuning television"; "peace, plenty, and prosperity"; "trick or treat"; "light up a Lucky"; "make money by mail"; "from the first you light to the last at night"; "Give us guns and save your sons."

A-5   SLOGANS, BROMIDES, AND CATCH PHRASES
(See also **D-2.3**)

Robert Louis Stevenson once said: "Man does not live by bread alone, but principally by catch-words." Following are some expressions which have been used to influence people's thinking: "Crime does not pay, but crime comics do." "Be happy, go Lucky." "Go West, young man, go West." "I'd rather be right than be president." "The only thing we have to fear is fear itself." "I disapprove of what you say, but I will defend to the death your right to say it." "I have nothing to offer but blood, toil, tears, and sweat." "Beauty is as beauty does." "There is no hope for the satisfied man." "Only the productive can be strong, and only the strong can be free." "All the news that's fit to print." "One man with courage makes a majority." "If ever there was a time when public relations were indispensable that time is now." "Our national strength is founded on a unified powerful morale." "Two world wars have brought unprecedented responsibilities to our nation, and economic, as well as social and political challenge to our democratic way of life."

Malcomb W. Bingay has said, "America must be getting damned sick and tired of all these platitudes, bromides, and catchwords that are mouthed over and over again by every politician of every party, by every editorial writer, by every preacher, by every orator or anybody who THINKS he is an orator. . . . Won't SOMEBODY who knows SOMETHING talk plain talk so we can understand? I'm fed up on this 'Sail-on-oh-ship-of-state' hokum."

A-6 UNWARRANTED ASSUMPTIONS (See also pp. 32–33)

An assumption is a supposition taken for granted without proof. People invent explanations of phenomena they do not understand. Many of these explanations are superstitions, non-scientific theories, or traditional beliefs. For instance, it is assumed by many people that a ring around the moon portends a change in the weather, that the number 13 is associated with ill fortune, or that when a baby smiles in its sleep angels are speaking to it. What we call "jumping to conclusions" is usually argument from unwarranted assumptions or beliefs. Many Americans, after World War II, predicted a financial depression on the assumption that "history repeats itself." A number of public opinion polling agencies falsely predicted that Thomas Dewey would win the 1948 presidential election, on the assumption that the population sampled had already made up their minds about how they would cast their votes.

One might argue that the newspaper is on its last legs because of the introduction of radio, television, and motion pictures. Yet it was reported in *Editor and Publisher* (1956) that circulation of daily newspapers increased during 1955 by more than 1,000,-000 copies. The year 1955 was called "the best in history for American newspapers."

People get into all kinds of trouble and distress because of such unwarranted assumptions as: that words have the same meanings for all people; that campaign promises will be fulfilled; that translations from one language to another can be made without loss of meaning; that dictionaries record the unchangeable meanings of words; that advertised products are superior to unadvertised products; that statistical calculations are foolproof; that illustrations in a mail-order catalogue are true representations of the advertised products; that wealthy people are most happy; that the life of a movie star is all glitter and glamour.

A-7   RUMOR AND WISHFUL THINKING   (See also Section 2.9)

Rumor, gossip, slander, whispering campaigns, and wishful thinking are all based on unwarranted assumptions related to strong needs, interests, or purposes. In other words, rumors are most useful in reflecting the motives of the people who spread them. Scandal appeals to sexual motives, and malicious gossip to revenge. Pipe dreams, fantasies, and wishful thoughts are clearly linked to hope and desire. Miraculous feats supposedly performed by folk heroes—Daniel Boone, Buffalo Bill, Davy Crockett, Johnny Appleseed—are easily explained as rumor. Margaret Chute shows how a biographer may be accused of starting a rumor:

> It is easy enough to make good resolutions in advance, but a biographer cannot altogether control his sense of excitement when the climax of his years of research draws near and he begins to see the pieces fall into place. Almost without his volition, A, B, and D fit together and start to form a pattern, and it is almost impossible for the biographer not to start searching for C. Something turns up that looks remarkably like C, and with a little trimming of the edges and the ignoring of one very slight discrepancy it will fit the place alloted for C magnificently.
>
> It is at this point that the biographer ought to take a deep breath and sit on his hands until he has had time to calm down. He has no real, fundamental reason to believe that his discovery is C, except for the fact that he wants it to be. He is like a man looking for a missing piece in a difficult jigsaw puzzle, who has found one so nearly the right shape that he cannot resist the desire to jam it into place.[13]

Rumor may also be employed as advertising propaganda. It has been rumored, for example, that foods cooked in aluminum

[13] "Getting at the Truth," *Saturday Review of Literature*, September 19, 1953.

kettles are poisonous. One medical authority has this to say in regard to the matter: "Far from being 'poisonous,' as peddlers of other kinds of kitchen ware would have customers imagine, aluminum is universally distributed in soils and plants and the available experimental evidence warrants but one conclusion, namely, that aluminum, occurring naturally in foods or introduced by utensils in which food is cooked or kept, is not a health hazard."[14]

How rumor may be used to defend political viewpoints and ideologies is shown by the mythical report of a Communist to his local Soviet: "Moreover, America is so desperate for food that her people have taken to the last resort of a starving nation. They are killing their dogs and eating them. . . . At the ball game, vendors in white jackets passed among the spectators shamelessly offering sandwiches of dog meat for sale, and crying out, 'Hot dogs!' "[15]

[14] William Brady in "Health Talks," *The State Journal* (Lansing, Michigan), January 28, 1956, p. 16.
[15] "Baseball a la Moscow," *American Magazine*, August, 1950, p. 119.

LOGICAL FALLACIES

Logical reasoning supplies no foolproof method of winning an argument, solving a problem, or convincing people. Logic, as we have shown in Chapter 8, is more useful for testing the validity of an argument than for discovering the truth. Logical formulas are altogether too rigid, too inflexible, too limited to be trusted in specifying the exact truth about the ever changing world of matter and of human relations. Logic can be used to deceive and mislead, as well as point up truth. The most common fallacies of logical reasoning include fallacies of induction, fallacies of deduction, faulty causal argument, and faulty analogy.

L-1 FALLACIES OF INDUCTION (See also Section 8.1)

L-1.1 Hasty or broad generalization

A hasty generalization is a sweeping statement about *all* of a given set of facts based on inspection of *some* of the facts. The following specifications for a typical man, determined in a scientific laboratory, generalize about all mankind from limited observations: "He weighs about 154 pounds; is about 43% muscle and 15% bone. His liver makes up almost two and one-half percent of his total weight whereas his brain is an even two percent. He consumes about two and one-half quarts of water a day, also gets fractional ounces of sodium, potassium, sulphur, zinc, copper and other metals. His lung capacity is five quarts. . . ."

James Thurber in Chapter 6 of *Thurber Country* humorously calls attention to some common varieties of sweeping statements which he classifies as true, untrue, half-true, debatable, ridiculous, fascinating but undemonstrable, and idiosyncratic. Here are some of the ones he collected: Women don't sleep very well. There are no pianos in Japan. People would rather drink than go to the theater. Architects have the wrong idea. Doctors don't know what they're doing. You never see foreigners fishing. People who break into houses don't drink wine. Peach ice cream is never as good as you think it's going to be.

Numerous examples of questionable generalizations may be found in commercial advertisements: X automobile breaks all records. The world's most popular soft drink. More people smoke X cigarettes than any other leading brand.

One type of broad generalization may be called "the public opinion myth." It is based on the questionable theory that "fifty million Frenchmen can't be wrong." What most of the people believe to be true is quite often considered to be the verifiable truth about a matter. Actually, of course, majorities can easily be and have often been wrong. That "everybody is doing it" is small justification for following suit. A thousand wrongs do not make a right. It doesn't make any difference how many people think that Friday the thirteenth is an unlucky day. The thinking of people about the day has little bearing on what will happen. We are too easily caught in the web of such mass illusions as: Hollywood is a city of glamour. Money can buy anything including happiness. Hard work is the surest guarantee of success. Teaching school is a soft job. Psychiatry is of dubious value in the treatment of mental disorders. Culture can be purchased with dollars and cents. All politicians are corrupt. The Democratic party has a fixed platform. Anything in print is true.

Another type of broad generalization may be called restricted identity, or labelomania. To disguise the true characteristics of persons, places, or things by slapping labels on them is to distort the facts. Name calling, evident in such sobriquets as *white-collar workers, pen-pushers, pill-rollers, foreigners, eggheads, have-nots, laymen, liberals,* and *stool pigeons,* is a highly unrealistic way of representing people. Any one of us play so many roles in life that it would be difficult to enumerate them: student, employee, Democrat, band leader, English major, pedestrian, voter, consumer. To identify a person by a single role he plays in life is to omit much that could be said of him. (See also Section 11.2)

L-1.2 Unfounded inference

An inference is a statement about the unknown made on the basis of the known. A good example is supplied by a manager of a home improvement company who expounded the following theory about pitted windshields: "Glass for windshields is made from silica. Silica sand abounds on Western United States beaches. Sand fleas abound in the sand. What actually happens is that in securing the sand for the windshield glass, sand flea eggs also are gathered. The eggs remain in the glass and, with the approach of warm weather, the windshields warm up, the eggs hatch, and the fleas have to chip the glass to get out."

Not all inferences, of course, are without foundation. Scientists of necessity make inferences from carefully observed facts in order to increase our knowledge of the universe. Scientific inferences, or hypotheses, when tested, confirmed, and established by verifiable evidence, take on the status of "truth." When subsequent experimentation and further observation fail to confirm or support initial inferences, scientists alter their theories in harmony with the best information at hand. The long-believed "continental drift" theory, which maintained that the continents of the earth were once one great land mass, has recently been discounted because of radical differences in the living and fossil animals of the various continents. Likewise the Darwinian theory of evolution has failed to stand up under continued research and investigation.

The kinds of inferences made by most people under average conditions are little more than irrational guesses—mere shots in the dark: That heavy people are jollier than slim ones; that red-headed people are temperamental; that writers of romantic books are exciting and stimulating people; that beauty is the criterion of Hollywood success; that a college education will insure vocational success; that figures never lie; that lightning never strikes twice in the same place; that a criminal always returns to the scene of his crime; that some people are just naturally born lucky; that once a criminal, always a criminal; that crime never pays.

L-1.3 Prediction

A prediction is a generalization that predicts an unknown series of events on the basis of factual observations: The National Resources Committee predicted in 1938 that the United States population, then in the neighborhood of 130,000,000, would soon level off. It might reach a peak, it was said, and start declining as early as 1955. Computations were made as to what would happen in the case of sixteen different possible combinations of fertility, mortality, and immigration. But not one of the sixteen estimates predicted a population as high as 155,000,000 by 1951—or even by 1955. Six of the sixteen predicted that the population would still be below 155,000,000 as late as 1980. One estimate for 1980 was only 127,947,000. The only possible explanation seems to be that people are still too unpredictable to be encompassed in neat formulas.

L-1.4 Stereotypes and sampling error

By careful selection of evidence regarding a given subject, you can "prove" almost anything about it. Suppose, for example, you want to prove that men are better cooks than women. You

merely select examples of famous chefs to bolster your contention. If you want to prove that women are better cooks than
men, select different examples, ones that will support this thesis.
The practice of using highly selective examples to prove a point
is often called "card-stacking." It is one of the most frequently
employed of the propagandists' tricks.

Since our own versions of the world are derived from personal
experience, we quite naturally form mental images of people,
places, and things which are distorted because they are generalizations from limited samples. You create in your own mind a
standardized or stereotyped picture of various nationalities of
people: Chinese, Indian, German, Turk, etc. A. Den Doolaard
poses a question which may help you to understand the nature
of stereotypes: "I am a Dutchman. Can you swear that this does
not evoke instantaneously the following surrealistic picture in
your mind: my head an Edam cheese, my left arm a tulip, my
right arm the wing of a windmill, whereas the rest of my anatomy
consists of baggy trousers and wooden clogs?"[16]

Mr. Doolaard goes on to paint a picture of Americans as seen
in the mind's eye of Europeans: "He will see enormous cars, sky-
scrapers that reach to the moon, monstrous combines rushing
through wheatfields bigger than his own small country, and girls
with endless legs digging their proudly pointed bosoms into his
ribs aching for the kind of love that the Johnson Office has
shelved between the coils of its hypercritical icebox. His wife will
see her American rival moving swiftly on four-inch heels through
her mechanized kitchen, deftly setting mysterious dials for a self-
cooking dinner. Then an elevator will deposit her on the bearskin
rug before her satin bed upon which a fresh pair of nylon stockings is waiting for her."

The trouble with such "pictures" of American people is that
they are based on extreme and unrepresentative cases. We, of
course, make just such ridiculous generalizations about Euro-

[16] A. Den Doolaard, "A Study in Misunderstanding," *Saturday Review of
Literature*, September 24, 1949.

peans, Orientals, and Eskimos. The mass media of communication—newspapers, magazines, radio, television, motion pictures—may easily foster the creation of stereotypes which can be relied upon to produce emotional responses that interfere with clear, straight thinking.

L-1.5 Black and white reasoning

We have a strong tendency to engage in what is called either-or thinking. For example, we think of money as either genuine or counterfeit. We think of movies as either exciting or boring; of college professors as either stimulating or dull; of politicians as either liberal or conservative. We seek "yes" or "no" answers to such questions as: Does cigarette smoking cause lung cancer? Is the government infiltrated with communists? Should people retire at age sixty-five? Will eating carrots improve one's eyesight? Is there a Santa Claus?

The most appropriate answer to any of these questions is best expressed in degrees of probability or certainty. Water is neither hot nor cold: its temperature is a matter of degree. Likewise, people are neither intelligent nor stupid but possess various degrees of intellectual capacity. The truth about any proposition may best be defined as some point between two extremes.

BLACK ———————————————————————————— WHITE

A scientist thinks of "truth" in degrees of probability. He asks himself: What degree of certainity do I have that my proposition is true? To what extent is this proposition always true? How much evidence may be produced to disprove my thesis? Have I considered all the available evidence?

L-1.6 Misapplications

When a generalization which is derived from one set of data is applied to situations or aggregations which were not sampled, we say the generalization is misapplied. Thus, if you derived from the population of New York City the number of foreign-born people and then used this figure as an index of the whole country, you would be guilty of this fallacy. Educational studies based on a small sample of students at one college often supply generalizations that are applied to all educational institutions in the country. In the final analysis, a generalization is true only for the sample from which it was derived, and at the time and place when the data were collected.

L-2 FALLACIES OF DEDUCTION (See also Section 8.2)

L-2.1 Dogmatic statements

Dogmatic statements are inflexible statements of assertion that offer no exceptions to hard and fast rules or principles. "Men are all alike" is such a statement. Dogmatic statements are usually unsupported expressions of opinion rather than conclusions from facts and, when employed as premises in a perfectly valid syllogism, have the appearance of truth:

> All policemen have flat feet.
> Jack Webb is a policeman.
> Therefore, Jack Webb has flat feet.

Here are a number of statements which need to be supported by evidence before they are used in argument:

> The atomic bomb will in itself constitute a cause of war.
> The people are too damn dumb to understand.
> The common denominator of all teen-age crimes is comic books.

L-2.2 Clichés, proverbs, and aphorisms (See A-5 and D-2.3)

Familiar expressions which take the form of generalizations are usually too oversimplified to be suitable as premises in an argument. Haste makes waste. The early bird gets the worm. Nothing ventured, nothing gained. A friend in need is a friend indeed. A picture is worth a thousand words. Nothing is too good for the Irish. God helps those who help themselves.

L-2.3 Authority (See also Section 8.3)

The principal fallacy of authority in deduction consists in quoting an eminent man on subjects outside his field of specialty. The opinions of a landscape designer on problems of child care would be of no more value than the opinion of someone selected at random from a telephone book. Authority at best represents a limited point of view which may or may not fit the purposes to which you bend it.

L-2.4 The undistributed middle

The middle term of a syllogism is the one that appears in each of the premises, but not in the conclusion. Undistributed means that some are unaccounted for with respect to the other term or class.

All G.I.'s wear dogtags.
I wear dogtags.
Therefore, I am a G.I. INVALID

All G.I.'s wear dogtags.
I am a G.I.
Therefore, I wear dogtags. VALID

L-2.5 The ambiguous middle

When the middle term of a syllogism is inadequately defined or equivocal, the argument will be false.

Religious people are not criminals.
Mr. X is a religious man.
Therefore, Mr. X is not a criminal.

In this syllogism the term *religious people* may have many possible meanings.

L-3 FALLACIES IN CAUSATION (See also pp. 148–152)

L-3.1 Post hoc

Post hoc, ergo propter hoc is a Latin expression meaning "after this, therefore because of this." In other words, it is fallacious to assume that because two events occur simultaneously or in chronological sequence one event causes the other. Given two such events, the possibilities are: (a) that any apparent relationship is coincidental; (b) that there is no relationship; (c) that both events are effects of an unestablished cause; (d) that one event did actually cause the other.

Much so-called circumstantial evidence is faulty for this reason. So is superstition. A mother who dreamed her boy was going to die just two weeks before he did tried to work out a cause-effect relationship. A woman in New Mexico who had her nude body dusted by a broom made of cut flowers claimed she was cured of a horrible disease. A group of boys who lost a five-dollar bill in a junk yard claimed that prayer helped them to find it. Farmers who plant crops which grow in the ground, like potatoes, claim better results when they plant in the waning phase of the moon than when they plant in the waxing phase.

Occasionally some freak of circumstance actually "proves" the validity of superstition. A black cat proved its reputation for bad luck, for a rural mail carrier and a woman passenger, when they swerved the car to avoid hitting the cat, thus losing control of the vehicle and causing serious damage to the car and themselves.

L-3.2 Selected single cause

It is erroneous to suppose that there is a single cause for complex events such as a declaration of war. To say that the sinking of the *Lusitania* caused America to declare war on Germany in 1917 is to ignore a large part of the whole truth. In any cause-effect relationship the following complexities exist: (a) There are many causes for a single effect. (b) There are many effects of a single cause. (c) Any single cause is one in an unbroken, unending series of causal relationships.

Here is an example of this type of fallacy: "The Republican victory in the 1952 presidential election brought about the end of the Korean conflict because the outcome of the election caused Russia to change her foreign policy."

L-3.3 Confused cause and effect

When two events take place almost simultaneously, the causal relations between them may be easily confused. Robert M. Hutchins, in "Gate Receipts and Glory," states, "Money is the cause of athleticism." Now it is certainly true that there is a great deal of money involved in intercollegiate sports. The question, however, is: Does the money cause the activity, or does the activity produce the money? Dr. Frederic Wertham, in "The Comics . . . Very Funny!" assigns comic books as the major cause of juvenile delinquency. Whether they actually are or not is extremely difficult to say. It may be that the reading of comic books is coincidental with delinquency. It may be that delinquency is followed by the reading of comic books.

L-4 FALSE ANALOGY (See also Section **7.5** and pp. **147–148**)

Analogy—argument which assumes that because two things are similar in some respects they are similar in all respects—is always false when it is offered as proof. Analogies like the following explain an idea but do not prove anything:

The parallels between Robinson Crusoe and our own nation are these: Like him, we are in a position where we can't look to anyone else for security, and we are in serious danger. If we are going to come through, we must do it by the use of our labor and our technology. Like Crusoe, we seek to raise our standard of living and to produce enough so that we may be secure through bad times as well as good. Crusoe was threatened by cannibals. We are threatened by enemies even less civilized. Crusoe was able—thanks to the products of his superior technology—to defeat his enemies in two major combats and he sought to rehabilitate those who had been their prisoners. We call our combats wars and we call our help to the erstwhile prisoners the Marshall Plan, but the parallels are there.

Crusoe, however, had one great advantage over us. His situation was uncomplicated with respect to where his true security lay. He knew. But too many Americans do not . . . they are apparently unaware that only technological expansion can guarantee the continuation of this very happy state of existence. . . .[17]

Such arguments are based on false assumptions. Few people ever bother to challenge the assumptions, and the argument appears valid, has a strong emotional appeal, and snares many unwary readers or listeners.

[17] William H. Ward, "The True Security," *Vital Speeches of the Day*, December 1, 1952, pp. 109–110.

PARAGRAPHS

A paragraph is a unit of discourse, not just a handy break in the continuity of an extended passage. It is a recognizable part of the total idea being communicated and deserves to be separated from the whole text as much as words deserve to be separated from each other. An effective paragraph has unity, continuity, and form. Paragraphing is in reality a method of punctuation that helps a reader understand an author's thought. It is, therefore, functional to meaning and not regulated by arbitrary rules governing its length, form, structure, or complexity. The division of an essay into paragraphs is guided by the marking off of blocks of meaning that are interrelated in the whole idea.

P-1 UNITY IN PARAGRAPHS

If a group of sentences may be properly called a paragraph, there is an interdependence among them which suggests that they belong together. The nucleus of thought, or central idea, is the unifying agent. Usually one sentence in the paragraph is a bare statement of the theme or thesis of the whole. It is called the topic sentence and may appear anywhere in the paragraph. If there is no such statement in a group of related sentences, the thesis may be implied by the structure of the paragraph or by the arrangement of sentences.

427

A paragraph may begin with a topic sentence:

"*History is a bath of blood.* The Iliad is one long recital of how Diomedes and Ajax, Sarpedon and Hector *killed.* No detail of the wounds they made is spared us, and the Greek mind fed upon the story. Greek history is a panorama of jingoism and imperialism—war for war's sake, all the citizens being warriors. It is horrible, because of the irrationality of it all—save for the purpose of making 'history'—and the history is that of the utter ruin of civilization in intellectual respects perhaps the highest the earth has ever seen."[18]

A paragraph may end with a topic sentence:

Among the countless thousands who flock, the nation over, on a bright Saturday of mid-November to witness a "big" football game in some nearby academic town, there must be a few who, in the interval between the halves, ask themselves, what is this amazing spectacle at which they are assisting? How vast a swarming multitude! Special trains by the score pour out their living freight; the roads of a dozen counties overflow their brims with the converging streams of motors; a battalion of special police keep crowds in order; countless hawkers stridently recommend stale edibles or "winning colors." And the occasion of it all is that two and twenty college youths are to play a friendly game of ball. While every autumn sets new records of congregated attendance, *there is,* I think, *a steadily growing sense of something not altogether right and normal in the great edifice of organized college athletics* of which the "big" game is the crowning pinnacle.[19]

The topic sentence may appear midway in a paragraph:

It's not that I want anybody protecting me, or supporting me, or giving me his seat in the subway. I just don't want them spitting in my eye the whole time. I've given up hope of having time to have a soul, but can't I have one tiny foible? My unemancipated great aunts had a great advantage: they could be eccentric. Right now, there's not one young female character in the whole vast breadth of these United States. A few old ones, mostly toothless, persist: everybody loves them and talks about them continuously. *I want to be a*

---

[18] William James, "The Moral Equivalent of War."
[19] Robert K. Root, "Sports versus Athletics," *Forum,* November, 1924.

character, too. I want to save string. I want to be scared of the telephone. I want to let my heels run over and not wear gloves. I want to make scenes. I want to write occasional verse. I want to be rude to fools, while I'm still young enough to do it without being described as a naughty old lady. I want to have crackpot notions, little ways, and one of my moods.[20]

The topic sentence, or central thought, may be implied rather than stated:

"Some years ago when I was the dinner guest of a famous club in Boston, the chairman of the evening introduced me in the following words: 'Our guest tonight is an economist. I need hardly remind you, gentlemen, of the large part played in our life of today by our economists. Indeed it has been calculated that if all the economists were laid out in a line, end to end, starting at the Mexican border, they would reach'—the orator paused impressively and added—'nowhere.' "[21]

P-2 CONTINUITY IN PARAGRAPHS

We tie the parts of words together by spacing letters and using hyphens; we tie the parts of sentences together by conjunctions. How are the parts of paragraphs linked together? What makes the sentences cohere? There are several devices: repetition of key words, pronoun and antecedent relationships, and transitional words and phrases. Besides making for continuity in single paragraphs, these devices connect one paragraph to another so that meaning flows smoothly from the beginning to the end of a complete discourse.

Transition words and phrases include such expressions as *therefore, however, for example, nevertheless, since, whereas, moreover, hence, thus, finally, and, but, or, for, this, that, these, those,* and numerical markers—*first, second, third.* Notice the devices used in the following two paragraphs:

[20] Sylvia Wright, "Whose World? . . . and Welcome to It," *Harper's Magazine,* May, 1955, p. 35.

[21] Stephen Leacock, "Has Economics Gone to Seed?" in *Too Much College,* New York, 1940, p. 109.

"A fact is a statement that can be checked. There are historical facts, observable facts, and experimental facts. Historical facts come to us by indirect evidence. Observable facts can be directly perceived by qualified witnesses. Experimental facts are subject to control. All facts are objective—that is, impersonal.

"An opinion cannot be checked; it is personal. An opinion is a guess, a hunch, a projection into the unknown. It is an opinion because all the facts are not in."[22]

Repetition of the key words *fact*, in the first paragraph, and *opinion*, in the second paragraph, glues the sentences together. Also the last sentence in paragraph one is a restatement of the thesis stated in the first sentence of that paragraph. The word *impersonal*, in the first paragraph, is contrasted by *personal*, in the second paragraph, thus connecting the two units. Coherence is also maintained in these paragraphs by their very structure, as we shall show.

P-3 FORM AND STRUCTURE IN PARAGRAPHS

The methods and arrangements for clarifying, supporting, and defending ideas apply to paragraphs as well as to whole essays. Thus a paragraph may be developed and structured chronologically, spatially, analytically, or climactically. Illustration, example, definition, comparison and contrast, analogy, and all other forms discussed in Chapters 7, 8, and 9 are appropriate frameworks for paragraph units. Consider the illustrative paragraphs quoted in the last section. The first one is developed analytically and at the same time is a unit in a larger analysis, as shown in this outline:

Evidence
A. Fact
   1. Historical fact
   2. Observable fact
B. Opinion

[22] Bess Sondel, "Everybody's Listening!" *National Parent-Teacher*, January, 1951.

Both paragraphs are developed by definition, and the two together by contrast and comparison. Parallel structure is evident in the wording of the first line of each paragraph:

(1) A fact can be checked . . .
(2) An opinion cannot be checked . . .

This device makes for unity as well as coherence.

Notice the parallel structure within the following paragraph, maintained by consistent use of verbs in the present tense (italics are supplied):

The simple theory . . . *harmonizes* . . . facts otherwise most perplexing, and *exhibits* the sequence and relation between phenomena that without reference to it are diverse and contradictory. It *explains* why improvements which increase the productive power of labor and capital increase the reward of neither. It *explains* what is commonly called the conflict between labor and capital, while proving the real harmony of interest between them. It *cuts* the last inch of ground from under the fallacies of protection, while showing why free trade fails to benefit permanently the working classes. It *explains* why want increases with abundance, and wealth tends to greater and greater aggregations. . . .[23]

a. Paragraphs may be developed by specific instances, examples, and illustrations:

A great critic is certainly more difficult to find in the present time than in a generation or two ago. It is the business of the critic to evaluate and create some order and sense out of the literature of his own generation. It is also his function to restore or bring to life neglected and misunderstood writers. Melville's "Moby Dick" was recognized as a work of genius by American critics many years after his death, and then only after English critics had set up a hue and cry about that forgotten man. William Faulkner had better luck. While our own book reviewers and the public were hesitating about the value of his work, to such an extent that in 1947 only three or

[23] Henry George, *Progress and Poverty.*

four of his novels were in print, French and Scandinavian critics were calling him our most creative and most significant writer.[24]

Well, it was lovely. Over the tops of the beach-plum bushes I could see the ocean lying calm in the morning sun, swinging to and fro forever. There was a sort of hum in the air that I remembered, a hum made up of the sounds of bees and of hummingbirds and the hum that the sun makes shining. Otherwise the morning was very still. I don't know where the children had gone. I could smell the sweet fern up on the moors; the scent came drifting down on the salty breeze. I still felt weak and rather ill, but peaceful; happy. I leaned my head back in the deck chair where I was sitting, and rested. It was such a beautiful morning, almost worth eating the bad clam for. I could have stayed resting in that chair all summer, while the white gulls wheeled over my head and slid down the air currents toward the sea.[25]

b.   Paragraphs may be developed by analogy:

Take the average normally intelligent child of eight. He has an astonishingly large vocabulary, and he speaks good English as naturally and as casually as he rides his bicycle. He has never heard of such outlandish terms as predicate nominative, indicative mode, verbal noun; nor is there any reason why he should know them, any more than he needs to know the abstruse scientific terms of the law of equilibrium in order to perform the extremely delicate and difficult feat of riding his bike "without hands."[26]

So much for the value of Latin as a mainstay for the technical study of language. But, to my thinking, a further reason for retaining it as the base of our education is because it can serve, so to speak, as ballast. It is the ballast in the hold of a ship, down in the dark and unseen, which governs every graceful dip and dive of the flag at the masthead and guarantees against disaster. Or we may take another metaphor from one of these odd little mantelpiece figures of man-

[24] Horace Sutton, "The Reviewer's Function," *Saturday Review of Literature,* December 19, 1953, p. 24.

[25] Nancy Hale, "The Coasts of New England," *The New Yorker,* September 10, 1955, p. 42.

[26] Frank Colby, *The Practical Handbook of Better English,* New York, 1944, p. 3.

darins or patriarchs whose nodding head rocks back and forward but never falls because of a controlling ball of lead suspended in his belly. For those of us trained in a classical education Latin is the ball of lead in our bellies which keeps our eyes properly focused on the horizon.[27]

c. Paragraphs may be developed by contrast and comparison:

The American space-sense, the American time-sense, the American sense of personal identity are not those of Europeans—and in particular, not those of the English. The English language was moulded to express the English experience of life. The literature written in that language is one of the greatest glories of the entire human adventure. That achievement went hand in hand with the comparable achievement of forging the language which conveyed so accurately their senses of space, time, and identity. Those senses are not ours and the American people and American writers have long been engaged in reshaping the inherited language to express our modes of apprehension.[28]

d. Paragraphs may be developed by suggestion and association:

Where have they gone, these old familiar phrases? The rocker has become a curio, a period piece, and is probably relegated to somebody's attic if it hasn't been split up for kindling wood. And the same holds for Great Aunt Lizzie's choice collection of aphorisms. Hers was a high standard of conduct up to which few of her friends, even relations, were able to measure. I can hear her saying: "The trouble with your uncle is that he simply has no git up and git," or "If you ask me Cousin Hattie is turning into a crashing bore" (obviously the result of her recent trip to England), or "What would you expect of old Farmer Brown? He's just plain ornery," or "I wouldn't trust him for a minute; he's only a fair-weather friend, a Good Time Charlie," or with sly innuendo, "Well, if you believe all you hear she's really no better than she should be."[29]

[27] Stephen Leacock, "What Good Is Latin?" in *Too Much College*, p. 50.
[28] Thornton Wilder, "Toward an American Language," *Atlantic Monthly*, July, 1952, p. 31.
[29] Dale Warren, "Aunt Lizzie's Lexicon," *Saturday Review of Literature*, December 5, 1953, p. 21.

e. Paragraphs may be developed by analysis:

For purposes of analysis, the comics may be divided into serial strips and strips which offer a different anecdote each day. The serials are the more interesting, since they present all the problems of the anecdotal strips as well as a number of their own. In these serials, the next larger unit after the daily installment might be called the narrative sequence. Narrative sequences correspond roughly to the chapters of a picaresque novel: the plot of each is complete in itself but the leading characters are carried over into the next sequence. The usual length of sequences is from forty to sixty installments. They often seem much longer, however, because strip time is so much slower than actual time—a unique artistic situation, since in novels, plays and movies, time usually moves faster for characters than for the reader. Only one strip, Frank King's Gasoline Alley, keeps real time: each daily installment corresponds roughly to a day in the lives of the characters, who age at the same rate as their readers.[30]

f. Paragraphs may be developed by definition or elucidation:

Some years ago, being with a camping party in the mountains, I returned from a solitary ramble to find every one engaged in a ferocious metaphysical dispute. The *corpus* of the dispute was a squirrel—a live squirrel supposed to be clinging to one side of a tree-trunk; while over against the tree's opposite side a human being was imagined to stand. This human witness tries to get sight of the squirrel by moving rapidly around the tree, but no matter how fast he goes, the squirrel moves as fast in the opposite direction, and always keeps the tree between himself and the man, so that never a glimpse of him is caught. The resultant metaphysical problem now is this: *Does the man go round the squirrel or not?* He goes round the tree, sure enough, and the squirrel is on the tree, but does he go round the squirrel? In the unlimited leisure of the wilderness, discussion had been worn threadbare. Every one had taken sides, and was obstinate; and the numbers on both sides were even. Each side, when I appeared, therefore appealed to me to make it a majority. Mindful of

[30] Ignatius G. Mattingly, "Some Cultural Aspects of Serial Cartoons," *Harper's Magazine*, December, 1955, p. 35.

the scholastic adage that whenever you meet a contradiction you must make a distinction, I immediately sought and found one, as follows: "Which party is right," I said, "depends on what you *practically mean* by 'going round' the squirrel. If you mean passing from the north of him to the east, then to the south, then to the west, and then to the north of him again, obviously the man does go round him, for he occupies these successive positions. But if on the contrary you mean being first in front of him, then on the right of him, then behind him, then on his left, and finally in front again, it is quite as obvious that the man fails to go round him, for by the compensating movements the squirrel makes, he keeps his belly turned towards the man all the time, and his back turned away. Make the distinction, and there is no occasion for any further dispute. You are both right and both wrong according as you conceive the verb 'to go round' in one practical fashion or the other."[31]

There's a tale told about a Hollywood producer who once asked a screen writer to think up a plot for an adventure picture. "Just what sort of adventure movie did you have in mind?" the writer asked. "Young man," said the producer, "by an adventure picture, I mean a love story with crocodiles." The producer's definition undoubtedly fits a good many movies that have come to our screens of late. And where are crocodiles to be found in abundance? In Africa, of course. So to Africa have gone many Hollywood safaris, with results that are sometimes entertaining, sometimes not.[32]

g. Paragraphs may be developed by giving directions:

Then, as summer progresses, you can get after the crab grass in a new way. The idea is to cut off the flowers so the stuff can't go to seed. This isn't easy because crab grass is smart. If you cut the lawn every week, it senses this and sends its seed stalks out sideways close to the ground. But you can fool it. In August you stop cutting the grass altogether. The crab grass is lulled into a false sense of security and sends its seed heads straight up. You watch them carefully, and as soon as the tiny flowers open and you can see the small yellow stamens, you mow the lawn as high as possible, just enough to lop off

---

[31] William James, "What Pragmatism Means."
[32] Hollis Alpert, "Adventure, Anyone?" *Woman's Day*, May, 1955, p. 16.

the flowers. You may even have to do this by hand. But don't cut it short. You want the second crop to grow upright too, so you can lop it off. There usually isn't time for a third crop. Some golf course keepers help this process along by pulling the seed heads up with a rake.[33]

h. Paragraphs may be developed by testimony or by factual evidence:

Harold Strong, who has spent his life studying boys who go wrong and is the director of Children's Village at Dobbs Ferry, New York, thinks a child's desire to belong to a group is one of the keys to the solution of juvenile delinquency. He has observed that children go from group to group until they find one that accepts them. If they are rejected by all the good groups, they can always find their place with a "bad" group. Refusal to steal a car, pick a pocket, or vandalize somebody's house can be antisocial behavior in a "bad" group. Man, as too many people idly observe, is a social animal. How can we insure a child's aligning himself with a "good" group?[34]

P-4 SUGGESTIONS FOR PLANNING PARAGRAPHS

a. Avoid making paragraphs 200 to 300 words in length. Keep them short, but do not limit them to single sentences except for transition paragraphs between larger units of material.

b. Use the beginning and ending of paragraphs for points of maximum emphasis.

c. Be sure to indent paragraphs clearly for the convenience of your readers.

d. Be consistent in your method of developing a paragraph, but use several methods simultaneously if you want to.

e. Take special pains to make transitions within a paragraph and between paragraphs smooth.

f. Make paragraphs consistent in tone, style, and mood.

[33] "The Art and Science of Cutting the Grass," *Changing Times*, June, 1955, p. 42.

[34] Croswell Bowen, "Why They Go Wrong," *Saturday Review of Literature*, February 27, 1954, p. 13.

g.   Use parallel arrangements in and among paragraphs in order to properly unify your thought.

h.   Make your topic sentence clear and emphatic. If it is implied rather than stated, leave no doubt as to your precise meaning.

SENTENCES

Communication skill may be defined as the ability to employ language in ways that will most efficiently and effectively transfer ideas from one person to another. The emphasis, as we have said many times, is on clarity. Clarity is a quality of verbal discourse that should transcend every element into which a given message can be analyzed. The author's meaning in a sentence is by far the most important consideration of the sentence. In fact, it is the only important thing about the sentence. Every aspect of the sentence should somehow contribute to this meaning. But meaning is not a simple thing; it is multi-dimensional and includes all of the following relationships:

a.   Relation between observer and thing observed. Sentences reflect the author's feelings or judgments of the thing he is talking about.
b.   Relation between the transmitter and receiver of the message. Sentences reflect the author's purpose in what he has to say.
c.   Relation between the author and the society of which he is a part. Sentences reflect meanings which are assigned words by community consent.
d.   Relation between words in a verbal context. The syntactical arrangement of words in sentences specifies an author's meaning.

S-1 SENTENCE UNITY: THE PERIOD FAULT

A sentence as a unit of discourse contains a unified thought. Such a thought may be a compound idea; it may be a modified idea. In any event, it is a complete idea, and every element in a sentence must be intimately related to this idea. If I say: "Niagara Falls separates Canada and the United States," I focus upon a single thought.

Sentence fragments are parts of a sentence which lose their meaning when isolated from the context in which they appear. The following statements are fragments:

> Because I love you.
> Since earliest times.
> Unaccustomed as I am to public speaking.
> Whenever in the course of human events.

Whenever a statement of this kind is presented as a sentence, we call it a period fault.

In oral discourse, we use sentence fragments without thinking, and there is no reason why we shouldn't, if our thought is clear. Notice the conversational fragments in the following:

> "Where's the Packard?"
> "They took the Packard."
> "Who drove?"
> "The Indian."
> "They're both Indians. Which of the brothers drove the car?"
> "The one who lived at this hotel."
> —William Saroyan

In written discourse it is customary to avoid sentence fragments, even though established writers sometimes use them for effect.

> "I don't feel well."
> "What specifically?"
> "Oh—aches and pains."
> "Where?"

"Oh—here, there, and everywhere."

"We'll run a few tests and I'll examine you. The nurse will get you undressed."

In written discourse it is customary to avoid sentence fragments except as they appear in conversational sequences such as the one quoted above. But since the line of demarkation between the spoken word and the written word is gradually becoming less distinct, more and more sentence fragments appear in written essays. Here is an example of a sentence fragment which appears in the writing of William Faulkner:

"Because that dream was man's aspiration in the true meaning of the word aspiration. It was not merely the blind and voiceless hope of his heart: it was the actual inbreathe of his lungs, his lights, his living and unsleeping metabolism, so that we actually lived the Dream."[35]

S-2   SENTENCE LENGTH

Some textbook writers defend the notion that sentences should be restricted to fourteen to twenty words. Others argue that the length of sentences should vary so as to avoid monotony. Sentence length is a matter of individual style: some authors write long sentences, others short ones. We seem to be writing shorter sentences today than authors of a century ago did. Notice the length of this sentence by John Henry Newman, written in 1873:

And then again, the first time the mind comes across the arguments and speculations of unbelievers, and feels what a novel light they cast upon what he has hitherto accounted sacred; and still more, if it gives in to them and embraces them and throws off as so much prejudice what it has hitherto held, and, as if waking from a dream, begins to realize to its imagination that there is now no such thing as law and the transgression of law, that sin is a phantom, and

[35] William Faulkner, "On Privacy—the American Dream: What Happened to It," *Harper's Magazine*, July, 1955, p. 34.

punishment a bugbear, that it is free to sin, free to enjoy the world and the flesh; and still further, when it does enjoy them, and reflects that it may think and hold just what it will, that "the world is all before it where to choose," and what system to build up as its own private persuasion; when this torrent of wilful thoughts rushes over and inundates it, who will deny that the fruit of the tree of knowledge, or what the mind takes for knowledge, has made it one of the gods, with a sense of expansion and elevation,—an intoxication in reality, still, so far as the subjective state of the mind goes, an illumination?

There are 206 words in the sentence, which is more than the number of words in an average paragraph these days.

Our concern, of course, is not with how other people have regulated sentence length but rather with how sentence length will help accomplish the specific purpose we have in mind in the communication of meaning. All matters of style are relative to purpose, and sentence length is certainly a matter of style.

For the average person who has trouble with sentences, we could arbitrarily rule that he should avoid:

S-2.1   Primer-type sentences

"This is a cat. The cat has whiskers. The cat's whiskers get into the milk."

S-2.2   Long, involved sentences with many dependent clauses and modifiers

"We do not understand the exact nature of the functional interdependence of culture and language as taught today by the metalinguists and general semanticists, but we do know that this interdependence is a fact, and we can accuse the makers of auxiliary languages of having substituted their subjective judgment for the cultural pole in the bipolar entity of what I have referred to as the functional interdependence of language and culture" (Alexander Gode).

S-2.3   Run-on sentences

". . . and this afternoon I went shopping. I started out and then I decided it was going to rain and went back and changed my hat; I was wearing that pink with the roses but I changed to the old blue—you know, the blue felt I got last fall when Millie was in town, with the veil. And when I walked into the butcher's, Joe, the nice one whose wife just lost her baby, with the little mustache, anyway, he looked at me and said, 'Mrs. Vance, you come at the right time, we just got in some more of those pork tenderloins you said you liked,' and . . ." (J. A. M. Meerloo).

S-2.4   Making sentences all the same length

Notice the variety in the following:

"Nonsense. The Casual Style is within everyone's grasp. It has now become so perfected by constant polishing that its devices may readily be identified, and they change so little that their use need be no more difficult for the novice than for the expert." (William H. Whyte, Jr.).

These rules cannot be expected to produce satisfactory results for all occasions and purposes. Notice, for example, the effective satire Eugene Field accomplished with primer sentences:

"Here we have an Oyster. It is going to a Church Fair. When it gets to the Fair, it will swim around in a big Kettle of Warm Water. A Lady will Stir it with a Spoon, and sell the Warm Water for Forty Cents a pint. Then the Oyster will move on to the next Fair. In this way, the Oyster will visit all the Church Fairs in Town, and Bring a great many Dollars into the Church Treasury. The Oyster goes a Great Way in a Good Cause." (*The Tribune Primer*).

S-3   POSITION OF MODIFIERS

Meaning is clarified by the position of modifiers—words, phrases, or clauses which limit, explain, or specify the essential elements of a sentence. The position of many modifiers is fixed by usage. Notice how the modifying element in the following sentences either precedes or follows the words modified:

The *proper* arrangement *of flowers* is important.
The man *in charge* is a newcomer.
The *two-story* house *on the left* is for sale.
Any *up and coming young* man will succeed *if he tries.*

Custom, however, has not fixed the position of all modifiers, so that the meaning of sentences can be greatly altered by shifting such elements from one position to another. Adverbial modifiers are, generally speaking, more movable than adjectival modifiers:

Anyone can succeed *if he tries.*
Anyone *if he tries* can succeed.
If he tries, anyone can succeed.

Whenever modifiers are misplaced, the expression is likely to become ambiguous:

No identification was found on the man lying in the street *by the police.*

When a modifier appears in a sentence with nothing to modify, it is said to "dangle." Dangling modifiers are usually participles, or verbal adjectives. Such statements as the following are illogical and confusing:

Playing and dancing on the lawn, our party was a great success.
(Corrected: Playing and dancing on the lawn, we had a successful party.)
Trying as hard as we could, the knot wouldn't come untied.
(Corrected: Trying as hard as we could we were unable to untie the knot.)

S-4 PARALLEL STRUCTURE

Parallelism in sentence structure means putting similar elements in similar forms. Thus, we say: *Swimming* and *skating* are my favorite sports. Not: *To swim* and *skating* are my favorite sports.

The thought is much clearer when the form and structure are regulated and controlled. Observe the parallelism in the following sentence:

Religion and *liberty*
                    are the two
great objects of defensive war. Cojoined, they
unite all the feelings, and *call forth* all the energies
of man.
In defense of them nations contend with the spirit of the Maccabees;
"*one* will chase a thousand, and *two* put ten thousand to flight."
                    —Timothy Dwight

Whenever items are listed in series, parallel structure should be observed in order to keep the thought from becoming muddled:

There be three things which are too wonderful for me, yea four which I know not:
    the way of an eagle in the air;
    the way of a serpent upon a rock;
    the way of a ship in the midst of the sea; and
    the way of a man with a maid.
                    —Proverbs 30:18–19

A fact is a statement that can be checked. There are
historical facts,
observable facts, and
experimental facts.
                    —Bess Sondel
Morale is largely a matter of keeping emotions at a certain pitch; and unfortunately
    fear,
    hatred,
    suspicion
            are among the emotions most easily aroused.
                    —John Dewey

When two elements are juxtaposed for comparison or contrast, parallel structure keeps the meaning clear:

The Lord will destroy the house of the proud, but he will establish the border of the widow.

—Proverbs 15:25

Sometimes parallel structure is purposely upset for special effects: In the following sentence, the form is parallel but the meaning or content is not:

"It was adventure, travel, danger, skill, grace, romance, comedy, peanuts, popcorn, chewing-gum and soda water" (William Saroyan, "The Circus").

In this sentence three sets of parallel items are thrown together helter-skelter to create the idea of orderly confusion of a circus: (a) adventure, travel, danger, romance, comedy; (b) skill, grace; (c) peanuts, popcorn, chewing-gum, soda water. Notice that the items in (a) are all abstract nouns; the items in (b) are attributes of people; and the items in (c) are specific nouns closely related.

S-5 COÖRDINATION

When elements in a sentence are of equal weight, we can show the equality by placing them in parallel structure, or by linking them together with coördinate conjunctions. In the familiar statement attributed to Julius Caesar—"I came, I saw, I conquered"—the equality is established by parallelism. Part of the meaning is, of course, obtained from the chronological and climactic arrangement of items. Here are a number of sentences from the writings of Emerson which demonstrate how independent elements are made of equal weight or coördinated by the use of conjunctions: "Man does not stand in awe of man, *nor* is his genius admonished to stay at home, to put itself in communication with the internal ocean, *but* it goes abroad to beg a cup of water of the urns of other men."

The close connection between the first and last clauses of the following sentence is established by the conjunction:

"Science . . . undergoes continual changes; it is barbarous, it is civilized, it is Christianized, it is rich, it is scientific; *but* this change is not amelioration."

Juxtaposed statements may be equated by the conjunction:

"The civilized man has built a coach, *but* has lost the use of his feet. He is supported on crutches, *but* lacks so much support of muscle. He has a fine Geneva watch, *but* he fails of the skill to tell the hour by the sun."

Here is an example of varied word order, parallel structure, and coördination:

"A Greenwich nautical almanac he has, and so being sure of the information when he wants it, the man in the street, does not know a star in the sky. The solstice he does not observe, the equinox he knows as little, and the whole bright calendar of the year is without a dial in his mind. His notebooks impair his memory; his libraries overload his wit; the insurance office increases the number of accidents; and it may be a question whether machinery does not encumber; whether we have lost not by refinement some energy, by a Christianity intrenched in establishments and forms, some vigor of wild virtue."

S-6 SUBORDINATION

When one element of a sentence is dependent upon another element, the relationship is shown by connecting the two with a subordinating conjunction, relative pronoun, or conjunctive adverb. In the following sentences the dependent element is in italics and the connective is underlined:

When *it is time to go,* you will be told.

As soon as *your mother* arrives, let me know.

Aside from such extreme measures there has to be definite organization, as *we saw in the two World Wars,* to keep up the morale of even noncombatants. [John Dewey]

It is not a good sign <u>when</u> *security officers resist fair-minded inquiry.*
Sound though *it is,* such advice is not likely to be warmly received.
But so <u>simple</u> and so clear is this truth, <u>that</u> *to see it once is always to recognize it.*
That *there is a common cause,* and <u>that</u> *it is either what we call* material progress or something *closely* connected with material progress, becomes more than an inference <u>when</u> *it is noted that the phenomena we class together and speak of as industrial depression are but manifestations of phenomena* which always accompany *material progress, and* <u>which</u> show *themselves more clearly and strongly as material progress goes on.*
[Henry George]

S-7   EFFECTIVE SENTENCES

Effective sentences are sentences which produce precisely the responses their author desires. As John Mason Brown has said: "The sentence and the paragraph, by means of which points are made, thoughts communicated, emotions transferred, pictures painted, personalities caught, rhythms established, and cadences varied, offer other challenges and should provide their own sources of delight and pride." How effective a sentence is depends almost entirely on the author's purpose in the context in which it is placed. Prescriptive rules for sentences are quite unrealistic because they must be broken so often in order to accomplish what an author has in mind. For example, one author uses short, primer-like sentences to produce a sense of movement and excitement; another uses run-on sentences to create an atmosphere of meditation and reverie; still another employs sentence fragments to give emphasis to what is said. Notice how effectively Mark Twain produces sound effects by a long succession of participles: "All day long he was singing, whistling, yelling, whooping, laughing—it was maddening, devastating, unendurable."

S-7.1 Split constructions

Sentence clarity requires that you keep logically related elements together. Split constructions include separation of subject and verb, verb and object, preposition and object, and other closely related elements.

> Subject and Verb: I, hoping to be the first one to class, hurried. (Improved: I hurried in order to be the first one to class.)
>
> Object and Verb: He turned off, with a gesture of defiance and disgust, the radio. (Improved: He turned off the radio with a gesture of defiance and disgust.)
>
> Preposition and Object: He jumped out of, because he was frightened, the car. (Improved: He jumped out of the car because he was frightened.)

S-7.2 Shifts that result in inconsistency of expression

a. Avoid needless shift in person or number.

> Shift in Person: When *you* are industrious, *one* can succeed. (Improved: When you are industrious, you can succeed.)
>
> Shift in Number: If a *person* tries hard enough, *they* will succeed. (Improved: If a person tries hard enough, he will succeed.)

b. Avoid shifts in voice, tense, or mood of verbs.

> Shift in Voice: Singing *could be heard* as we *approached* the house. (Improved: We could hear singing as we approached the house.)
>
> Shift in Tense: She *sat* down in the rocker and *begins* to knit. (Improved: She sat down in the rocker and began to knit.)
>
> Shift in Mood: *Finish* your homework, and then you *should* practice your music. (Improved: Finish your homework and then practice your music.)

S-7.3 Mixed and illogical constructions

Do not expect your reader or listener to untangle your illogical thinking or your involved constructions.

a. Avoid superfluous *that*: We know *that* even though we are late *that* we won't be penalized. (Improved: We know that even though we are late we won't be penalized.)

b. Avoid double negatives. Although colloquial usage permits double negatives, and although some double negatives enforce rather than dispute statements of fact, a careful writer avoids such constructions as:

"*No* fotch-on preacher *ain't never* come to this here meetin'-house."

"I *ain't never* done *nothin'* to nobody."

"I *can't scarcely* hear him." (Improved: I can scarcely hear him. Or: I can't hear him.)

c. Avoid mixed, illogical syntax. Although the language is full of all kinds of grammatical inconsistencies—such as *children* as a plural for *child*, and to *center around* for *center in*—there seems little reason to throw logic to the winds and hope people will comprehend our meaning regardless of what we say. Examples of syntactical confusion include:

Irregardless of what we say, people will misunderstand. (Improved: Irrespective of what we say, people will misunderstand. Or: Regardless of what we say, people will misunderstand.)

Some of the methods used were physical exertion. (Improved: One of the methods used was physical exertion.)

d. Avoid unfinished grammatical construction.

After showing all my credentials, we went to the police station. (Improved: After showing all my credentials to the officer, I accompanied the others to the police station.)

S-8 WORD ORDER

Word order is one of the simplest means we have of clarifying meaning. The response you make to the following statements is in each case determined largely by the order in which the words appear:

> You are going!
> Are you going?
> Going, are you?
> Hit me, Jack.
> Jack hit me.

The last of these sentences is stated in normal or SVO (subject-verb-object) order. Here are additional examples:

Subject	Verb	Indirect Object	Direct Object or Complement
Shakespeare	wrote		plays.
Columbus	discovered		America.
Wilson	wrote	his wife	a letter.
My sister	sings.		
	Stop		the train.
	Give	me	your word.

Variations from normal word order accompany substitutions for the subject:

> *There* was an old lady from Podunk.
> *It* is time to go.
> *That* is what you think.

Variations from normal word order accompany passive voice of verbs:

> The letter *was delivered* by the postman.
> The proposal *was approved* by the committee.

S-8.1 Variations from normal word order for questions, emphasis, or special effects

a. Word order is varied for questions: Are you going?

b. Word order is varied for emphasis:

> That, I do not believe.

Could be that you are mistaken.
Came the dawn.
The money is all I want.
Happiness, money will not buy.
Here is your share.
In single file came the soldiers.
On top of the house was my child.
So do I.
Neither is he.

S-8.2 Variations from normal word order for negation, rarity, or improbability

Never was I so embarrassed.
Nowhere have I seen such beauty.
Little does he realize that I followed him.
Only twice have I seen him flinch.

Change word order of sentences for variety:

We live the time that a match flickers; we pop the cork of a ginger-beer bottle, and the earthquake swallows us on the instant. Is it not odd, is it not incongruous, is it not, in the highest sense of human speech, incredible, that we should think so highly of the ginger-beer, and regard so little the devouring earthquake? The love of life and fear of Death are two famous phrases that grow harder to understand the more we think about them. It is a well-known fact that an immense proportion of boat accidents would never happen if people held the sheet in their hands instead of making it fast; and yet, unless it be some martinet of a professional mariner or some landsman with shattered nerves, every one of God's creatures makes it fast.
—Robert L. Stevenson, "Aes Triplex"

In the following sentence, inverted word order of the "this was" variety is used to emphasize the subject by putting it sharply in focus:

"This was the American Dream: a sanctuary on the earth for individual man: a condition in which he could be free not only of the old established closed-corporation hierarchies of arbitrary power which had oppressed him as a mass, but free of that mass into which the hierarchies of church and state had compressed and held him individually thralled and individually important" (William Faulkner).

Too often, however, this type of inversion is cumbersome and wasteful, and thwarts rather than clarifies thought:

"There are indications that the influence of critical groups has become disproportionate to the amount of wisdom contained in their criticisms." The sentence might better begin thus: "Facts indicate that . . ."

If you want to produce a sense of movement, dramatic action, or direction, normal word order will be most suitable:

"The little old lady has lived in a third-floor room for fifteen years. Her family cannot remember when she last came out of it. She has a rocker, and can be heard rocking herself to sleep right after lunch. She is an avid reader, and has a vast collection of magazines dating back to 1907" (Walter Kerr).

CONVENTIONS OF GRAMMAR AND SYNTAX

Part of the business of clarifying meaning in language is accomplished by respecting certain arbitrary conventions of grammar and syntax, regulated by usage but less subject to change than the meanings of words or their pronunciations. The principles discussed under this heading are selected because of the frequency of disorders resulting from improper understanding of them. A Glossary of Grammatical Terms appears at the close of the section.

G-1 AGREEMENT AND REFERENCE OF PRONOUNS

G-1.1 Agreement with antecedent in person, number, and gender

Person: The policeman (third person) has lost his (third person) badge.

Number: The girls (plural) have given their (plural) consent.

Gender: The boy (masculine) has removed his (masculine) shoes.

453

G-1.2   Indefinite pronouns

Indefinite pronouns are either singular or plural depending on the author's meaning: *All, some, none, everyone,* and *everybody* may be either singular or plural. *Anyone, nobody, somebody, someone, either, neither,* and *each* are usually singular.

Singular: Everyone is expected to do his duty.
Plural: Everyone walked out on the speaker and I couldn't blame them.
Singular: Some child is crying his eyes out.
Plural: Some craftsmen refuse to reveal their trade secrets.
Singular: Each man is held responsible for his valuables.
Singular: Neither of the contestants has kept his balance.

G-1.3   Collective nouns

A collective noun used as an antecedent takes either a singular or plural pronoun, depending on the sense of the sentence.

Singular: The audience takes its time applauding.
Plural: The audience took their seats.
Singular: The faculty has canceled its meeting.
Plural: The faculty will wear their caps and gowns.

G-1.4   Agreement with one of two antecedents

A pronoun should agree with the nearest of two antecedents when one is singular and one is plural.

Neither the teacher nor the students had brought their books.

G-2   AGREEMENT OF SUBJECT AND VERB

G-2.1   Agreement in person and number

Scientists revise their theories from time to time. (*Scientists* and *revise* are in third person and plural in number.)
You are too short to qualify. (*You* and *are* are in second person and singular or plural in number.)

G-2.2   Agreement when separated

A verb should agree with its subject even though another noun separates them.

I, the candidate, have decided to abide by majority opinion.
The criminal as well as his friends is in hiding.

G-2.3 More than one subject

Two or more subjects joined by *and* take a plural verb, unless
the two subjects form a single idea or have a closely related meaning.

Plural: A pencil and paper are all you need.
Singular: The sum and substance of his thought is clear.

G-2.4 Subjects in plural form

Nouns plural in form but singular in meaning take a singular
verb; subjects plural in form which indicate a unity take a singular verb.

Economics is my favorite subject.
No news is good news.
The whereabouts of the suspect is not known.
Two and two is four.
Five miles is a long walk.

G-2.5 Indefinite singular pronouns

Indefinite singular pronouns take singular verbs: *each, everyone, everybody, anyone, someone, somebody, no one, nobody,
one, another, anything, either, neither. None* may be followed
by either a singular or a plural verb.

Each student has his own book.
Someone is whistling a tune.
One of you is wrong.
None of the freshmen are eligible.
None (no one) is expected to leave without permission.

G-2.6 Collective nouns

A collective noun is followed by a singular or plural verb depending on the intended sense.

The family is in favor of the marriage.
The family were seated around the table.
The faculty is having a meeting.
The faculty were furious about the decision.

G-2.7 Relative pronouns

When relative pronouns have plural antecedents they take plural verbs.

He is one of the students who are most likely to succeed.

G-3 CASE OF NOUNS AND PRONOUNS

Case is a characteristic of nouns and pronouns which shows the relationship between the noun in question and other parts of the sentence in which it occurs.

G-3.1 Nominative case

The subject of a finite verb and a predicate complement are in the nominative case.

Subject: I like college very much.
Predicate complement: It is I. (Colloquial usage permits "It is me," contrary to the conventional rule.)

G-3.2 Objective case

The object of a verb or preposition and the subject, object, and objective complement of an infinitive are in the objective case.

Object of verb: My father blames me.
Indirect object: Give me the flowers.
Object of preposition: A group of us met the boat.
Subject of infinitive: I asked him to play.
Object of infinitive: My desire to please him is sincere.
Objective complement: Did you think Roger to be me?

G-3.3 Possessive case

A pronoun which modifies a gerund is in the possessive case.

We objected to his calling us names.
John came without my inviting him.

G-3.4 Case of relative pronouns

The case of a relative pronoun is determined by its use in a sentence.

Admit whoever comes. (*whoever* is the subject of *comes; you* [understood] is the subject of *admit*)
Invite whomever you wish. (object of *invite*)
Give the reward to whoever wins. (subject of *wins,* not object of preposition *to;* the clause *whoever wins* is object of the preposition)
Whom did you wish to see? (object of infinitive *to see:* "You did wish to see whom?")

G-4 DEGREE OF ADJECTIVES AND ADVERBS

Adjectives and adverbs have three degrees of emphasis or force: positive, comparative and superlative.

G-4.1 Degree for two things or for three or more

In formal discourse, use the comparative degree when two things are compared; use the superlative degree when three or more things are involved.

Jack is the taller of the two boys.
This is the best book in the collection.

G-4.2 No comparison possible

Do not invent comparative or superlative forms for words which admit of no comparison: unique, true, perfect, empty, full, fatal, dead, excellent, perpendicular, round.

G-4.3   One form only of comparative or superlative degree

Do not say, "I am the most happiest person in town." Say, "I am the happiest person in town."

G-4.4   Care with comparisons

Do not use the positive degree of adjectives and adverbs when a comparison is intended.

> Awkward: The dormitories at this college are the largest and picturesque as any in the state.
> Improved: Largest and most picturesque.

G-5   SUBJUNCTIVE MOOD OF VERBS

Mood of verbs establishes a speaker's or writer's mood about the actuality of an event. The indicative mood indicates the truth of what is said. The subjunctive mood implies doubt or uncertainty.

G-5.1   Wish, supposition, or doubt

Use the subjunctive mood of verbs when you want to express a wish, supposition, or doubt.

> I wish I were back home.
> If need be, I'll arrange the details myself.

G-5.2   Conditions contrary to fact

Use the subjunctive mood of verbs for conditions contrary to fact or probability.

> If I were you, I'd go in a minute.

G-5.3   Recommendations or demands

Use the subjunctive mood of verbs for recommendations and demands.

> I move the meeting be adjourned.
> It is mandatory that the applicant be of age.

G-6 TENSE OF VERBS

Tense refers to the time of happening of an event specified in a verbal statement: present time, past time, future time.

G-6.1 Statement of fact

Use the present tense in a dependent clause to state a fact.

Some students would not believe *that Reno is west of Los Angeles.*

G-6.2 Adjustment of tense to coincide with thought

The following sentences are examples of approved usage:

I am going to go to New York. (sometime in the future)
I am going to New York. (announcement of decision)
I shall go to New York. (determination)
I intend to go with you. (future intention)
I intended to go with you. (not *to have gone*)
I lay on the couch for an hour. (past tense)
We play in San Francisco tomorrow. (future tense)

G-6.3 Past tense, past participle

Form the past tense and past participle of verbs according to approved usage. Most verbs form the past tense and past participle by adding *-ed* or *-d* to the infinitive:

arm	armed	armed	make	made	made
bat	batted	batted	pay	paid	paid
climb	climbed	climbed	talk	talked	talked
flee	fled	fled	tell	told	told
have	had	had	want	wanted	wanted
lay	laid	laid	yank	yanked	yanked

Some verbs form the past tense and past participle by adding *-t* and making some other change in pronunciation:

bring	brought	brought	keep	kept	kept
buy	bought	bought	lose	lost	lost
catch	caught	caught	sleep	slept	slept
deal	dealt	dealt	teach	taught	taught
feel	felt	felt			

Some verbs form the past tense and past participle by changing vowels within the word:

bind	bound	bound	hold	held	held
bleed	bled	bled	shoot	shot	shot
dig	dug	dug	sit	sat	sat
fight	fought	fought	win	won	won
grind	ground	ground			

Some verbs do not change to form the past tense and past participle:

bet	bet	bet	hit	hit	hit
bid	bid	bid	let	let	let
burst	burst	burst	quit	quit	quit
cast	cast	cast	set	set	set
cut	cut	cut	split	split	split

Some verbs form the past participle with -n:

bear	bore	born	drive	drove	driven
bite	bit	bitten	get	got	gotten
blow	blew	blown	go	went	gone
choose	chose	chosen	lie	lay	lain
do	did	done	see	saw	seen

G-7   VOICE OF VERBS

Voice indicates whether the subject of a sentence acts (active voice) or is acted upon (passive voice.)

G-7.1 Passive voice

Use the passive voice when it is idiomatic, when emphasis is desired, or when the active voice would be awkward.

> Dinner is served.
> The president was shot by an actor.
> The pictures were taken from the interior of the car.

G-7.2   Active voice

Prefer the active voice for most communication, when you want to be direct and forceful.

> We climbed the mountain. (Not "The mountain was climbed by us.")
> He showed a color film which he had taken. (Not "A color film, taken by him, was shown.")

GLOSSARY OF GRAMMATICAL TERMS

Active voice: A characteristic of verbs which denotes that the subject performs the action expressed.

Adjective: A word, phrase, or clause used to modify a noun. Possessive nouns and pronouns are adjectives by this definition.

Adverb: A word, phrase, or clause used to modify a verb, a gerund, an adjective, or another adverb.

Antecedent: The noun or pronoun to which a pronoun refers.

Appositive: A noun added to another by way of explanation, identification, or definition. Example: *Lincoln, the Civil War President, was assassinated.*

Case: A characteristic of nouns which shows their relation to other words in a sentence. Three principal cases have survived in English: nominative, possessive (or genitive), and objective (or accusative).

Clause: A group of words containing its own subject and predicate. Clauses may be independent or dependent. Both types of clauses appear in this sentence: When I was young (dependent), I could run a mile without tiring (independent). Dependent clauses function as single parts of speech. The dependent clause in the sentence above is adverbial.

Comparison: Changes in form of adjectives and adverbs to indicate degrees of quality, quantity, or manner. Three degrees of comparison are:

Positive	Comparative	Superlative
large	larger	largest
little	less	least
good	better	best
bad	worse	worst
beautiful	more beautiful	most beautiful

Complement: A noun or adjective which follows a linking verb, or copula. Example: Grass is *green.*

Complex sentence: A sentence with one independent and one or more dependent clauses.

Compound sentence: A sentence containing two or more independent clauses.

Compound-complex sentence: A sentence containing two or more independent clauses and at least one dependent clause.

Conjunction: A word used to join words, phrases, or clauses. Conjunctions are either coördinating or subordinating. Coördinating conjunctions include *and, but, or, either, neither, nor, not only, but also.* Subordinating conjunctions include *although, whereas, because, if.*

Conjunctive adverb: An adverb which is used as a conjunction. Examples: *also, furthermore, nevertheless.*

Context: A series of related words cast in a sentence or sentences.

Copula: A linking verb which shows the relation between a subject and its complement.

Finite verb: A verb capable of making a complete and independent assertion. (Verbals are not finite verbs.)

Gender: The classification of nouns according to sex. There are four principal genders: Masculine, feminine, neuter, and common. In the early English language, as in Modern German, gender had little if any thing to do with sex.

Gerund: A verbal noun ending in *-ing.* It has the same form as the present participle of the verb from which it is derived.

Grammar: A systematic science of language which explains the relationships of words in context.

Idiom: A customary way of putting words together. Examples: *Dinner is served, about face, back up, sing out.*

Infinitive: The basic form of a verb preceded by *to,* the sign of the infinitive. Examples: *to go, to jump, to run, to be.*

Interjection: An exclamatory word interjected into a sentence without affecting the grammatical structure. Examples: *well, oh, ouch, curses.*

Intransitive verb: A verb which does not require a direct object to complete its meaning. Examples: *Birds fly. Flowers bloom. I lie on the bed.*

Linking verb: See Copula.

Mood: A characteristic of verbs which establishes a speaker's or writer's mood about the actuality of an event.

Number: The change in form of a noun or pronoun to indicate whether one or more than one is spoken of.

Object: A noun or its equivalent which receives the action of a transitive verb. Example: I read the *book*.

Participle: A form of a verb which may be used as an adjective. Participles are either present or past:

Present participle: Books in *running* brooks.

Past participle: The inverted page.

Person: The modification of the form of a verb to indicate whether the person is speaking (first person), is spoken to (second person), or is spoken of (third person). Examples:

First person: *I* am the one you want to see.

Second person: *You* bring me the slate.

Third person: *He* is always late.

Phrase: A group of related words having no subject or predicate used as a part of speech. Phrases are classified according to form as infinitive phrase, participial phrase, and prepositional phrase.

Infinitive phrase: to go alone.

Participial phrase: running wild.

Prepositional phrase: in a little while.

Phrases are classified according to function as noun phrases, adjective phrases, adverbial phrases, and verb phrases.

Predicate: The active verb in a sentence together with its modifiers, objects, and complements. Example: The train *runs on schedule most of the time.*

Preposition: A word which relates a noun or its equivalent to the word it modifies. Examples: *to, in, by, from, for, about, under.*

Simple sentence: A sentence with one independent clause and no subordinate clauses. Example: I see a horse.

Subject: The noun or pronoun in a sentence about which an assertion is made. Example: My *courses* are not difficult.

Substantive: Nouns or noun equivalents, including pronouns, infinitives, gerunds, noun phrases, noun clauses.

Syntax: A name for the grammatical relations among words in sentences or contexts.

Transitive verb: A verb accompanied by a direct object, or one which requires a direct object to complete its meaning.

Voice: The change in the form of a verb to indicate whether the subject is the doer of the action (active) or the receiver of the action (passive.)

MECHANICS

Punctuation is a mechanical device used by writers to help clarify the meaning they want to transmit. There are five principal functions of punctuation: (a) to link words and groups of words: colon, semicolon, dash, hyphen; (b) to separate sentences and parts of sentences: period, question mark, exclamation point, comma; (c) to terminate statements: period, question mark, exclamation point; (d) to enclose sentences or parts of sentences: commas, dashes, parentheses, brackets, quotation marks; (e) to indicate omissions: apostrophe, periods, dashes.

The following conventional marks are used:

,	comma	-	hyphen
.	period	'	apostrophe
?	question mark	" "	double quotation marks
;	semicolon	' '	single quotation marks
:	colon	( )	parentheses
!	exclamation point	[ ]	brackets
—	dash	*	asterisk

M-1 COMMA

M-1.1 Between independent clauses

Place a comma before a coördinating conjunction which joins two independent clauses.

465

The administration building will not be completed this spring, but it should be ready by fall.

The board of examiners will prepare an examination, and it will be administered to all freshmen.

M-1.2 To set off introductory clauses and long introductory phrases

While I was home during vacation, I had a chance to see a Broadway play.

During the most exciting movie ever to appear in our town, my brother fell asleep.

M-1.3 To set off nonrestrictive elements, parenthetical statements, and mild interjections

H. L. Mencken, who wrote *The American Language*, died recently.

The girls, believe it or not, have been waiting for us.

Herman Melville, as everyone knows, wrote *Moby Dick*.

You will have the good sense, I hope, to act your age.

He is, however, under age.

One of the students, curiously enough, came in street clothes.

Dear me, will I ever get this problem solved?

M-1.4 To set off contrasted elements

The author of *Winterset* was Maxwell Anderson, not Sherwood Anderson.

The part of a sentence essential to the meaning is restrictive, not nonrestrictive.

M-1.5 To set off words in apposition

John Herbert, the vice-president of the club, will introduce the speaker.

My sister, Mrs. Edmond Clifford, has returned from South America.

M-1.6 To set off vocatives, or nominatives of direct address, and yes and no

Mary, will you please set the table.

I would hire you, Mr. Jones, but your experience is not sufficient.

Don't worry, pal, you will get what is coming to you.

Yes, I am coming when I get ready.

M-1.7 To set off absolute expressions

The radio being turned on full blast, I couldn't hear a word you said.

We were afraid we would lose our way, the road being so poorly marked.

M-1.8 To separate items listed in series

He ran up the stairs, into the house, and to his room.

Melville wrote *Moby Dick, Typee, Omoo,* and *White Jacket.*

The following prices are effective: 10 cents for the small size, 25 cents for the large size, 59 cents for the economy size.

I came, I saw, I conquered.

A long, squirmy, reddish worm peered out at me.

M-1.9 To separate elements in dates, addresses, and direct quotations

I answered your letter on May 17, 1956, and sent it to 515 South Vernon Street, Albany 5, New York, as you requested.

You said, "I love you," three times.

"Wait a minute," said Betty, "I haven't finished my coffee."

M-2 SEMICOLON

M-2.1 Between independent clauses not joined by a coördinating conjunction

A college student must budget his time; learning doesn't take place without effort.

I took a cab to the city; I reached the office by noon; I found your letter on my desk.

M-2.2   Between independent clauses joined by a conjunctive adverb

Follow the adverb with a comma.

> We started on time; nevertheless, we will have to work overtime.
> I didn't know you were coming; however, you are perfectly welcome.
> He came early; so I told him to take off a few minutes. (When *so* and *that* appear together, no semicolon is necessary: He came early so that he could get finished on time.)

M-2.3   When one clause has internal punctuation

Use a semicolon with a coördinating conjunction to join independent clauses if one of the clauses contains internal punctuation.

> Many students, with little effort, conquer mathematics; but writing requires practice.

M-2.4   To group items in a series

> The officers are Walter Crawford, president; Tom King, vice-president; and Mary Martin, secretary.

M-2.5   Before special expressions

Use a semicolon before such expressions as *namely, for example, for instance,* and *that is,* when they introduce a second independent clause.

> He was often excited; for example, he broke the dishes purposely without provocation.

M-3   PERIOD, QUESTION MARK, AND EXCLAMATION POINT

M-3.1   To end sentences

Use a period to end declarative and imperative sentences.

> I shall return.
> Do come back soon.

M-3.2 After indirect questions

Use a period after an indirect question.

He asked me if I had ever tasted a raw oyster.

M-3.3 With abbreviations

Use a period after an abbreviation.

Mr. Mrs. Dr. Ph.D. C.O.D. Mich. etc.

M-3.4 For ellipses

Use periods to indicate an ellipsis. Three periods are used in addition to whatever other punctuation is part of the context.

"I care not what course others make take. . . . Give me liberty or give me death."

M-3.5 Uses of question marks

Use a question mark after a direct question, or within parentheses to indicate doubt or uncertainty.

Where are you going with that package?
The questions to be answered are when? where? how? why?
He blurted out, "Whom do you think I am?" and then left the room.
A passage in the second part of *The Return from Parnassus*, 1601 (?), seems to indicate that Shakespeare had worsted Jonson in satirical encounter.

M-3.6 Uses of exclamation points

Use an exclamation point to indicate surprise, command, emphasis, or emotional feeling.

What a thrill!
Are you going? Wonderful!
Leave the room at once!
Ouch! That hurt.

M-4 COLON AND DASH

M-4.1 For introduction

Use a colon to introduce a list, a long quotation, a formal question, words following an introductory statement.

> Your equipment should include the following: a pen, paper, dictionary, and English handbook.
> Andrew Jackson is reputed to have said: "It's a damned poor mind that can think of only one way to spell a word."
> The purpose of the paper is: to determine to what extent atomic energy has revolutionized modern living.
> For sale: one riding pony.
> Resolved: That patent medicines should be outlawed.

M-4.2 For separation

Use a colon to separate parts of titles, references, numerals, publications from publishers, salutation from text of a letter.

> *Principles of Composition: A College Text.*
> Luke 24:13
> 9:17 P.M.
> Dear Sir:
> New York: Harper & Brothers.

M-4.3 To show a break or omission

Use a dash to show a sudden break in thought, or omission of letters.

> He started out: "Once upon a time—."
> Well, if that is how you are going to act—.
> D—n the redcoats, we'll put them in their places.

M-4.4 For parenthetical words or emphasis

Use a dash to set off parenthetical statements or to emphasize an appositive.

> He has only one interest—sports.
> This picture—believe it or not—has been banned.

M-5   PARENTHESES AND BRACKETS

M-5.1   Parenthetical statements

Use parentheses to set off a statement or material which obviously is outside the main scope of the sentence.

His story (I can't understand why) won first place in the contest.
The reporter used such words as *fresh* (in the sense of *saucy*),
to figure (in the sense of *to believe*), and *to grill* (in the sense
of *to question*).

M-5.2   To enclose letters, etc.

Use parentheses to enclose letters, figures, references, question
marks.

Life insurance is important for three reasons: (1) to protect the
family income; (2) to save money consistently; and (3) to
safeguard the future of those you love.
Joel Barlow's "Columbiad" (1807) loosed a terrifying geyser of
abuse.
I paid ten dollars ($10.00) for a series of dance lessons.
Readers of *Tom Jones* will remember the visit of Jones and
Partridge to the playhouse (Bk. XVI, Ch. V).
Thomas Kyd, 1589 (?), wrote a play on the Hamlet story.

M-5.3   Brackets

Use brackets to enclose editorial remarks, stage directions, or
sic to indicate errors in quoted passages.

At that time he [Milton] still had his eyesight.
HELENA: Good-bye, dear boy. [She lightly kisses his head as he
bends over her hand, and goes out.]

M-6   APOSTROPHE

M-6.1   To indicate omissions in the spelling of words

don't—do not
o'clock—of the clock

class of '56—class of 1956.
it's—it is
I'm goin' to sleep on the rocks.

M-6.2 To indicate possessive case of nouns

This is really the same rule as M-6.1.

John's father—John his father

Use an apostrophe and *s* to form the possessive of a noun not ending in *s*.

My boy's dog is here.

Use an apostrophe alone to form the possessive of a plural noun ending in *s*.

My boys' bicycles are in the shed.

Use the apostrophe alone, or with *s*, to form the possessive of singular nouns ending in *s*.

Jesus' (Jesus's) disciples went to the mountain.

M-6.3 To form the plural of words, letters, numbers, or symbols

She uses too many *and*'s.
My roommate received straight A's.
He wrote during the 1880's.
His 3's and 5's look alike.
Use +'s or −'s to indicate your answers on the test.

M-7 QUOTATION MARKS

M-7.1 For exact quotation

Use double quotation marks to indicate the exact words of a quoted passage.

Horace Greeley popularized the expression, "Go West, young man, and grow up with the country."

M-7.2 Special uses

Use quotation marks to enclose technical terms in nontechnical contexts or to indicate special senses of a word.

> I have a "high-fidelity" wife.
> She is a veritable "queen."

M-7.3 Single

Use single quotation marks to enclose a quotation within a quotation.

> My mother complains, "I simply can't understand a child who says, 'I am not hungry.' "

M-7.4 To indicate the titles of chapters in a book, magazine articles, or the definition of words

> "Is Man an Absurdity?" is an essay in the book *Patterns for Living.*
> *Ichthyology* is "the department of zoology that treats of fishes."

M-8 HYPHENS, ITALICS, CAPITALS, NUMERALS, AND ABBREVIATIONS

M-8.1 Hyphens

Use hyphens to form compound words, compound numbers, or to avoid ambiguity. Today we write either separately or as single units many words which were formerly hyphenated: commander in chief, undertake. Consult a dictionary to determine acceptable usage.

> It was a well-paved highway.
> There are thirty-two students in the class.
> Two-thirds of the students are girls.
> My brother has re-enlisted in the military service.

M-8.2 Italics

Use italics (underlining) to indicate titles of magazines, newspapers, books, long poems, plays, the names of ships, foreign words, or words spoken of as words.

> The *Neversink* is out to sea.
> *Collier's* is a so-called "slick" magazine.
> Everyone should read Wendell Johnson's *My Most Enchanted Listener.*
> Nincompoop is derived from the Latin *non compos mentis.*
> Although *ain't* appears in the dictionary, it is not approved as acceptable usage.

M-8.3 Capitals

Use capital letters to indicate the beginning of a sentence; proper nouns or words derived from proper nouns; the first word of every line of poetry; the important words in the titles of books, plays, magazine articles, or musical compositions.

> My father came down with diphtheria.
> This looks like a Shakespearean sonnet.
> *Paradise Lost* is an epic.
> All candidates are required to know French.
> Thomas Hardy wrote *The Return of the Native.*

M-8.4 Numerals

Use numerals according to the following rules:

Use words to indicate numbers composed of one or two words, when an ordinal number is less than 100, and when it is part of a compound adjective.

> My uncle owns two hundred acres of land.
> I learned by memory the Twenty-Third Psalm.
> We finally won an eight-hour day.

Use figures for numbers which cannot be expressed in one or two words, for dates, addresses, telephone numbers, percentages, hours.

> The opponent won 1738 votes.
> The hotel was built in 1890.

My telephone number is ED 2–6914.
He works at 215 American Avenue.
Turn to page 1798.
I was born April 16, 1939.
The interest is 6 percent.
It is 11:45 P.M. now.

Do not begin a sentence with a figure.

One hundred and one men are not enough to win the battle.

M-8.5 Abbreviations

Abbreviate titles before and after proper names, with dates and numerals, with idiomatic phrases, and to designate government agencies, books, magazines, or clubs.

Mr. Jones is coming to dinner.
Frederic Reeve, Ph.D., is in Europe.
The Norman Conquest occurred in 1066 A.D.
My room is No. 617.
The dress cost $5.69.
Publishers discourage the use of *i.e., viz., e.g., vs.,* and *etc.*
The AFL and CIO have merged.
The Strategic Air Command, SAC, is important in national defense.
OED (Oxford English Dictionary) is a ten-volume set.

M-9 PARAGRAPH MECHANICS

M-9.1 Indentation

Indent the first line of every paragraph.

Every American child should learn at school the history of the conquest of the West. The names of Kit Carson, of General Custer and of Colonel Cody should be as household words to them. These men as truly helped to form an empire as did the Spanish Conquistadores.

—Robert Graham

M-9.2 Dialogue

In writing dialogue, paragraph each speech separately.

"Then why are we campin' here?" Johnny asked.

"You'll have to ask Tabby. Utes are funny sometimes. I told Tabby about it but he just says, 'No rain tonight. Clear skies. You sleep on the rocks, Tomas. I sleep on the grass and be comfortable.' So . . ."

"So," Johnny said, "you're goin' to sleep on the rocks."

—Forrester Blake

M-10 SPELLING

Unfortunately there is no consistent logic in spelling. If we altered the spelling of words as we alter meanings and pronunciations, we would have less difficulty with this convention of language. But spelling of words is quite arbitrarily fixed and every student of language must learn to spell words by whatever system seems most profitable. Sometimes the pronunciation of a word is a true indication of its spelling. Sometimes the etymology of a word furnishes a clue. Some people find it useful to associate words of similar derivation in order to remember how they are spelled. Some general rules for spelling particular types of words are useful. A good dictionary is a sure guide.

A student who understands the nature of language, how words are formed, how they are derived, how they are adapted to new situations stands a much better chance of spelling words correctly than one who depends solely on memory. A student who reads much, who possesses a good visual memory, and who is curious about words will usually spell words correctly most of the time. A student who reads little, writes less, and pays little attention to how words are employed in writing and speaking is usually a poor speller.

There was a time when spelling was not standardized and a man could spell a word any way that appealed to him. Andrew Jackson is credited with saying, "It's a damn poor mind that can think of only one way to spell a word." But in our day inaccurate spelling is considered a sign of an uneducated man. So you must learn to spell the simple words which cause so much trouble.

M-10.1 Visualizing

Visualize words as well as hear them. Errors in spelling accounted for by failure to visualize words correctly include: *accept* for *except, breath* for *breathe, quiet* for *quite, sychology* for *psychology.*

M-10.2 Pronunciation

Pronounce words correctly. Avoid adding vowels or extra syllables to words, or omitting consonants or syllables. Failure to pronounce words correctly accounts for such misspellings as *atheletics* for *athletics, libary* for *library, pome* for *poem.*

M-10.3 Accuracy of observation

Avoid mistaking one word for another: *desert* for *dessert, forth* for *fourth, later* for *latter, peace* for *piece, to* for *two* or *too, weather* for *whether.*

M-10.4 Practice

Practice writing the words which cause you difficulty. Spelling is a matter of written rather than oral communication. Make a list of words which you misspell and drill yourself with paper and pencil.

M-10.5 Dictionary

Use a dictionary whenever you are in doubt of the approved spelling of a word.

Following is a list of frequently misspelled words:

absence	acquaintance	all right	analyze
accidentally	acquire	almost	athletics
accommodate	across	always	beginning
achievement	advice	among	believe

benefited
business
category
comparative
conceivable
conscientious
criticize
curiosity
deceive
definite
description
effect
embarrass
environment
erroneous
exaggerate
experience
fascinate
finally
forty
government

governor
grammar
height
immediately
irresistible
its (it's)
laboratory
led
loneliness
lose
necessary
noticeable
occasion
occurrence
parallel
pastime
peaceable
possession
precede
principal
principle

privilege
procedure
professor
quiet
quite
receive
recognize
recommend
repetition
rhythm
ridiculous
sacrilegious
schedule
seize
sense
separate
sergeant
shining
similar
succeed
superintendent

suppression
synonym
tendency
tragedy
tries
truly
twelfth
unnecessary
until
unusual
usually
vacuum
varies
vengeance
village
villain
weird
whether
won't
writing
you're

INDEX

INDEX

INDEX